Single Camera Video

From Concept to Edited Master

Focal Press is an imprint of Butterworth Publishers.

Library of Congress Cataloging-in-Publication Data

Schihl, Robert J.
    Single camera video: from concept to edited master /
Robert J. Schihl.
        p.   cm.
    Bibliography: p.
    Includes index.
    ISBN 0-240-80039-7
    1. Television—Production and direction.   2. Video
recordings—Production and direction.   I. Title.
PN1992.75.S35   1989
791.45'0232—dc19   88-31599

British Library Cataloguing in Publication Data

Schihl, Robert J.
    Single camera video : from concept to edited master.
    1. Videorecordings. Production—Manuals
    I. Title
    778.59'92

    ISBN 0-240-80039-7

Butterworth Publishers
80 Montvale Avenue
Stoneham, MA 02180

10 9 8 7 6 5 4 3 2 1

Printed in the United States of America   46142

Contents

Preface

Single camera video production refers to those varying video projects that create the product of the single camera video technology, for example, the news piece, the documentary, the teleplay, the commercial, the music video, the instructional video, the industrial video, and the public relations video. Admittedly, some of these video genres are not standard fare for television production facilities whether professional or educational. Today more producers in the television industry are using video technology to produce these various genres.

It is necessary for beginning producers, directors, teachers, and students to be aware of the similarities and differences among the varying video genres and the preproduction, production, and postproduction processes required in the television industry for their development.

Over the past few years, academic programs in television production, both undergraduate and graduate, have sought to introduce more single camera video genres into courses in video production because of the growing need to be skilled in these video products in some fashion in the future of the television industry. Many television production academic programs are using single camera video production instead of full studio video production. This changeover is often based on financial considerations. Single camera video technology is far less expensive than multiple camera studio technology. Another compelling reason for changing to single camera video production in television education is the changing directions within the television industry itself—more videos produced today utilize single camera production techniques than full studio production techniques.

Many beginning producers and directors constantly search at industry conventions and conferences for some text or workbook that teaches both production design and the processes for accomplishing some basic single camera video genres. Television producers and directors require information on the procedural and organizational flow in creating a video product from preproduction start to postproduction finish—and all the necessary steps in between. These producers and directors also want task organizing forms that facilitate preproduction, production, and postproduction. Furthermore, the home video hobbyist is experimenting with video equipment and wondering how to produce different video genres with a home video camera, videotape recorder, and videotape editor.

This text is for all these people—undergraduates, graduates, beginning professional producers and directors, and the home video hobbyist. This text includes the definition and description of five genres of single camera video production: the news piece, the documentary, the teleplay, the commercial, and the music video. Readers will also find each video genre treated singularly with its unique preproduction, production, and postproduction steps and the procedural processes and organizing forms for achieving these steps successfully.

This single camera video production text is designed for the intermediate level in television production education. This text assumes a basic familiarity with single camera video equipment, remote videotaping experience, and postproduction videotape editing.

There are other single camera video genres growing in popularity and demand that are not specifically covered in this text. Some such genres are industrial, instructional, and public relations video pieces. Although these video genres are not treated separately in this text, they are adaptations of both the soft news video product and the video documentary product, which are covered.

The approach taken in this text can be considered a "how to" approach for single camera video production. Those who have taught video production know that the first steps in quality education, the first questions asked of students, and, therefore, the first approach good instructional direction takes is an approach that is reassuring, organizing, procedural, and progressive. That is the structure of this text.

In this book each single camera video production genre is treated (1) in flowchart and checklist fashion—in chronological order by production roles (above- and below-the-line); (2) in a descriptive process format—in chronological order by field production tasks; and (3) in functionally designed organizational and procedural forms—the paperwork requisite at all stages of video preproduction, production, and postproduction, and instructions on how to complete these forms.

Some decisions on the size of video production crews in single camera video production had to be made in presenting the processes of single camera video production. Professionally, the size of production crews and the roles utilized are a function of the available skilled crew members and the money available in the budget for the production. Producing roles and production crew size created in this text can be altered to meet the number of available producing or production students or skilled videographers and the available financing for the production.

Currently, the video production industry is not standardized in the procedural manner in which its video products are created. This text, although it appears to recommend standardized approaches to achieving video products, does not imply that the industry is standardized, nor is it an attempt to standardize the industry. The presentation of ordered production steps is merely academic, a way of teaching and learning required stages in video production. The video product is the result of a creative process and should remain that way.

This text provides order and organization to five video genres for beginning producers, directors, teachers, and students of video production. Once someone becomes familiar with the process of any video genre, then that person is encouraged to use what works and facilitates the task, and to drop or rethink those elements that do not work or no longer facilitate the task.

I have taught both multiple and single camera produc-

tion for almost 20 years at both undergraduate and graduate levels in broadcast education. I was responsible for initial curriculum development in two new television production departments, one at the undergraduate and the other at the graduate level of education. I have developed and taught unique genres of video production for television: the full length teleplay and the music video.

For eight years I have served as originator and executive producer for a nationally satellited newscast staffed entirely by graduate students. I also piloted a preschool children's television program, which is in the research and development stage at present. My television commercials have been seen on national cable television.

I am currently a full professor and senior television faculty member at CBN University, Virginia Beach, Virginia.

Acknowledgments

I am indebted to my wife Joanne and our sons, Joel and Jonathan, for the hours of time away from them in the production of this text and the remote video productions over the years during which the knowledge and experience was gained to write this text.

I am also indebted to the following chairpersons and deans who were instrumental in encouraging a dedication to television production education: Dr. Charles R. Petrie, Dr. Julia Paquette, Dr. David W. Clark, and Dr. Jack Keeler.

Finally, there was a small army of graduate assistants to whom I owe the challenge to write this text if only to facilitate their work load: Marshall Thomas, Cynthia Glaser, David Webster, Rob Cody, Bill Cox, Rick Hardy, Barry Boardman, Janet Boyd, John Boswell, Sam Ebersole, Mike Hartsfield, Stan Jeter, Bob Claster, Jim Chiero, Mike Torres, Mark Vermilion, and David Payton. Many thanks to musician and graduate student Joseph Ciccarello for his assistance with creating the music video storyboard.

A.M.D.G.
Robert J. Schihl

Chapter 1

Television News Production

INTRODUCTION

• Role of Video in News Production

The need for a portable video camera technology for the production of television news was the spark that precipitated the development of the equipment itself. Television news production probably still makes up the most use of the remote video camera technology. The need to capture fast breaking news events and the creation of longer news packages of video stories is currently a great demand on the single camera video technology.

In the mid-1970s, local news stations distinguished themselves as forerunners in their broadcast market by trumpeting the fact that they had the "mini-cam," the first portable video camera. Then to speed the video to the station or on-the-air, the microwave technology was developed and championed. Like any new technology, the first use of the mini-cam was unsophisticated and overused. Single camera video technology was on center stage and was featured; the form of its product and the process used to create it had to wait.

Currently, the single video camera in television news production is at the level of art form and is the subject of many video awards ceremonies for quality production in the reporting of news.

• Types of Video News

The use and development of electronic news gathering (ENG) [as the single video camera is called in news production] procedures created a division of types of news and in turn established processes that further distinguished these types. Two types of the video news genre divide according to whether the content is perceived as

hard news or soft news. *Hard news* is defined as the fast breaking kind of immediate information that should be transmitted to the public on the next newscast. One of the best examples of hard news is the video piece that accompanies an accident or other civil emergency reported on any daily television newscast. *Soft news* is defined as the more undated (often called evergreen) timeless kind of information that can be produced at a more leisurely pace than hard news can tolerate. A good example of soft news is the "PM Magazine" style video pieces, which form the latter portion of most television newscasts.

THE PREPRODUCTION PROCESS: HARD NEWS

Unlike other genres of single video camera production, the hard news video piece is governed and controlled by forces that leave little to established videotaping procedures and production polish. The nature of the hard news event, e.g., car accident, a murder, demands a basic coverage, which in turn is determined by the nature of the event. For example, an automobile accident is a fast occurrence followed by police control and the swift removal of crash vehicles for safety reasons. Hence, the producer/news reporter and camera/videotape recorder operator have to be equally fast and as thorough in their news event coverage as conditions allow.

• Personnel

The minimum remote production crew generally utilized in the television news production today is the two person crew: producer/news reporter and camera/videotape recorder operator.

FLOWCHART AND CHECKLIST FOR HARD NEWS VIDEO PRODUCTION

PREPRODUCTION	PRODUCTION	POSTPRODUCTION

PRODUCER/NEWS REPORTER (P/NR)

PREPRODUCTION	PRODUCTION	POSTPRODUCTION
☐ (1) Researches news topic	☐ (1) Meets newsmaker	☐ (1) Arranges postproduction schedule and facilities
☐ (2) Makes appointment with newsmaker	☐ (2) Plans shoot with camera operator	☐ (2) Writes voice-over script/records voice-over copy
☐ (3) Accepts assigned or chooses C/VTRO	☐ (3) Meets with interviewee(s)	☐ (3) Reviews source tapes/records editing work sheets (editing work sheet)
☐ (4) Meets with C/VTRO	☐ (4) Preps interviewee(s)	☐ (4) Coordinates editing cue sheets with script (editing cue sheet)
	☐ (5) Supervises camera set-up	☐ (5) Edits or supervises TD
	☐ (6) Supervises lighting set-up	☐ (6) Adds music and effects; mixes and sweetens audio track
	☐ (7) Supervises audio set-up and mike check	☐ (7) Writes character generator copy (edited master clipsheet)
	☐ (8) Calls for take and wrap	☐ (8) Times edited master
	☐ (9) Keeps location log/continuity sheets (location log form)	☐ (9) Coordinates clock times with character generator copy
	☐ (10) Calls for location strike	

CAMERA/VIDEOTAPE RECORDER OPERATOR (C/VTRO)

PREPRODUCTION	PRODUCTION	POSTPRODUCTION
☐ (1) Requisitions remote videotaping equipment	☐ (1) Arranges equipment pick-up/delivery	☐ (1) Returns remote videotaping equipment; reports damage, loss, malfunction
☐ (2) Meets with P/NR	☐ (2) Sets up location camera and videotape recorder	
	☐ (3) Lights location site	
	☐ (4) Sets up audio and performs a mike check	
	☐ (5) Follows producer's directions	
	☐ (6) Videotapes take	
	☐ (7) Takes responsibility for the location strike	

If the producer/new reporter does not edit:

TECHNICAL DIRECTOR/EDITOR (TD/E)

☐ (1) Edits from editing cue sheet under the supervision of the P/NR
☐ (2) Adds music and effects; mixes and sweetens audio track
☐ (3) Labels edited master

Producer/news reporter (P/NR). In television news operations, the news reporter serves as the producer and director and performs the combined tasks of both a producer and a director. Because hard news coverage cannot wait for treatments and preproduction scripts, the producer/news reporter is responsible for what background research any news reporter should have or breaking news story requires, and contacts with the newsmaker, which involves access to the news location. Some producer/news reporters may choose their own camera/videotape recorder operator.

Camera/videotape recorder operator (C/VTRO). The camera/videotape recorder operator who accompanies the producer/news reporter on location is responsible for requisitioning equipment and checking it out, knowing how to set up camera, videotape recorder, audio, and lighting on location, and knowing what the producer/reporter wants from the location shoot and how to properly videotape it.

Other crew members. There are news operations where other crew members may be assigned to location shoots. These crew members may include at least a grip, and perhaps additional talent (e.g., the anchor of the newscast).

• **Preproduction Stages**

Preproduction of the hard news story can require as little as the preparation in the mind and experience of a producer/news reporter and camera/videotape recorder operator. They know simply that they will need adequate video and audio to create a fast edited video piece to be run with the news reporter's audio copy. When a hard news story allows more production time, there are preproduction stages that should be part of a professional producer/news reporter's operating agenda.

Researching the news (P/NR 1). A producer/news reporter should not be far removed from the news research and background information that make up the essence of news reporting. That research is a combination of a journalist's sense for news and the quality of keeping up on breaking news stories.

Contacting the newsmaker (P/NR 2). The producer/news reporter also functions with the sources of news—the newsmaker. In the face of a news story, the producer/news reporter makes contact (usually by telephone) with the newsmaker as a step to setting up an interview or simply to access the location of a breaking news story.

Choosing a camera/videotape recorder operator (P/NR 3). Given the opportunity of a news story, the producer/news reporter must either choose a camera/videotape recorder operator or accept an operator assigned by the news organization. A producer/news reporter knows that there are many advantages to working with a familiar camera operator who understands the producer's process and style of covering a news story. Fostering a working relationship as such translates into communication, cooperation, and generally a better final video product.

Requisitioning equipment (C/VTRO 1). The camera/videotape recorder operator has the responsibility of requisitioning and picking up the video production equipment necessary to cover the remote shoot. Equipment to be requisitioned usually includes the video camera, videotape recorder, microphone(s), lighting instruments, and accessories to the equipment such as cables and adapters. The camera/videotape recorder operator is responsible for procuring the videotape cassette(s) for the shoot.

Professional operators set up all equipment and power it all up before accepting it for a shoot. Even with well-maintained equipment, an operator should want to know that the combination of equipment and accessories received from storage/maintenance is in working order. For example, the gentle movement of cable connections may reveal a power short unnoticed during maintenance checks. There are few greater frustrations than getting to a breaking news story to find equipment malfunctioning.

Meeting with the camera/videotape recorder operator (P/NR 4). The producer/news reporter should see to it that some time is spent with the camera/videotape operator before arrival at the remote location. Most camera/videotape operators are not accomplished news reporters and can be ill-informed on breaking news events. The producer/news reporter should share details of the news event with the camera/videotape recorder operator and indicate what objectives should be achieved with the video and audio to be recorded on location. Sharing common details and objectives can make a great difference in cooperation and the accomplishment of goals on the shoot. If the producer/news reporter has not worked with the camera/videotape recorder operator before, the communication of producing styles and video aesthetics can also pave the way to a good working arrangement in the field.

Meeting with the producer/news reporter (C/VTRO 2). With even the tightest working schedules in busy newsrooms, it is important for the producer/news reporter to find time to meet with the camera/videotape recorder operator before the shoot. Communication is a key ingredient to success on even the fastest location shoots. It may be that the only time available to the producer/news reporter and camera/videotape recorder operator is the travel time to a location. Some dialogue on key points of a shoot and the objectives of the news story will serve to facilitate the working arrangement of producer/news reporter and camera/videotape operator and the success of the video product.

THE PRODUCTION PROCESS: HARD NEWS

A production rule for single camera work is to shoot for the edit. Thus, the videographer approaches any videotaping situation with the final edited video piece in mind. For the hard news video piece, the time constraints of a breaking news event make covering the event with video even more challenging. It is wise on fast breaking news event coverage to videotape (1) coming on the scene of the event (XLS and/or LS), (2) gathering some normal

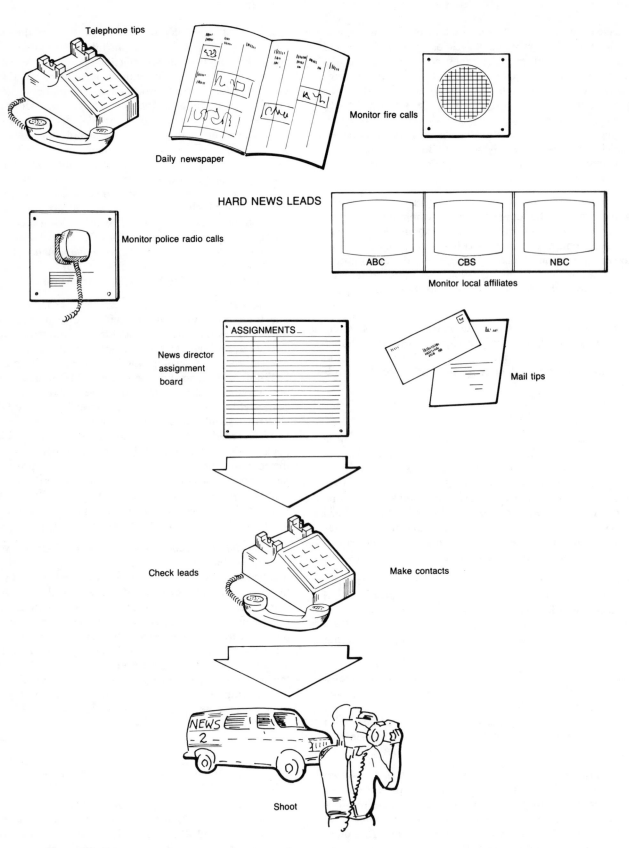

FIGURE 1–1
Hard news leads/sources. There are many sources for leads to the hard news video story. The
news reporter takes a lead, checks on the lead, and makes contacts, with an eye to shooting
videotape.

sight range video footage (MS), (3) using some video of the main elements/persons of the scene (CU), and (4) then ending with video that takes leave of the scene (MS and LS or XLS). When basic video coverage is complete, then interviews with newsmakers can be videotaped with some leisure, after which, videotaping generic cut-aways can be done.

• Personnel

Producer/news reporter (P/NR). The producer/news reporter handles all a producer's responsibilities on the remote news shoot. Preproduction stages carry over to the location. Any details on the newsmaker or the breaking news story are the producer's responsibilities. The producer/news reporter also serves as a director on the remote news location. As director, specific instructions to the camera/videotape recorder operator are expected.

Camera/videotape recorder operator (C/VTRO). The camera/videotape recorder operator has camera, videotape recorder, audio, and lighting responsibilities on location. The operator also looks to the producer/news reporter as the director of the shoot. During the shoot the operator has to operate the videotape recorder and monitor audio and video while videotaping the shoot. The camera/videotape recorder operator is responsible for the videotape cassette(s) on location, their proper labeling, and removing the record button after videotaping.

Other production personnel. It is not uncommon for a grip to be assigned to facilitate some of the work of the camera operator on a remote news location. The grip should be ready to assist in any of the equipment set-ups for which the operator is responsible. The grip may also be required to operate the videotape recorder during the shoot as well as monitor audio and video input levels.

Additional talent may be part of the remote news location videotaping. Often a producer/news reporter may be performing the producer's role for a special news correspondent or the newscast anchor. The talent then is also the responsibility of the producer/news reporter and should look to the producer for direction on location.

• Production Stages

Meeting with the newsmaker (P/NR 1). Whatever the news story, in some manner there is a newsmaker, whether VIP, victim, emergency personnel, or perpetrator. It is the producer/news reporter's responsibility to contact the newsmaker on the location. This may be facilitated if arrangements are made during preproduction. Meeting the newsmaker serves to orient the producer/news reporter to details of a news story not previously known. It is this step that may best begin to organize and give direction to the news story for the producer/news reporter. Important information to be gleaned by the producer/news reporter from a newsmaker is the basic news questions: who, what, where, when, why, and how. Then imaging the video news story can begin.

Picking up/taking delivery of equipment (C/VTRO 1). If the requisition of equipment is separated from the actual pickup and/or the delivery of rented equipment, the camera/videotape recorder operator begins production requirements by facilitating the acquisition of all necessary equipment. A good checklist makes this task manageable. There are many equipment accessories that comprise a good video shoot, and accurate accounting of every piece of equipment received can be difficult.

Planning the shoot (P/NR 2). Once the basics of the story are cleared, a producer/news reporter should confer with the camera/videotape recorder operator and begin planning the visual approach—imaging—to covering the story. A working relationship is thus beneficial. With experience, a camera/videotape recorder operator knows how a producer/news reporter thinks and how the producer builds a story with video images. Precious news coverage time can be saved on location when each professional knows, respects, and trusts each other professionally.

Meeting with the interviewee (P/NR 3). Besides the details of a news event itself, most remote news video pieces include an interview on location. The interviewee may be the newsmaker or someone contacted through a lead from the newsmaker. The producer/news reporter has a twofold responsibility regarding the interview: (1) meeting the

News reporter/producer

Camera/videotape recorder operator

FIGURE 1–2
The two-person hard news video crew. The most common hard news remote video crew consists of the news reporter/producer and the camera/videotape recorder operator.

interviewee and securing the interview, and (2) prepping the interviewee before videotaping.

Meeting the interviewee may or may not be difficult, but often interpersonal tact and skill are required. News events have a way of making a newsmaker defensive. Foremost among interpersonal skills a producer/news reporter should learn is the ability to disarm the defensive posture of an interviewee. An interviewee may be disarmed by being put at ease by knowing what questions will be asked during an interview. It may also be disarming to an interviewee for a producer/news reporter to ask an interviewee what questions should *not* be asked during an interview.

Prepping the interviewee (P/NR 4).   Preparing the interview means to prep the interviewee. Prepping the interviewee requires a sensitivity toward the newsmaker. Many newsmakers may never have been through the experience of being interviewed on camera. Interviewees need to know what is required of them. They should be briefly introduced to the process of location videotaping, the microphone (e.g., holding it, attaching it to themselves, talking across it), the lens of the camera (e.g., where it is, whether to look into it or not), where to stand, and how to answer the questions.

Setting up location camera/videotape recorder (C/VTRO 2).   While the producer/news reporter meets with a newsmaker, the camera/videotape recorder operator should be unloading and setting up the camera, videotape recorder, lights, and microphone(s). The faster the news is breaking, the faster the set-up must be. Many camera operators handle partially assembled equipment in a mobile vehicle or assemble the equipment en route to a location.

Lighting the location site (C/VTRO 3).   After the camera and videotape recorder are set, the camera/videotape recorder operator is responsible for lighting the location. The fastest method is to use a light attached to the front of the camera or one handheld.

Given more time, especially for interviews, better lighting set-ups can be accomplished. Three-point lighting—key, fill, and back—might still be easily utilized.

Setting up the audio equipment (O/VTRO 4).   The final set-up for which the camera/videotape recorder operator is responsible is to mike the talent. At a minimum this may require one microphone, a handheld mike, for the producer/news reporter. A single microphone can also be attached to the front of the video camera. Perhaps two will be needed: one for the producer/news reporter and another for the newsmaker.

The camera/videotape recorder operator should conduct a mike check with the producer/news reporter and any other talent. Input levels for each mike and for each talent should be noted and set.

An important detail for the camera/videotape recorder operator is to know beforehand what ambient audio the producer/news reporter may need from the location to be used in postproduction editing. During the shoot the camera/videotape recorder operator should monitor the audio input by way of a headset plugged into the videotape recorder. Audio levels can be maintained by watching the audio VU meter on the videotape recorder. The VU meter monitors the audio input in decibels. The camera/videotape recorder operator can help the location shoot by being aware of ambient noises (e.g., airplanes, car exhausts) to which the producer/news reporter may not be sensitive.

Supervising camera set-up (P/NR 5).   In keeping with the role of producer, the producer/news reporter should make a supervising check on camera set-up. The producer/news reporter should have an image in mind of the final edited video as a major field responsibility. Camera placement

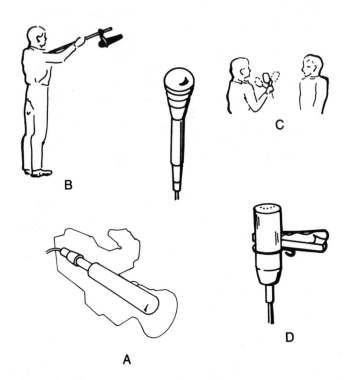

FIGURE 1–4
Hard news audio instruments and techniques. (A) The mike is attached to the camera. (B) The mike is attached to a fishpole and handheld. (C) The mike is handheld by the news reporter/producer. (D) The mike is clipped to clothing.

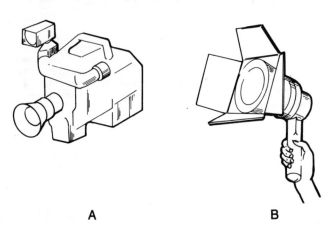

FIGURE 1–3
Hard news video lighting instruments and techniques. (A) The light is attached to the top of the camera. (B) The light is handheld.

may have to be changed. It is common for the producer to look through the viewfinder of the camera to check framing and zooming.

Supervising lighting set-up (P/NR 6). A producer/news reporter's responsibility is over the entire shooting environment. Another critical eye added to the camera operator's can make for a well-lighted scene. The producer/news reporter should look for how and where shadows fall; where microphones may be placed and how microphone shadows may fall are some preproduction elements that should be of interest to the producer/news reporter.

Supervising audio set-up and mike check (P/NR 7). As with other location responsibilities, the producer/news reporter should check the audio equipment set-up and make note of the correct type and necessary number of mikes. The physical placement of mikes should also be observed at this time. This would be important if some form of a fishpole is being used to hold and extend a microphone into the videotaping environment. Lastly, after supervising the audio set-up, the producer/news reporter should have a mike check for the mike(s) being used for the shoot. At this point in the production process both the producer/ news reporter and talent should have microphones on or in hand and ready for the first take.

Following the producer/news reporter's directions (C/VTRO 5). Because the producer/news reporter serves as a location director also, the camera/videotape recorder operator should follow the producer/news reporter's direction on location. It is the producer who is ultimately responsible for the final edited video piece and should have the edited master in mind.

Calling for a take (P/NR 8). Depending on the news story, there may or may not be time for a lot of prevideotaping details. If the pressure of the news event or story allows some prevideotaping details, the producer/news reporter should take charge and coordinate the takes with the interviewee(s) and the location environment. Because the producer/news reporter is responsible for all production details, he or she is best qualified to call everything in readiness. If other talent is present, the producer/news reporter directs their contribution to the videotaping also.

Many producer/news reporters write some of their final news story script copy while still on location. Then they can videotape segments of the story while the camera is still set-up. At least three segments of a location news piece are appropriate from the news location: (1) the news story lead, (2) internal summaries and/or bridges, and (3) stand-up summary and/or tag. These segments of the location news story can be videotaped and used with audio and video or as a voice-over only. The great advantage to videotaping these segments on location is to add the location ambience to the whole news story. This adds to the appreciation of the live quality of immediacy to television news reporting.

Videotaping the take (C/VTRO 6). The camera/videotape recorder operator records the shoot as planned with the producer/news reporter. The operator/videotape recorder operator is responsible for monitoring video and audio levels during taping. After final videotaping the camera/ videotape recorder operator should remove the record button from all recorded videotape cassettes. This is especially necessary if the remote crew will move on to other news events and locations with the likelihood of continuing videotaping. Irreplaceable video can be lost by inserting the recorded videocassette with the record button in place into the recorder at a later location.

Location log and continuity (P/NR 9). The producer/news reporter's responsibility includes some record of the video and audio takes made on location and their relationship to the news story. A location log records basic location details that will facilitate the preparation of postproduction editing. (See the location log form.)

A location log or continuity record is a written account

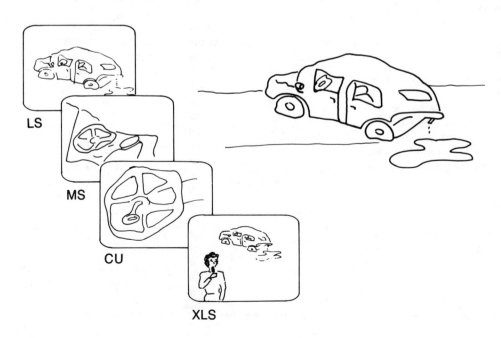

FIGURE 1–5
Covering the hard news event with video. Basic hard news video coverage of the remote news event is the LS, MS, CU, and XLS.

LS

MS

CU

XLS

of the following: (1) the number of takes videotaped on the location, (2) notes on the audio content of each take, (3) notes on the video content of each take, (4) the full text and spelling of the name and title of interviewees for character generator copy, and (5) some judgment notation regarding the usability of each take. If time permits during videotaping, and presupposing that the videocassette was rewound and the counter set to zero when videotaping began, the counter number for each take will allow rapid searching for the take before editing.

Calling for location strike (P/NR 10). It is the responsibility of the producer/news reporter to alert the camera/videotape recorder operator when it is perceived that the news story and the news location have been adequately covered. A location strike should not be called until sufficient cutaways have been videotaped. Even if time does not permit, the sequence of basic video shots (LS, MS, CU, MS, LS) of the news location might well serve for cut-aways. However, producers and camera operators should listen carefully to the content of interviews and let that suggest which cut-aways would be appropriate in a final edited master.

Being responsible for the location strike (C/VTRO 7). The camera/videotape recorder operator has the final responsibility of the location strike when the producer/news reporter calls for it. This is an opportunity for the camera/videotape recorder operator to make note of any damage, loss, or malfunction to equipment or accessories.

THE POSTPRODUCTION PROCESS: HARD NEWS

The stages of postproduction of the hard news video piece can be "fast and dirty." It is not uncommon for the producer/news reporter to edit the piece. This is true especially for small news markets. Given some time for script and location log work by the producer/news reporter, an assigned editor may do the actual editing with the producer/news reporter as a supervisor.

• Personnel

Producer/news reporter (P). In some news organizations, the producer/news reporter is responsible for editing the hard news video piece. All postproduction tasks then fall to the producer/news reporter. This includes responsibility for the source tapes, their content, logging source tapes, final editing decisions, timing the final edited video, and writing the character generator copy for the broadcast of the video piece.

Technical director/editor (TD/E). In some television news operations, a technical director or editor may be assigned to do the actual editing of the source tapes. In such a case, the producer/news reporter assists in the editing suite and is expected to know the content of the source tapes and to make editing decisions.

Camera/videotape recorder operator (C/VTRO). The camera/videotape recorder operator has the final responsibility of

returning the videotape equipment and alerting equipment maintenance to any source of technical problems or malfunction.

• Postproduction Stages

As with any postproduction process, it is necessary for the producer/news reporter to be prepared to go into the videotape editing process. Even for fast news coverage, some sense of the order and content of the source tape(s), which is the responsibility of the producer/news reporter, is a prerequisite in the editing suite.

Arranging postproduction scheduling and facilities (P/NR 1). The producer/news reporter takes the responsibility of arranging the time and editing facility for videotape editing purposes. This may involve meeting the availability of a technical director or editor if the producer is not doing the editing.

Writing the script (P/NR 2). The producer/news reporter begins to function more as the news reporter at this stage than as the producer. The story covered on location principally on videotape must now be written. Often this is a task begun while returning to the newsroom and broadcast studio. The news reporter will have to consider writing copy for a voice-over to be recorded at the studio or in the editing suite before videotape editing begins. This may be in place of or in addition to the stand-ups (lead, bridges, summary, tag) already recorded on location.

Creating the editing work sheets (P/NR 3). If the standard process of location news coverage (LS, MS, CU, MS, LS) was followed, then editing preparation can be made swiftly, even from memory. In the process of writing the news story to accompany the video for the news story, the producer/news reporter can draw from the location log sheet kept during videotaping while on location. Depending on the thoroughness of these notations, it is possible that the producer would not even have to review the source tapes before editing. Sometimes the demands of fast breaking news and the immediacy of a broadcast deadline preclude much more time. Some technical director/editors, if time permits, will insist on editing work sheets before an editing session begins. A producer will have to (1) go through source tape(s) and review all the video, (2) make note of every video take on the source tape, (3) make some value judgment about the quality of each take, and (4) record videotape counter numbers, clock times, or SMPTE code frames for each bite of video/audio on the source tape(s). (See the editing work sheet.)

Designing the editing cue sheets (P/NR 4). If there is a lot of time before an editing deadline, a producer/news reporter or an editor may require an editing cue sheet for the proposed edited master. The editing cue sheet is a written format of the order of the proposed edited master from the editing work sheet. The producer uses the editing cue sheet to juxtapose the bites of video and audio from various portions of the source tape(s) into the proposed order of the final edited master. Completing the editing cue sheet before editing saves editing suite time (and money) because editing decisions are made in advance of

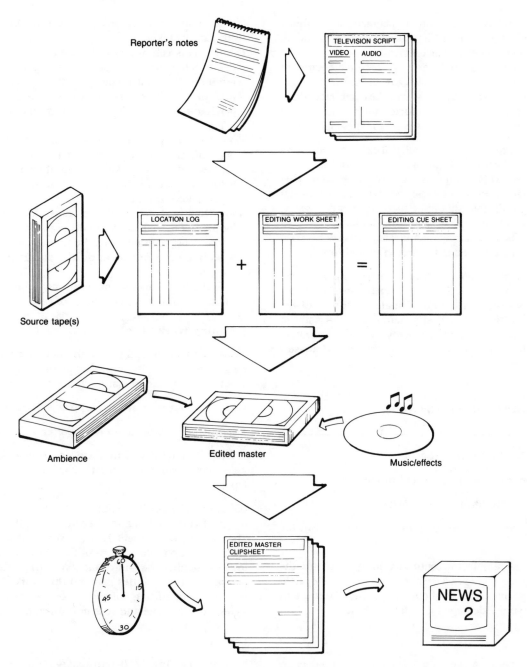

Reporter's notes

TELEVISION SCRIPT
VIDEO | AUDIO

Source tape(s)

LOCATION LOG + EDITING WORK SHEET = EDITING CUE SHEET

Ambience   Edited master   Music/effects

EDITED MASTER CLIPSHEET

NEWS 2

FIGURE 1–6
Postproduction stages in the preparation of the hard news video piece for broadcast.

an editing session and the entire final edited master can be designed on paper before actual editing begins. (See the editing cue sheet.)

Editing the news piece (P/NR 5). The producer/news reporter has the final responsibility for the edited news piece. In an editing session either alone or with a technical director/editor, the producer should take the authority for all editing decisions. This does not mean that a producer does not or should not listen to the advice of others, but final decisions belong to the producer.

Mixing/sweetening of the edited master (P/NR 6). When first edits are finished, other audio effects are edited in.

Ambience may be needed, music might be used, and so on. Some broadcast facilities require that the two audio tracks used in editing be mixed down to one.

Writing character generator copy (P/NR 7). When the edited master is complete, the producer knows what sound bites are being used, and character generator copy should be written for each screen image needing such text. Good location log records should have the proper spelling and correct titles for every interviewee. Character generator copy should be included on a reporting form often called a clipsheet. The names and titles typed and checked for accuracy are included for entry into the character generator. Any other copy, e.g., text of a document, a telephone number, credit for video or film, should also be included. (See the edited master clipsheet form.)

The last step for a producer/news reporter entails an accounting of the edited master for the news telecast. Before a producer/news reporter gives the completed video news assignment to a news director for inclusion in a newscast, some remaining tasks have to be completed.

Timing the edited master (P/NR 8). The producer/news reporter should make a final and accurate timing of the edited master. This timing is usually made from first audio to final audio. If for some creative reason the first audio is delayed, note should be made of this difference. The same exception holds true for final audio cue. At this stage of the project, timing should always be done with a stopwatch. (See the edited master clipsheet form.)

Coordinating timing with the character generator copy (P/NR 9). The last task before handing over the master videotape to a news director is to coordinate the timing of the edited video with the character generator copy so a studio director knows where all text copy will be accurately inserted during the newscast. (See the edited master clipsheet form.)

VIDEO PRODUCTION ORGANIZING FORMS

• Remote Log/Continuity Form

Production process: Hard news field production

Responsibility: Producer/news reporter

Purpose: To record videotaping production details in the field.

Objective: The remote log/continuity form facilitates the time consuming need to view source videotapes after field production to make notes about the quality, extent, and content of every videotaped take from the field.

Glossary

News Story Slug A descriptive word or two used as an abbreviated label for a news story. A slug is most often used at the heading of a written news story.
Location The remote site where the videotaping was done.
VTR Counter/Timer/Code This column notes the measure used to clock the length of every videotape take. One method of measuring the length of a videotaped take is to read the built-in digital counter on the videotape recorder. Another measure is to use a stopwatch as a timer. Still another measure is to stripe the source videotape with SMPTE time code and record frames as a measure of the length of a take. Place a check in the correct box to indicate the type of measure used to time the source tape.
Location Because the environment used for videotaping on a location can change, e.g., interior, exterior, this

column allows notation of changes within the location for various takes.
Talent This column allows notation to be made of the person or persons videotaped during a take. This is a reminder that full name, correct spelling, and proper title of videotaped talent are required for character generator copy later in postproduction editing or news telecast.
Take No. It is not uncommon for more than a single take of any event or interview on location to be videotaped. If the takes are numbered consecutively, recording that number here will facilitate easier recall of the take during editing.
Good/No Good This column allows for a judgment on location of the various takes during videotaping. Having a comment recorded saves the time of viewing takes to make the same judgment during postproduction preparation for editing.
Video/Audio This column encourages some notation on the video and/or audio content of each take.

• Editing Work Sheet

Note: If adequate and thorough notes were made on the remote log continuity form, completing the editing work sheet may not be necessary.

Production process: Hard news postproduction

Responsibility: Producer/news reporter

Purpose: To prepare for postproduction editing of the video news story to a master tape from source videotape(s).

Objective: The editing work sheet records in videotaping order all video and/or audio recordings on the source tape. The editing work sheet is a transcription of the source tape(s). An accurate account of the source tape(s) saves a lot of searching the source tape(s) during editing. Many postproduction facilities demand this work before access is allowed to editing suites. For the producer this stage saves valuable time and cost in postproduction.

Glossary

News Story Slug A descriptive word or two used as an abbreviated label for a news story. The term slug is most often used at the heading of a written news story in journalism.
Audio: Channel 1/Audio: Channel 2 The producer of the package should indicate the correct audio channel or channels and their use on the source tape(s). Because the choice can vary between channel 1 or channel 2 for field recording, the designation should be made of the channel on which audio recording was made in the field.
Tape No. The number of the videocassette tape being logged should be entered here.
VTR CNTR Clock SMPTE Because some measure should be made of the videotape content on the source tape(s) it is helpful to note what that measure is. Choices include the digital counter on the videotape recorder/

playback unit, reading from a stopwatch, or reading SMPTE time code. Source videotapes can be striped during videotaping or as a first step in postproduction prior to beginning the editing work sheet. These measures should be consecutive measures made from the beginning (rewound) of the source videotape(s). The VTR counter and stopwatch should be set to begin at zero. SMPTE time code is easiest to use when also set to zero at the beginning of striping.

IN/OUT   These columns allow the producer to indicate the beginning and ending measures (VTR counter, clock, or SMPTE) for the particular videotape units being noted.

Notes   Any meaningful notation about the content of the video and/or audio on the source tape(s). This is the place to make value judgments about the quality and usability of each particular take.

Segment Clock Time   This column should record the real clock time length of each particular video and/or audio bite being noted. Depending on the desired content of any particular video and/or audio bite, judgment should be made whether the time should be from first video to final video or first audio to final audio.

• **Editing Cue Sheet**

Production process: Hard news postproduction

Responsibility: Producer/news reporter

Purpose: To prepare for postproduction editing of the news video piece to master tape from source videotape(s).

Objective: The editing cue sheet is a postproduction preparatory stage that creates the format and order of edits of the proposed master videotape from the editing work sheet. The editing cue sheet juxtaposes takes from the editing work sheet into the proposed order of edits for postproduction editing. This step permits a lot of creative work and quality time on the proposed final edited piece without tying up a videotape editing suite.

Glossary

News Story Slug   A descriptive word or two used as an abbreviated label for a news story. The term slug is most often used as the head of a written news story in journalism.

Audio: Channel 1/Audio: Channel 2   The producer of the package should indicate the correct audio channel or channels and their proposed use on the edited master tape(s). Because the choice can vary between channel 1 or channel 2 and mixed channels, the designation should be made of the channel on which final audio recording will be made.

Tape No.   The number of the videocassette tape being logged should be entered in this column.

VTR CNTR Clock SMPTE   Because some measure should be made of the videotape content on the edited master SMPTE tape(s), it is important to note what that measure is. Choices include the digital counter on the videotape recorder/playback unit, the reading from a stopwatch, or SMPTE time code. SMPTE time code can

be striped on the edited master tape(s) as a first step in postproduction prior to actual editing. These measures should be consecutive measures made from the beginning (rewound) of the master videotape(s). The VTR counter and stopwatch should be set to begin at zero. SMPTE time code is easiest to use when also set to zero at the beginning of striping.

IN/OUT   These columns allow the producer to indicate the beginning and ending measures (VTR counter, clock, SMPTE) for the particular videotape bites being used from the source tape(s) as noted on the editing work sheet.

Notes: In-cue Out-cue   This space should indicate the video and/or audio in-cues and out-cues from the proposed bites noted on the editing work sheet from the source tape(s). This space will allow the producer to create the proposed edited order of videotape bites from the source tape(s) to the master tape. The in-cues and out-cues may be either video cues and/or audio cues. Video cues briefly describe the content of the beginning or end of the bite being considered; audio cues are the first few words of the beginning of the proposed bite or final few words at the end of the bite being considered.

Segment Clock Time   This column should record the real clock time length of each particular video and/or audio bite being proposed. Depending on the desired content of any particular video and/or audio bite, judgment should be made whether the time should be from first video to final video, first audio to final audio, or first audio to final video. When all entries recorded in this column are summed up, the total should approximate the length of the final edited video piece.

• **Edited Master Clipsheet**

Production process: Hard news postproduction

Responsibility: Producer/news reporter; videotape editor

Purpose: To record all character generator copy necessary for the telecast of the edited master video news piece.

Objective: The edited master clipsheet facilitates for the producer or editor all possible character generator screen text necessary to accompany the edited master video for telecast. The form serves as a summary listing of all essential information not already contained on the edited master video piece.

Glossary

News Story Slug   A descriptive word or two used as an abbreviated label for a news story. A slug is most often used at the heading of a written news story.

Title   Some news video pieces are more properly titled as a way to describe the content and expanded use of the video.

Audio: Channel 1, 2 Mixed   Indication should made of the final audio channel used for editing. Some producers edit using both audio channels and expect that the edited master uses the mixed audio playback option. Other producers mix the two audio channels down to either one of the two available channels. The choice made in editing should be indicated.

Length The total edited length of the news piece should be timed. Timing is most often from first audio to final audio. A producer might intend to begin the news piece with a video image before first audio begins. This is the point where that choice should be indicated.

Out-cue In the broadcast situation in which a video piece is to be B-rolled into a longer program, a control room director will need a video or audio out-cue, a description of the intended final video, or the final few words of the audio track. This out-cue should be indicated here.

Character Generator Copy This section of the form records for the producer or control room director all the character generator copy for matting on the news video piece during the telecast.

Videotape/Film Credit When a producer uses video or film footage from another source, screen credit may be required. This entry may be as simple as "File Footage" or "Courtesy of ABC-TV."

In ___:___/Out ___:___ For every screen of character generator copy the producer or editor will have to provide a clock time from the beginning of the video piece at which the character generator copy is to be matted over the video and when the matte is to be removed (i.e., the length of time to remain on the screen).

Reporter Lower Third This character generator copy gives the name of the reporter whether the reporter is to be seen on screen or whether the reporter only does a voice-over. Following are examples of reporter lower third:

JOHN DOE
_____

News at 5:00

and

JOHN DOE
Reporting

Interviewee/Actuality Lower Third When newsmakers appear on screen, character generator copy is expected. An example of an interviewee/actuality lower third is

REV. JOHN DOE
Pastor

Voice of When a newsmaker does not appear on screen and/or the interview is done over the telephone, the correct form for character generator copy is to indicate that the audience is hearing the voice of the person only. Here is an example of character generator copy for this:

Voice of
SEN. JOHN P. DOE
(R) Virginia

Transcription Occasionally, transcribed text copy has to appear on the screen over the video image. If a news-

maker is speaking in a foreign language, if a newsmaker has a very heavy accent, or if the audio quality is very poor, a transcription of a portion of the audio track may have to be matted on the screen over the interview or actuality. A quotation from a book or a number of statistics from a survey may have to be matted on the screen. This is the place to indicate that text copy.

Trade Credit Perhaps some favor or permission adding to the quality of the news piece production warrants an on-screen credit. This is called a trade. This is the place to indicate that text. An example of a trade credit is:

Reporter's clothes
provided by
FOR MEN ONLY

Video Credits Some news operations provide the opportunity to attach individual credits to a news piece itself, or provide room at the end of a news program for individual piece credits. Even if no provision is made on the news program, adding the proper credits to the clip sheet provides a record of credits for the video piece for future reference. Following is an example of video credits for a news video piece:

JOHN DOE
_____

Producer

MARY SMITH
_____

Camera Operator

BILL JONES
_____

Videotape Editor

THE PREPRODUCTION PROCESS: SOFT NEWS

The soft news video piece is called a package in some television production operations. Soft news generally involves a longer process of production development. Because the content of soft news is less immediate, more "evergreen," the process of the production of soft news in turn can take more time and often demands longer time in video production. These differences determine the separate nature of the content of soft news over hard news video production. One of the better known local soft news television program examples is the "PM Magazine" program. Some of the better known national soft news television programs are "60 Minutes," "West 57th Street," and "20/20."

• Personnel

The production crew of a soft news video piece usually has the advantage of a crew larger than the hard news video production crew. A soft news video preproduction crew might include a producer and a camera and videotape recorder operator.

Producer (P). The producer is the person responsible for the development and success of the soft news video piece.

FLOWCHART AND CHECKLIST FOR SOFT NEWS VIDEO PRODUCTION

PREPRODUCTION	PRODUCTION	POSTPRODUCTION

PRODUCER (P)

PREPRODUCTION
- (1) Researches topic
- (2) Writes treatment (treatment form)
- (3) Scouts location (location site survey form)
- (4) Writes preproduction script (television script form)
- (5) Sketches storyboard (storyboard form)
- (6) Does script breakdown (script breakdown form)
- (7) Creates shot list (shot list form)
- (8) Designs production schedule (production schedule form)
- (9) Accepts assigned or chooses C/VTRO
- (10) Meets with C/VTRO
- (11) Obtains copyright clearances, insurance coverage; notifies police

PRODUCTION
- (1) Meets with production crew at crew call
- (2) Meets with location host
- (3) Handles all location details
- (4) Meets with interviewees/talent
- (5) Supervises camera/videotape recorder set-up
- (6) Supervises lighting set-up
- (7) Supervises audio recording set-up
- (8) Preps the interviewee/rehearses the scene
- (9) Calls for take and wrap
- (10) Keeps location log/continuity sheets (location log form)
- (11) Calls for location strike (talent release form)

POSTPRODUCTION
- (1) Arranges postproduction editing schedule and facilities
- (2) Prepares source tapes
- (3) Prepares master tape
- (4) Views source tapes/records editing work sheets (editing work sheet form)
- (5) Writes final production script (production script form)
- (6) Creates editing cue sheet (editing cue sheet form)
- (7) Edits or supervises TD
- (8) Adds music and effects/mixes audio tracks
- (9) Times final edited master
- (10) Writes character generator copy
- (11) Coordinates character generator copy with timed edited master (edited master clipsheet form)
- (12) Labels edited master

CAMERA/VIDEOTAPE RECORDER OPERATOR (C/VTRO)

PREPRODUCTION
- (1) Meets with producer
- (2) Creates equipment/accessories list (equipment checklist form)
- (3) Requisitions equipment
- (4) Works shot list and location notes

PRODUCTION
- (1) Arranges equipment pick-up/delivery
- (2) Sets up camera/videotape recorder
- (3) Supervises grip
- (4) Sets up location lighting equipment/lights set
- (5) Follows producer's directions
- (6) Videotapes take
- (7) Supervises location strike/strikes camera, videotape recorder, lighting equipment

POSTPRODUCTION
- (1) Returns camera, videotape recorder, and lighting equipment and accessories
- (2) Reports equipment damage, loss, malfunction, repair, and replacement

AUDIO DIRECTOR (AD)

PRODUCTION
- (1) Knows preproduction script and shot list
- (2) Sets up audio recording equipment/makes mike check
- (3) Monitors sound recording during videotaping
- (4) Records location ambience track
- (5) Strikes audio equipment and accessories

POSTPRODUCTION
- (1) Returns audio equipment and accessories
- (2) Reports equipment damage, loss, malfunction, repair, and replacement

GRIP (G)
- (1) Assists C/VTRO in equipment set-up
- (2) May be required to operate videotape recorder, monitor VU meters, etc.
- (3) Assists in equipment and location strike

TALENT (T)
- (1) Meets with producer
- (2) Readies make-up and clothing appearance
- (3) Is responsible to the producer for location direction

TECHNICAL DIRECTOR/EDITOR (TD/E)

If the producer does not edit:
- (1) Edits from editing cue sheet under supervision of producer
- (2) Adds music and effects/mixes audio tracks
- (3) Labels edited master

The producer is often the creative individual who takes the initiative to propose the content of the video piece. The producer writes the treatment and the preproduction script, breaks out the shot list, designs the storyboard for the camera operator, and makes all preproduction contacts and production schedules. The producer serves as a director on location.

Camera/videotape recorder operator (C/VTRO). The camera/videotape recorder operator is responsible to the producer and determines camera and videotape recording equipment needs and availability. Until production day, the camera/videotape recorder operator performs preproduction tasks for other crew members who will join the crew at production, the audio director, and perhaps a grip. The producer and camera/videotape recorder operator must be open to communication. A meeting before a shoot is usually required. During this meeting the preproduction stages become a means to better understand what is required and expected on a location shoot.

• **Preproduction Stages**

Beginning stages of any video production (preproduction) are steps that are often neglected and treated as busy work. Experience and discipline have proven that a successful video product is a direct function of thorough and quality preproduction. Preproduction—treatment, preproduction script and/or storyboard, script breakdown, and shot list—are designed to encourage creative development and discourage the serendipity syndrome, the expectation that good video can regularly be achieved without really planning for it. Some quality news operations require preproduction stages to force the structure proven so necessary to quality video packages.

Researching a topic (P 1). Good soft news video packages begin with an idea. Ideas in a television market can be gleaned from many sources. An ongoing television program made up of soft news video packages will self-generate ideas called in or written in by program viewers. Keeping abreast of softer news articles from the local newspapers and magazines will also generate ideas for soft news video packages. In many cases of ideas taken from other sources, much of the background research may be already done for the producer. A good source of creative ideas is the producer who learns to be sensitive and aware of the soft news video package ideas in life: the people and the environments around us in everyday living.

Writing the treatment (P 2). The treatment is a verbal statement of goals and objectives of the video package, basic production values, and content elements of the proposed video package. This stage is often required as an in-house proposal style step to encourage individual creativity and initiative among reporters and producers. Generally, the treatment or synopsis is required before program directors or news producers allow a project to be funded or authorized. It follows that the better and more professional a treatment is conceived and written,

the better the chances for the authorization of the video project.

A treatment should contain the following: (1) the name of the producer, (2) a proposed title for the video piece, (3) the proposed length of the piece, (4) goals and objectives to be achieved, (5) the target audience for the content of the piece, (6) the organization or outline of the content of the piece, (7) proposed contacts or interviewees, (8) proposed remote location(s), (9) proposed shooting date, and (10) the suggested air date. (See the treatment form.)

Scouting the location (P 3). For many soft news video packages scouting for remote shooting locations is an important preproduction requirement. The producer should search out environments that will serve as a shooting location for the video project. Often the content of the soft news piece will dictate a location environment. Whether a location must be sought for the shoot or is immediately available by the nature of the content of the package, the producer or assigned location scouts should visit the proposed location to determine a number of production needs. Those needs include (1) the actual shooting space, (2) location contact personnel, (3) lighting requirements, (4) suitable power resources, and (5) the audio environment. The location visit will serve to evaluate crew needs and to determine the location equipment, security, and safety necessary for the shoot. (See the location site survey form.)

If the location shoot will take place outdoors or indoors with windows, a compass will be needed to accurately determine due east and the position of the sun as a determinant of camera placement and the need for reflectors and color correcting gels. Instant developing film and camera permit fast photos of a location for creating camera angles and other preproduction planning and evaluation after location scouting. (See the location site survey form.)

Writing a preproduction script (P 4). Some video production operations find it advantageous to require a more refined step before production—a preproduction script. This step serves to flesh out the treatment to the extent that a producer can begin to image the proposed video package.

The preproduction script contains (1) the lead (sometimes even the proposed lead-in if the video package is a portion of a larger television program), (2) the proposed video content, (3) the questions to be asked of an interviewee, (4) the bridges or internal summaries, (5) video or audio transitions, (6) proposed cut-aways, (7) proposed ambience and/or music, and (8) talent summary and/or stand-up tag. (See the preproduction script form.)

Sketching the storyboard (P 5). Once a producer realizes that communication problems with a crew on location are minimized with accurate communication, many opt for a storyboard. Given that "one picture is worth a thousand words," it should follow that television aspect frames containing a sketch of the camera framing and the content of a shot can best convey a producer's intent to a camera operator. A thorough storyboard should also indicate video transitions (e.g., dissolves, zooms) and cut-aways,

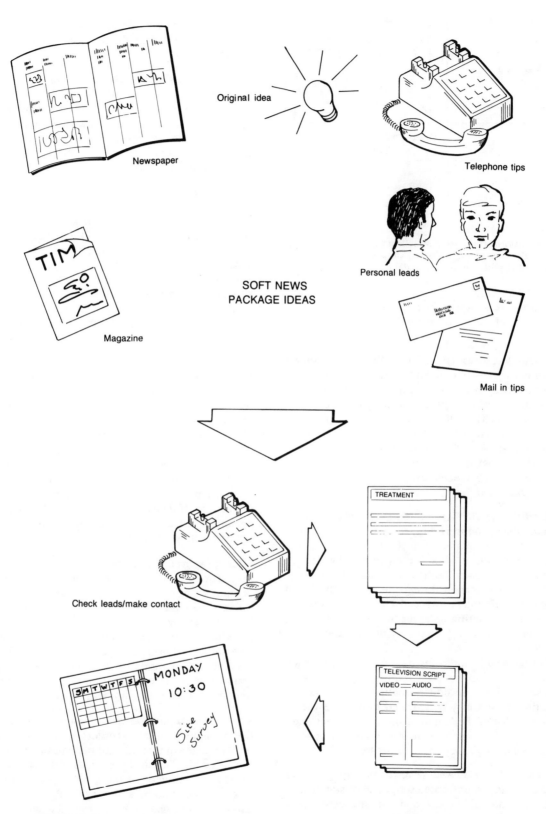

FIGURE 1-7
Soft news video package idea sources. Soft news video package ideas come from a variety of sources. The producer checks possibilities and writes a treatment and a preproduction script, then makes an appointment for shooting the package.

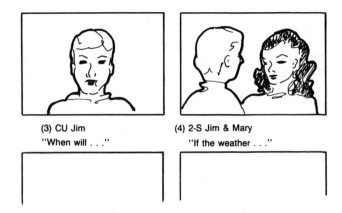

(3) CU Jim
"When will . . ."

(4) 2-S Jim & Mary
"If the weather . . ."

FIGURE 1–8
A preproduction storyboard. A storyboard contains aspect ratio frames with sketches of the proposed subject and framing, and a framing symbol with audio copy under each frame.

which in turn give a camera operator a sense of the pacing and the length of video to be shot. (See the storyboard form.)

Doing the script breakdown (P 6).   After the script and/or a storyboard is completed, doing a breakdown of the script takes the project a step closer to production. Because the video and audio of a script and/or storyboard are in a proposed final edited order, it is necessary for a producer to break the script and/or storyboard down into the order of efficient videotaping. The breakdown entails listing the proposed video from the same environment and/or with the same talent to be videotaped at the same time. (See the script breakdown form.)

Creating the shot list (P 7).   It is a current efficient preference that remote video producers and crews work from a shot list. The shot list is created from the breakdown of the preproduction script. A shot list organizes the camera shots required from each location shoot and the order of the shots to be videotaped during the shoot. The listed shots include both interviews and cut-aways. This list serves to create a shooting order for the remote shoot and facilitates communication between a producer and a camera operator.

    The shot list also includes the framing desired for each shot (e.g., MS), the content of the framing (e.g., the doctor at his desk), and any secondary motion (e.g., zooming, panning, tilting) that may be required during the videotaping. Some idea of the length or pacing of a shot (e.g., an interview, or a zoom of :05) also serves to move a videotape shoot along. (See the shot list form.)

Designing the production schedule (P 8).   Once the producer has completed the preproduction script and/or storyboard, the script breakdown, and the shot list, and when location(s) have been scouted and firmed up, a production schedule can be drawn up and set. Production schedules contain the following information: (1) the day and date(s) for the location shoot, (2) crew call times, (3) production meeting times, (4) location arrival times, (5) equipment set-up deadlines, (6) talent call, (7) meal breaks, (8) location host contact names and telephone numbers, and

(9) anticipated strike time. For outdoor shoots, rain dates are often included in the schedule. (See the production schedule form.)

Accepting an assigned or choosing a camera/videotape recorder operator (P 9).   Policy differs from news operation to operation. In some production facilities, a producer chooses a camera/videotape recorder operator; in others, they are assigned. There are advantages both ways; in either case, a producer should arrange to meet with the camera/videotape recorder operator.

Meeting with the camera/videotape recorder operator (P 10).   The producer should meet with the camera/videotape recorder operator to discuss production goals and objectives and the video production values of the proposed shoot. Other content of this meeting between the producer and camera/videotape recorder operator is the preproduction script, storyboard, script/storyboard breakdown, shot list, and production schedule. Because the camera/videotape recorder operator is also responsible for lighting the location and audio recording for the shoot, these elements should also be included for discussion in this preproduction meeting.

Meeting with the producer (C/VTRO 1).   The first requirement of a camera/videotape recorder operator is to meet with the producer of the soft news package. The sooner the camera/videotape recorder operator is involved in preproduction stages, the better planning can occur for the location shoot itself. The camera operator should have copies of the preproduction script, storyboard, shot list, location site survey, and the production schedule. These allow a camera operator to begin planning for the location production. If the choice is the camera/videotape recorder operator's to make, an audio director might be discussed at this meeting.

Creating equipment/accessories list (C/VTRO 2).   When the production schedule is firmed up, crew members with equipment responsibilities (e.g., camera operator, audio director) should prepare equipment needs lists. These lists contain available equipment/accessories, equipment/accessories that need to be purchased, and equipment/accessories that need to be rented. An equipment checklist suggests and reminds the camera/videotape recorder operator of needed equipment and accessories for the location shoot. (See the equipment check list.)

Requisitioning equipment and accessories (C/VTRO 3).   Once the camera/videotape recorder operator has determined the available equipment, and the equipment needed to be rented or purchased, these needs of the production have to be requisitioned. In most video production facilities, this means that notification of available equipment needs, dates, and times has to be submitted to some supervisory/maintenance personnel. Those needs that have to be rented or purchased should be submitted also to proper personnel to be authorized and obtained to meet the production schedule.

Working the shot list (C/VTRO 4).   After the production meeting, the camera/videotape recorder operator is able to creatively prepare the location shoot with the shot list and notes from the location scouting. The camera/video-tape recorder operator can plan camera and videotape recorder set-up placement, lighting design and placement, audio recording design and microphone placement, and power sources and cable runs before getting to the location site.

Obtaining clearance, insurance, and notifying police (P 11). Once the preproduction stages are complete, the producer has a better idea of the creative needs of the final video package. These needs can often include the choice of music, published text, or visuals (e.g., photographs). The producer must know what video and/or audio elements intended for the video package are copyrighted and who holds the copyright for each element. It is the producer's responsibility to clear all copyrighted material for the news package for use in the proposed video. It is the producer who begins the process of copyright clearance. Copyright clearance usually takes more time than a phone call to a publisher. Many copyright owners require the copyright clearance request to be made in writing before production use of copyrighted materials. This requires a lengthy lead time. Once the production schedule is firm, other production needs can be attended to, such as insurance and police notification. Insurance coverage (equipment, bodily injury, and property) should be covered by the producer for all location sites, cast, and crew. A production facility has probably already provided for coverage, and the only thing needed by the producer is notification of the insurance holder of dates, names, places, and an equipment list.

When some location sites include public exteriors, local police departments need to be notified and, when necessary, arrangements have to be made in advance for closing streets and/or regulating traffic. Even if the production does not need exterior locations of public places, the size of a production crew can be so large when invading a neighborhood it is good practice to notify police that you are there and that you have authorization.

THE PRODUCTION PROCESS: SOFT NEWS

The challenging nature of the soft news video package is to successfully accomplish the preproduced remote location video package. The remote location production process in video as in film is all too often a tedious experience with constant breakdowns in communication among responsible crew; this need not always be the case. If quality preproduction has occurred to this point, a conscious attempt to live by and follow through with preproduced details will affect a smooth flowing and pleasant field production experience. From a preproduced project, a well-prepared crew, and an efficient field production, a quality video package can emerge.

• Personnel

Producer (P). The producer is responsible for all location details pertaining to the video production and the crew.

This responsibility to the location began when a location was scouted for production values. The location choice decision should have been followed up with a confirmation mailing to the location personnel. A telephone call reminder to the location host should be made the day before the shoot is planned. The producer fulfills a director's role on location. The producer should keep the crew on schedule, relate with the talent, and decide the videotaped take, wrap, and location strike.

Camera/videotape recorder operator (C/VTRO). The camera/videotape recorder operator has the responsibility for all required remote video production equipment. Depending on the needs expressed on the equipment list, the camera/videotape recorder operator is responsible to get all requisitioned equipment, whether available, rented, or purchased, to the location. The next obligation of the camera operator/videotape recorder operator is the set-up and test of the camera and videotape recording equipment. Following camera set-up, the camera/videotape recorder operator is required to light the location set. Lighting is generally the longest set-up on a location shoot and should be facilitated the most. The camera/videotape recorder operator should have the shot list, which is helpful in preparing for videotaping. The production schedule should contain deadline times for set-ups.

Audio director (AD). The audio director joins the crew on the production day and works closely with the camera/videotape recorder operator. The producer should have given the audio director the preproduction script and shot list. The audio director is responsible for audio pick-up and recording equipment set-up. During a take the audio director monitors the audio input level into the videotape recorder. The audio director may be required to start rolling and stop the videotape recorder during videotaping. The audio director may also serve as mike grip also, holding the microphone extension pole during a shoot. This can be done while monitoring audio levels with a headset. For the location strike, the audio director is responsible for striking and loading all audio equipment.

Grip (G). The grip has to be ready to assist wherever needed. Much work is required during set-up. The grip may have to bounce from camera set-up to lighting to audio recording preparation. A grip may also be called upon to handle a fishpole with the microphone during videotaping or be responsible for rolling and stopping the videotape recorder.

Talent (T). Many soft news video packages are part of a larger television program format with talent who also serve as on-air studio hosts. The same host/talent may go on location with the remote production crew. These talent are usually called upon to do the interviewing, the stand-up lead, bridges, and stand-up tag for the video package. Talent is directly responsible to the producer. Depending on the custom of the production crew, the talent may either report to the location in make-up and proper dress or may be given time after arrival to prepare.

• Production Stages

Crew call (P 1). Although it may not seem important, a crew call for the entire crew serves many production purposes. Besides affording a rendezvous for the entire crew, a producer should use the occasion for a production meeting. This is an opportunity to set goals and objectives for the project as well as deadlines for stages of the shoot. This may be a time for a producer to share preproduction paperwork in the form of handouts to the crew to facilitate communication for the day.

The advantages of collective travel and arrival at a location cannot be overlooked. Traveling together means not getting lost on the way and arriving at the same time with the producer who has had public relations contact with the host location. Details and requirements for unloading and hauling of equipment from the unloading area to the shooting area are usually handled by the producer.

Part of the crew call can deal with the pick-up and transportation of equipment. An experienced crew will not leave an equipment pick-up site without first testing all the equipment and even recording and viewing some video. More shoots have been saved because a conscientious producer insisted on knowing before departing a rendezvous site that all equipment was in working order. A slight wiggle on every cable may help determine an electrical short while the cable can still be replaced or repaired.

Meeting location hosts (P 2). The producer has the responsibility to meet with representatives of the location site, personnel, or security. It is important to review all location needs as requested at the time the location was scouted and confirmed by a follow-up mailing. A telephone call should have been made to the location hosts as a reminder the day before the scheduled shoot.

Location hosts are often fascinated by video production details and techniques and are usually grateful to be introduced to crew and talent, and to be informed regarding the equipment and its contribution to the video production. Small courtesies to and involvement of the location host at this stage of a shoot can pay dividends to the producer and crew at a later time.

Handling all location details (P 3). All location details should go through the producer. It is important for the producer to stand firmly on what was agreed upon with the location host during scouting regarding the environment of the location. This includes any proposed changes to be made in moving furniture, wall decorations, window dressing, and so on. Many egos and sensitivities have been hurt and generosity bruised by liberties taken on location sites. It is always proper to check with the location representatives before making any changes or presuming any liberty to the location environment.

If rearrangements to the location site have been agreed upon, it is good to take instant developing film photographs of the location site before changing the environment as an aid in returning the site at the end of a shoot to the way it was upon arrival. It is also a good practice to check on security for personal belongings and nonutil-

ized equipment during a stay at a location. Frequently, host personnel has arranged for a secure room for that purpose.

Arranging equipment pick-up/delivery (C/VTRO 1). The camera/videotape recorder operator created the equipment list during preproduction and noted available equipment, equipment to be rented and equipment to be purchased. At that time some arrangements were probably made for pick-up and delivery of purchased and rented equipment on the day of production. These arrangements need to be checked and followed up close to the production day.

The camera/videotape recorder operator should know from the location scouting form where replacement equipment and accessories can be purchased in the geographic vicinity of the location shoot. Knowing where a hardware or electronics store is in the area of the shoot can come in handy when some equipment or accessory needs to be repaired or replaced during the location shoot.

Setting up the camera and videotape recorder (C/VTRO 2). Once unloading the equipment has been accomplished, and the crew knows from the producer and/or the shot list what the first videotaped take will be, work can proceed on respective equipment set-ups. It is good practice to keep the producer informed on the progress of each set-up and be alerted to any problems encountered and time estimates for correction or repair. The production schedule noted deadlines for completing equipment set-up and check. These should be striven for and met.

Assisting the camera/videotape recorder operator (G 1). The grip is initially assigned to the camera/videotape recorder

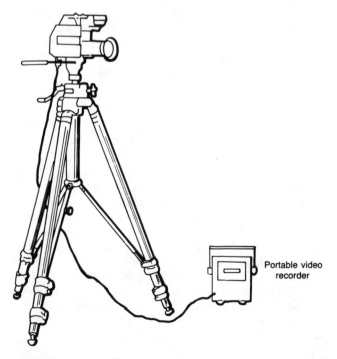

Portable video recorder

FIGURE 1–9
Equipment set-up. The minimum equipment required for the soft news video shoot are the camera, tripod, and videotape recorder. The tripod is not used in handheld camera videotaping.

operator to assist wherever necessary. A lot of assistance is needed during equipment set-up time and location lighting. During videotaping a grip may be asked to operate the videotape recorder, to monitor video levels, or to monitor audio input levels.

Supervising the grip (C/VTRO 3). The grip assigned to a remote video crew is usually under the supervision of camera/videotape recorder operator. The grip usually helps setting up any needed equipment.

Setting up lighting (C/VTRO 4). Without a lighting director, the camera/videotape recorder operator is responsible for lighting the location environment. The camera/videotape recorder operator knows what is required for lighting with the advance preparation of the preproduction script and shot list.

The camera/videotape recorder operator has the responsibility to choose the correct lighting instruments; run power cables; place lighting stands with lighting instruments mounted; aim, focus, and control the lights; make gel and scrim choices; and test the lighting on camera with the talent in place.

Knowing the preproduction script and shot list (AD 1). The audio director begins audio recording set-up by having a copy of the preproduction script and the shot list. These forms provide the audio director with the flow and demands of audio required for the production of the soft news video package.

The preproduction script informs the audio director of all the sound requirements for the entire production. Sound requirements may require more than location audio recording. Location sound requirements may include location playback demands such as a radio in the background, television audio sounds, or a music track. The shot list contains the order of the shooting takes. The shot list also facilitates the role of the audio director in planning audio pick-up and recording needs.

Setting up and checking location audio equipment and accessories (AD 2). The audio director should check with the camera/ videotape recorder operator for the equipment needed for audio recording on location. The camera/videotape recorder operator created the audio equipment needs in the equipment check list during preproduction.

Once the videotape recorder is set up and operating,

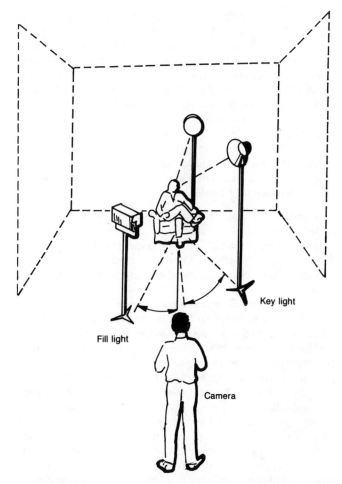

FIGURE 1–10
Basic soft news package remote lighting instruments and technique. The three-point lighting technique is a basic lighting pattern for the soft news video package.

audio cables can be connected and audio mike checks made. The audio equipment set-up requires the cooperation of the videotape recorder operator because microphone cable connections and the audio monitoring headset connection are made into the videotape recorder. The audio director should make a set-up check by having run cables, checking microphones for batteries, setting gain levels with talent or stand-ins, and listening carefully for

FIGURE 1–11
Soft news package audio equipment and techniques. (A) The mike is attached to a fishpole, which is extended into the videotaping set. (B) The talent may wear a lavaliere mike attached to clothing. (C) The producer or host may choose to use a handheld mike.

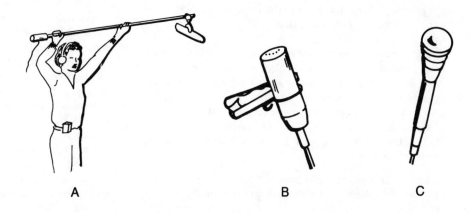

A   B   C

ambience sound that may be unacceptable or intolerable to the scene. The audio levels for voice recording can be made by watching the VU meter for audio input level and monitoring the audio by headset. When everything checks out, the producer should be notified. The audio director should be aware that a deadline was set on the production schedule for completing equipment set-up and checks. If some form of boom microphone is being used during videotaping, it will require set-up and checking as well as practice with a mike grip and talent. When the shoot will make use of a microphone boom, special attention has to be made of boom and mike shadows from lighting and from camera framing.

Directing talent/interviewee(s) (P 4). The producer takes directorial charge of the talent and interviewee(s) on location. The relations with the talent should be attended to as soon as possible. Talent have a need to know what to do, what is expected, and how long videotaping will take.

People who will be interviewed on location (newsmakers) need more attention from the producer than the crew. Usually, interviewees are new to the process and demands of location videotaping. Interviewees need to be coached and prepped to what is expected of them, where to look, what questions may be asked, what content is to be covered, how to answer, make-up and appearance, and so on. Often an assuring word is all that is needed. It is also a good idea to prepare interviewees to the tedium of many takes, camera replacement, poor sound recording, and relighting the location. It is good public relations to be able to tell talent exactly (as one can) when they will be needed for videotaping. It is equally good policy to have another stand-in for talent while setting lights and testing the camera and the microphone. The producer should call for some videotaping to be shot before calling talent. The need to troubleshoot technical problems while talent has to wait is a sign of an amateur crew. When it is time to videotape, the talent should be called and shown where to stand, sit, move, and look. Anticipating the questions of talent can save a lot of time, videotape stock, and patience.

Meeting with the producer (T 1). The initial responsibility of the talent for the soft news video package is to meet with the producer. The producer is in charge of the location production and serves as field director. The producer knows what is expected from all talent and is the primary source for that information. The producer will expect to meet with the talent and provide directorial information.

The talent should also have questions concerning their role. Questions are expected after the producer conveys what is to be expected from talent on location. It has to be assumed that persons performing roles in the production of a video project have some idea of what is expected of them. Even if the talent are the newsmaker, that role itself defines some of the expectations from talent during the location shoot.

Following the producer's directions (C/VTRO 5). Because the producer fills the role of a director on location, the camera/

videotape recorder operator should look for and follow all the production directions of the producer. The producer has the responsibility for the final videotape project and should know what is needed to accomplish that goal.

Supervising camera/videotape recorder set-up (P 5). Because the producer doubles as the director on location, it is the producer's responsibility to check both the camera and videotape recorder for placement and operating efficiency. This means checking for white balance and registration and "taking some pictures" to test all cable connections, looking through the viewfinder to check on camera position and framing, and so on.

When some videotape is recorded, the producer should play back the recorded tape and check the quality of the video. A sample of what the audience will eventually see is the best check of the camera placement, framing, and operation.

Supervising lighting set-up (P 6). Again, the producer takes a director's role and checks the lighting set-up. Because the producer has the completed concept of the soft news video package in mind, the producer should also check the set by eye through the viewfinder and even some recorded videotape for all aspects of lighting instruments, levels, design, mood, and shadows. The ultimate test of location lighting is to see the effect of the lighting as the audience will see it on some video playback check.

Supervising audio recording set-up and mike check (P 7). The producer should make the final set-up check with audio. This entails checking the microphones chosen to be used, verifying that they are picking up sound, noting how they are held (e.g., attached to a fishpole, pinned to a garment), and checking for cast shadows from some pole mounted mike. Some sound produced on a test bite of playback videotape is the best test.

Being prepared with make-up and clothing appearance (T 2). Talent for the soft news video package usually come to the location environment in make-up and with required clothing. Required clothing may be an actor's costume or ordinary street clothes. Location make-up may also be provided. The least make-up all talent should use is translucent powder for the touch-up of oily skin and perspiration. Common baby powder is a good translucent powder to use.

One rule for talent is "hurry up and wait." Video location shoots are notorious for delays. The person most vulnerable to delay is the talent. Delays take the edge off readiness and spontaneity. It is professional for the talent to be aware of demands on time and preparedness on a location shoot. Talent should hold themselves to expect delays and to be always ready. It is good practice to distance oneself from all the equipment set-up and testing activity but still be immediately present.

Talent are frequently called upon to stand in place while lighting is adjusted and while microphones are checked for levels. Talent should be available for these technical demands and at the same time be able to absent themselves for recuperation and preparation.

Prepping the interview (P 8). Often an interview will have to be prepped in detail. This means placing the talent and interviewee in the lighted area and creating some dialogue to test microphone levels and check for shadows. The interview should be prepped for good responses. This entails coaching the interviewee to reword a talent's question in their response. With this kind of prepping, an interviewer's questions need not always be required on the edited master.

Being responsible to the producer for direction (T 3). Talent is responsible to the producer while on location. The producer functions as the director of talent on location. The producer will decide when to call talent to the set, when to begin, when to stop, when to redo a take, when to leave the set, and when videotaping is complete. Talent should be ready to respond to the needs of the other technical crew at the same time. The camera/videotape recorder operator and audio director may have to make requests of the talent before, during, and after a take.

Being required to perform any number of production tasks (G 2). The grip may be asked to perform any number of production tasks that do not need a lot of experience. Videotape recorder operation, i.e., rolling the tape, stopping the tape, is one such task. Another task might be to monitor the VU meters for audio or video level input; another, to mike grip—hold the microphone mount in the recording environment. The grip then is responsible to the crew member to whom the grip is assigned.

Calling for a take and a wrap (P 9). When the producer is assured that all equipment set-ups are complete and talent are ready, a take can be called for. Taping an interview requires less preparation than does an action take or dramatized scene. Interviews are staged either seated or standing, but usually without movement. Because an interviewee is an important subject of the videotape, that person's position should be featured. This means attempting to shoot the face as straight as possible. Placing the camera beside and slightly behind the interviewer allows the best image. This camera position can also permit an over-the-interviewer shoulder shot of the interviewee. Cheat shots of the interviewer, if necessary, can be taped after the interview proper.

A point for conducting interviews without the dialogue sounding like a television talk show is to ask the talent to repeat all questions before answering them. Then in editing more attention can be paid to the interviewee and little or no attention to the interviewer's questions.

During videotaping it is important again to be reminded that on single camera remote shoots, it is helpful to shoot for the edit. Untimely zooms or subject framing adjustments during an interview can create serious problems during an editing session. Because it is incorrect to cut from secondary movements (pan, tilt, dolly, truck, arc, zoom) to a static shot, it will be necessary for the camera operator to complete movements swiftly and give the postproduction editor some established video pad in which to effect an edit. A problem with framing adjustments during an interview is that a jump cut may result during editing; jump cuts create an edit that can be difficult to cover. The producer can direct the interview and call for the take from an off-camera position. Some standardizing directorial language and cueing is as follows:

Producer: "Stand by for a take."

Producer: "Ready to roll tape."

Audio director: "Ready to roll tape."

Producer: "Roll tape."

Audio director: "Tape is rolling."

Producer: "Action" or "First question."

Talent (pauses): Asks first question.

Producer (when interview is complete): "Cut."

Audio director: Stops videotape recorder.

Producer: Checks video and audio levels; replays tape on playback monitor. Announces intentions: "Take it again," "That's a wrap," "Next set-up," or "Strike the location."

If the shoot involves some action or drama, the producer is usually required to rehearse the various elements of the shoot. The producer should block the talent in the lighted area for the shoot, rehearse the talent alone, block the camera for the shot, rehearse both the talent and the camera, check both audio recording and lighting for changes, rehearse again if changes need to be made, and then call for a standby and take.

Producer: "Stand by for a take."

Producer: "Ready to roll tape."

Audio director: "Ready to roll tape."

Producer: "Roll tape."

Audio director: "Tape is rolling."

Producer (pauses): "Action!"

Talent (pauses): Begins action or dialogue.

Producer (records beyond edit point): "Cut!" Checks audio and video levels; replays tape on playback monitor. Announces intentions: "Take it again," "That's a wrap," "Next set-up," or "Strike the location."

The producer should determine what additional environments (interiors, exteriors), objects (photographs, posters, signs), or events (reenactments) might serve as cutaways during editing. Videotaping additional images usually is done after a primary videotape session. The same determination should be made about needed audio ambience. Uniform ambience should be used for any location voice-over copy, talent lead, bridges, or talent tag. The final determination of a wrap on location is the responsibility of the producer. It is the producer's choice whether another take should be made or not. Nonprofessional talent tire faster than professionals. All efforts should be made to get a take on the first try with nonprofessionals.

Videotaping the take (C/VTRO 6). When the scene has been rehearsed or the interview prepped, the producer should call for a take. The responsibility of the camera/videotape recorder operator is to follow directions and prepare to record the scene. During videotaping the camera/videotape recorder operator will have to monitor video levels occasionally while keeping an eye on the focusing and framing of the camera lens.

Monitoring audio during videotaping (AD 3). Similar to monitoring video levels during videotaping, audio levels need monitoring during a take. It is customary for an audio director to monitor audio by watching the VU meter on the videotape recorder and having set acceptable mean levels to monitor audio input over a headset all during the take. This monitoring can be done even while holding a microphone boom.

Recording location ambience (AD 4). Before a strike call the audio director has the responsibility to record some continuous, uninterrupted location ambience sound to use in postproduction mixing. It is the audio director's responsibility to remind the crew of this need and to get a good recording from the location environment.

Keeping a location log/continuity (P 10). An aid to the producer in preparation for postproduction editing is some accounting notation (a log) on all videotaped takes on location. This process is closely related to continuity note taking for drama production. The location log notes each consecutively numbered take, the content of each take, and a judgmental record of the production value of the take. The location log relates to both the shot list and the preproduction script. (See the location log form.)

If the location log is accurate, the tedious process of reviewing all source tape after production and before postproduction can be eliminated because a record of the shoot is contained in the log. The log should also record the videotape recorder counter number as each take begins and ends. This implies that the counter was reset to zero and each videotape rewound at the beginning of each shoot. The producer will have to request this information from the videotape recorder operator.

Calling for a location strike (P 11). One of the final responsibilities of the producer on location is to determine when videotaping is complete. When all necessary video is complete, i.e., scripted copy, interviews, cut-aways, and ambience audio, the producer can call for a strike. A strike call should occasion a reminder to the crew of special directions from the location host on returning the location environment to its original appearance. Special departure instructions may be required by the location host, for example, using a freight elevator, a particular exit door, or loading dock. Some remote production crews carry a box of cleaning chemicals and cloths to clean the environment before they leave. Generally, this entails washing, dusting, and cleaning any surfaces handled or taped during production. This is a courtesy that may be rewarded with location access permission when a return visit to the location may be necessary for the present shoot or some future shoot. The location strike may signal the last chance a producer has for obtaining necessary talent release signatures. (See the talent release form.)

Supervises the location strike (C/VTRO 7). The camera/videotape recorder operator has the final responsibility of supervising the strike of the camera, videotape recorder, and lighting equipment. Lighting instruments should be allowed to cool down before striking. A sudden jar to very hot light bulbs can break filament and cause a loss of light life. The strike entails the supervision by the camera/videotape recorder operator of both the grip and audio director in the breakdown and repacking of all other equipment. The camera operator has the added responsibility of removing the record button from all the videocassettes and properly labeling each recorded videocassette with the title of the project, the producer, location, talent, and date before striking the equipment.

Striking location audio (AD 5). The audio director has the responsibility to strike the audio equipment after the final take. Microphones need the most immediate care in handling because of their sensitivity. Mikes are more vulnerable with the rush of talent to leave a set and the call to strike a location by the crew. An audio director should retrieve microphones first and return them to secure casings as soon as possible after a wrap or strike call.

Assisting in the equipment and location strike (G 3). The grip should take an active part in all equipment and location strikes. This means asking crew members where their inexperienced help could be best utilized. The grip should ask questions about the proper breakdown of equipment before plunging into the strike if striking a location is new to them.

THE POSTPRODUCTION PROCESS: SOFT NEWS

The postproduction stages of the soft news video production package are not under the deadline pressure of the hard news video production. Because soft news pieces are evergreen, the need to edit swiftly does not usually exist. Quality preparation for postproduction editing is beneficial in the completed master.

• Personnel

Producer (P). The producer of the soft news video package is responsible for postproduction details: preparing the source videotapes for editing, reserving facilities, and scheduling the editing suite. In some postproduction operations, the producer may also serve as editor; in other operations, a videotape editor/technical director is assigned to the project. In any case, the producer has the responsibility to make final editing decisions.

Camera/videotape recorder operator (C/VTRO). With the production of the soft news video package completed, there are only summary tasks remaining for the camera/videotape recorder operator. The return and accountability of video production equipment accessories remain the final responsibility of the camera/videotape recorder operator.

Audio director (AD). The audio director has final responsibilities due at postproduction time: returning equipment and reporting damage, loss, and malfunctioning.

Videotape editor/technical director (E/TD). It is the requirement of some editing facilities to require an editor/technical director. In such a case, the producer will have to work with the editor/technical director during editing sessions. The responsibility of editing decisions is still that of the producer.

• Postproduction Stages

Arranging postproduction editing schedule and facilities (P 1). Because the full responsibility of the soft news video piece rests with the producer, the producer is required to schedule editing time given adequate preparation time beforehand and to reserve the requisite editing suite. Postproduction facilities usually do permit "walk-in" editing time and equipment. Adequate advance scheduling for both an editing timetable and editing suite is more important if a technical director/editor must also be scheduled.

Returning remote video equipment and accessories (C/VTRO 1). It is the responsibility of the camera/videotape recorder operator to return to maintenance/storage facilities all the equipment used during the remote location shoot. Rented equipment would have to be returned to the equipment rental agency. Equipment purchased for the shoot should be reported separately to maintenance/storage personnel.

Returning audio equipment and accessories (AD 1). The responsibility of the audio director is to return all remote audio recording equipment and accessories to maintenance/storage facilities.

Reporting damaged, lost, or malfunctioning equipment (C/VTRO 2). As a final obligation to the soft news video shoot, the camera/videotape recorder operator should report any equipment or accessory that may have been damaged during the location shoot. This report should also include any loss of equipment or accessories. Most equipment maintenance/storage personnel also appreciate a written report of any equipment or accessory that may have malfunctioned during the location shoot. It is good practice to report any repair or replacement made to equipment during the shoot.

Reporting damaged, lost, or malfunctioning equipment (AD 2). The final responsibility of the audio director is to report any damaged equipment, lost equipment, or equipment that is malfunctioning. Maintenance personnel also expect a report of any repair that was made on location and any replacement that had to be done while on location.

Preparing the source tapes (P 2). The producer begins preparing the source tapes from the location shoot by reorganizing all source tapes according to the preproduction script and the location log. Location shoots are usually videotaped out of order from the preproduction script. They must be put in order of editing needs. The source tapes should be striped with SMPTE time code if editing is to be done with time code. This step simply requires the time to run all the tapes, master tape also, through a videotape recorder that is programmed to record SMPTE time code on one of the two audio tracks of the videotape. If editing is not going to be done with time code, when video was laid on the source tapes during videotaping, a

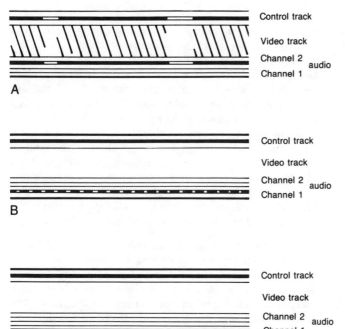

A

B

C

Control track

Video track

Channel 2
Channel 1 } audio

FIGURE 1-12
Source and master tape control tracks and SMPTE track. (A) Source tape with interrupted control track with interrupted video and audio taping. (B) Master tape uninterrupted SMPTE code striping (and control track). (C) Master tape with uninterrupted control track.

control track was also laid along with the video and audio tracks, and they function as a basic code for postproduction editing.

Preparing the master videotape (P 3). The producer should designate a fresh, high quality videotape as the master tape. This tape will have to be striped with SMPTE time code. If time code is not being used, the master tape will have to be striped with a control track.

Viewing source tapes and recording editing work sheets (P 4). If location log sheets were not accurately kept on location, or if the producer or editor deems it necessary, all the source tapes will have to be viewed and described on editing work sheets. The editing work sheet is a verbal description of each source videotape listing of all location takes with some form of measurement, with either videotape recorder counter notation, clock time from a stopwatch, or SMPTE time code, and some judgmental remark indicating the quality of each video take. (See the editing work sheet.)

The main purpose of the editing work sheet is to make

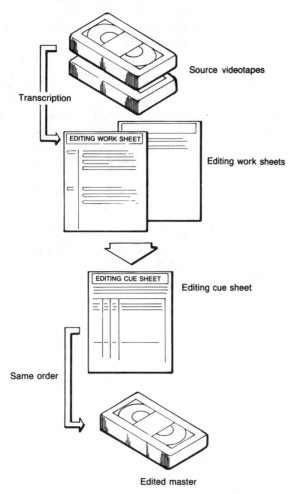

FIGURE 1–13
The relationship of the editing work sheet to the source tapes and the editing cue sheet to the edited master. The editing work sheet is a descriptive transcription of the source tapes; the editing cue sheet is a format of the edited master tape.

the video editing sessions proceed smoothly and swiftly. The more information about the content of the source videotapes and where that content is on the source videotapes that can be made at this stage, the fewer questions in editing sessions, thus saving valuable time and money. Some producers prefer to make a transcription of the content of interviews to better assist them in making editing content decisions later.

Writing a script (P 5). At this stage the producer may realize that the location shoot deviated from the preproduction script or the interviews went in an unanticipated direction so that a new script will have to be written. With the preproduction script as a point of reference, and the content of the interviews and location video in mind, the producer should write a final production script.

Creating an editing cue sheet (P 6). From the editing work sheet and the final production script the producer should create the editing cue sheet. The editing cue sheet is an enormous time-saving step in postproduction. The editing cue sheet is a written format of the proposed final edited master organized from the editing work sheet according to the final production script. The editing cue sheet contains the chosen video and/or audio bites from the editing work sheet with in-cues and out-cues of each bite indicated, and the length of each bite in the juxtaposed order of the final production script. (See the editing cue sheet.)

Because the storyboard is a communication aid from the producer to the camera operator, the editing cue sheet is a communication aid from a producer to the editor in the editing suite. The advantage of the editing cue sheet is that expensive editing suite time can be saved outside the editing suite in preparation for editing. On the editing cue sheet, a producer can construct the format of the proposed edited master tape on paper from the editing work sheet before entering an editing session.

The editing session: editing or supervising editing (P 7). It is usually not necessary to perform a rough edit before attempting a final edit for the soft news video package. Unlike the television commercial, there is usually not a specific time length accuracy to be achieved with the soft news video package, which would necessitate a rough edit first. When all the proper preparation work has been done for the editing session, master videotape editing can move swiftly. Maximum advantage should be taken of the editing work sheet and editing cue sheets. If an associate producer can be employed in the editing suite, source tape video can be fast searched for the good video bites indicated on the editing work sheets while the producer and/or editor are performing a previous edit.

Mixing: adding music, effects, and ambience (P 8). If SMPTE time code is being used in editing, the second audio track cannot be utilized until the last stage of editing because the track will have to be erased of the time code signal to make additional use of the second audio track. The producer will save music, sound effects, or location ambience track as a final editing task. In control track editing only, the second audio track is free to be used for a second audio track without having to wait until last. For some telecast requirements, when two audio tracks have been used in the editing process they will be required to be mixed down into one track before broadcast. It is important to know from broadcast operations which of the two audio channels will have to hold the new mixed audio track.

Timing the final edited master (P 9). The producer has to make a final and accurate timing of the master tape from first audio to last audio. There may be exceptions to this if the real starting point (or ending point) of the piece is not an audio cue. If such is the case, that should be noted to the program producer or studio director. This timing has to be made with a stopwatch in real clock time. (See the edited master clipsheet.)

Writing character generator copy (P 10). There remain some final tasks for the producer before the soft news video package can be turned over to the broadcast program producer. The producer of the package is responsible for the correct character generator copy to be inserted over the soft news video during telecast. Accuracy of this copy should entail spelling of proper names, and the full and correct title of the person being labeled. Much of this information should be recorded on the location log records or the continuity records. (See the edited master clipsheet.)

Coordinating character generator copy with the timed master tape (P 11). The clock timing of the edited video package and the character generator copy must be coordinated. This entails making in and out time notation for insert matting each character generator text screen over the correct video at the proper time during telecast.

Beginning with the stopwatch at zero and the first audio cue of the video package, time consecutively to the point where each character generator screen text should be inserted. Record both matte in-point and out-point video for the period the character generator copy should remain on the video screen. Continue consecutive timing to the next text insert and record those in- and out-points. (See edited master clipsheet.)

Labeling the edited master videotape cassette and cassette case (P 12). It is an important practice for the master videotape cassette and video cassette case to be accurately labeled. Labels should contain at least the title of the video package, the producer's name, the date, and the length. Both the cassette label and the case label should contain identical information.

VIDEO PRODUCTION ORGANIZING FORMS

• Treatment Form

Production process: Soft news preproduction

Responsibility: Producer

Purpose: To propose a soft news video package to video production managing personnel, executive producer, or news director.

Objective: The treatment form attempts to focus elements of the proposed video package for the producer as a step to presenting the idea or concept to production management personnel for approval. The basic needs required by production management to judge the appropriateness of a video package include goals and objectives for the video package and some verbal description of the proposed visual imaging.

Glossary

Proposed Title A working title is appropriate to the proposed video package described in the treatment. There is an advantage to titling a proposed video package. In the synthesis of a simple title can be contained a concept or idea that paragraphs cannot convey.

Proposed Length Committing to a time length for the video package is a good discipline for the video producer. In many video production operations, all video packages will have to fall within a given range of time length. The time length commitment gives management personnel a grasp of the likelihood of the success of the video package and its content in terms of its length.

Proposed Shooting Date Most video production managers have to operate in terms of a calendar of video packages for broadcast purposes. Thus, the commitment to a shooting date allows more information in the judgment of approving supervisory personnel.

Proposed Completion Date Another bit of information for a video production manager is the estimated date for the completion of the video package. Many completion dates depend on the content and challenge of videotaping a topic and editing the source tapes.

Production Statement A production statement is a brief emotional or rational verbal expression that functions as a reminder during all stages of the project's production of the specific goal or objective of the video package. The production statement is meant to be a constant reminder to crew members of the precise goal of the message of the production. An example of a production statement for a video package on senior citizen exercise groups is "Being senior is being strong."

Communication Goals and Objectives of the Production Stating communication goals and objectives for the proposed video package should contain the rationale for doing the proposed video, who the target audience is, the audience needs for the video package in terms of the topic, and the interests in the topic on the part of the audience. The more information that can be given in this section of the treatment aids the video manager in judging the suitability of the proposed video package for broadcast.

Package Treatment The treatment itself is the verbal description of the proposed video including proposed interviewees, questions for the interview, proposed cutaways for the piece, and proposed locations for shooting. The more information that is available at this stage of preproduction, the better a video production manager can judge the treatment for approval. The treatment should be seen as a synopsis of the proposed video

easily rented if needed. Caution must be exercised with the use of a power generator. They are a source of unwanted noise in the environment, which can be difficult to control.

Audio Problems Defined This area of the form focuses on details that will affect the production of audio recording in the proposed location environment.

Interior Environmental Sounds This entry should contain all perceived sound that is audible in the interior of the proposed location environment. This means careful listening for hums and buzzes from air conditioning, refrigerators, freezers, sound speakers, copying machines, fluorescent lights, and so on. All sounds should be noted. Note should also be made of the ability to control or turn off the sounds.

Ceiling Composition The composition of a ceiling can determine the quality of sound recordings made in the proposed location environment. For example, a hard composition ceiling will reflect sound; sound proofing materials on a ceiling will absorb sound. Both can make a difference in the quality of recorded sound.

Wall Composition The composition on the walls of a proposed location environment will also make a difference in the quality of sound recorded in that environment. For example, cork, carpet or cloth, and sound proofing will absorb sound; tile, mirror, and plaster will reflect sound.

Exterior Environmental Sounds Location scouts must listen carefully to both interior and exterior sounds in an environment. Exterior sounds will affect both an exterior and an interior shoot. For example, some common exterior sounds that can affect an interior shoot are airplanes, emergency vehicles, a school playground, a busy highway, and a noisy manufacturing plant. Make note of every perceivable sound.

Floor Covering Composition The composition of a floor will also have an effect on sound recording in an environment. For example, a polished hardwood or tile floor will reflect sound as well as create sound (e.g., footsteps). Deep pile carpeting will absorb sound.

Cast and Crew Needs This area of the form reminds location scouts that care and consideration of cast and crew needs will have to be accounted for during a location shoot.

Restroom Facilities Restroom facilities for men and women will have to be provided. Part of the location site survey is to note, perhaps on the diagram of the location, where the restroom facilities are closest to the shooting area.

Green Room Availability A green room is a theater term for a waiting area for actors. Some such waiting area may also be required for the cast for the video production. This should be a room close to the shooting area, but separate from the shooting area where cast can relax and await their blocking and videotaping call.

Parking Arrangements A remote video production crew and cast can create a parking space demand on a neighborhood or public parking area. During scouting the question of special parking should be addressed. This may occasion some parking privileges or special directions or restrictions.

Freight Elevator In some location environments, the number of crew, cast, and equipment involved in video production may require the use of a freight elevator in a facility. The location of the freight elevator should be part of a location environment diagram giving directions from the freight elevator to the shooting area.

Eating Facilities When the length of a shooting day will require a meal on location, some eating facility, special room, or vending machines should be noted. Some facilities may prohibit any eating on the premises. Notation then will have to be made of restaurants in the vicinity of the proposed location.

Make-up Facilities If the video production requires that cast or talent appear in make-up, some facility will have to be provided for the application of the make-up. Ideally, make-up application requires mirrors, adequate lighting, and sinks. Restroom facilities make decent make-up preparation accommodations. If nothing else is available, a double set of restrooms can be designated for make-up and costuming.

Loading/Unloading Restrictions The amount of equipment needed for a remote video production may require special unloading and loading requirements at a location site, e.g., an outside loading dock area. Such an unloading dock may also be close to a freight elevator. Location personnel should always be made aware of the great amount of equipment video production requires. They should be the judge of any special circumstances that might be required for so much equipment.

Hardware Store Because remote video production demands so much hardware equipment, there is often the need to purchase supplies or replace broken, lost, or forgotten supplies. Facilities representatives may be the persons to know where the closest hardware store is in the vicinity of the proposed location environment.

Civil Emergency Services This area of the form lists essential civil services in the service of both the production cast and crew and the location site.

Police Station The address and phone number of the police station that services the proposed location site is important contact information. With the number of individuals a remote video production crew involves, the amount of equipment and the use of an environment warrants the sensitivity to police presence and availability.

Fire Station The same holds true for the fire protection station within the environmental area of the proposed location shoot site. The heavy use of electrical power for a remote video production shoot should alert both producer and production crew to the potential dangers of so much power use. This holds especially true for an older facility such as a private home used as a location site. The address and phone number of the fire station should be entered here.

Location Security and Equipment Safety This area of the form records important information on general personal and property security and safety.

Facility Security This entry records the general security of crew and cast and equipment during the production shoot. Some proposed locations in highly public areas such as a shopping mall will present security risks;

confined production sites such as a private home would be more secure. Note should be made of apparent security in general for all production elements.

Personnel Values Security　Record should be made of the arrangements made with facilities personnel for the safety and security of personal belongings while crew and cast are involved in production. This includes wallets and purses especially. Facilities personnel often can provide a locked and secure room for the deposit of personal valuables during production.

Equipment Safe Storage　Arrangements should be made for the security of unused equipment and accessories that should be safely stored until needed or stored after use until the location strike. The facilities personnel can often provide a locked and secure room for equipment storage.

Overnight Storage/Security　Often remote location shoots will take place over the period of more than one day. This will entail the safe and secure storage of equipment overnight. Complete breakdown of all location equipment and loading, transport, and unloading a second day can result in the loss of valuable time and energy. Facilities personnel can often provide adequate overnight storage that is both safe and secure.

Other Relevant Information　This area of the form records other important information that falls outside the other areas of location details.

Public Area Power Source　Often in public areas such as a city park, the local power company may already provide a power box with electrical outlets for private use. This service has to be requested from the power company and a deposit made to secure power costs at the end of the production shoot. Location scouts should search a public area for some sign of power source facility. It may serve the site survey to make a call to the local power company and request a listing of outdoor power sources.

Clearance/Insurance　Personal security for the crew and talent and property damage insurance coverage should be secured before video production. Academic programs have personal insurance coverage for students and property damage and loss coverage for school equipment that is active when the shoot is a valid academic project with a supervising faculty present. Other remote video production projects can easily receive coverage by contacting a reliable insurance agent. Some potential location facilities personnel require verification of insurance coverage before approval of their location for a shoot. Anticipating insurance notification before facilities personnel require it is a sign of professional competence.

Photographs Taken　When more than one location environment is being scouted for a shoot and a decision must be made away from a potential site, a producer will have to judge from the location scout's report. An important part of a location site survey is photographs of the proposed location. Instant developing film is most convenient. When adequate photographs of a location site are part of a survey, these photographs help a producer and camera operator plan a shoot and assist a crew after a location strike in replacing a location environment to the arrangement and condition it was before the production crew arrived. The photographs taken should be listed. The photographer's camera position and direction of the lens of the photographed site should be noted on the location diagram as an aid in designing the video camera shots and lens framing for the production.

Location Environment Drawing/Map　Another important product of location scouting is a drawing or map of the proposed location site. This entails a rough pacing off of all environments, both interior and exterior, that are being considered as a video setting. Windows should be placed, compass direction indicated, power outlets and circuits noted, and existing furniture and other properties sketched. Everything should be included that may enter into the use of the location from the needs of the production and the adaptability of the location environment.

Traffic Control　At some exterior location environments, the extent of a video production crew, talent, and equipment will necessitate some control of vehicular traffic. For example, parking restriction may be required along the area of a shooting set, moving traffic may have to be redirected during a shoot, or a street may have to be closed off entirely from traffic. Most police departments are cooperative to such requests, but they will need adequate advance time notification. In some instances the approval of a city or town council may be required. This also requires adequate lead time to process the request and get it to the council in good time for the shoot or a change of plans if the request should be denied.

Exterior Compass Direction　If the remote location site is an exterior shoot, an accurate assessment of the compass directions of the area should be made with respect to the proposed shooting site. The sun is the principal light source to an exterior shoot and that source is in constant movement. Knowing the direction the sun takes from east to west on a proposed location environment is a most important variable to designing an outdoor video shoot. A compass is a necessity to scouting a location site. Many location personnel are not accurate about their recollection of east and west directions and are not reliable sources of information, given the importance that the sun's direction has on a remote video shoot.

Other Comments/Observations　This area should record any other details not covered in the form to this point. It is important to record all impressions of a proposed location site. Sometimes the smallest detail missed or the smallest detail included can become either an obstacle or an asset to the production later. When in doubt about including a detail, include it.

● **Storyboard Form**

Production process:　Soft news preproduction

Responsibility:　Producer

Purpose:　To assist in the imaging, flow, and pacing of a proposed soft news video package.

Objective: The storyboard form coordinates in aspect ratio form each change of screen image and audio copy in sequential manner. The storyboard facilitates the communication of concept and image of a video project to camera operators and editors. A storyboard encourages a producer to make a commitment to video elements of screen content, framing, and picturization.

Notes on use: Each aspect ratio frame should be sketched with basic form or design of proposed video content. The basic form or design should approximate the desired video framing expected by the camera. A new frame should be sketched for every significant proposed image change. Transitions between frames other than the cut can be indicated in the space between frames. Frames should be numbered consecutively for reference purposes. Below each frame corresponding audio copy should be recorded.

- **Video Script/Storyboard Form**

Production process: Soft news preproduction

Responsibility: Producer

Purpose: To coordinate a verbal description of the proposed video and the proposed audio copy with corresponding storyboard frames.

Objective: The video script and storyboard combination form is an alternative script form in which each corresponding storyboard frame is coordinated with the verbal visual description and audio copy.

Glossary

Video This column is used similarly to the video column in the two column script form. It should contain a simplified verbal description of the video content, camera framing, edit transition, and character generator copy of the proposed video project.

Storyboard Frame Those storyboard frames should be used that coordinate with the entry in the video column. Not all frames will be used or needed. Simply skip those frames that do not match video and audio entries. See the directions for using storyboard aspect ratio frames on the storyboard form.

Audio This column is used similarly to the audio column in the two column script form. It contains all audio copy for the proposed video package. As with any television script, audio copy should be written first; then the video descriptions opposite the respective audio cue should be created. On this form the storyboard frame should then be sketched corresponding to the first line of each new VIDEO column entry description.

- **Script Breakdown Form**

Production process: Soft news preproduction

Responsibility: Producer

Purpose: To break the preproduction script down into production units usually according to common location or talent requirements.

Objective: The script breakdown form organizes the preproduction script from the proposed edited order of a final video to a shooting order according to differing common criteria for the shoots, e.g., location similarity and talent. The breakdown form helps organize the shooting units by script pages or number of script lines criteria for managing the remote production.

Glossary

Length This entry records the estimated length of the final soft news package.

Script Length The length of the preproduction script in number of script pages is recorded here.

Script Pages Script pages is one of several modes of measuring the length of a remote shooting unit. This method uses the number of whole or partial pages of script copy as a determinant of length of a shooting unit.

No. of Script Lines The number of lines of script copy is another determinant of length of a shooting unit. The count should be every line of talent copy to be recorded during the unit shoot.

Int/Ext These abbreviations stand for interior/exterior referring to the script demands for shooting indoors or outdoors. Whether the shoot is an interior or an exterior shoot can also be a determinant for the script breakdown and shooting unit.

Time The time of day or night required by the location and interior/exterior setting should be recorded here.

Setting The specific area of a required location site, e.g., a setting would be the parents' bedroom for the Smith's home location site.

Location The location column records the remote location environment at which the setting is to be found. For example, the Smith's home is the location site for the parents' bedroom.

Talent This entry records by name the specific talent who are required in the setting at the location for a particular shoot.

Shooting Order When the entire script is broken down into shooting units, then the producer can determine the units for individual shoots and the consecutive shooting order for the entire remote project.

- **Shot List Form**

Production process: Soft news preproduction

Responsibility: Producer or camera operator

Purpose: To translate the preproduction script from the script breakdown into location shooting units or camera takes.

Objective: The shot list form organizes each proposed videotape take on location into shooting units. The shooting units generate the necessary video to create the proposed soft news video package as designed on the preproduction script. This preproduction task facilitates the ''what's next'' syndrome during location productions. The shot list should exactly define each and every camera set-up, lens framing, and video shot needed to achieve that video.

Glossary

Location   Every planned location site camera set-up and change of location site camera set-up should be noted in this column.

Shot No.   From the script breakdown form, every necessary shot needed to create the imaging of the preproduction script should be numbered consecutively. The respective number should be recorded here.

Master Shot   If a proposed shot is a master shot or establishing shot (e.g., XLS) for a scene, it should be noted here. For example, a master shot might be an XLS of a couple walking toward the camera during dialogue.

Cut-in Shot   If a proposed shot is a cut-in (from a master shot), it should be noted in this column. For example, a cut-in might be a CU shot of one of the couple in the master shot.

Cut-away Shot   Unlike the cut-in (to a master shot), the cut-away shot is relevant but extraneous to (usually away from) the master scene shot. An example of a cut-away would be generic footage of a city street.

Shot Framing   Shot framing directions for every proposed shot should make use of the symbols for the basic camera shot framing: XLS, LS, MS, CU, XCU. This would communicate to the camera operator the lens framing for the proposed shot.

Shot Motion   Shot motion directions should indicate the kind of movement desired in the proposed shot. Movement in a shot can be either primary movement (on the part of the talent in front of the camera) the blocking of the talent, or secondary movement (on the part of the camera itself) the pan, tilt, arc, truck, dolly, pedestal, or zoom.

Content Notes   Any particular details of any shot that are not covered in the previous directions can be noted here. An example of a content note would be to direct the camera operator to defocus the lens during the shot.

• **Equipment Checklist Form**

Production process: Soft news preproduction

Responsibility: Camera/videotape recorder operator

Purpose: To suggest and account for all possible equipment and accessories necessary for a successful remote video shoot.

Objective: The equipment checklist form is an all-inclusive checklist for equipment and accessories hardware that may be needed on a video production location site. The checklist notes first the equipment available to the production crew, usually the equipment owned by the production facility. Second, the list notes the equipment that may have to be purchased for the shoot. Third, the

checklist allows for notation for any equipment that may have to be rented for the shoot. There are blank lines in equipment groups to personalize the checklist for an individual production or facility.

Glossary

Location(s)   The location(s) for which the equipment will be needed should be noted here.

Avl   This abbreviation stands for available equipment that may be owned by the production facility itself. A check in this column indicates that the equipment or accessory is available to the production crew and free to be used on the scheduled production day.

Pch   This abbreviation stands for purchase and indicates that the needed equipment or accessory will have to be purchased for the production project. Items checked as needed to be purchased will probably require some other requisition step and approval. The checklist also does not imply when the purchasing will be done or by whom. This is the responsibility of the production crew member.

Rnt   This abbreviation stands for rent and indicates that the needed equipment or accessory is not available, perhaps too expensive to purchase for the shoot, and will have to be rented from a supplier. Similar to items checked in the purchase column, additional steps may be required in the process of obtaining the rented equipment. Some requisition may have to be made, approval received, and rental details made.

Camera/Recorder/Tripod/Test Equipment/Audio/Power Supplies/Lighting/Cables   These areas of the form listed are an attempt to anticipate all possible equipment and accessories needs for a remote video production. Many items may be superfluous. They are listed as an attempt to suggest all possible production needs, and equally to suggest the use of some hardware that could be needed during a remote location shoot. One way to use this checklist is to permit it to suggest hardware elements to make the experience of a remote video shoot smooth and productive.

Miscellaneous   This area of the form is the result of years of remote video production experience and represents many production disasters during which these elements could have made a difference. Some items are redundant; some may suggest some use not before anticipated. Most items are helpful to the good order and task facilitation on location.

• **Production Schedule Form**

Production process: Soft news preproduction

Responsibility: Producer

Purpose: To organize and schedule the videotape production of individual script and location units of the video news package.

Objective: The production schedule form organizes the elements of each remote location into production days and dates for videotaping. The form serves to notify the production crew and talent of specific location addresses, dates, times, and script pages of scheduling the videotape production of the news package. The schedule also sets alternate dates, projected equipment set-up and location strike times, and approximate times for completing the shoot.

Glossary

Shooting Day 1 This area of the form sets the specific date (weekday, month, and day) for the first shooting day. The production schedule form also firms up an alternate rain date.

Location Site The remote environment/place approved for the shoot after site survey was completed should be noted here. This names the building and geographic area where the videotaping is to take place.

Location Map No. This notation relates the location site and address to a municipal map of the geographic area (e.g., H-3).

Location Host The name of the location personnel responsible for the facility/area where the shoot is to occur should be recorded here. This is the everyday contact person with whom the producer will cooperate on details of the location and the shoot. A contact telephone number where the location host can be reached should be included.

Crew Call The time and place of the production crew starting crew call should be entered here.

Talent Call The time and place for the arrival call for talent is also listed. Because the talent do not need the lead time for equipment set-up as the production crew do, the talent call can be up to an hour later than the production crew call. Time should be allotted for make-up if make-up is being required for the talent.

Set-up This entry is a range of time including a deadline for the production crew to complete all equipment set-up and checks of the equipment.

Projected Strike Time This time sets an approximate termination hour for completing the shoot and striking the location.

Shoot Order Units If the preproduction script was arranged in script units, this column records the order in which the script units will be shot.

Script Pages This column records the script pages that will be produced during the shoot.

Setting The specific setting within the location where the videotaping will occur is listed here.

Approx. Time A range of hours and minutes approximating the time needed to complete the script units and script pages proposed for production during that shooting day.

Cast The talent or cast who will be a part of the videotaping are listed here.

Action Properties On many location shoots, some action properties are required, e.g., an automobile, an animal. Those action properties required for the respective script units/pages are recorded here.

Comments The comments section allows the producer the opportunity to make any additional notes to be called to the attention of the crew or talent.

- **Remote Log/Continuity Form**

Production process: Soft news production

Responsibility: Producer

Purpose: To record videotaping production details in the field.

Objective: The remote log/continuity form facilitates the time consuming need to view source videotapes after field production to note the quality, extent, and content of every videotaped take from the field.

Glossary

Location The location is the remote site where the videotaping was done.

VTR Counter/Timer/Code This column notes the measure used to clock the length of every videotape take. One method of measuring the length of a videotaped take is to read the build-in digital counter on the videotape recorder. Another measure is to use a stopwatch as a timer. Still another measure is to stripe the source videotape with the SMPTE time code and record frames as a measure of the length of a take. Place a check in the correct box to indicate the type of measure used to time the source tape.

Location Because the environment used for videotaping on a location can change, e.g., interior versus exterior, this column allows notation of changes within the location for various takes.

Talent Note should be made of the person or persons videotaped during a take. This is a reminder that the full name, correct spelling, and proper title of videotaped talent will be required for character generator copy later in postproduction editing or news telecast.

Take No. It is not uncommon for more than a single take of any event or interview on location to be videotaped. All takes should be numbered consecutively and the number of each take recorded. The number will facilitate easier recall of the take during editing.

Good/No Good A judgment should be made on location of the various takes during videotaping. Having a recorded comment on the quality of each take as it is completed saves the time of viewing all videotaped takes to make the same judgment during postproduction preparation for editing.

Video/Audio Some notation might be made on the video or audio content of each take in this column.

- **Talent Release Form**

Production process: Soft news production

Responsibility: Producer

Purpose: To give the producer legal rights over the video and audio recording of individual talent.

Objective: The talent release form is a legal document, which when filled out and signed by talent, gives to the producer and the producing organization the legal right to use both video and/or audio recording of an individual for publication. This form is especially necessary in cases of video package content on controversial issues, but its use is recommended whenever any talent is being featured in video and audio taping.

Glossary

Talent Name This entry should contain the name of the individual talent recorded on video or audio.
Recording Location The location site of the video or audio recording should be entered here.
Producer The name of the supervising producer should be entered here.
Producing Organization The incorporated name of the video producing organization should be entered here.

Note: The expression "For value received" may imply that some remuneration, even a token remuneration, be required for the form to be legally binding. When there is any doubt about the legal nature of the document, consult a lawyer.

• Editing Work Sheet

Note: If adequate and thorough notes were made on the remote log/continuity form, completing the editing work sheet may not be necessary.

Production process: Soft news postproduction

Responsibility: Producer

Purpose: To prepare for postproduction editing of the video package to a master tape from source videotape(s).

Objective: The editing work sheet records in videotaping order all video and/or audio recordings on the source tape. The editing work sheet is a transcription of the source tape(s). An accurate account of the source tape(s) saves a lot of searching the source tape(s) during editing. Many postproduction facilities demand this work before access is allowed to editing suites. For the producer this stage saves valuable time and cost in postproduction.

Glossary

Audio: Channel 1/Audio: Channel 2 The producer of the package should indicate the correct audio channel or channels and their use on the source tape(s). Because the choice can vary between channel 1 or channel 2 for field recording, the designation should be made of the channel on which audio recording was made in the field.
Tape No. The number of the videocassette tape being logged should be entered here.
VTR CNTR/Clock/SMPTE Because some measure should be made of the videotape content on the source tape(s), it is helpful to note what that measure is. Choices include the digital counter on the videotape recorder/playback unit, reading from a stopwatch, or reading SMPTE time code. Source videotapes can be striped during videotaping or as a first step in postproduction prior to beginning the editing work sheet. These mea-

sures should be consecutive measures made from the beginning (rewound) of the source videotape(s). The VTR counter and stopwatch should be set to begin at zero. SMPTE time code is easiest to use when also set to zero at the beginning of striping.
IN/OUT These columns allow the producer to indicate the beginning and ending measures (VTR counter, clock, or SMPTE) for the particular videotape units being noted.
Notes Any meaningful notation about the content of the video and/or audio on the source tape(s). This is the place to make value judgments about the quality and usability of each particular take.
Segment Clock Time This column should record the real clock time length of each particular video or audio bite being noted. Depending on the desired content of any particular video and/or audio bite, judgment should be made whether the time should be from first video to final video, or first audio to final audio.

• Editing Cue Sheet

Production process: Soft news postproduction

Responsibility: Producer

Purpose: To prepare for postproduction editing of the news package to master tape from source videotape(s).

Objective: The editing cue sheet is a postproduction preparatory stage that creates the format and order of edits of the proposed master videotape from the editing work sheet. The editing cue sheet juxtaposes takes from the editing work sheet into the proposed order of edits for postproduction editing. This step permits a lot of creative work and quality time on the proposed final edited piece without tying up a videotape editing suite.

Glossary

Audio: Channel 1/Audio: Channel 2 The producer of the package should indicate the correct audio channel or channels and their proposed use on the edited master tape(s). Because the choice can vary between channel 1 or channel 2 and mixed channels, the designation should be made of the channel on which final audio recording will be made.
Tape No. The number of the videocassette tape being logged should be entered here.
VTR CNTR/Clock/SMPTE Because some measure should be made of the videotape content on the edited master SMPTE tape(s), it is important to note what that measure is. Choices include the digital counter on the videotape recorder/playback unit, the reading from a stopwatch, or SMPTE time code. SMPTE time code can be striped on the edited master tape(s) as a first step in postproduction prior to actual editing. These measures should be consecutive measures made from the beginning (rewound) of the master videotape(s). The VTR counter and stopwatch should be set to begin at zero. SMPTE time code is easiest to use when also set to zero at the beginning of striping.

IN/OUT These columns allow the producer to indicate the beginning and ending measures (VTR counter, clock, SMPTE) for the particular videotape bites being used from the source tape(s) as noted on the editing work sheet.

Notes: In-cue/Out-cue This space should indicate the video or audio in-cues and out-cues from the proposed bites noted on the editing work sheet from the source tape(s). This space allows the producer to create the proposed edited order of videotape bites from the source tape(s) to the master tape. The in-cues and out-cues may be either video cues or audio cues. Video cues briefly describe the content of the beginning or end of the bite being considered; audio cues are the first few words of the beginning of the proposed bite or final few words at the end of the bite being considered.

Segment Clock Time This column should record the real clock time length of each particular video or audio bite being proposed. Depending on the desired content of any particular video or audio bite, judgment should be made whether the time should be from first video to final video, first audio to final audio, or first audio to final video. When all entries recorded in this column are summed up, the total should approximate the length of the final edited video piece.

• Edited Master Clipsheet

Production process: Soft news postproduction

Responsibility: Producer

Purpose: To record all character generator copy necessary for the telecast of the edited master video news package.

Objective: The edited master clipsheet facilitates for the producer all possible character generator screen text necessary to accompany the edited master video for telecast. The form serves as a summary listing of all essential information not contained on the edited master video package. This form also serves to prompt the producer to create possible character generator screen text for an edited package.

Glossary

Package Title This entry records the title of the news package as proposed on the preproduction forms. This is the title that labels the edited package.

Audio: Channel 1, 2, Mixed Indication should be made of the final audio channel used for editing. Some producers edit using both audio channels and expect that the edited master use the mixed audio playback option. Other producers mix the two audio channels down to either one of the two available channels. The choice made in editing should be indicated.

Length The total edited length of the news package should be timed. Most often, timing is from first audio to final audio. A producer might intend to begin the news package with a video image before first audio begins. This is the point where that choice should be indicated.

Out-cue In the broadcast situation in which a video piece is to be B-rolled into a longer program, a control room director will need a video or audio out-cue, a description of the intended final video, or the final few words of the audio track. This out-cue should be indicated here.

Character Generator Copy This section of the form records for the producer or control room director all the character generator copy for matting on the news video package during telecast.

Videotape/Film Credit When a producer uses video or film footage from another source, screen credit may be required. This entry may be as simple as "File Footage" or "Courtesy of ABC-TV."

In __:__/Out __:__ For every screen of character generator copy the producer will have to provide real clock time from the beginning of the video package at which point the character generator copy is to be matted over the video and when the matte is to be removed (i.e., the length of time to remain on the screen).

Reporter Lower Third This character generator copy gives the name of the reporter or talent whether the reporter or talent is to be seen on-screen or whether the reporter or talent only does a voice-over. Examples of reporter/talent lower third follow:

JOHN DOE
News at 5:00

and

JOHN DOE
Reporting

Interviewee/Actuality Lower Third When interviewees appear on screen, character generator copy is expected. Here is an example of an interviewee/actuality lower third:

REV. JOHN DOE
Pastor

Voice of When an interviewee does not appear on screen or the interview is done over the telephone, the correct form for character generator copy is to indicate that the audience is hearing the voice of the person only. Following is an example of character generator copy for this:

Voice of
SEN. JOHN P. DOE
(R) Virginia

Transcription Occasionally, transcribed text copy has to appear on the screen over the video image. For example, if an interviewee is speaking in a foreign language, if an interviewee has a very heavy accent, or if the audio quality is very poor, a transcription of a portion of the audio track may have to be matted on the screen over the interview or actuality. A quotation from a book or a number of statistics from a survey may have to be matted on the screen. This is the place to indicate that text copy.

Trade Credit Perhaps some favor or permission adding to the quality of the news package production warrants on-screen credit. This screen credit is called a trade. This is the place to indicate that text. An example of a trade credit is

Reporter's clothes
provided by
FOR MEN ONLY

Video Credits Some news operations provide the opportunity to attach individual credits to a news package itself or provide room at the end of a news program for individual package credits. Even if no provision is made on the news program, adding the proper credits to the clipsheet form provides a record of credits for the video package for future reference. Following is an example of video credits for a news video package:

JOHN DOE
_____
                    Producer

MARY SMITH
_____
              Camera Operator

BILL JONES
_____
              Videotape Editor

REMOTE LOG/CONTINUITY

HARD NEWS VIDEO PRODUCTION

Producer/News Reporter:

Camera Operator:

News Story Slug:

Location:

Date: /   /

Page   of

VTR COUNTER/ TIMER/CODE	LOCATION	TALENT	TAKE NO.	GOOD/ NO GOOD	VIDEO/AUDIO

| HARD NEWS VIDEO PRODUCTION REMOTE LOG/CONTINUITY | Page | of |

VTR COUNTER/ TIMER/CODE	LOCATION	TALENT	TAKE NO.	GOOD/ NO GOOD	VIDEO/AUDIO

EDITING WORK SHEET

HARD NEWS VIDEO PRODUCTION

Producer:	News Story Slug:
	Date: / /
Camera Operator:	Audio: Channel 1
	Audio: Channel 2
	Page of

TAPE No.	VTR CNTR CLOCK SMPTE		NOTES	SEGMENT CLOCK TIME
	IN	OUT		
				:
				:
				:
				:
				:
				:
				:
				:
				:
				:
				:
				:
				:
				:
				:
				:
				:
				:
				:
				:
				:
				:
				:
				:
				:
				:
				:
				:
				:

HARD NEWS VIDEO PRODUCTION EDITING WORK SHEET			Page	of	

T A P E No.	VTR CNTR CLOCK SMPTE		NOTES	SEGMENT CLOCK TIME
	IN	OUT		
				:
				:
				:
				:
				:
				:
				:
				:
				:
				:
				:
				:
				:
				:
				:
				:
				:
				:
				:
				:
				:
				:
				:
				:
				:
				:
				:
				:
				:
				:
				:
				:
				:
				:
				:
				:
				:

EDITING CUE SHEET

HARD NEWS VIDEO PRODUCTION

Producer:

Camera Operator:

News Story Slug:
Date: /   /
Audio: Channel 1
Audio: Channel 2
Page   of

TAPE No.	VTR CNTR CLOCK SMPTE IN	OUT	NOTES	SEGMENT CLOCK TIME
			IN CUE	:
			OUT CUE	
			IN CUE	:
			OUT CUE	
			IN CUE	:
			OUT CUE	
			IN CUE	:
			OUT CUE	
			IN CUE	:
			OUT CUE	
			IN CUE	:
			OUT CUE	
			IN CUE	:
			OUT CUE	
			IN CUE	:
			OUT CUE	
			IN CUE	:
			OUT CUE	
			IN CUE	:
			OUT CUE	
			IN CUE	:
			OUT CUE	
			IN CUE	:
			OUT CUE	
			IN CUE	:
			OUT CUE	
			IN CUE	:
			OUT CUE	
			IN CUE	:
			OUT CUE	

T A P E No.	VTR CNTR CLOCK SMPTE IN	OUT	NOTES	SEGMENT CLOCK TIME
HARD NEWS VIDEO PRODUCTION EDITING CUE SHEET			Page	of
			IN CUE	:
			OUT CUE	
			IN CUE	:
			OUT CUE	
			IN CUE	:
			OUT CUE	
			IN CUE	:
			OUT CUE	
			IN CUE	:
			OUT CUE	
			IN CUE	:
			OUT CUE	
			IN CUE	:
			OUT CUE	
			IN CUE	:
			OUT CUE	
			IN CUE	:
			OUT CUE	
			IN CUE	:
			OUT CUE	
			IN CUE	:
			OUT CUE	
			IN CUE	:
			OUT CUE	
			IN CUE	:
			OUT CUE	
			IN CUE	:
			OUT CUE	
			IN CUE	:
			OUT CUE	
			IN CUE	:
			OUT CUE	
			IN CUE	:
			OUT CUE	
			IN CUE	:
			OUT CUE	

EDITED MASTER CLIPSHEET

HARD NEWS VIDEO PRODUCTION

Producer/News Reporter: News Story Slug:
Camera Operator: Date: /   /
Video Editor: Audio: Channel 1 ☐   2 ☐   Mixed ☐

News Story Slug/Title:

_____

Length: (first audio ☐ /video ☐ to final audio ☐ /video ☐)
_____ : _____

Out cue:

_____

Character Generator Copy: Notes
   Videotape/Film Credit   In ___:___
                             Out___:___

_____

   Reporter Lower Third   In ___:___
                             Out___:___

_____

   Interviewee/Actuality Lower Third In ___:___
                             Out___:___

_____

_____

   Interviewee/Actuality Lower Third In ___:___
                             Out___:___

_____

_____

   Voice of   In ___:___
                             Out___:___

_____

_____

Character Generator Copy (continued)	Notes

Transcription #1   In ___:___
           Out___:___

_____

_____

_____

_____

Transcription #2   In ___:___
           Out___:___

_____

_____

_____

_____

Trade Credit   In ___:___
           Out___:___

_____

_____

_____

Video Credits   In ___:___
           Out___:___

_____ Producer

_____ Camera Operator

_____ Videotape Editor

TREATMENT

SOFT NEWS VIDEO PRODUCTION

Producer:	Proposed Title:
Camera Operator:	Proposed Length: :
	Proposed Shooting Date: / /
Date: / /	Proposed Completion Date: / /
Locations:	
	Page of

Production Statement

Communication Goals and Objectives of the Package; Most Important Questions

Package Treatment

(Continue on reverse side.)

TELEVISION SCRIPT

SOFT NEWS VIDEO PRODUCTION

Producer:	Package Title:
Camera Operator:	Length: : Date: / / Page of

VIDEO	AUDIO

SOFT NEWS VIDEO PRODUCTION TELEVISION SCRIPT	Page	of
VIDEO	AUDIO	

LOCATION SITE SURVEY

SOFT NEWS VIDEO PRODUCTION

Producer:	Package Title:
Location Scout(s):	Script Page(s):
	Script Unit(s):
Approval:	Date: / /

Location: Site Identification:
Local Contact Person: Comments:
  Name:
  Title:
  Address:
  City: State:
  Phone No.: ( )   -
Facilities Personnel: Comments:
  Name:
  Position Title:
  Address:
  City: State:
  Phone No.: ( )   -

LIGHTING PROBLEMS DEFINED

Light contrast ratios   Existing light control

Lighting intensity   Lighting use

Ceiling height   Floor description

Windows/Compass direction   Special consideration

POWER PROBLEMS DEFINED

Number of power outlets	Number of outlet prongs
Number of separate circuits	Location of circuit breakers
Types of fuses	Portable generator need

AUDIO PROBLEMS DEFINED

Interior environmental sounds	Exterior environmental sounds
Ceiling composition	Floor covering composition
Wall composition	

CAST AND CREW NEEDS

Restroom facilities	Eating facilities
Green room availability	Make-up facilities
Parking arrangements	Loading/unloading restrictions
Freight elevator	Hardware store

CIVIL EMERGENCY SERVICES

Police station   Fire station

LOCATION SECURITY AND EQUIPMENT SAFETY

Facility security   Equipment safe storage

Personnel values security   Overnight storage/security

OTHER RELEVANT INFORMATION

Public area power source   Traffic control

Clearance/Insurance needed   Exterior compass direction

Photographs taken   Location environment drawing/map

Other information:

OTHER COMMENTS/OBSERVATIONS

STORYBOARD

SOFT NEWS VIDEO PRODUCTION

Producer:

Package Title:
Page   of

54

VIDEO SCRIPT/STORYBOARD

SOFT NEWS VIDEO PRODUCTION

Producer:

Package Title:

Camera Operator:

Length: :
Date: /   /
Page   of

VIDEO	AUDIO

VIDEO	AUDIO

SCRIPT BREAKDOWN

SOFT NEWS VIDEO PRODUCTION

Producer:

Camera Operator:

Package Title:

Length: :
Script Length: pages
Page   of
Date: /   /

SCRIPT PAGES	NO. OF SCRIPT LINES	INT/ EXT	TIME	SETTING	LOCATION	TALENT	SHOOT- ING ORDER

					Page of		
SCRIPT PAGES	NO. OF SCRIPT LINES	INT/ EXT	TIME	SETTING	LOCATION	TALENT	SHOOT- ING ORDER

SHOT LIST

SOFT NEWS VIDEO PRODUCTION

Producer:	Package Title:
Camera Operator:	Date: / / Page of

LOCATION	SHOT						CONTENT NOTES
	NO.	MASTER	CUT-IN	CUT-AWAY	FRAMING	MOTION	

| | Page | of | |

LOCATION	SHOT						CONTENT NOTES
	NO.	MASTER	CUT-IN	CUT-AWAY	FRAMING	MOTION	

EQUIPMENT CHECKLIST

SOFT NEWS VIDEO PRODUCTION

Producer: \
Camera Operator: \
Videotape Recorder Operator: \
Audio Director: \
Location(s):

Package Title:

Date: /   /

Avl Pch Rnt

CAMERA
- Video Camera
- Lenses
- Filters
- AC/DC Monitor
- Lg Screen Monitor
- _____

RECORDER
- Videotape Recorder
- VTR Backup
- _____

TRIPOD
- Tripod w/Head
- Camera Head Adapter
- Dolly
- _____

TEST EQUIPMENT
- Waveform Monitor
- Vectorscope
- Grey Scale
- Registration Chart
- White Card
- Headphones
- _____

AUDIO
- Shot gun Microphone
- Lavaliere Microphone
- Hand-held Microphone
- Fishpole
- Wind screens

Avl Pch Rnt

AUDIO (continued)
- Mixer
- Adapter plugs
- Earphone
- Headphones
- _____
- _____

POWER SUPPLIES
- Batteries for Camera
- Batteries for Recorder
- Batteries for Monitor
- AC Power Converter
- Microphone Batteries
- _____

LIGHTING
- Light Kit
- Soft Light Kit
- Barn Doors
- Spun Glass Filters
- Blue Gels
- Orange Gels
- Screens
- Scrims
- ND Filters
- Aluminum Foil
- Wooden Clothes Pins
- Light Meter
- Reflector
- Spare Bulbs: Qty
- _____
- _____

Avl	Pch	Rnt	

CABLES

Avl	Pch	Rnt	
☐	☐	☐	Multi-pin Cable Camera to Recorder
☐	☐	☐	Video Cable Camera to Recorder
☐	☐	☐	Video Cable Camera to Waveform Monitor/ Scope
☐	☐	☐	Video Cable Scope to Monitor
☐	☐	☐	Audio Mixer Cable to Recorder
☐	☐	☐	Audio Extension Cables
☐	☐	☐	_____

MISCELLANEOUS

Avl	Pch	Rnt	
☐	☐	☐	Video tape
☐	☐	☐	Teleprompter
☐	☐	☐	Teleprompter Script
☐	☐	☐	Cue Card Paper
☐	☐	☐	Duct Tape
☐	☐	☐	Masking Tape
☐	☐	☐	Spare Fuses
☐	☐	☐	Tool Kit
☐	☐	☐	Stopwatch
☐	☐	☐	Slate
☐	☐	☐	Chalk
☐	☐	☐	Eraser
☐	☐	☐	Bullhorn
☐	☐	☐	Walkie-Talkie
☐	☐	☐	Dulling Spray
☐	☐	☐	Talent Release Forms
☐	☐	☐	Step Ladder
☐	☐	☐	Lens Cleaner and Tissue

Avl	Pch	Rnt	
☐	☐	☐	Sewing Kit
☐	☐	☐	Paper, Pens, Felt Markers
☐	☐	☐	Rope
☐	☐	☐	Barrier Cones
☐	☐	☐	Poster Board
☐	☐	☐	Flashlight
☐	☐	☐	Scissors
☐	☐	☐	100' Power Cords
☐	☐	☐	Staple Gun and Staples
☐	☐	☐	Power Outlet Boxes
☐	☐	☐	_____
☐	☐	☐	_____
☐	☐	☐	_____
☐	☐	☐	_____
☐	☐	☐	_____
☐	☐	☐	_____
☐	☐	☐	_____
☐	☐	☐	_____
☐	☐	☐	_____
☐	☐	☐	_____
☐	☐	☐	_____
☐	☐	☐	_____
☐	☐	☐	_____

PRODUCTION SCHEDULE

SOFT NEWS VIDEO PRODUCTION

Producer:	Package Title:
Camera Operator:	Date: / / Page of

SHOOTING DAY 1   **RAIN DATE**
___/___/___

_____, _____, _____
(Weekday)   (Month)   (Day)

Location Site:_____   Location Map No._____

Address:_____
          City_____   State _____

Location Host:_____
Phone No.: (___)____-_____

Crew call:___:___ AM/PM
    Address:_____

Talent call:___:___ AM/PM
    Address:_____

Set-up:___:___ to ___:___   Projected Strike Time:____:____

SHOOT ORDER UNITS	SCRIPT PAGES	SETTING	APPROX. TIME	CAST	ACTION PROPERTIES
			: to :		
			: to :		
			: to :		
			: to :		
			: to :		

Comments:

SHOOTING DAY 2   RAIN DATE

_____, _____, _____   ___/___/___
(Weekday)   (Month)   (Day)

Location Site:_____ Location Map No. _____

Address: _____
       City_____ State _____

Location Host:_____
Phone No.: (___)___-_____

Crew call:___:___AM/PM
    Address:_____

Talent call:___:___AM/PM
    Address:_____

Set-up:___:___ to___:___   Projected Strike Time:___:___

SHOOT ORDER UNITS	SCRIPT PAGES	SETTING	APPROX. TIME	CAST	ACTION PROPERTIES
			: to :		
			: to :		
			: to :		
			: to :		
			: to :		

Comments:

REMOTE LOG/CONTINUITY

SOFT NEWS VIDEO PRODUCTION

Producer:

Camera Operator:

Package Title:

Location:

Date: /   /

Page   of

VTR COUNTER/ TIMER/CODE	LOCATION	TALENT	TAKE NO.	GOOD/ NO GOOD	VIDEO/AUDIO

Page of					
VTR COUNTER/ TIMER/CODE	LOCATION	TALENT	TAKE NO.	GOOD/ NO GOOD	VIDEO/AUDIO

TALENT RELEASE FORM

SOFT NEWS VIDEO PRODUCTION

Talent Name: _____
(Please Print)

Project Title: _____

For value received and without further consideration, I hereby consent to the use of all photographs, videotapes or film, taken of me and/or recordings made of my voice and/or written extraction, in whole or in part, of such recordings or musical performance

at _____ on _____ 19___
   (Recording Location)   *(Month)*   *(Day)*   *(Year)*

by_____ for_____
      (Producer)   *(Producing Organization)*

and/or others with its consent, for the purposes of illustration, advertising, or publication in any manner.

Talent Name_____
                        (Signature)

Address_____ City_____

       State _____ Zip Code _____

       Date:____/____/____

If the subject is a minor under the laws of the state where modeling, acting, or performing is done:

Guardian _____ Guardian _____
            (Signature)   *(Please Print)*

Address _____ City _____

       State _____ Zip Code _____

       Date:____/____/____

EDITING WORK SHEET

SOFT NEWS VIDEO PRODUCTION

Producer:

Camera Operator:

News Package Title:
Date: /   /
Audio: Channel 1
Audio: Channel 2
Page   of

T A P E No.	VTR CNTR CLOCK SMPTE		NOTES	SEGMENT CLOCK TIME
	IN	OUT		
				:
				:
				:
				:
				:
				:
				:
				:
				:
				:
				:
				:
				:
				:
				:
				:
				:
				:
				:
				:
				:
				:
				:
				:
				:
				:
				:
				:
				:
				:
				:

	SOFT NEWS VIDEO PRODUCTION EDITING WORK SHEET			Page	of	

T A P E No.	VTR CNTR CLOCK SMPTE		NOTES	SEGMENT CLOCK TIME
	IN	OUT		
				:
				:
				:
				:
				:
				:
				:
				:
				:
				:
				:
				:
				:
				:
				:
				:
				:
				:
				:
				:
				:
				:
				:
				:
				:
				:
				:
				:
				:
				:
				:
				:

EDITING CUE SHEET

SOFT NEWS VIDEO PRODUCTION

Producer:

Camera Operator:

News Package Title:
Date: / /
Audio: Channel 1
Audio: Channel 2
Page   of

TAPE No.	VTR CNTR CLOCK SMPTE IN	OUT	NOTES	SEGMENT CLOCK TIME
			IN CUE	:
			OUT CUE	
			IN CUE	:
			OUT CUE	
			IN CUE	:
			OUT CUE	
			IN CUE	:
			OUT CUE	
			IN CUE	:
			OUT CUE	
			IN CUE	:
			OUT CUE	
			IN CUE	:
			OUT CUE	
			IN CUE	:
			OUT CUE	
			IN CUE	:
			OUT CUE	
			IN CUE	:
			OUT CUE	
			IN CUE	:
			OUT CUE	
			IN CUE	:
			OUT CUE	
			IN CUE	:
			OUT CUE	
			IN CUE	:
			OUT CUE	
			IN CUE	:
			OUT CUE	

SOFT NEWS VIDEO PRODUCTION EDITING CUE SHEET			Page	of	
TAPE No.	VTR CNTR CLOCK SMPTE		NOTES		SEGMENT CLOCK TIME
	IN	OUT			
			IN CUE		:
			OUT CUE		
			IN CUE		:
			OUT CUE		
			IN CUE		:
			OUT CUE		
			IN CUE		:
			OUT CUE		
			IN CUE		:
			OUT CUE		
			IN CUE		:
			OUT CUE		
			IN CUE		:
			OUT CUE		
			IN CUE		:
			OUT CUE		
			IN CUE		:
			OUT CUE		
			IN CUE		:
			OUT CUE		
			IN CUE		:
			OUT CUE		
			IN CUE		:
			OUT CUE		
			IN CUE		:
			OUT CUE		
			IN CUE		:
			OUT CUE		
			IN CUE		:
			OUT CUE		
			IN CUE		:
			OUT CUE		
			IN CUE		:
			OUT CUE		
			IN CUE		:
			OUT CUE		

EDITED MASTER CLIPSHEET
SOFT NEWS VIDEO PRODUCTION

Producer/News Reporter: Package Title:
Camera Operator: Date: /   /
Video Editor: Audio: Channel 1 ☐   2 ☐   Mixed ☐

Package Title:
_____

Length: (first audio to final audio)
_____ : _____

Outcue:
_____

Character Generator Copy: Notes
    Videotape/Film Credit   In __:__
                             Out __:__

    _____

    Reporter Lower Third   In __:__
                             Out __:__

    _____

    Interviewee/Actuality Lower Third   In __:__
                             Out __:__

    _____
    _____

    Interviewee/Actuality Lower Third   In __:__
                             Out __:__

    _____
    _____

    Voice of   In __:__
                             Out __:__

    _____
    _____

Transcription #1   In __:__
                                Out__:__

_____

_____

_____

_____

Transcription #2   In __:__
                                Out__:__

_____

_____

_____

_____

Trade Credit   In __:__
                                Out__:__

_____

_____

_____

Video Credits   In __:__
                                Out__:__

_____ Producer

_____ Camera Operator

_____ Videotape Editor

Chapter 2

Video Documentary Production

INTRODUCTION

One of the earliest video genres to find a home in the medium of television was the documentary. Documentary communication by definition seeks to initiate a process that culminates in some public action. The documentary should present a call to some social action and complete the process by making the presentation persuasive.

The roots of the documentary can be found in film for the movie theatre. The first film documentaries were produced for movie theatre circulation. It was clear very early that the general public was not inclined to pay the cost of admission to sit through a documentary film instead of an entertaining film.

With the coming of television as the mass medium, documentary production was taken over by the news departments of television stations and networks. The television documentary gives producers a longer forum in which to air in-depth topics.

THE PREPRODUCTION PROCESS

• Personnel

The production of the documentary is similar to the production of the soft news video package. The crew for documentary production is small, similar to the crew size for the soft news video package.

Producer (P). The person around whom a documentary is usually conceived and created is the producer. A documentary producer can be a part of a larger organization such as the news department of a local television newscast or may be simply an independent producer or documentary freelancer.

Most documentaries have a sponsoring organization, e.g., the news department of a television network or affiliate, or the organization sponsoring the topic/subject of the documentary. This unique basis for documentary production creates the first demand on the producer, substantial preproduction work. This preproduction work means principally a proposal to the sponsoring organization. Most documentary productions hinge on initial success at this level, i.e., getting a proposal accepted by a sponsoring organization. The producer oversees all facets of the documentary preproduction including the choice of a camera operator and a videotape operator, components of the basic documentary production crew.

Camera operator (CO). The camera operator has the responsibility of listing, requisitioning, and/or purchasing the necessary equipment for videotaping on location. This list should include lighting equipment and accessories also. The camera operator may participate in the choice of a videotape recorder operator because they will have to work together closely. The camera operator should arrange to meet early in the preproduction process with the producer to review production plans and needs. When the producer has completed the shot list, the camera operator can begin planning the location shoot.

Videotape recorder operator (VTRO). The videotape recorder operator begins preproduction responsibilities by estimating and ordering videotape stock for the documentary shoot. The videotape recorder operator should list and make arrangements for all equipment needed for video and audio recording on location. This is a good occasion to meet with the camera operator and coordinate equip-

FLOWCHART AND CHECKLIST FOR VIDEO DOCUMENTARY PRODUCTION

PRODUCER (P)

	PREPRODUCTION	PRODUCTION	POSTPRODUCTION
	☐ (1) Writes proposal	☐ (1) Meets location host(s)	☐ (1) Arranges postproduction schedule and facilities
	☐ (2) Researches topic	☐ (2) Handles all location details	☐ (2) Reorders source tapes with preproduction script
	☐ (3) Scouts location site (location site survey form)	☐ (3) Meets with crew	☐ (3) Reviews source tapes/records editing work sheets (editing work sheet form)
	☐ (4) Writes treatment (treatment form)	☐ (4) Supervises location arrangement	☐ (4) Transcribes source tape interview(s)
	☐ (5) Constructs budget (budget form)	☐ (5) Meets with interviewees	☐ (5) Writes final documentary script (documentary script form)
	☐ (6) Writes preproduction script (television script form)	☐ (6) Preps interviewer(s) and interviewee(s)	☐ (6) Creates editing cue sheets with script (editing cue sheet form)
	☐ (7) Does script breakdown (script breakdown form)	☐ (7) Supervises equipment set-up	☐ (7) Edits or supervises TD
	☐ (8) Develops shot list (shot list form)	☐ (8) Calls for take and wrap	☐ (8) Adds music/effects and mixes
	☐ (9) Designs production schedule (production schedule form)	☐ (9) Keeps location log/continuity notes (location log/continuity notes form)	☐ (9) Adds titling and credits (edited master clip sheet form)
	☐ (10) Chooses and meets with CO	☐ (10) Calls for location strike (talent release form)	☐ (10) Transcribes finished documentary
	☐ (11) Obtains clearances for all copyrighted material		
	☐ (12) Obtains insurance coverage		

CAMERA OPERATOR (CO)

	PREPRODUCTION	PRODUCTION	POSTPRODUCTION
	☐ (1) Meets with producer	☐ (1) Arranges camera and lighting equipment/accessories pick-up/delivery	☐ (1) Returns remote camera and lighting equipment and accessories
	☐ (2) Chooses and meets with VTRO	☐ (2) Sets up and checks location camera	☐ (2) Reports damaged, lost, malfunctioning equipment or accessories
	☐ (3) Prepares camera and lighting equipment/accessories list (equipment checklist form)	☐ (3) Sets up and checks location lighting	
	☐ (4) Works shot list	☐ (4) Follows producer's directions	
		☐ (5) Strikes camera and lighting equipment/accessories	

VIDEOTAPE OPERATOR (VTRO)

	PREPRODUCTION	PRODUCTION	POSTPRODUCTION
	☐ (1) Meets with CO	☐ (1) Arranges videotape recorder and audio equipment/accessories pick-up/delivery	☐ (1) Returns remote videotape and sound recording equipment and accessories
	☐ (2) Prepares videotape recording and audio equipment/accessories list (equipment checklist form)	☐ (2) Sets up and checks location videotape recorder and sound recording	☐ (2) Reports damaged, lost, malfunctioning equipment or accessories
	☐ (3) Orders videotape stock	☐ (3) Responds to producer's directions	
	☐ (4) Labels and organizes tape stock	☐ (4) Videotapes take(s)	
		☐ (5) Monitors video and audio levels during taping	
		☐ (6) Labels videotapes and removes record button	
		☐ (7) Strikes videotape recorder and sound recording equipment/accessories	

TALENT

	PRODUCTION
	☐ (1) Follows producer's directions

TECHNICAL DIRECTOR/EDITOR (TD/E)

If the producer does not edit:

☐ (1) Edits from editing cue sheet and final script under the supervision of the producer
☐ (2) Adds music/effects and mixes channels
☐ (3) Labels edited master

ment lists. The videotape recorder operator will also be listing audio recording needs because audio recording on location will be the responsibility of the videotape recorder operator.

• Preproduction Stages

There is a growing recognition among professionals that the days of serendipity documentary work are over. The cost of videotape stock (or film) and the high cost of postproduction time in handling a lot of videotape has forced more thorough preproduction work on the documentarist.

For the documentarist, the beginning of the genre is the preproduction proposal, which defines the whole project to a sponsoring organization. In other words, preproduction is a built-in necessity for successful documentary production.

Writing the proposal (P 1). The first preproduction stage is the proposal to a sponsoring organization. The proposal is a document consisting essentially of the following items: (1) a treatment, (2) a proposed budget, (3) a video format (outline) or preproduction video script, and (4) proposed production schedule. As is evident from its label—a proposal—the documentary is proposed to an organization for funding and/or authorization to operate in the name of the organization. It should be clear from the nature of this preproduction stage that the more thorough the proposal, the better the chances of the documentary being approved. Yet before undertaking the proposal another step is required—research.

Researching a topic (P 2). Before a producer begins a proposal, quality research into the topic or subject of the proposed documentary should begin. What a producer needs to write a proposal is a knowledge of the subject of the proposed documentary. The more the producer knows the subject to be covered in a documentary, the better a funding or authorizing organization is likely to look favorably upon a producer and the documentary idea. Sloppy research breeds a lack of confidence and credibility. It should be assumed that the authorizing organization probably knows the topic well. Skimpy or negligent research will be easily apparent. It may be necessary for the producer to hire a knowledgeable researcher in the field of the subject of the proposed documentary.

Research usually means a good library. Currently, with high tech prepared bibliographies and computer searches for topics, research is easier and faster than ever, but good research is time-consuming. One of the best ways to do quality research is to organize. The whole subject of logos (order or organization) from Aristotelian persuasion bears upon the researcher/producer. If a producer organizes the topic carefully from the beginning, then the whole organization of further research, the format or outline of the documentary, the preproduction script, and the order of videotaping the documentary will be created at the same time.

Quality research can also reveal potential locations for videotaping, available prerecorded videotape and film,

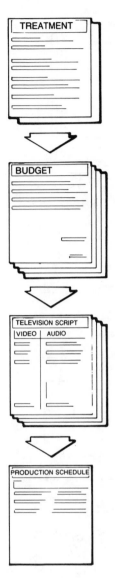

FIGURE 2–1
Stages of the documentary proposal. The documentary proposal includes the treatment, the budget, the preproduction script, and a proposed production schedule.

the acquisition of still photographs, contact persons, and potential interviewees, besides the content nature of the topic itself. There are simply no cogent reasons for not doing a good job at research.

Scouting the location site (P 3). The order in which a producer may choose to perform necessary preproduction stages may vary. Scouting out a location site for videotaping the documentary or at least searching out the place to interview the interviewee/spokespeople should at least follow adequate research into the subject for the documentary. The availability and suitability of a remote videotaping location may make the difference in a number of other preproduction decisions, e.g., the treatment and budget. A producer may have to pay for the scouting trip beforehand and recoup the expense later in the proposed budget. There are many requirements of a good shooting location to be scouted including available interiors and

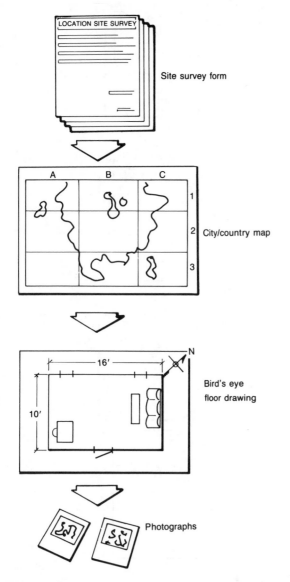

FIGURE 2-2
The location site survey. The location site survey includes the survey forms, a map of the proposed location site, bird's eye view sketches of proposed videotaping set locations, and photographs of the proposed location set areas.

exteriors, use permits, accessibility, and travel distances. (See the location site survey form.)

Once a location site has received approval both of the producer and the location host, a follow-up confirmation mailing should be sent to the host. This mailing should detail all agreed upon elements of the shoot and the environment requirements. The date and arrival time of the crew should also be noted. It is excellent practice for the producer to contact the location host a day or two before production crew arrival on location as a final detail check and as a courtesy reminder to the host.

Writing the treatment (P 4). The treatment portion of a proposal is a verbal description of the suggested topic or subject of the documentary. The content of the treatment should cover the topic and why it should be the focus of

a documentary. It should also contain a proposed title, the proposed length, and the goals and objectives for the documentary. It is helpful to include the target audience and the reasons for targeting them and suggested production values to reach that audience.

Once the producer has set goals and objectives for the documentary, a production statement can be written to accurately define in an emotional or rational few words the rationale for the documentary. The production statement then serves as a precise reminder during every stage of the production of the rationale for the documentary.

A good help to the treatment section of the proposal is a format or outline of the proposed documentary. If research has been beneficial, some sort of progressive flow to the information of the documentary should be apparent. This can then develop into the reasonable, logical order of the documentary. An outline (or format) solidifies in the mind of a reader of the proposal the direction (beginning, ending, and flow) of the proposed documentary project. (See the treatment form.)

Constructing a budget (P 5). The producer of the proposed documentary has to set the financial accountability necessary in television production. A preproduction budget must be generated. One reason for the proposal is to seek funding from an authorizing organization. Hence a handle on finances in the form of a proposed budget is necessary to the proposal.

Most budgets are a matter of organizing essential expenses both from producing personnel and from the projected costs of documentary production and postproduction. There are many models of budgets available and most budget forms serve the purpose of suggesting the items of expense to be considered. The basis for much equipment and facility costs can be obtained from a rate card, which most video production facilities and equipment suppliers make available to potential clients. Even academic production facilities have a cost figure for equipment use per hour. (See the budget form.)

Writing the preproduction script (P 6). With research completed and format for the documentary finished, a preproduction script is not difficult to write at this stage. It is to be kept in mind that a script at this stage is only a preproduction step and not a final production script. Yet with the advantage of research and information leads from research, a script is advantageous at this point. Major elements to be included in the preproduction script are topic lead, proposed interviewees, bridges between segments, proposed video, proposed cut-aways, internal summaries, and final summary. (See the television script form.)

Doing a script breakdown (P 7). As in most preproduction stages, the preproduction script serves as a master design or blueprint for the final project. From that master design, the producer breaks out the shooting order of the documentary from the proposed preproduction script. A script breakdown should list individuals to be interviewed and where they are located (the locations of the proposed interview(s)) and the cut-aways to be taken at the location. The script breakdown clusters portions of the script by proposed location shoots and available interviewees. (See the script breakdown form.)

Developing the shot list (P 8). From the script breakdown, the producer can readily create a listing of shots to be videotaped and in the order in which they might most economically be shot on the proposed location. The shot list should contain a consecutively numbered listing of proposed video shots indicating the content of each shot (e.g., the vice-president of the corporation), the framing of each shot (e.g., XCU), and some indication of secondary motion required (e.g., a zoom, a pan). (See the shot list form.)

Designing the production schedule (P 9). With the preproduction work completed, the producer can now design a production schedule on the basis of available locations and available interviewees and travel arrangements. It is difficult to estimate the length of a production schedule for a documentary. Every documentary project has its different production needs. A separate production schedule may have to be created for every interviewee or for every trip. There is no standard. There are often many people to be interviewed on the subject of the documentary. That need to interview people will necessitate travel to distant locations. Production schedule information should include the following: (1) dates of each individual videotape shoot, (2) places for travel, (3) transportation plans, (4) crew accommodations, (5) location sites, and (6) interviewee names and titles. There is also need for crew members to have phone numbers at location sites for emergency contact purposes. (See the production schedule form.)

Choosing and meeting with the camera operator (P 10). Most often producers have the right to choose principle crew members especially the camera operator and videotape operator. If budgets allow, other production team members could be utilized, e.g., associate producer, director, lighting director, and grip, but they would not be necessary. Given that most documentary production involves travel, "the smaller and lighter, the better . . . and less expensive," is a good guideline.

Meeting with the producer (CO 1). The first requirement of a camera operator is to meet with the producer of the documentary. The sooner the camera operator is involved in preproduction stages, the better planning can occur for the location shoot itself. The camera operator should have copies of the preproduction script, shot list, location site survey forms, and the production schedule. These allow a camera operator to begin planning for the production.

Choosing and meeting with the videotape recorder operator (CO 2). The choice of a videotape recorder operator can be a joint decision of both the producer and the camera operator. The videotape recorder operator should be someone known and trusted by both the producer and camera operator. Besides working together and trusting each other professionally, travel and lodging together make other demands on crew members individually. The videotape recorder operator should have the experience of a

location videotaping shoot and be able to handle audio recording on location also.

Meeting with the camera operator (VTRO 1). The videotape recorder operator should arrange to meet with the camera operator. These crew members will have to work closely during the location shoot. At the preproduction stage, the camera operator has a lot of information about the documentary production, which should be shared with the videotape recorder operator. The preproduction script, the shot list, and the location survey will allow the videotape recorder operator to begin work on planning videotape stock needs and audio recording requirements.

Preparing camera and lighting equipment/accessories list (CO 3). It is the responsibility of the camera operator and the videotape recorder operator to survey the needs for their respective positions for available equipment. In some operations there is the necessity to reserve remote camera equipment in advance. These reservations should be made.

For equipment not available, arrangements will have to be made for rental or purchase. It is convenient to inquire from the proposed location site(s) in which interviewing and videotaping will be done for video equipment/accessories rental and purchasing possibilities. Renting on location can save some of the problems found in transporting fragile and expensive video production equipment. (See the equipment checklist form.)

Preparing videotape and audio recording equipment and accessories list (VTRO 2). After meeting with the camera operator and sharing preproduction information, the videotape recorder operator's first responsibility is to determine the videotape and sound recording equipment and accessories needed for location videotape production. (See equipment checklist.)

Ordering videotape stock (VTRO 3). One of the production necessities that requires lead time for ordering and purchasing is the videotape stock necessary for the project. The most probable videotape stock is the ¾ inch videotape size. The small cassette unit is 20 minutes in length. This will vary if recording is to be done on 1 inch videotape or broadcast quality ½ inch videotape. Because shooting ratios for video vary from 3:1 to 4:1 (compared to 8:1 to 9:1 for film), the length of the preproduction script might be some indication of the amount of stock tape necessary for the production. A 3:1 ratio of shooting generally means that three video takes may be necessary to get the one that is needed.

Labeling and organizing videotape stock (VTRO 4). A preproduction requirement for the videotape recorder operator is to create a coding system that will facilitate handling and organizing videotape stock on location and in postproduction. A simple code might involve the initials of the title of the documentary (e.g., POW for "A Perspective on War"), followed by consecutive numbering (e.g., POW-01 for the first videocassette). Labeling involves identical coding on both the cassette itself and the videotape carrying case. The consecutive numbering organizes the videotapes for accurate and swift reordering after production only if the videotapes are used in consecutive order during production. The coding system should also be shared with the producer or whoever will keep the location log for the coordination of videotapes and location takes on the log for the shoot itself.

Working the shot list and other preproduction details (CO 4). The camera operator should take the opportunity to work with the shot list and the location site survey to begin specific planning for the location shoot. The camera operator should design camera placement and lighting plots on location drawings. These preproduction tasks save invaluable location production time.

Obtaining clearances for copyrighted materials (P 11). The producer should select music and any special sound effects for the final production on the basis of the preproduction script. Lead time is going to be required to obtain necessary legal clearance for copyrighted recordings. Copyright clearances also have to be obtained from the copyright owners of any copyrighted still photographs, materials from books, films, or videotapes that may be proposed for the documentary.

Obtaining insurance coverage for the location shoot (P 12). The producer has the responsibility to obtain insurance coverage for the personal safety of the crew, for the theft, loss, and destruction of equipment, and for property damage for the location. Some location hosts may make such insurance coverage a prerequisite to location use. Police and public safety officials may also make such a demand on the production crew. Academic programs usually have insurance coverage, both personal coverage for faculty and students as well as property coverage for the loss or damage of equipment. This coverage is automatic if a faculty member is present and the project is authorized by the school. Insurance coverage for other documentary production crews is easily obtained from a reliable insurance agent or insurance company.

THE PRODUCTION PROCESS

The process of the documentary production is similar to the production of the soft news remote video package.

• Personnel

The production crew for remote videotaping for the documentary can be as small as the crew for the remote production of the soft news package, or larger depending on the extent of the documentary and the budget allotted.

Producer (P). The producer holds the key position on the location shoot for the documentary. The producer serves as the director for the videotaping, i.e., calling the shots. The producer is responsible for all production details. Many producers also serve as talent for the documentary and thus serve a multifaceted role on location as the principle interviewer.

Camera operator (CO). The camera operator follows the directions of the producer on location as the camera

operator would follow the director. Primary among responsibilities of the camera operator is the acquisition and transportation of the video camera, its location set-up, and proper functioning.

On most documentary shoots, especially the smaller production, the camera operator serves as lighting director and is thus responsible for lighting equipment, its set-up, and design. Acquisition and transportation of that equipment are also among the camera operator's responsibilities.

Videotape recorder operator (VTRO). Responsible to the camera operator and to the producer is the videotape recorder operator. The location task for the videotape operator is the acquisition, transportation, set-up, and operation of the videotape recorder. After videotape recorder set-up, the videotape operator is responsible for the audio cables and microphones and their proper set-up and functioning. During videotaping the videotape operator monitors both video and audio input recording levels.

Other production crew members. Given the extent of some documentary productions, other crew members may be added to spread the work responsibility. A director might take the location production responsibility from the producer. A lighting director might take the location lighting demands from the camera operator as an audio director might monitor and control all sound production and recording on location.

Talent (T). On some documentary productions, the producer is the talent/interviewer for the project. This usually follows from the involvement in the research and the preproduction stages of the project. On other documentaries, talent may be hired to serve as voice-over announcer/

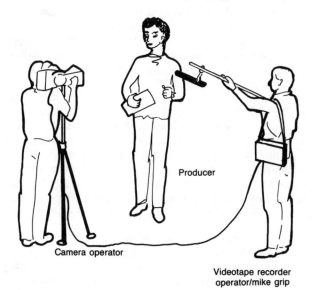

FIGURE 2–3
The three-person documentary production crew. The basic documentary production crew is the producer, the camera operator, and the videotape recorder operator. The videotape recorder operator also handles sound recording.

interviewer/on-camera talent. They would be responsible to the producer as they would be to a director on location.

• Production Stages

Meeting with location host(s) (P 1). The producer's first responsibility upon arrival at a location site for videotape production is to meet with the location personnel. The proper respect to people in charge of remote location facilities is beneficial throughout the location shoot. It is simple courtesy to ask what the normal procedures are for the location environment. All previous requests made at the time of location scouting should be reiterated again and reviewed for the benefit of the host.

It is presumed that the location personnel received a mailed confirmation following location scouting and final approval from the producer of the documentary. If location scouting, site approval, and confirmation by mail are separated from the shooting schedule by a period of time, location hosts should be notified again. This second notification should be made closer to crew arrival and the scheduled shoot either by phone or by mail as an additional courtesy. This pre-arrival/shoot notification should reaffirm those details of the shoot agreed upon at location scouting time.

Handling all location details (P 2). The producer should see to all location details from relations with host personnel and security personnel to the needs of crew and talent. Most location details should have been checked at site scouting time and confirmed by mail or by phone with the host. A sensitive issue with some location hosts is the rearrangement of location environment, i.e., moving furniture, which may be necessary to set lights and place the camera. Requesting all changes beforehand from the host will save bruised egos and request denials later. The use of electrical power and other environmental elements should have been cleared during location scouting and confirmation. The producer handles all details on the location shoot. This involves keeping the shoot on schedule, keeping interviewees informed of progress, calling breaks for the crew, calling ahead for other remote locations, and checking on security for equipment and valuables on the site.

Meeting with the production crew (P 3). Small documentary crews will likely travel together to all location shoots. Meeting and travelling together allows time for a production meeting and coordination of production goals and objectives. Last minute changes and unanticipated details should be shared before the production crew begins location and equipment set-up.

Supervising location arrangement (P 4). There are very few location video shoots that could be accomplished without some adaptation of the location environment. This entails changes that begin to disturb location hosts if the changes were not anticipated beforehand and approval gained from host personnel. The producer should have secured permission from location personnel for all changes in the environment no matter how slight the changes may seem to be. The producer should also have seen to it that notes or instant developing film pictures were made of the environment before changes were made to ensure the return of the environment to its original position after the location strike. Because the producer secured the necessary permission from the host, the producer has the responsibility to supervise the changes agreed upon.

Arranging camera and lighting equipment pick-up and/or delivery (CO 1). The camera operator should have made arrangements for the acquisition and transportation of equipment needs to complete a successful location shoot before the production day. Some equipment may need to be picked up and stored while other equipment may have to be rented and delivered or picked up on the day of shooting. This is especially true if the rental is made in a locality other than the home base for the production crew.

Arranging for videotape recorder and audio recording equipment pick-up and/or delivery (VTRO 1). The videotape recorder operator has the responsibility for the videotape recorder and audio recording equipment and accessories. As with the camera operator, arrangement must be made for rented and/or purchased equipment and accessories and its delivery or pick-up. These details are more important if the equipment is coming from vendors in an unfamiliar locality. Checks and double checks on details of delivery and pick-up should be the normal course of procedure.

Meeting with interviewees (P 5). One of the reasons for the remote location shoot for a documentary is to interview individuals of interest and importance to the content of the documentary, usually in their own environment. It is important for the producer to contact the interviewee/talent immediately upon arrival on location. The producer should relay details of the shoot to the talent, including the approximate time until they will be needed for videotaping. Other details, such as the need for make-up or special clothes (i.e., a costume, a uniform), should be settled as soon as possible.

Setting up camera equipment (CO 2). The camera operator should prepare equipment responsibilities for videotaping. The camera operator should know from the shot list and preproduction stages where the first camera shot will be taken and can begin camera placement accordingly. The camera operator has to work closely with the videotape recorder operator to assure coordinated technical responses.

Lighting the location set (CO 3). The camera operator is responsible for lighting the location set. This allows the camera operator to set the lights with an eye to camera framing and light levels. When lights are set, the camera should be white balanced and ready for the producer's check.

Setting up the videotape recorder (VTRO 2). The videotape recorder operator must work in tandem with the camera operator in setting up on location. Power sources will have to be shared, power cables run in parallel, equipment operation checked, and so on. When videotape recorder set-up is complete, the producer should be informed.

Setting up location audio recording equipment (VTRO 3). The videotape recorder operator has the responsibility to record location sound. This entails knowing the requirements of the preproduction script for audio recording. Microphones, microphone extension cables, and microphone stands or holders (e.g., a fishpole) are all the responsibility of the videotape recorder operator during set-up. A test audio recording is a check to be made before talent is brought to the set.

Prepping the interview (P 6). When the crew indicates that they are ready to videotape, the producer should call for the talent. It is important for the crew to have a sensitivity toward talent who are new to documentary production and may have never been through the experience of location videotaping. This sensitivity should cover every aspect of what is about to occur. Talent need to know where to sit, where to look, how to handle a microphone, how to talk into a microphone, and so on. A producer with an eye to final editing should prep the talent with a request that an interviewee repeat each question asked of him or her as a preface to a response. This allows the

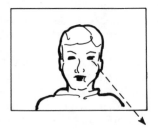

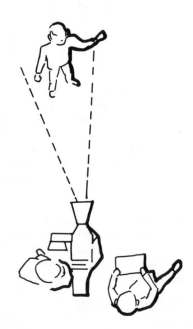

FIGURE 2–4
Staging the documentary interview videotaping. To have the interviewee face forward but not address the lens, place the producer/interviewer next to the camera and have the interviewee speak to the producer/interviewer.

final video and audio editing to flow better and not appear similar to a talk show—question and answer conversation.

The stress on the part of talent of videotaping interviews can be relieved by a producer if openness and candor are part of the preparation of interviewees. People being interviewed need to know what is expected of them in the way of questions, sensitive content, and even the right not to answer or talk about some areas of content. A sensitivity to these areas can go far to create a good interviewing experience and contribute to the documentary in general.

Supervising equipment set-ups (P 7). Because the producer is ultimately responsible for the production and serves in the role of director on location, the producer should oversee the set-up of camera and its placement, the lighting design, and audio pick-up. These technical elements are the means to achieving the goals and objectives of the video for the documentary (the look) the producer has in mind. To check set-ups allows the producer a final critical look at everything as a step in accomplishing what the crew set out to achieve. There is little question that the best equipment set-up check is to test record some audio and video and play it back on a playback monitor. What the producer sees on the playback monitor—ultimately what the viewing audience will see—is the best check for location set-ups.

Calling for a take and a wrap (P 8). Whether the producer serves as an interviewer or not, the control of videotaping is the producer's responsibility. The need to call out direction is the same as other shoots: the location should be readied with a "stand by" command; the videotape roll should be readied and recording begun; a countdown (10, 9, 8 . . .) to the first audio should be made without the last two seconds being audible.

If the producer is also the interviewer, then the video should be controlled for the edit, i.e., pauses should be held after directions are called to allow for a postproduction edit point. This holds especially true for a pause at the end of an interview before calling for a "cut." The producer knows all the videotape shots to be completed: leads, interviews, cut-aways, bridges, summaries, and tags. A "wrap" is called when all shots for that location are videotaped.

Following the producer's directions (T 1). The talent have the responsibility to be aware of the producer's intentions on the set and to be prepared to respond with whatever the producer calls for in the way of a take or retake, change of shot, or redoing responses.

Following the producer's directions (CO 4). Because the producer serves as a director for the production on location, the camera operator must follow the producer's directions regarding production values during the shoot. This includes changing camera placement, lighting design, shot framing and movement, and retakes.

Responding to the producer's directions and videotaping takes (VTRO 4). The videotape recorder operator should be ready to roll the tape recorder (i.e., to start the recorder in record mode) and be prepared to respond to the producer's call to roll tape for recording (to actually start the recorder). The videotape recorder operator also must be sensitive to the producer's call to cut and be prepared to stop the videotape recorder.

Monitoring video and audio levels during taping (VTRO 5). The videotape recorder operator must also monitor the audio input by listening to the audio signal over a headset during videotaping. The videotape recorder operator should keep an eye on the VU meters, which are another check on audio and video input signals during videotaping. The videotape recorder operator should be sensitive to extraneous location sounds, such as airplanes and sirens, during a videotape take. These should be called to the producer's attention usually at the end of a take for evaluation and possibly a retake.

Keeping the location log/continuity notes (P 9). It is good practice for the producer to keep a location log and/or record continuity notes. A log written on location records the order and content of takes, as well as some note of the quality of the take. The log should also keep record of the code of the videotape cassette being recorded. If dramatizations are part of a documentary location shoot, the need to keep continuity notes from take to take becomes essential. Continuity notes record the many details of talent, their lines, body positions, and costuming from shot to shot to ensure good edits (continuity editing) of a scene during postproduction. (See the location log form and continuity notes form.)

Calling for a location strike (P 10). The producer calls for a strike of the location shoot when appropriate. A strike of a location calls for extreme care and courtesy. Many remote documentary locations are environments where people continue to move around and work. The faster a crew strikes, the more courtesy the crew appears to extend to location hosts.

The supervision of the location strike is the responsibility of the producer. Care should be taken in removing tape, mike holders, lighting stands, and gels so that no damage occurs.

Any rearrangement of location elements such as furniture should be replaced with diligence. Reference to location survey notes or instant developing film pictures taken before a location environment was rearranged facil-

itates the restoration of the environment at strike time. The strike is often the last opportunity the producer may have to obtain legal releases from interviewees. (See the talent release form.)

Supervising the equipment strike (CO 5). With the responsibility the camera operator assumes for equipment, it is the camera operator who should supervise the location strike and the replacement and storage of all location equipment. This is the time to refer to an equipment checklist to account for everything brought to a location environment. The camera operator has the additional responsibility to strike location lighting equipment. Care must be exercised that incandescent bulbs in lighting instruments cool down adequately before striking them. Hot bulbs are sensitive to jarring. Jarring a hot bulb can destroy the filament and lessen the light life of the bulb.

Labeling videotapes and removing record buttons (VTRO 6). The videotape recorder operator has the responsibility to remove record buttons from recorded tapes and properly label the videotape cassettes and cassette cases. It is helpful to communicate with the producer and coordinate location log notes with videotape labels. Details such as these serve to save a lot of time in the preparation for postproduction editing.

Assisting in the location strike (VTRO 7). The videotape recorder operator is responsible for the strike and repackaging of all videotape recorder and audio equipment and accessories.

THE POSTPRODUCTION PROCESS

There is little question that the extent of the postproduction process for documentary video production is a function of the length of the individual project. For most documentaries the producer is the only crew member to work postproduction on the project. Depending on the facility in which postproduction is done, the presence of a required technical director/editor may preclude whether the producer does the editing of the documentary.

• Personnel

Producer (P). The producer assumes sole responsibility for the final stages of the documentary project. Many producers are qualified to undertake the editing process and prefer to work alone. Some producers function as an editing decision-maker while an editor or technical director will do the actual "button pushing" at the editing console. Whether the producer works alone or with an editor, the responsibility of the preparatory work that precedes the editing sessions falls on the producer.

Camera operator (C/VTRO). With the production of the documentary package completed, there are only summary tasks remaining for the camera operator. The return and accountability of remote camera and location lighting equipment and accessories remain the final responsibility of the camera/videotape recorder operator.

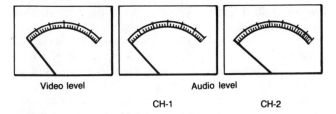

Video level   Audio level

CH-1   CH-2

FIGURE 2–5
Monitoring VU meters during videotaping. The videotape recorder operator must monitor the video and audio input VU meters.

Videotape recorder operator (VTRO). Similar to the camera operator, the only remaining tasks of the videotape recorder operator is to return videotape recording and sound recording equipment and note any losses, damage, or malfunctioning equipment or accessories.

Technical director/editor (TD/E). When a facility requires or the budget affords the luxury, a technical director/editor in the editing suite is employed to do the actual editing of source videotapes to a master tape.

- **Postproduction Stages**

Arranging postproduction schedule and facilities (P 1). The producer has the responsibility to anticipate editing facility needs, including scheduling and personnel. Often the producer does the editing on the documentary. Then there is only the need to plan on preparation time to postproduction. If a technical director/editor is to be used, then scheduling has to account for the availability of another. Besides editing suite availability, accounting has to be made for the amount of time needed to complete the editing. This can be a conservative estimate if preparation of source tapes, editing work sheets, editing cue sheets, and the final documentary script are complete.

Returning remote video and lighting equipment and accessories (CO 1). It is the responsibility of the camera operator to return to maintenance/storage facilities all the camera and lighting equipment used during the remote location shoot. Rented equipment would have to be returned to the equipment rental agency. Equipment purchased for the shoot should be reported separately to maintenance/storage personnel.

Reporting damaged, lost, or malfunctioning equipment (CO 2). As a final obligation to the video documentary shoot, the camera operator should report any equipment or accessory that may have been damaged during the location shoot. This report should also include any loss of equipment or accessories. Most equipment maintenance/storage personnel also appreciate a written report of any equipment or accessory that may have malfunctioned during the location shoot. It is a good practice to report any repair or replacement made to equipment during the shoot.

Returning videotape and sound recording equipment and accessories (VTRO 1). It is the responsibility of the videotape recorder operator to return to maintenance/storage facilities all the videotape and sound recording equipment used during the remote location shoot. Rented equipment would have to be returned to the equipment rental agency. Equipment purchased for the shoot should be reported separately to maintenance/storage personnel.

Reporting damaged, lost, or malfunctioning equipment (VTRO 2). As a final obligation to the video documentary shoot, the videotape recorder operator should report any equipment or accessory that may have been damaged during the location shoot. This report should also include any loss of equipment or accessories.

Most equipment maintenance/storage personnel also appreciate a written report of any equipment or accessory that may have malfunctioned during the location shoot. It is a good practice to report any repair or replacement made to equipment during the shoot.

Recording source tapes with the preproduction script (P 2). Sometime after the location strike, the producer should take charge of the source tapes from the videotape recorder operator. Preproduction preparation requires that the source tapes be put in the order of the preproduction script, no longer in shooting order. If the producer was faithful to the preproduction work put into the script, script breakdown, and shot list, then this reordering is a simple step to preparing for editing. If SMPTE time code is to be used in editing, each of the source tapes will have to be striped. The master tape will also have to be striped with time code. If time code will not be used in editing, the master tape will still have to be striped with a control track. A control track was laid on the source tapes during videotaping.

Reviewing source tapes and recording editing work sheets (P 3). Even though location log sheets were kept during production, it is necessary for a producer to preview all source tapes as a prelude to editing. This step allows the producer to study video and audio responses from location talent. This is the first step in the editing process—deciding what might be used in the documentary and what will not—and the beginning of a final script for the documentary.

The editing work sheets are a listing of all the video on the coded source tapes with notations of in-cues and out-cues, length of segments, some videotape recorder counter numbers, stopwatch time, or SMPTE code, and some judgmental notations on the relative value of takes on the source tapes. (See the editing work sheet.)

Transcribing the interviews (P 4). It is customary in documentary production to verbally transcribe the content of interviews from the source videotapes. The reasons for this are twofold. First, exact verbal transcriptions of interviews gives the producer a deeper research edge in writing the final production script. Because the interviewee by nature is an expert in the topic or subject of the documentary, the interviewee's response to questions is important. Simply reviewing (listening and viewing) the source videotapes is insufficient to adequately weigh the import of what was said. Second, the written transcription of interviews permits a more accurate editing of the content of the interview. The producer can indicate in the transcribed text exact edit points in the content. This also allows a finer final production script. It is also helpful to have an exact transcription of the content of interviews, especially if the subject matter is extremely controversial and if the producer could be subject to a libel suit or misrepresentation of facts during editing.

To save wear and tear on source tapes during transcribing, a dub should be made of the source tapes. A copy of the source tapes on ½ inch videocassettes or on audio cassettes will facilitate transcriptions and preserve the security and quality of the source tapes.

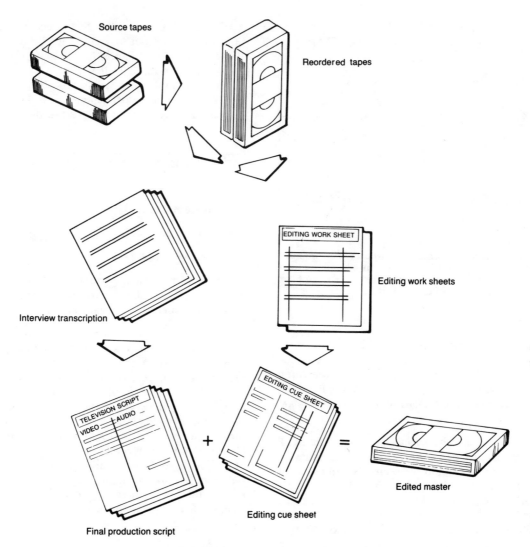

Source tapes

Reordered tapes

Interview transcription

EDITING WORK SHEET

Editing work sheets

TELEVISION SCRIPT

VIDEO | AUDIO

EDITING CUE SHEET

Edited master

Editing cue sheet

Final production script

FIGURE 2–6
Documentary postproduction preparation.

Writing the final script for the documentary (P 5). Now that the producer has seen and noted all takes videotaped on the editing work sheets, all elements are in order for a final production script. Although the preproduction script has served an important service, it gives way to the final script. It can still serve as a frame of reference and a basic framework for the final script, but with the dynamics of location shoot and interviewing, many elements first considered important give way to new elements often more important or creative. The preproduction script gives way to the material gathered on location.

An important addition to the writing of the final production script for the documentary will be the transcriptions of the content of the location interviews from the source videotapes.

Coordinating editing cue sheets with the final production script (P 6). After each source tape has been reviewed, work sheets completed, and the final production script written, the producer can spend quality time apart from the tapes and

video monitors and, with the final script, begin assembling from the editing work sheets and the transcription of the interviews to the editing cue sheets the juxtaposed segments for the proposed edited documentary. In other words, the editing cue sheets should look like a written format for the soon-to-be-edited documentary.

The editing cue sheets contain juxtaposed video segments from the editing work sheets, the video/audio in-cues and out-cues for each segment with the aid of the transcriptions, the clock length of each segment, the source tape label/code number, and the approximate counter number, stopwatch time, or SMPTE code for the segment from the source tape. Given the cost of postproduction time spent in an editing suite, the thoroughness of the editing cue sheets can reduce the hours from the cost of editing time. (See the editing cue sheet.)

Editing or supervising the editing session (P 7). With the majority of editing decisions already made on the editing cue sheets and with the editing work sheets to aid in

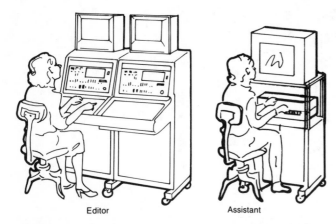

Editor   Assistant

FIGURE 2–7
Postproduction editing and editing assistance. The producer
or the technical director does the editing. An editing assistant
saves time in the editing suite by quickly searching editing bites
from source tapes before the editor needs them.

swift recovery of videotape segments from the source
tapes, editing can begin. There is an advantage to some
other personnel assistance in the editing suite searching
out subsequent videotape segments on an auxiliary fast
search videotape playback deck as previous segments are
being edited.

*Adding music and effects and mixing the audio channels (P
8).* After the master tape has been edited, and assuming
that most synchronous audio bites are also edited with
the video, the second audio track is ready for voice-over
tracks, location ambience tracks, music, or sound effects.
This should be the final editing pass on videotape because
in the course of laying this audio track in place, SMPTE
time code will be erased and replaced with the music and
effects track. In some telecast facilities, a mixed audio
track is required. This means that audio channel 1 (dialogue track) and audio channel 2 (music and effects) will
have to be mixed down to one channel track. It will be
the responsibility of the producer to ascertain on which
of the two audio channels the telecast facility prefers the
mixed track.

Adding titling and credits (P 9). After the master tape is
complete, then titles and credits can be matted on the
video. Some producers may matte the character generator
copy in the editing suite over the proper video images as
they are being edited onto the master. Other producers
prefer to add character generator copy to the edited master
through a studio control room switcher. This can also be
done while the two audio tracks are being mixed down.
The producer can prepare for proper titling and credits'
matte keying by completing an accurate timing of the
master tape from the first audio cue. The character generator copy can then be written and the timed insert
points for matte keying included on the script. (See the
edited master clipsheet.)

Final script transcription for the documentary (P 10). Many
documentary sponsoring organizations may wish to have

a transcribed copy of the final documentary for legal
purposes in addition to a videotaped dub of the master.
If the sponsoring organization or some interviewee was
granted editing rights in lieu of their participation in the
documentary, then they would require a copy of the final
audio text of the documentary from which to make
corrections or revisions to the text of the documentary.

VIDEO PRODUCTION ORGANIZING FORMS

• Treatment Form

Production process: Video documentary preproduction

Responsibility: Producer

Purpose: To propose a documentary video production to
managing personnel, executive producer or new director,
or potential sponsoring organization.

Objective: The treatment form attempts to focus elements
of the proposed video documentary for the producer as a
step to presenting the idea or concept to production
management personnel or sponsoring organization for
approval. The basic needs required by production management or sponsors to judge the appropriateness of a
video documentary include a production statement cap-
turing the concept of the production, the goals and
objectives for the documentary, some verbal description
of the proposed documentary, and an outline or format of
the proposed documentary. For a documentary, the treatment is the first of three basic documents that comprise a
proposal to production management or potential sponsors.

Glossary

Proposed Title   A working title is appropriate to the
proposed documentary described in the treatment. There
is an advantage to titling a proposed documentary. In
the synthesis of a simple title can be contained a concept
or idea that paragraphs cannot convey.

Proposed Length   Committing to a time length for the
documentary is a good discipline for the video producer.
The time length commitment gives management personnel and potential sponsors a grasp of the likelihood
of the success of the video documentary and its content
in terms of its length.

Proposed Shooting Date   Some indication of the proposed starting date for beginning shooting the proposed
documentary should be made. The commitment to a
beginning shooting date allows more information in
the judgment of approving supervisory personnel.

Proposed Completion Date   Another bit of information
for a video production manager is the estimated date
for the completion of the documentary. The completion
date will depend on the content and challenge of
videotaping the topic of the documentary and editing
source tapes.

Production Statement   A production statement is a
brief emotional or rational verbal expression that will

function as a reminder during all stages of the project's production of the specific goal or objective of the documentary. The production statement is meant to be a constant reminder to crew members of the precise goal of the message of the production. An example of a production statement for a documentary on Canada is "Canada is foreign, friendly, familiar, and near."

Communication Goals and Objectives of the Documentary Stating communication goals and objectives for the proposed documentary should contain the rationale for doing the proposed video, who the target audience is, the audience needs for the documentary in terms of the topic, the interests in the topic on the part of the audience, and so on. The more information that can be given in this section of the treatment aids the production management or sponsors in judging the suitability of the proposed documentary for production.

Documentary Description The treatment itself is the verbal description of the proposed video including proposed interviewees, questions for the interview, proposed cut-aways for the piece, and proposed locations for shooting. The more information that is available at this stage of preproduction, the better a video production manager or sponsor can judge the treatment for approval.

Documentary Outline/Format Helpful in judging the extent of research put into the proposed documentary is the ability to outline or format the content, organization, and flow of the proposed documentary. A good outline or format distinguishes sections of materials and places them in logical progression. Determine the relative importance of points within sections; a logical hierarchy of material ensures a smooth flow to the documentary. Create outline or format hierarchies with the use of alphanumeric heading designations. For example,

I. Major Section
   A. Sub Section
      1. Major Point
         a. Minor Point

- **Production Budget Form**

Production process: Video documentary preproduction/proposal

Responsibility: Producer

Purpose: To realistically estimate all possible costs of the production of the proposed video documentary from preproduction to postproduction.

Objective: The budget form is a blank model of a budget for the production of a video documentary. The form is meant to organize all facets of documentary production into estimated expenses and actual expenses. It serves to suggest possible cost items across the whole spectrum of video production, personnel, equipment, labor, and materials. The form should be used to suggest expenses and to call attention to possible hidden costs.

Notes on use: The form should be studied for line items that might pertain to a proposed video documentary shoot. Only applicable line items for the proposed documentary need to be considered. Use the suggestion of line items to weight possible costs for the project. Note that all sections of the budget are summarized on the front page of the form. The subtotal of costs from the individual sections are brought forward to be listed in the summary.

Some costs are calculated by the number of days employed, the hourly rate of pay, and overtime hours. Other costs are calculated by the number of items or people by allotted amount of money per day for the item. The cost of materials is calculated by the amount of material(s) by the cost of a unit.

Projected costs to be applied to the budget can be found from a number of sources. One source of equipment rental and production costs is the rate card of a local video production facility. Salary estimates and talent fees can be estimated from the going rates of relevant services of equivalent professionals or from their agencies. Phone calls to providers of services and materials will also produce cost quotes. Travel costs can be obtained by a phone call to travel agencies or airline companies. There is no question that preparing a good budget is going to involve a lot of time and research.

Glossary

No. Preproduction Days Estimate the number of days to complete the necessary preproduction stages for the documentary. This time includes quality research on the documentary subject, writing the proposal (treatment, preproduction script, budget, location scouting), script breakdown, shot list, equipment checklist, and the production schedule.

No. Studio Shoot Days/Hours Estimate the number of days and hours for which a studio and/or control room facilities may be needed. This time estimate accounts for any in-studio videotaping (e.g., talent on a set) or the use of control room switcher or character generator for postproduction effects.

No. Location Days/Hours Estimate the number of shooting days and hours that may be required on location.

Location Sites List the proposed location shooting sites at which the previous days and hours were estimated.

No. Postproduction Days/Hours Estimate the number of days and hours that will be spent in postproduction in completing the video documentary.

First Shooting Date Indicate the first date proposed to begin videotaping the documentary.

Completion Date Indicate the projected completion of the documentary project. This date should include all postproduction tasks.

Summary of Production Costs This summary area brings forward the subtotals of costs from the respective sections within the budget form. Note that each line unit 1 through 13 is found as section heads within the budget form. When the individual units are completed within the budget, the subtotal is listed in the summary table.

Contingency This term refers to the practice of adding a contingency percentage to the subtotal of subtotals as a padding against the difference in actual final costs from the estimated costs of all line items. The customary contingency percentage is 15%. Multiply the subtotal of line 16 by 0.15 to determine the contingency figure. That result added to line 16 becomes the grand total of the budget costs.

Preproduction Costs The preproduction costs section refers to those personnel who are involved in tasks at the preproduction stage of production.

Crew A number of essential crew personnel (producer, camera operator, videotape recorder operator) are listed in this section as well as other suggested personnel (e.g., associate producer, location director) who could be added to the preproduction crew. Blank lines are available to add other crew members unique to a specific production or project.

Estimated The estimated category refers to costs that can only be projected before the production. Rarely are the estimated costs the final costs to be incurred because of the number of variables that cannot be anticipated. Every attempt should be made to ensure real estimated cost figures and to ensure the consideration of as many variables to the cost as possible. The challenge of estimated budget costs is to project as close as possible to actual costs when they are known.

Actual The actual category of a budget records the costs that are finally incurred for the respective line items during or after the documentary production is completed. The actual costs are those costs that will really be paid out for the production. The ideal budget seeks to have actual costs come as closely as possible—either at or preferably under—to the estimated costs for the production.

Production Costs This production costs section refers to crew personnel and the time spent during the actual production of the video documentary production. Also included in this section are all possible projected costs that might be incurred during the production of the documentary.

Crew This section of the budget refers to elements of crew personnel during the production of the documentary.

Production Materials and Expenses This unit of the budget refers to the many cash needs during production. The line item per diem is the term used to signify the cash allotted to each crew member to cover their own daily meals on location when meals are not provided. Working meals refer to meals that are provided, usually catered to the crew on location. An example of a per diem allotment might be $20 to cover breakfast, lunch, and supper for one day for every crew member.

Location Expenses This section of the budget refers to those costs incurred with the location(s) for the documentary production. This section covers both preproduction location scouting and the actual location site use for production.

Equipment Rental Equipment that may have to be rented for the documentary production is accounted for in this section. A number of possible rental items are suggested. Blank lines are provided for other rental equipment.

Videotape Stock This section of the budget accounts for all the videotape stock that may be needed for the production of the documentary.

Miscellaneous Costs Miscellaneous costs are those items that fall outside the other structured sections of the budget. In some instances the line items cover the whole range of the project (e.g., telephone, insurance).

Talent Expenses The cost of talent for the video documentary should be accounted for in this section of the budget. This section also provides for the transportation of talent to and from location sites during production.

Postproduction Costs Postproduction expenses refer to those costs to be incurred after the production stage of the documentary and during the videotape editing process.

Editing This unit of the budget provides for expenses incurred during videotape editing. Editing facilities and special effects are all accounted for.

Sound A separate section of the budget accounts for the special category of costs incurred for sound production and recording.

Editing Personnel This section of the budget accounts for the cost of postproduction personnel and their hourly rate.

Art Work The artwork unit of the budget accounts for any animated sequences that may be required for the production of the documentary. This unit also takes into account any art work, including computer graphics, which may be required for the documentary.

- **Television Script Form**

Production process: Documentary preproduction and postproduction

Responsibility: Producer

Purpose: To coordinate in side-by-side columns audio copy and a verbal description of the video imaging of the video documentary.

Objective: As a preproduction script, the proposed audio copy and the verbal description of the proposed video documentary can be expressed in acceptable video script form. It is the first format stage in solidifying a proposed video project. As a final production script in postproduction, the two-column form coordinates the final draft of the documentary drawn from the preproduction script, the editing work sheets, and interview transcriptions from the source tapes.

Glossary

Documentary Title The title of the video documentary as it will be known.

Length For the preproduction script, the entry for the length of the proposed video documentary is an estimate. For the final production script, the entry for the length should be more accurate.

Video The video column should contain an abbreviated verbal description of the video elements of the video documentary. This column should contain image content descriptions and framing (e.g., XLS of New York City Skyline), editing transitions (e.g., dissolve, cut, fade) and special effects (e.g., DVE rotation), cut-ins, cut-aways, and character generator copy. For example,

VIDEO

XLS New York City Skyline;
Diss to MS house front;
Cut to CU Mrs. Betty Kasper
Super LT   MRS. BETTY KASPER
                        Artist

Audio   The audio column should contain the full verbal copy to accompany the video described in the VIDEO column. Audio copy is written first in the development of a script. Audio copy should be typed in all caps. All talent and production directions should be typed in upper and lower caps. All audio copy should be introduced with the label of the talent intended to deliver the copy. The AUDIO column should also record the use of sound effects, music, and ambience. In the preproduction script, proposed interview questions should be included. In the final production script, audio bites from source tapes should be transcribed and included in the audio column. For example,

SFX: City street traffic sounds.

ANN: NOT EVERYONE LIVING IN NEW YORK CITY SUFFERS FROM THE IMPERSONALIZATION OF THE BIG APPLE.

• Script Breakdown Form

Production process: Video documentary preproduction

Responsibility: Producer

Purpose: To break the preproduction script down into production units usually according to common location or talent requirements.

Objective: The script breakdown form organizes the preproduction script from proposed edited order of a final video to a shooting order according to differing common criteria for the shoots, e.g., similar location, available talent. The breakdown form will help organize the shooting units by script pages or number of script lines criteria for managing the remote production.

Glossary

Length   This entry records the estimated length of the final video documentary.
Script Length   The length of the preproduction script in number of script pages is recorded here.
Script Pages   Script pages is one of several modes of measuring the length of a remote shooting unit. This method uses the number of whole or partial pages of script copy as a determinant of length of a shooting unit.
No. of Script Lines   The number of lines of script copy is another determinant of length of a shooting unit. The

count should be every line of talent copy to be recorded during the unit shoot.
Int/Ext   These abbreviations stand for interior/exterior referring to the script demands for shooting indoors or outdoors. Whether the shoot is an interior or an exterior shoot can also be a determinant for the script breakdown and shooting unit.
Time   The time of day or night that the location and interior/exterior setting requires should be recorded here.
Setting   Setting means the specific area of a required location site, e.g., a setting would be the vice president's office at ABC Corporation Headquarters' location site.
Location   The location column records the remote location environment at which the setting is to be found. For example, the ABC Corporation Headquarters is the location site for the vice president's office setting.
Talent   The specific name of the talent who is required in the setting at the location for a particular shoot. For example, the name of the individual being interviewed would be entered here.
Shooting Order   When the entire script is broken down into shooting units, then the producer can determine the units for individual shoots and the consecutive shooting order for the entire remote project.

• Location Site Survey Form

Production process: Video documentary preproduction

Responsibility: Producer

Purpose: To organize and facilitate the survey of possible remote video production location environments.

Objective: The location site survey form is designed to assist the producer or location scouts who have to search out and describe potential remote environments for video production purposes. Because many sites may have to be evaluated for any particular shoot, details of each site will have to be recorded to be evaluated and approved at a later time usually away from the site by the producer. The form is designed to raise all possible production needs and location details for a successful remote video production. The form serves to organize and record location site details for later evaluation away from the site.

Glossary

Location Scout(s)   This entry should list those other than the producer who have been recruited to help scout potential locations for the production of the video documentary.
Script Page(s)   This entry should coordinate the location being scouted with the page from the preproduction script that calls for the use of the location.
Script Unit(s)   Some television scripts are divided into shooting units for production location purposes. These script units are numbered consecutively. This entry records the script unit numbers that will be videotaped at the scouted location.
Location   The entry should record the actual environ-

ment called for in the script. For example, the vice president's office.

Site Identification This entry should correspond with a city map (e.g., H-3) or name of the location environment (e.g., ABC Corporation Headquarters).

Local Contact Person The name of the responsible owner, manager, or supervisory officer of a proposed location. This person is the individual who is the location scout(s)' contact person at the highest level of authority over a proposed location site. This person is the use-granting authority for the location. The name, title, address, city, state, and phone number of the contact person should be accurately recorded. All this information including the proper title will be needed for mail correspondence purposes. The "comments" space allows for any notes about the contact person (e.g., executive secretary's name) that would be relevant.

Facilities Personnel The facilities personnel information is a record of the person who is the individual with whom the producer and production crew will work on the location. For example, the maintenance engineer, office manager, and janitor are the individuals responsible for the everyday operation of the proposed location. The name, position title, address, city, state, and phone number of each should be recorded. This information becomes the most practical to the production crew and the producer. This is the information most utilized once the location is chosen for use. The "comments" space should be used for any other relevant information about the facilities personnel. For example, the directions to the facilities personnel office at the location site or maintenance workshop should be recorded here.

Lighting Problems Defined This area of the form focuses attention on those details of the proposed location that can affect lighting of the environment for videotape production.

Light Contrast Ratios Scouts should note any extreme light areas of the environment. A light meter can read and record the extreme lighting intensity of any existing areas of the environment. For example, one end of the proposed location site may have no windows and no ceiling lights. The light reading for this end of the room will be low to nonexistent. The other end of the room may be flooded with light from a number of windows. The light reading at this end of the room will be high. These readings form the contrast ratio between the most existing light and least existing light for this room.

Lighting Intensity This entry records the highest light level reading in the proposed location environment. This information will tell the producer that some controls will have to be used on the light source or other light will have to be created to balance this light intensity.

Ceiling Height The height of an existing ceiling is important information. For example, ceiling height indicates the available height for lighting stands for lighting instruments to be used. A low ceiling allows light to be bounced, or a high ceiling means that light is absorbed. High ceilings also demand a lot of light if the ceiling needs to be lit.

Windows/Compass Direction Knowing the number of windows opening to the exterior of the location is an important location consideration. Many windows may demand correcting incandescent lights with filters or the need to gel the windows. Another important fact regarding a location environment with windows is the compass direction they face. East facing windows can expect a flood of strong morning sunlight that can push the lighting intensity in the location environment. West facing windows will create the same problem in the afternoon. When working remote locations the strongest source of light is the sun, and the sun is a constantly moving light source. Knowing the direction of that moving light source is important. Shadows and reflections change constantly. It is a good practice to have a compass when scouting locations and to take an accurate reading of due east.

Existing Light Control A question to ask facilities personnel during location scouting is the control of existing lighting. For example, in an all fluorescent lighting environment, there may be one master switch; it would be important to know where it is. Simple wall switches for other light control should also be noted.

Lighting Use Notation should be made as to how some existing lighting is used. For example, lighted display cases in the environment, parking lot lights, and night lights are conditions of lighting use in the location environment. Such light use cannot be controlled.

Floor Description The description of the type of flooring in a proposed location environment can have consequences for set lighting design. For example, a highly polished floor covering reflects light; a dark carpet absorbs light or reflects unwanted hues.

Special Consideration Use this space to record for any other specific location detail that might affect lighting design in the environment for the production. For example, a pool of water could reflect light or a mirror on a wall.

Power Problems Defined This area of the form focuses attention on and records the details that have to do with electrical power sources. Video production equipment relies heavily on available power sources.

Number of Power Outlets Count should be made of the number of electrical power outlets in the immediate environment of the proposed shoot. An additional count should also be made of the outlets that can be accessed by power cable runs.

Number of Separate Circuits It is important to know how many separate electrical circuits are represented by the power outlets. This is a question for the facilities personnel/maintenance engineer. The power outlets and separate circuits should be noted on a location diagram.

Types of Fuses One liability of heavy electrical needs for video production equipment is the frequent blown fuse. In some facilities restoring power is not a matter of resetting a circuit, but replacing a fuse. A good example of the need for fuses is the older private home location environment. Fuses come in many sizes and wattages. It is important to know both size and wattage for the proposed location.

Number of Outlet Prongs There are at least two common types of electrical outlets: the two-prong and the three-prong. Many older environments have only the two-prong outlets. Almost all video production equipment utilize the three-prong plug. Hence, adapters will have to be used on all two-prong outlets. The number of two-prong outlets will have to be known during location scouting so that adapters can be provided.

Location of Circuit Breakers Given the common occurrence of overloading electrical circuits with video production equipment needs, the location of fuse boxes and circuit breakers should be known. Often crew members will have to reset breakers and replace blown fuses.

Portable Generator Need It may happen that there is no power source available in a proposed location environment. The only possible source of electricity may be that generated by the production crew itself with a portable power generator. Power generators can be easily rented if needed. Caution must be exercised with the use of a power generator. They are a source of unwanted noise in the environment, which can be difficult to control.

Audio Problems Defined This area of the form focuses on details that will affect the production of audio recording in the proposed location environment.

Interior Environmental Sounds This entry should contain all perceived sound that is audible in the interior of the proposed location environment. This means careful listening for hums and buzzes from air conditioning, refrigerators, freezers, sound speakers, copying machines, fluorescent lights, and so on. All sounds should be noted. Note should also be made on the ability to control or turn off the sounds.

Ceiling Composition The composition of a ceiling can determine the quality of sound recordings made in the proposed location environment. For example, a hard composition ceiling reflects sound; sound proofing materials on a ceiling absorb sound. Both can make a difference in the quality of recorded sound.

Wall Composition The composition on the walls of a proposed location environment will also make a difference in the quality of sound recorded in that environment. For example, cork, carpet or cloth, and sound proofing absorb sound; tile, mirror, and plaster reflect sound.

Exterior Environmental Sounds Location scouts must listen carefully to both interior and exterior sounds in an environment. Exterior sounds will affect both an exterior and an interior shoot. For example, some common exterior sounds that can affect an interior shoot are airplanes, emergency vehicles, a school playground, a busy highway, and a noisy manufacturing plant. Make note of every perceivable sound.

Floor Covering Composition The composition of a floor will also have an effect on sound recording in an environment. For example, a polished hardwood or tile floor reflects sound as well as creates sound (e.g., footsteps). Deep pile carpeting absorbs sound.

Cast and Crew Needs This area of the form reminds location scouts that care and consideration of cast and crew needs will have to be accounted for during a location shoot.

Restroom Facilities Restroom facilities for men and women will have to be provided. Part of the location site survey is to note, perhaps on the diagram of the location, where the restroom facilities are closest to the shooting area.

Green Room Availability A green room is a theatre term for a waiting area for actors. Some such waiting area may also be required for the cast for a video production. This should be a room close to the shooting area, but separate from the shooting area where cast can relax and wait their blocking and videotaping calls.

Parking Arrangements A remote video production crew and cast can create a parking space demand on a neighborhood or public parking area. During scouting, the question of special parking should be addressed. This may occasion some parking privileges or special directions or restrictions.

Freight Elevator In some location environments, the number of crew, cast, and equipment involved in video production may require the use of a freight elevator in a facility. The location of the freight elevator should be part of a location environment diagram giving directions from the freight elevator to the shooting area.

Eating Facilities When the length of a shooting day requires a meal on location, some eating facility, special room, and/or vending machines should be noted. Some facilities may prohibit any eating on the premises. Notation then will have to be made of restaurants in the vicinity of the proposed location.

Make-up Facilities If the video production requires that cast or talent appear in make-up, some facility will have to be provided for the application of the make-up. Ideally, make-up application requires mirrors, adequate lighting, and sinks. Restroom facilities make decent make-up preparation accommodations. If nothing else is available, a double set of restrooms can be designated for make-up and costuming.

Loading/Unloading Restrictions The amount of equipment needed for a remote video production may require special unloading and loading requirements at a location site, e.g., an outside loading dock area. Such an unloading dock may also be close to a freight elevator. Location personnel should always be made aware of the great amount of equipment video production requires. They should be the judge of any special circumstances that might be required for so much equipment.

Hardware Store Because remote video production demands so much hardware equipment, there is often the need to purchase supplies or replace broken, lost, or forgotten supplies. Facilities representatives may be the persons to know where the closest hardware store is in the vicinity of the proposed location environment.

Civil Emergency Services This area of the form lists essential civil services in the service of both the production cast and crew and the location site.

Police Station The address and phone number of the police station that services the proposed location site is important contact information. With the number of individuals a remote video production crew involves, the amount of equipment and the use of an environment warrants the sensitivity to police presence and availability.

Fire Station The same holds true for the fire protection station within the environmental area of the proposed location shoot site. The heavy use of electrical power for a remote video production shoot should alert both producer and production crew to the potential dangers of so much power use. This holds especially true for an older facility such as a private home used as a location site. The address and phone number of the fire station should be entered here.

Location Security and Equipment Safety This area of the form records important information on general personal and property security and safety.

Facility Security This entry records the general security of the crew, cast, and equipment during the production shoot. Some proposed locations in highly public areas such as a shopping mall present security risk; confined production sites such as a private home would be more secure. Note should be made of apparent security in general for all production elements.

Personnel Values Security Record should be made of the arrangements with facilities personnel for the safety and security of personal belongings while crew and cast are involved in production. This includes wallets and purses especially. Facilities personnel often can provide a locked and secure room for the deposit of personal valuables during production.

Equipment Safe Storage Arrangements should be made for the security of unused equipment and accessories that should be safely stored until needed, or stored after use until the location strike. The facilities personnel can often provide a locked and secure room for equipment storage.

Overnight Storage/Security Often remote location shoots take place over the period of more than one day. This entails the safe and secure storage of equipment overnight. Complete breakdown of all location equipment and loading, transport, and unloading a second day can result in the loss of valuable time and energy. Facilities personnel can often provide adequate overnight storage that is both safe and secure.

Other Relevant Information This area of the form records other important information that falls outside the other areas of location details.

Public Area Power Source Often in public areas, such as a city park, the local power company may already provide a power box with electrical outlet for private use. This service has to be requested from the power company and a deposit made to secure power costs at the end of the production shoot. Location scouts should search a public area for some sign of power source facility. It may serve the site survey to call the local power company and request a listing of outdoor power sources.

Clearance/Insurance Personal security for the crew and talent and property damage insurance coverage should be secured before video production. Academic programs have personal insurance coverage for students and property damage and loss coverage for school equipment, which is active when the shoot is a valid academic project with a supervising faculty present. Other remote video production projects can easily receive coverage by contacting a reliable insurance agent. Some potential location facilities personnel require verification of insurance coverage before approval of their location for a shoot. Anticipating insurance notification before facilities personnel require it is a sign of professional competence.

Photographs Taken When more than one location environment is being scouted for a shoot, and a decision may be made away from a potential site, a producer will have to judge from the location scout's report. An important part of a location site survey is photographs of the proposed location. Instant developing film is most convenient. When adequate photographs of a location site are part of a survey, these photographs help a producer and camera operator plan a shoot and assist a crew after a location strike in replacing a location environment to the arrangement and condition it was before the production crew arrived. The photographs taken should be listed. The photographer's camera position and direction of the lens of the photographed site should be noted on the location diagram as an aid in designing the video camera shots and lens framing for the production.

Location Environment Drawing/Map Another important product of location scouting is a drawing or map of the proposed location site. This entails a rough pacing off of all environments both interior and exterior that are being considered as a video setting. Windows should be placed, compass direction indicated, power outlets and circuits noted, existing furniture and other properties sketched, and so on. Everything should be included that may enter into the use of the location from the needs of the production and the adaptability of the location environment.

Traffic Control At some exterior location environments, the extent of a video production crew, talent, and equipment will necessitate some control of vehicular traffic. For example, parking restriction may be required along the area of a shooting set, moving traffic may have to be redirected during a shoot, or a street may have to be closed off entirely from traffic. Most police departments are cooperative to such requests, but they need adequate advance time notification. In some instances the approval of a city or town council may be required. This too requires adequate lead time to process the request and get it to the council in good time for the shoot or a change of plans if the request is denied.

Exterior Compass Direction If the remote location site is an exterior shoot, an accurate assessment of the compass directions of the area should be made with respect to the proposed shooting site. The sun is the principal light source to an exterior shoot, and that source is in constant movement. Knowing the direction the sun takes from east to west on a proposed location environment is a most important variable to designing an outdoor video shoot. A compass is a necessity to scouting a location site. Many location personnel are not accurate about their recollection of east and west directions and are not reliable sources of information, given the importance that the sun's direction has on a remote video shoot.

Other Comments/Observations This area should record any other details not covered in the form to this point. It is important to record all impressions of a proposed location site. Sometimes the smallest detail missed or the smallest detail included can become either an obstacle or an asset to the production later. When in doubt about including a detail, include it.

• **Production Schedule Form**

Production process: Video documentary preproduction

Responsibility: Producer

Purpose: To organize and schedule the videotape production of individual script and location units of the video documentary.

Objective: The production schedule form organizes the elements of each remote location into production days and dates for videotaping. The form serves to notify the production crew and talent of specific location addresses, dates, times, and script pages of scheduling the videotape production of the news package. The schedule also sets alternate dates, projected equipment set-up and location strike times, and approximate times for completing the shoot. Because the video documentary production often requires crew travel, the production schedule form records travel means, departure and arrivals, and accommodations.

Glossary

Shooting Day This area of the form sets the specific date (weekday, month, and day) for the first shooting day. The production schedule form also firms up an alternate rain date.

Location Site The remote environment/place approved for the shoot after site survey was completed should be noted here. This names the building and geographic area where the videotaping is to take place.

Location Map No. This notation relates the location site and address to a city map of the geographic area (e.g., H-3).

Location Host The name of the location personnel responsible for the facility/area where the shoot is to occur should be recorded here. This is the everyday contact person with whom the producer will cooperate on details of the location and the shoot. A contact telephone number where the location host can be reached should be included.

Emergency Phone No. An emergency contact telephone number is made available for the family of the crew.

Travel: Departure All details for production crew departure are recorded here. The choice of mode of travel and other pertinent information should also be included.

Accommodations The details of living accommodations during overnight shoots are recorded here.

Travel: Return The details for the production crew's return are recorded here. Again, mode of travel and other information are to be included.

Shoot Order Units If the preproduction script was arranged in script units, this column records the order in which the script units will be shot.

Script Pages This column records the script pages that will be produced during the shoot.

Setting The specific setting within the location where the videotaping will occur is listed here.

Approx. Time A range of hours and minutes approximating the time needed to complete the script units or script pages proposed for production during that shooting day.

Talent/Interviewee The talent or interviewees who will be a part of the videotaping are listed here.

Properties On many location shoots, some kind of properties are required, e.g., an automobile, an animal. Those properties and any other set elements required for the respective script units/pages are recorded here.

Crew Call The time and place of the production crew starting crew call should be entered here.

Talent Call The time and place for the arrival call for talent is also listed. Because the talent do not need the lead time for equipment set-up as the production crew do, the talent call can be up to an hour later than the production crew call. Time should be allotted for make-up if make-up is required for the talent.

Set-up This entry is a range of time including a deadline for the production crew to complete all equipment set-up and checks of the equipment.

Projected Strike Time This time sets an approximate termination hour for completing the shoot and striking the location.

• **Shot List Form**

Production process: Video documentary preproduction

Responsibility: Producer or camera operator

Purpose: To translate the preproduction script from the script breakdown into location shooting units or camera takes.

Objective: The shot list form organizes each proposed videotape take on location into shooting units. The shooting units will generate the necessary video to create the proposed documentary as designed on the preproduction script. This preproduction task facilitates the "what's next" syndrome during location productions. The shot list should exactly define every camera set-up, lens framing, and video shot needed to achieve that video.

Glossary

Location Every planned location site camera set-up and change of location site camera set-up should be noted in this column.

Shot No. From the script breakdown form, every necessary shot needed to create the imaging of the preproduction script should be numbered consecutively. The respective number should be recorded here.

Master Shot   If a proposed shot is a master shot or establishing shot (e.g., XLS) for a scene, it should be noted here. For example, a master shot might be an XLS of a couple walking toward the camera during dialogue.

Cut-in Shot   If a proposed shot is a cut-in (from a master shot) it should be noted in this column. For example, a cut-in would be a CU shot of one of the couple in the master shot.

Cut-away Shot   Unlike the cut-in (to a master shot), the cut-away shot is relevant but extraneous to (usually away from) the master scene shot. An example of a cut-away would be generic footage of a city street.

Shot Framing   Shot framing directions for every proposed shot should make use of the symbols for the basic camera shot framing: XLS, LS, MS, CU, and XCU. This would communicate to the camera operator the lens framing for the proposed shot.

Shot Motion   Shot motion directions should indicate the kind of movement desired in the proposed shot. Movement in a shot can be either primary movement (on the part of the talent in front of the camera) which is the blocking of the talent; or secondary movement (on the part of the camera itself) which can be the pan, tilt, arc, truck, dolly, pedestal, or zoom.

Content Notes   Any particular details of any shot that are not covered in the previous directions can be noted here. An example of a content note would be to direct the camera operator to defocus the lens during the shot.

• Equipment Checklist Form

Production process: Video documentary preproduction

Responsibility: Camera operator and videotape recorder operator

Purpose: To suggest and account for all possible equipment and accessories necessary for a successful remote video shoot.

Objective: The equipment checklist form is an all-inclusive checklist for equipment and accessories hardware that may be used or needed on a video production location site. The checklist notes first the equipment that is available to the production crew, usually the equipment owned by the production facility. Second, the list notes the equipment that may have to be purchased for the shoot. Third, the checklist allows for notation for any equipment that may have to be rented for the shoot. There are blank lines in equipment groups to personalize the checklist for an individual production or facility.

Glossary

Location(s)   The location(s) for which the equipment will be needed should be noted here.

Avl   This abbreviation stands for "available" equipment that may be owned by the production facility. A check in this column indicates that the equipment or accessory is available to the production crew and free to be used on the scheduled production day.

Pch   This abbreviation stands for "purchase" and indicates that the needed equipment or accessory will have to be purchased for the production project. Items checked as needed to be purchased will probably require some other requisition step and approval. The checklist also does not imply when the purchasing will be done or by whom. This is the responsibility of the production crew member.

Rnt   This abbreviation stands for "rent" and indicates that the needed equipment or accessory is not available, perhaps too expensive to purchase for the shoot, and will have to be rented from a supplier. Similar to items checked in the purchase column, additional steps may be required in the process of obtaining the rented equipment. Some requisition may have to be made, approval received, and rental details made.

Camera/Recorder/Tripod/Test Equipment/Audio/Power Supplies/Lighting/Cables   These areas of the form listed are an attempt to anticipate all possible equipment and accessories needs for a remote video production. Many items may be superfluous. They are listed as an attempt to suggest all possible production needs, and equally to suggest the use of some hardware that could be needed during a remote location shoot. One way to use this checklist is to permit it to suggest hardware elements to make the experience of a remote video shoot smooth and productive.

Miscellaneous   This area of the form is the result of years of remote video production experience and represents many production disasters during which these elements could have made a difference. Some items are redundant; some may suggest some use not before anticipated. Most items are helpful to the good order and task facilitation on location.

• Remote Log/Continuity Form

Production process: Video documentary production

Responsibility: Producer

Purpose: To record videotaping production details in the field.

Objective: The remote log/continuity form facilitates the time-consuming need to view source videotapes after field production to note the quality, extent, and content of every videotaped take from the field.

Glossary

Location   The location is the remote site where the videotaping was done.

VTR Counter/Timer/Code   This column notes the measure used to clock the length of every videotape take. One method of measuring the length of a videotaped take is to read the built-in digital counter on the videotape recorder. Another measure is to use a stopwatch as a timer. Still another measure is to stripe the source videotape with the SMPTE time code and record frames as a measure of the length of a take. Place a check in the correct box to indicate the type of measure used to time the source tape.

Location Because the environment used for videotaping on a location can change, e.g., interior versus exterior, this column allows notation of changes within the location for various takes.

Talent Note should be made of the person or persons videotaped during a take. This is a reminder that the full name, correct spelling, and proper title of videotaped talent will be required for character generator copy later in postproduction editing or news telecast.

Take No. It is not uncommon for more than a single take of any event or interview on location to be videotaped. All takes should be numbered consecutively and the number of each take recorded. The number will facilitate easier recall of the take during editing.

Good/No Good A judgment should be made on location of the various takes during videotaping. Having a recorded comment on the quality of each take as it is completed saves the time of viewing all videotaped takes to make the same judgment during postproduction preparation for editing.

Video/Audio Some notation might be made on the video or audio content of each take in this column.

• **Video Continuity Notes**

Production process: Documentary production

Responsibility: Producer or continuity secretary

Purpose: To record during videotaping the details of all elements of the production as an aid to reestablishing details for sequential shots. The need is to facilitate a continuity of production details so that editing across shots is continuous.

Objective: The video continuity form is a record of all possible video production details (e.g., location, talent, properties, dialogue) that must carry over from shot to shot and across edits in postproduction. The nature of single camera production is the fact that although video-taped shots are separate in production, the final video editing of various shots must look continuous. The continuity form records specific details at all facets of production and records them to reestablish the detail in subsequent videotaping.

Notes on use: The form is designed to be used for each separate shot being taken in single camera remote field production. This means that for any single shot with many takes, one continuity notes page should be used. In preparing for a lengthy remote shoot involving many shots to be achieved, as well as many camera and lighting set-ups, many copies of this form will have to be made.

The person keeping continuity notes should be observant. The role demands attention to the slightest detail of the production that may have to be reestablished in another camera take. The role needs a crew person with 100% of the time spent on note taking.

Admittedly, the immediacy of replaying video on a playback monitor on location is a fast check on any detail in a previous videotaped take. Although playback is fast, it is time-consuming, and it is not a habit that a producer should become accustomed to. Careful continuity notes are still a requirement in remote single camera video production.

Glossary

Slate No. A slate can be numbered consecutively. That number is recorded here.

Continuity Secretary If the producer does not keep the continuity notes, someone else is designated the continuity secretary. His or her name should be recorded here.

Set-up/Location A description or sketch of the location or the set-up of the environment is required here. Note should be taken of things that were moved (e.g., action properties) and need to be replaced.

Interior/Exterior These choices allow the notation whether the shoot is indoor or outdoor.

Day/Night These choices allow the notation of time of day.

Sync Cam 1/2 This alternative is the indication that the shoot is video and audio synchronous recording and indicates which audio channel is being used for recording the audio signal, channel 1 or channel 2.

Silent This choice indicates that the camera is taking video without recording any audio signal.

Wildtrack Wildtrack means that audio signals are being recorded without video. For example, to record a portion of location ambience for later audio mixing would not require video signals also.

WT with Cam This alternative, wildtrack with camera, indicates that a wildtrack is being recorded with a video signal also.

Sequence No. Some remote production video units are parts of a numbered sequence. This entry is used to record the sequence number being videotaped.

Shot No. When a shot list is being followed on location, the sequential number of the shot being videotaped is recorded here.

Script Page No. For a script being produced with numbered pages, the page number of the script page being videotaped is recorded in this space.

Shot List Page No. When a lengthy shot list is being videotaped, the page number of the shot list being videotaped is recorded here.

Costume/Make-up/Properties Notes The area should be used to verbally record all details noticed during production that may have to be reestablished for a subsequent take. Note should be taken of any costume use (e.g., a tie off-centered, a pocket flap tucked in), make-up detail (e.g., smudged lipstick, position of a wound), or property use (e.g., half-smoked cigarette in the right hand between the index and middle finger, or fresh ice cream cone in the left hand).

Tape No. This should be a record of the numerically coded videotape being recorded for this take. This record should coordinate this take with a particular videocassette.

Circle Takes (1–10) This area of the form facilitates record of each subsequent take of a shot or scene. The best use of these boxes is to circle each number representing the take in progress until the take is satisfactorily videotaped.

End Board The normal practice of indicating on the videotape what take in a scene is being recorded is to use the slate. If a particular take is flubbed or messed up for a minor problem (e.g., an actor missing a line), a producer might simply indicate that instead of stopping taping and beginning from scratch the crew keep going by starting over without stopping. When this occurs, because the slate was not used to record the beginning of the retake, an end board is used; the slate is recorded on tape at the end of the take instead of at the beginning. This note will alert the postproduction crew not to look for a slate at the beginning of that take but at the end.

Timer/Counter This area of the form should be used to record either a consecutive stopwatch time or the consecutive videotape recorder digital counter number. Both of these times should be a record of the length into the videotape. Therefore, the stopwatch and/or the counter should be at zero when the tape is rewound to its beginning at the start of the tape. It is a good practice for the videotape recorder operator to have the habit of calling the counter numbers out loudly to the continuity note taker at the beginning of every take.

Reason for Use/Not Good The benefit of the continuity notes is that it saves the tedium of reviewing all takes after a shoot to make a determination of the quality of each take. If conscientious notes are taken here and a judgmental notation on the quality of each take is recorded, one postproduction chore is complete. Usually, a producer makes a judgment on location anyway in determining whether to retake a shot or to move on to a new shot. The continuity secretary should note whether the take is good or not, and the reason for that judgment.

Action Continuity details on any action during the take should be noted here, e.g., the direction talent takes when turning, or the hand used to open a door.

Dialogue An area of continuity interest can be the dialogue of the script. Here notation should be made of any quirk of dialogue used in a take that may have to be repeated in a take intended for a matched edit.

• Talent Release Form

Production process: Video documentary production

Responsibility: Producer

Purpose: To give the producer legal rights over the video and audio recordings of individual talent.

Objective: The talent release form is a legal document, which when filled out and signed by talent gives to the producer and the producing organization the legal right to use both video and/or audio recording of an individual for publication. This form is especially necessary in cases of video documentary content on controversial issues, but its use is recommended whenever any talent is being featured in video and audio taping.

Glossary

Talent Name This entry should contain the name of the individual talent recorded on video or audio.

Recording Location The location site of the video and/or audio recording should be entered here.

Producer The name of the supervising producer should be entered here.

Producing Organization The incorporated name of the video producing organization should be entered here.

Note: The expression "For value received" may imply that some remuneration, even a token remuneration, be required for the form to be legally binding. When there is any doubt about the legal nature of the document, consult a lawyer.

• Editing Work Sheet

Note: If adequate and thorough notes were made on the remote log/continuity form, completing the editing work sheet may not be necessary.

Production process: Video documentary postproduction

Responsibility: Producer

Purpose: To prepare for postproduction editing of the video package to a master tape from source videotape(s).

Objective: The editing work sheet records in videotaping order all video and/or audio recordings on the source tape. The editing work sheet is a transcription of the source tape(s). An accurate account of the source tape(s) saves a lot of searching the source tape(s) during editing. Many postproduction facilities demand this work before access is allowed to editing suites. For the producer, this stage saves valuable time and cost in postproduction.

Glossary

Audio: Channel 1/Audio: Channel 2 The producer of the documentary should indicate the correct audio channel or channels and their use on the source tape(s). Because the choice can vary between channel 1 or channel 2 for field recording, the designation should be made of the channel on which the audio recording was made in the field.

Tape No. The coded number of each videocassette should be recorded here. This coordinates all source videotapes to the editing work sheets.

VTR CNTR/Clock/SMPTE Because some measure should be made of the videotape content on the source tape(s), it is helpful to note what that measure is. Choices include the digital counter on the videotape recorder/playback unit, reading from a stopwatch, or reading SMPTE time code. Source videotapes can be striped during videotaping or as a first step in postproduction prior to beginning the editing work sheet. These measures should be consecutive measures made from the beginning (rewound) of the source videotape(s). The VTR counter and stopwatch should be set to begin at zero. SMPTE time code is easiest to use when also set to zero at the beginning of striping.

IN/OUT These columns allow the producer to indicate the beginning and ending measures (VTR counter, clock, or SMPTE) for the particular source videotape units being noted.

Notes Any meaningful notation about the content of the video and/or audio on the source tape(s). This is the place to make value judgments about the quality and usability of each particular take.

Segment Clock Time This column should record the real clock time length of each particular video or audio bite being noted. Depending on the desired content of any particular video or audio bite, judgment should be made whether the time should be from first video to final video or first audio to final audio.

• **Editing Cue Sheet**

Production process: Video documentary postproduction

Responsibility: Producer

Purpose: To prepare for postproduction editing of the video documentary to master tape from source videotape(s).

Objective: The editing cue sheet is a postproduction preparatory stage that creates the format and order of edits of the proposed master videotape from the editing work sheet. The editing cue sheet juxtaposes takes from the editing work sheet into the proposed order of edits for postproduction editing. This step permits a lot of creative work and quality time on the proposed final edited piece without tying up a videotape editing suite.

Glossary

Tape No. The coded number of the source videotape from which each individual edit or bite will be taken should be noted here. Because the editing process will juxtapose many video bites from numerous video takes, many source tapes will be drawn from. The coded enumeration on all recorded source videocassettes is now useful and necessary to avoid confusion.

Audio: Channel 1/Audio: Channel 2 The producer of the package should indicate the correct audio channel or channels and their proposed use on the edited master tape(s). Because the choice can vary between channel 1 or channel 2 and mixed channels, the designation should be made of the channel on which final audio recording will be made.

VTR CNTR/Clock/SMPTE Because some measure should be made of the videotape content on the edited master SMPTE tape(s), it is important to note what that measure is. Choices include the digital counter on the videotape recorder/playback unit, the reading from a stopwatch, or SMPTE time code. SMPTE time code can be striped on the edited master tape(s) as a first step in postproduction prior to actual editing. These measures should be consecutive measures made from the beginning (rewound) of the master videotape(s). The VTR counter and stopwatch should be set to begin at zero. SMPTE time code is easiest to use when also set to zero at the beginning of striping.

IN/OUT These columns allow the producer to indicate the beginning and ending measures (VTR counter, clock, SMPTE) for the particular videotape bites being used from the source tape(s) as noted on the editing work sheet.

Notes: In-cue/Out-cue This space should indicate the video or audio in-cues and out-cues from the proposed bites noted on the editing work sheet from the source tape(s). This space will allow the producer to create the proposed edited order of videotape bites from the source tape(s) to the master tape. The in-cues and out-cues may be either video cues or audio cues. Video cues briefly describe the content of the beginning or end of the bite being considered; audio cues are the first few words of the beginning of the proposed bite or final few words at the end of the bite being considered.

Segment Clock Time This column should record the real clock time length of each particular video or audio bite being proposed. Depending on the desired content of any particular video or audio bite, judgment should be made whether the time should be from first video to final video, first audio to final audio, or first audio to final video. When all entries recorded in this column are summed up, the total should approximate the length of the final edited video piece.

• **Edited Master Clipsheet**

Production process: Video documentary postproduction

Responsibility: Producer

Purpose: To record all character generator copy necessary for the telecast of the edited master of the video documentary.

Objective: The edited master clipsheet facilitates for the producer all possible character generator screen text necessary to accompany the edited master video for telecast. The form serves as a summary listing of all essential information not contained on the edited master video documentary. This form also serves to prompt the producer to create possible character generator screen text for an edited documentary.

Glossary

Package Title This entry records the title of the video documentary as proposed on the preproduction forms. This is the title that will label the edited documentary from this point on.

Audio: Channel 1, 2, Mixed An indication should be made of the final audio channel used for editing. Some producers edit using both audio channels and expect that the edited master use the mixed audio playback option. Other producers mix the two audio channels down to either one of the two available channels. The choice made in editing should be indicated.

Length The total edited length of the documentary should be timed. Most often, timing is from first audio to final audio. A producer might intend to begin the documentary with video images before first audio begins. This is the point where that choice should be indicated.

Out-cue In the telecast situation where the documentary may be B-rolled into a longer program, a control room director will need the video or audio out-cue of the documentary. The out-cue is a description of the intended final video or the final few words of the audio track. This out-cue should be indicated here. If there are to be other breaks during the telecasting of the documentary (e.g., commercial breaks), then the out-cues of each break will have to be provided as well as out-cue and in-cue times.

Character Generator Copy This section of the form records for the producer or control room director all the character generator copy for matting on the video documentary during telecast.

Videotape/Film Credit When a producer uses video or film footage from another source, screen credit may be required. This entry may be as simple as "File Footage" or "Courtesy of ABC-TV."

In __:__/Out __:__ For every screen of character generator copy the producer will have to provide real clock time from the beginning of the documentary at which the character generator copy is to be matted over the video and when the matte is to be removed (i.e., the length of time to remain on the screen).

Reporter Lower Third This character generator copy gives the name of the producer or talent. This copy is needed whether the producer or talent is to be seen on screen or whether the producer or talent simply does a voice-over. Examples of producer/talent lower third follow:

JOHN DOE
_____

Producer

and

JOHN DOE
Producer

Interviewee/Actuality Lower Third When interviewees appear on-screen, character generator copy is expected. Here is an example of an interviewee/actuality lower third:

Mr. WILLIAM B. SMITH
Vice President
ABC Corporation

Voice of When the interviewee does not appear on screen or the interview is recorded over the telephone,

the correct form for character generator copy is to indicate that the audience is hearing the voice of the person only. Following is an example of character generator copy for this:

Voice of
SEN. JOHN P. DOE
(R) Virginia

Transcription Occasionally, transcribed text copy has to appear on the screen over some video image. For example, if an interviewee is speaking in a foreign language, or if an interviewee has a very heavy accent, or the audio quality of a sound bite is very poor, a transcription of a portion of the audio track may have to be matted on the screen over the interview or actuality. A quotation from a book or a number of statistics from a survey may have to be matted on the screen. This is the place to indicate that text copy.

Trade Credit Perhaps some favor or permission adding to the quality of the documentary production warrants an on-screen credit. This screen credit is called a trade. This is the place to indicate that text. This is an example of a trade credit:

Mr. Smith's clothes
provided by

FOR MEN ONLY

Video Credits Documentary production requires the listing of all credits to the video documentary itself. There is no standardized manner in which credits are to appear. Some sponsoring organizations may request lead credit, even before the title of the documentary appears, for example, "ABC Corporation presents." Some producers require their credit at the lead of the documentary also. Most often, production crew credits follow the documentary in a trailer fashion. Credits sometimes are listed in a hierarchical order of crew responsibilities. Just as often credits are listed in reverse hierarchical order. Besides crew credits, video, film, photograph, and music credits will also have to be placed on the documentary. People and organizations that have contributed to the production are also listed and thanked.

TREATMENT

VIDEO DOCUMENTARY PRODUCTION

Producer:

Proposed Title:

Proposed Length: :
Proposed Shooting Date: /   /
Date: /   /   Proposed Completion Date: /   /
Locations:

Page   of

Production Statement

Communication Goals and Objectives of the Documentary

Documentary Description

Documentary Outline/Format

(Continue on reverse side.)

PRODUCTION BUDGET

Producer: Documentary Title:

Camera Operator:

Videotape Recorder Operator: Length: :

No. Preproduction Days: [ ] Hours: [ ]   First Shooting Date: /   /

No. Studio Shoot Days: [ ] Hours: [ ]   Completion Date: /   /

No. Location Days: [ ] Hours: [ ]   Location Sites:

No. Post Production Days: [ ] Hours: [ ]

SUMMARY OF PRODUCTION COSTS	ESTIMATED	ACTUAL
1. Preproduction costs		
2. Production crew		
3. Production materials and expenses		
4. Location expenses		
5. Equipment rental		
6. Videotape stock		
7. Miscellaneous		
8. Talent costs and expenses		
9. Sub total		
10. Post production editing		
11. Sound		
12. Editing Personnel		
13. Artwork		
14.		
15.		
16. Sub total		
17. Contingency		
18. Grand total		

COMMENTS:

PREPRODUCTION COSTS

CREW	ESTIMATED				ACTUAL			
	Days	Rate	O/T Hrs	Total	Days	Rate	O/T Hrs	Total
1. Producer								
2. Assoc Producer								
3.								
4. Location Director								
5.								
6. Camera Operator								
7. VTR Operator								
8. Grip								
9.								
10. Location Scout								
11. Prod Asst								
12.								
Sub-Total								

PRODUCTION COSTS

CREW	ESTIMATED				ACTUAL			
	Days	Rate	O/T Hrs	Total	Days	Rate	O/T Hrs	Total
13. Producer								
14. Assoc Producer								
15.								
16. Location Director								
17.								
18. Camera Operator								
19. VTR Operator								
20. Grip								
21.								
22. Location Scout								
23. Prod Asst								
24.								
Sub-Total								

PRODUCTION MATERIALS AND EXPENSES	ESTIMATED	ACTUAL
25. Auto Rentals: No. of Cars		
26. Air Fares: No. of People ( ) x Amt per Day ( )		
27. Per Diems: No. of People ( ) x Amt per Day ( )		
28.		
29. Working Meals		
30.		
Sub-Total		

LOCATION EXPENSES	ESTIMATED	ACTUAL
31. Location Fees		
32. Permits		
33. Insurance		
34. Vehicle Rental		
35. Parking, Tolls, and Gas		
36. Shipping/Trucking		
37. Scouting		
Travel		
Car Rental		
Housing		
Per Diem		
38. Gratuities		
39. Miscellaneous		
40.		
Sub Total		

EQUIPMENT RENTAL	ESTIMATED	ACTUAL
41. Camera Rental		
42. Videotape Recorder Rental		
43. Audio Rental		
44. Lighting Rental		
45.		
46. Generator Rental		
47. Crane/Cherry Picker Rental		
48. Walkie Talkies/Bull Horn(s)		
49. Dolly Rental		
50. Mobile Unit Rental		
51. Camera Plane/Chopper Rental		
52. Camera Car(s) Rental		
53. Camera Boat(s) Rental		
54. Production Supplies		
55.		
56. Miscellaneous		
57.		
Sub Total		

VIDEOTAPE STOCK	ESTIMATED	ACTUAL
58. Videotape:		
1" (:) x ($)		
3/4" (S 20:00) x ($)		
3/4" (30:00) x ($)		
3/4" (60:00) x ($)		
59.		
60. Miscellaneous		
Sub Total		

MISCELLANEOUS COSTS	ESTIMATED	ACTUAL
61. Petty Cash		
62. Air Shipping/Special Carriers		
63. Telephones/Cables		
64. Billing Costs		
65. Special Insurance		
66. Miscellaneous		
Sub Total		

TALENT EXPENSES	ESTIMATED	ACTUAL
67. Per Diems: No. of Days ( ) x Amt per Day ( )		
68. Air Fare: No. of People ( ) x Amt per Fare ( )		
69. Taxis/Other Transportation		
70. Miscellaneous		
71.		
Sub Total		

POST PRODUCTION COSTS

EDITING	ESTIMATED				ACTUAL			
	Days	Rate	O/T Hrs	Total	Days	Rate	O/T Hrs	Total
72. SMPTE Time Coding								
73. On-Line Editing								
74.								
75. DVE Special Effects								
76. Tape-to-tape Duping								
77. Audio Mixing								
78. Audio Sweetening								
79. Sound Effects								
80. Character Generator								
81. Master(s)								
82. Dub(s)								
83. Tape Stock and Reels								
84. Paint Box								
85.								
86. Miscellaneous								
87.								
Sub Total								

SOUND	ESTIMATED				ACTUAL			
	Days	Rate	O/T Hrs	Total	Days	Rate	O/T Hrs	Total
88. Narration Recording								
89. Sound Effects								
90. Stock Music Search								
91. Stock Music Fee								
92. Mixing								
93.								
94. Miscellaneous								
Sub Total								

EDITING PERSONNEL	ESTIMATED				ACTUAL			
	Days	Rate	O/T Hrs	Total	Days	Rate	O/T Hrs	Total
95. Editor								
96. Asst Editor								
97.								
98. Miscellaneous								
Sub Total								

ART WORK	ESTIMATED				ACTUAL			
	Days	Rate	O/T Hrs	Total	Days	Rate	O/T Hrs	Total
99. Art Work								
100. Animator(s)								
102.								
103. Animation Materials								
104. Animation Photography								
105. Miscellaneous								
106.								
Sub Total								

COMMENTS

TELEVISION SCRIPT

VIDEO DOCUMENTARY PRODUCTION

Producer:	Documentary Title:
	Length: :
	Date: / /
	Page of

VIDEO	AUDIO

VIDEO DOCUMENTARY PRODUCTION VIDEO SCRIPT	Page	of
VIDEO	AUDIO	

SCRIPT BREAKDOWN

VIDEO DOCUMENTARY PRODUCTION

Producer:

Documentary Title:

Length: :
Script Length: pages
Page   of
Date: /   /

SCRIPT PAGES	NO. OF SCRIPT LINES	INT/ EXT	TIME	SETTING	LOCATION	TALENT	SHOOT- ING ORDER

VIDEO DOCUMENTARY PRODUCTION SCRIPT BREAKDOWN				Page	of		
SCRIPT PAGES	NO. OF SCRIPT LINES	INT/ EXT	TIME	SETTING	LOCATION	TALENT	SHOOT-ING ORDER

LOCATION SITE SURVEY

VIDEO DOCUMENTARY PRODUCTION

Producer:	Documentary Title:
Location Scout(s):	Script Page(s): Script Unit(s):
Approval:	Date: / /

Location: Local Contact Person: Name: Title: Address: City: State: Phone No.: ( ) - Facilities Personnel: Name: Position Title: Address: City: State: Phone No.: ( ) -	Site Identification: Comments: Comments:

LIGHTING PROBLEMS DEFINED

Light contrast ratios	Existing light control
Lighting intensity	Lighting use
Ceiling height	Floor description
Windows/Compass direction	Special consideration

POWER PROBLEMS DEFINED

Number of power outlets	Number of outlet prongs
Number of separate circuits	Location of circuit breakers
Types of fuses	Portable generator need

AUDIO PROBLEMS DEFINED

Interior environmental sounds	Exterior environmental sounds
Ceiling composition	Floor covering composition
Wall composition	

CAST AND CREW NEEDS

Restroom facilities	Eating facilities
Green room availability	Make-up facilities
Parking arrangements	Loading/unloading restrictions
Freight elevator	Hardware store

CIVIL EMERGENCY SERVICES

Police station   Fire station

LOCATION SECURITY AND EQUIPMENT SAFETY

Facility security   Equipment safe storage

Personnel values security   Overnight storage/security

OTHER RELEVANT INFORMATION

Public area power source   Traffic control

Clearance/Insurance needed   Exterior compass direction

Photographs taken   Location environment drawing/map

Other information:

OTHER COMMENTS/OBSERVATIONS

PRODUCTION SCHEDULE

VIDEO DOCUMENTARY PRODUCTION

Producer: _____ Documentary Title: _____

Camera Operator: _____ Date: __ / __ / __
Page ___ of ___

SHOOTING DAY   **RAIN DATE**

_____ , _____ , _____   __ / __ / __
(Weekday)   (Month)   (Day)

Location Site:_____ Location Map No. _____

Address: _____

     City_____ State _____

Location Host:_____
Phone No.: (__)___-_____
Emergency Phone No.: (__)___-_____

Travel: Departure
☐ Airline:_____ Date:__/__/__ Flight:_____ Time:__:__AM/PM
☐ Car: Date:__/__/__ Depart Point:_____ Time:__:__AM/PM
☐ Other:_____ Date:__/__/__
Accomodations:
   Hotel/Housing:_____ Address:_____
     City:_____ State:_____ Phone No.:(__)___-_____
Travel: Return
☐ Airline:_____ Date:__/__/__ Flight:_____ Time:__:__AM/PM
☐ Car: Date:__/__/__ Depart Point:_____ Time:__:__AM/PM
☐ Other:_____ Date:__/__/__

SHOOT ORDER UNITS	SCRIPT PAGES	SETTING	APPROX. TIME	TALENT/ INTERVIEWEE	PROPERTIES, ETC.
			: to :		
			: to :		
			: to :		
			: to :		

Crew call: __:__AM/PM   Set-up:__:__ to __:__AM/PM
   Address:_____

         Approximate Strike:
Talent call:__:__AM/PM   __:__ to __:__AM/PM
   Address:_____

VIDEO DOCUMENTARY PRODUCTION	Page	of

SHOOTING DAY   RAIN DATE
                                                  __/__/__
_____, _____, _____
    (Weekday)   (Month)   (Day)

Location Site:_____ Location Map No._____

Address: _____

       City_____ State _____

Location Host:_____
Phone No.: (__)___-_____
Emergency Phone No.: (__)___-_____

Travel: Departure
☐Airline:_____ Date:__/__/__ Flight:_____ Time:___:___AM/PM
☐Car: Date:__/__/__ Depart Point:_____ Time:___:___AM/PM
☐Other:_____ Date:__/__/__
Accomodations:
  Hotel/Housing:_____ Address:_____
     City:_____ State:_____ Phone No.:(__)___-_____
Travel: Return
☐Airline:_____ Date:__/__/__ Flight:_____ Time:___:___AM/PM
☐Car: Date:__/__/__ Depart Point:_____ Time:___:___AM/PM
☐Other:_____ Date:__/__/__

SHOOT ORDER UNITS	SCRIPT PAGES	SETTING	APPROX. TIME	TALENT/ INTERVIEWEE	PROPERTIES, ETC.
			: to :		
			: to :		
			: to :		
			: to :		

Crew call: ___:___AM/PM   Set-up:___:___ to ___:___AM/PM
  Address:_____
                                     Approximate Strike:
Talent call:___:___AM/PM   ___:___ to ___:___AM/PM
  Address:_____

COMMENTS:

SHOT LIST

VIDEO DOCUMENTARY PRODUCTION

Producer:

Documentary Title:

Camera Operator:

Date: / /
Page of

LOCATION	SHOT						CONTENT NOTES
	NO.	MASTER	CUT-IN	CUT-AWAY	FRAMING	MOTION	

VIDEO DOCUMENTARY PRODUCTION SHOT LIST							Page	of

LOCATION	SHOT						CONTENT NOTES
	NO.	MASTER	CUT-IN	CUT-AWAY	FRAMING	MOTION	

EQUIPMENT CHECKLIST
VIDEO DOCUMENTARY PRODUCTION

Producer: _____

Camera Operator: _____

Videotape Recorder Operator: _____

Documentary Title: _____

Date: /   /

Location(s): _____

Avl Pch Rnt

CAMERA
☐ ☐ ☐ Video Camera
☐ ☐ ☐ Lenses
☐ ☐ ☐ Filters
☐ ☐ ☐ AC/DC Monitor
☐ ☐ ☐ Lg Screen Monitor
☐ ☐ ☐ _____

RECORDER
☐ ☐ ☐ Videotape Recorder
☐ ☐ ☐ _____
☐ ☐ ☐ _____

TRIPOD
☐ ☐ ☐ Tripod w/Head
☐ ☐ ☐ Camera Head Adapter
☐ ☐ ☐ Dolly
☐ ☐ ☐ _____

TEST EQUIPMENT
☐ ☐ ☐ Waveform Monitor
☐ ☐ ☐ Vectorscope
☐ ☐ ☐ Grey Scale
☐ ☐ ☐ Registration Chart
☐ ☐ ☐ White Card
☐ ☐ ☐ Headphones
☐ ☐ ☐ _____

AUDIO
☐ ☐ ☐ Shot gun Microphone
☐ ☐ ☐ Lavaliere Microphone
☐ ☐ ☐ Hand-held Microphone
☐ ☐ ☐ Fishpole
☐ ☐ ☐ Wind screens

Avl Pch Rnt

AUDIO (continued)
☐ ☐ ☐ Mixer
☐ ☐ ☐ Adapter plugs
☐ ☐ ☐ Earphone
☐ ☐ ☐ Headphones
☐ ☐ ☐ _____

POWER SUPPLIES
☐ ☐ ☐ Batteries for Camera
☐ ☐ ☐ Batteries for Recorder
☐ ☐ ☐ Batteries for Monitor
☐ ☐ ☐ AC Power Converter
☐ ☐ ☐ Microphone Batteries
☐ ☐ ☐ _____

LIGHTING
☐ ☐ ☐ Light Kit
☐ ☐ ☐ Soft Light Kit
☐ ☐ ☐ Barn Doors
☐ ☐ ☐ Spun Glass Filters
☐ ☐ ☐ Blue Gels
☐ ☐ ☐ Orange Gels
☐ ☐ ☐ Screens
☐ ☐ ☐ Scrims
☐ ☐ ☐ ND Filters
☐ ☐ ☐ Aluminum Foil
☐ ☐ ☐ Wooden Clothes Pins
☐ ☐ ☐ Light Meter
☐ ☐ ☐ Reflector
☐ ☐ ☐ Spare Bulbs
☐ ☐ ☐ Flags
☐ ☐ ☐ _____
☐ ☐ ☐ _____

Avl	Pch	Rnt	
			CABLES
☐	☐	☐	Multi-pin Cable Camera to Recorder
☐	☐	☐	Video Cable Camera to Recorder
☐	☐	☐	Video Cable Camera to Waveform Monitor/ Scope
☐	☐	☐	Video Cable Scope to Monitor
☐	☐	☐	Audio Mixer Cable to Recorder
☐	☐	☐	Audio Extension Cables
☐	☐	☐	_____

Avl	Pch	Rnt	
			MISCELLANEOUS
☐	☐	☐	Video tape
☐	☐	☐	Teleprompter
☐	☐	☐	Teleprompter Script
☐	☐	☐	Cue Card Paper
☐	☐	☐	Duct Tape
☐	☐	☐	Masking Tape
☐	☐	☐	Spare Fuses
☐	☐	☐	Tool Kit
☐	☐	☐	Stopwatch
☐	☐	☐	Slate
☐	☐	☐	Chalk
☐	☐	☐	Eraser
☐	☐	☐	Bullhorn
☐	☐	☐	Walkie-Talkie
☐	☐	☐	Dulling Spray
☐	☐	☐	Talent Release Forms
☐	☐	☐	Step Ladder
☐	☐	☐	Lens Cleaner and Tissue

Avl	Pch	Rnt	
☐	☐	☐	Sewing Kit
☐	☐	☐	Paper, Pens, Felt Markers
☐	☐	☐	Rope
☐	☐	☐	Barrier Cones
☐	☐	☐	Poster Board
☐	☐	☐	Flashlight
☐	☐	☐	Scissors
☐	☐	☐	100' Power Cords
☐	☐	☐	Staple Gun and Staples
☐	☐	☐	Power Outlet Boxes
☐	☐	☐	_____
☐	☐	☐	_____
☐	☐	☐	_____
☐	☐	☐	_____
☐	☐	☐	_____
☐	☐	☐	_____
☐	☐	☐	_____
☐	☐	☐	_____
☐	☐	☐	_____
☐	☐	☐	_____
☐	☐	☐	_____
☐	☐	☐	_____
☐	☐	☐	_____
☐	☐	☐	_____

REMOTE LOG/CONTINUITY
VIDEO DOCUMENTARY PRODUCTION

Producer:	Documentary Title:
Camera Operator:	Location:
	Date: / /
Videotape No.:	Page of

VTR COUNTER/ TIMER/CODE	LOCATION	TALENT	TAKE NO.	GOOD/ NO GOOD	VIDEO/AUDIO

VIDEO DOCUMENTARY PRODUCTION REMOTE LOG/CONTINUITY			Page	of	
VTR COUNTER/ TIMER/CODE	LOCATION	TALENT	TAKE NO.	GOOD/ NO GOOD	VIDEO/AUDIO

VIDEO CONTINUITY NOTES

VIDEO DOCUMENTARY PRODUCTION

DOCUMENTARY TITLE:				SLATE NO.
PRODUCER:	CONTINUITY SEC'Y:			DATE / /

SET-UP/LOCATION				
	INTERIOR	DAY	SYNC Cam 1/2 SILENT	SEQUENCE NO.
	EXTERIOR	NIGHT	WILDTRACK WT with Cam	SHOT NO.
	SCRIPT PAGE NO.		SHOT LIST PAGE NO.	

COSTUME/MAKE-UP/PROPERTIES NOTES

TAPE NO.										
CIRCLE TAKES	1	2	3	4	5	6	7	8	9	10
END BOARD										
TIMER										
COUNTER										
REASON FOR USE/ NOT GOOD										

ACTION   DIALOGUE

TALENT RELEASE FORM

VIDEO DOCUMENTARY PRODUCTION

Talent Name: _____
(Please Print)

Documentary Title:_____

For value received and without further consideration, I hereby consent to the use of all photographs, videotapes or film, taken of me and/or recordings made of my voice and/or written extraction, in whole or in part, of such recordings or musical performance

at _____ on _____ 19___
(Recording Location) *(Month)* *(Day)* *(Year)*

by_____ for_____
(Producer) *(Producing Organization)*

and/or others with its consent, for the purposes of illustration, advertising, or publication in any manner.

Talent Name_____
(Signature)

Address_____ City_____

State _____ Zip Code _____

Date:____ /___ /___

If the subject is a minor under the laws of the state where modeling, acting, or performing is done:

Guardian _____ Guardian _____
(Signature) *(Please Print)*

Address _____ City _____

State _____ Zip Code _____

Date:____ /____ /___

EDITING WORK SHEET

VIDEO DOCUMENTARY PRODUCTION

Producer:

Documentary Title:
Date: /   /
Audio: Channel 1
Audio: Channel 2
Page   of

T A P E No.	VTR CNTR CLOCK SMPTE		NOTES	SEGMENT CLOCK TIME
	IN	OUT		
				:
				:
				:
				:
				:
				:
				:
				:
				:
				:
				:
				:
				:
				:
				:
				:
				:
				:
				:
				:
				:
				:
				:
				:
				:
				:
				:
				:
				:

TAPE No.	VTR CNTR CLOCK SMPTE		NOTES	SEGMENT CLOCK TIME
	IN	OUT		
				:
				:
				:
				:
				:
				:
				:
				:
				:
				:
				:
				:
				:
				:
				:
				:
				:
				:
				:
				:
				:
				:
				:
				:
				:
				:
				:
				:
				:
				:
				:
				:

VIDEO DOCUMENTARY PRODUCTION EDITING WORK SHEET   Page   of

EDITING CUE SHEET

VIDEO DOCUMENTARY PRODUCTION

Producer:

Documentary Title:
Date: /   /
Audio: Channel 1
Audio: Channel 2
Page   of

T A P E No.	VTR CNTR CLOCK SMPTE		NOTES	SEGMENT CLOCK TIME
	IN	OUT		
			IN CUE	:
			OUT CUE	
			IN CUE	:
			OUT CUE	
			IN CUE	:
			OUT CUE	
			IN CUE	:
			OUT CUE	
			IN CUE	:
			OUT CUE	
			IN CUE	:
			OUT CUE	
			IN CUE	:
			OUT CUE	
			IN CUE	:
			OUT CUE	
			IN CUE	:
			OUT CUE	
			IN CUE	:
			OUT CUE	
			IN CUE	:
			OUT CUE	
			IN CUE	:
			OUT CUE	
			IN CUE	:
			OUT CUE	
			IN CUE	:
			OUT CUE	
			IN CUE	:
			OUT CUE	

VIDEO DOCUMENTARY EDITING CUE SHEET				Page of	

T A P E No.	VTR CNTR CLOCK SMPTE		NOTES	SEGMENT CLOCK TIME
	IN	OUT		
			IN CUE	:
			OUT CUE	
			IN CUE	:
			OUT CUE	
			IN CUE	:
			OUT CUE	
			IN CUE	:
			OUT CUE	
			IN CUE	:
			OUT CUE	
			IN CUE	:
			OUT CUE	
			IN CUE	:
			OUT CUE	
			IN CUE	:
			OUT CUE	
			IN CUE	:
			OUT CUE	
			IN CUE	:
			OUT CUE	
			IN CUE	:
			OUT CUE	
			IN CUE	:
			OUT CUE	
			IN CUE	:
			OUT CUE	
			IN CUE	:
			OUT CUE	
			IN CUE	:
			OUT CUE	
			IN CUE	:
			OUT CUE	
			IN CUE	:
			OUT CUE	
			IN CUE	:
			OUT CUE	

EDITED MASTER CLIPSHEET
VIDEO DOCUMENTARY PRODUCTION

Producer:
Camera Operator:
Video Editor:

Documentary Title:
Date: /   /
Audio: Channel 1 ☐   2 ☐   Mixed ☐

Final Documentary Title: (to appear on the video)

_____

Length: (first audio ☐ /video ☐ to final audio ☐ /video ☐)
         _____ : _____

Out cue:

_____

Character Generator Copy: Notes
   Videotape/Film Credit   In ___:___
                                    Out___:___

   _____

   Reporter Lower Third   In ___:___
                                    Out___:___

   _____

   Interviewee/Actuality Lower Third In ___:___
                                      Out___:___

   _____

   _____

   Interviewee/Actuality Lower Third In ___:___
                                      Out___:___

   _____

   _____

   Voice of   In ___:___
                                    Out___:___

   _____

   _____

Notes

Transcription #1   In ___:___
                                    Out___:___

_____
_____
_____
_____

Transcription #2   In ___:___
                                    Out___:___

_____
_____
_____
_____

Trade Credit   In ___:___
                                    Out___:___

_____
_____
_____

Video Credits   In ___:___
                                    Out___:___

_____
                    Sponsoring Organization

_____
                        Executive Producer

_____
                                 Producer

_____
                          Camera Operator

_____
                 Videotape Recorder Operator

_____
                          Videotape Editor

_____
                          Special Thanks to:

Chapter 3

Remote Drama Production

INTRODUCTION

• Role of Video in Drama Production

There is an expanding role being played by the single video camera in the production of drama. The new role can be seen in the concurrent use of video with the film camera in major film productions today. In April 1988 CBS completed videotaping the teleplay, "Innocent Victims," the first made-for-television movie produced using high definition video technology. With the introduction and marketability of high definition television, it is wise for the teacher and student of video to prepare now for what is already upon us—the production of full length drama production in video, in other words, applying single camera film techniques to the single video camera production of drama.

It is not uncommon to see attempts in television education today to bridge the experiences of theater and video. This is occurring especially in undergraduate colleges where there is both a theater department and a television department. This bridge is as much the product of companion media and a relatively inexpensive recording technology as it is the vanguard of the future of the medium.

• Video: Convenient and Advantageous

In many ways the marriage of single camera film techniques to video camera technology is a marriage of convenience. It is convenient because the single camera video drama experience is achievable with a small crew, a small budget, and less time—less time both in the location production itself and in the speed of final editing.

Another advantage of video drama to both the amateur

and the professional is the ability to see the dramatic performance immediately after videotaping it. This is an advantage to academic goals in the short span of class and semester/quarter time periods. It is an advantage to the video student who has to see a problem production technique to improve or correct it while cast and crew are still around. It is an advantage to actors who rarely have a chance to see their own acting performance and to improve or correct it. Video drama productions can be critiqued while class is still in session; lighting design can be changed, audio corrected, camera framing adjusted; the actor can correct delivery and blocking, cheat shots, and check continuity immediately. These advantages become the checkpoints for a better production generally and a quality dramatic product in the long run.

THE PREPRODUCTION PROCESS

• Personnel

Because single camera video production is the marriage of two media, theater/drama and television, the breakdown of personnel falls according to the demands of the two media, which provide the division of personnel for production consideration. For the purposes of this text, the description of the video drama production process will concentrate on video production personnel only.

• Production Personnel

Producer (P). The producer for video drama production is responsible for the day-to-day business of the drama production. The producer is the principal contact between the creative elements such as the drama ensemble and the

FLOWCHART AND CHECKLIST FOR VIDEO DRAMA PRODUCTION

PREPRODUCTION	PRODUCTION	POSTPRODUCTION
PRODUCER (P)		
(1) Makes teleplay script selection	(1) Supervises crew call	(1) Arranges postproduction schedule and facilities
(2) Constructs budget (drama budget form)	(2) Meets location host/personnel/security	(2) Supervises posting preparation
(3) Chooses director	(3) Handles location rearrangement	(3) Observes editing with director
(4) Casts teleplay with director	(4) Handles crew and cast details	(4) Writes copy/designs titling and credits
(5) Supervises cast/crew interpretive reading	(5) Secures talent release signatures (talent release form)	
(6) Directs location scouting (location site survey form)		
(7) Creates production schedule (production schedule form)		
(8) Secures insurance coverage		
(9) Obtains copyright clearances		
(10) Notifies municipal police		
DIRECTOR (D)		
(1) Meets with producer	(1) Holds production meeting with crew	(1) Supervises postproduction preparation
(2) Casts teleplay with producer	(2) Supervises location rearrangement	(2) Reorders/edits master script: makes editing decisions
(3) Does script breakdown (script breakdown form)	(3) Supervises equipment set-ups	(3) Edits a rough edition
(4) Does/supervises location site scouting (location site survey form)	(4) Blocks actors without lines	(4) Reviews the rough edit
(5) Creates master script: designs blocking plots (blocking plots/storyboard form)	(5) Rehearses actors with lines	(5) Makes final edit
(6) Creates master script: designs storyboard (blocking plots/storyboard form)	(6) Blocks camera	(6) Labels edited master
(7) Develops the shot list (shot list form)	(7) Rehearses both camera and actors	
(8) Chooses/meets with camera operator	(8) Makes changes/rehearses	If the director does not edit:
(9) Chooses/meets with lighting director	(9) Calls for a take	**TECHNICAL DIRECTOR/EDITOR (TD/E)**
(10) Chooses CS	(10) Announces intentions: take/wrap/strike	(1) Edits from editing cue sheet under the supervision of the producer
		(2) Adds music/effects and mixes channels
		(3) Labels edited master
CAMERA OPERATOR (CO)		
(1) Meets with producer and director	(1) Arranges camera equipment/accessories pick-up/delivery	(1) Returns remote camera and lighting equipment and accessories
(2) Works master script and shot list	(2) Sets up location camera and performs check	(2) Reports damaged, lost, malfunctioning equipment or accessories
(3) Prepares camera equipment/accessories list (equipment checklist form)	(3) Blocks camera position with actors	
(4) Chooses/meets with VTRO and AD	(4) Rehearses camera with actors	
	(3) Videotapes take	
	(4) Strikes camera equipment/accessories	

LIGHTING DIRECTOR (LD)

- [ ] (1) Meets with director
- [ ] (2) Works master script and shot list, and location site survey
- [ ] (3) Designs lighting plots (lighting plot form)
- [ ] (4) Prepares lighting equipment/accessories list (equipment checklist form)

- [ ] (1) Arranges lighting equipment/accessories pick-up/delivery
- [ ] (2) Sets up location lighting and performs lighting check
- [ ] (3) Strikes lighting equipment/accessories

- [ ] (1) Returns remote videotape and sound recording equipment and accessories
- [ ] (2) Reports damaged, lost, malfunctioning equipment or accessories

VIDEOTAPE RECORDER OPERATOR (VTRO)

- [ ] (1) Meets with CO
- [ ] (2) Prepares vtr equipment/accessories lists (equipment checklist form)
- [ ] (3) Orders videotape stock
- [ ] (4) Labels/organizes tape stock

- [ ] (1) Arranges videotape recording equipment/accessories pick-up/delivery
- [ ] (2) Sets up location videotape recording and performs recording check
- [ ] (3) Monitors vectorscope
- [ ] (4) Responds to director's call for roll tape
- [ ] (5) Strikes videotape recording equipment/accessories

- [ ] (1) Removes record buttons/labels source videotapes/stripes source videotapes
- [ ] (2) Reorders source tapes to master storyboard
- [ ] (3) Returns remote camera and lighting equipment and accessories
- [ ] (4) Reports damaged, lost, malfunctioning equipment or accessories

AUDIO DIRECTOR (AD)

- [ ] (1) Meets with CO
- [ ] (2) Works master script/shot list
- [ ] (3) Designs audio plots (audio plot form)
- [ ] (4) Prepares audio equipment/accessories list (equipment checklist)
- [ ] (5) Chooses music/effects

- [ ] (1) Arranges audio recording equipment/accessories pick-up/delivery
- [ ] (2) Sets up location audio recording and performs recording check
- [ ] (3) Monitors audio input: dialogue and noise, mike in frame
- [ ] (4) Responds to director's directions
- [ ] (5) Strikes audio recording equipment/accessories

- [ ] (1) Returns remote videotape and sound recording equipment and accessories
- [ ] (2) Reports damaged, lost, malfunctioning equipment or accessories
- [ ] (3) Oversees audio quality of location dialogue
- [ ] (4) Adds music/effects/ambience; mixes and sweetens

CONTINUITY SECRETARY (CS)

- [ ] (1) Prepares continuity sheets (continuity notes form)
- [ ] (2) Coordinates with VTRO

- [ ] (1) Observes and records continuity details
- [ ] (2) Releases actors after cut
- [ ] (3) Establishes details before next shot

- [ ] (1) Reorders continuity sheets to master storyboard

ACTORS/TALENT (T)

- [ ] (1) Reads and interprets script with cast and crew
- [ ] (2) Learns lines, develops characterization
- [ ] (3) Checks costumes, tests make-up

- [ ] (1) Prepares for costuming, make-up, stand-in
- [ ] (2) Follows director: blocking, rehearsal, action, cut, freeze, take
- [ ] (3) Checks with CS
- [ ] (4) Is available/out-of-the-way

SLATE PERSON (SP)

- [ ] (1) Handles and updates slate
- [ ] (2) Coordinates with CS and VTRO
- [ ] (3) Follows director/slates video leader

MICROPHONE BOOM GRIP/OPERATOR (MBG/O)

- [ ] (1) Observes blocking/rehearsals/lighting instruments
- [ ] (2) Observes CU/LS framing/shadows
- [ ] (3) Mikes dialogue during take

production crew, and oversees all preproduction details. Some primary responsibilities in preproduction are the choice of script, budgeting, the production schedule, location scouting and site survey, contacts with site personnel, and supervising crew assignments.

The producer deals directly with location site hosts and personnel. The producer has to deal with municipal police when the location is a public exterior location. Whether a location site is exterior or interior, the producer must secure insurance coverage (theft, bodily harm, property) for crew, cast, equipment, and location property before production begins.

Director (D). The director is chosen by the producer. The director's primary preproduction responsibility is twofold: the choice and supervision of the remote video production crew and the master script. The director is the creative force behind the script, both in its interpretation and in production design. Script interpretation at the preproduction stage involves casting, script breakdown, and the creation of the master script (storyboarding, actor blocking plots, and camera shots). Production design at the preproduction stage involves choosing a camera operator and a lighting director (both creative crew appointments) and supervising location scouting and site survey.

Camera operator (CO). The camera operator is usually an appointment by the director. The preproduction tasks of the camera operator are the listing and reservation of camera equipment and accessories necessary for the remote production. This may entail available equipment, and/or renting or purchasing equipment. The camera operator chooses a videotape recorder operator and an audio director.

Lighting director (LD). The lighting director begins preproduction work by studying the script and determining the mood of all proposed camera shots. This can begin once the director has location site survey drawings completed. After a check of the location sites, lighting needs and lighting plots can be designed.

Videotape recorder operator (VTRO). The videotape recorder operator is responsible to the camera operator and oversees the acquisition and functioning of the videotape recorder. The videotape operator is responsible for videotape stock for the production and the proper labeling and coding of videotapes to coordinate slate and continuity records during production.

Audio director (AD). The audio director begins preproduction responsibilities by planning audio production and recording from the script. Preproduction audio planning entails checking location sites and knowing the audio requirements of the script. This may require choosing music and sound effects for the production. Audio production planning requires an equipment and accessories checklist.

Continuity secretary (CS). The continuity secretary is responsible for the proper and detailed note taking necessary to record all production detail elements of the location shoot. Preproduction responsibility entails organizing a structured approach to record notes of the production. The continuity secretary will need a set of note recording forms, lists of crew and actors, and the videotape stock code.

- **Drama Personnel**

Drama director. A director of drama takes the responsibility for all the preproduction drama side of the production. A drama director may participate in actor preparation, costume and make-up decisions, hand properties acquisition, and so on.

Actors. Once actors are cast for the teleplay, they can begin to learn their lines and develop their respective characters. Blocking should not be a concern to the actor in single camera drama production. Blocking is not created until the shoot itself.

Wardrobe master/mistress. The appointment of a wardrobe person removes the concern of costuming from the video production crew.

Make-up artist. Having a make-up artist may be important to a producer and facilitates proper appearances on video for the cast.

Property master/mistress. A property master or mistress assumes the responsibility for both hand and action properties required of the teleplay.

- **Preproduction Stages**

There is little disagreement among professionals that the secret to a good video production is preproduction. This holds doubly true for single camera video drama production. A successful production and a quality product are a direct function of the thoroughness of preproduction. The extent of the project both in length of the proposed product (usually 30:00 or longer) and the number of people involved (counting both technical production crew and acting ensemble) create perhaps the largest single camera remote video experience.

Choosing a script (P 1). The first step in video drama production is the choice of a script. A producer weighs the demands of any script, e.g., casting needs against available actors, location demands against available environments, in choosing a script. Because all scripts are not written in teleplay format, a script may have to be adapted to the medium of single camera video. The producer could involve the director in the process of script selection. After teleplay selection it is the director who will become the creative force in the interpretation and design of the production. In some productions an executive producer may have a script and choose the producer as a catalyst to get it produced.

Constructing a budget (P 2). After a creative decision in selecting a script for production, the producer has to turn to the mundane task of constructing a budget. Whatever or whoever is the funding agency for the production, the budget is critical to building a production staff and crew and determining the extent of video production values. A model budget form helps a producer consider the many details that need funding. (See the drama budget form.)

Choosing a director (P 3). The choice of a director for the production can follow the approval of a budget. A producer chooses a director for creative abilities and production management skills. The choice of a script may precipitate the type of director to be chosen. The period, mood, and style of the script could determine the qualities in a director suited for the production.

Meeting with the producer (D 1). The director should meet with the producer as the first step in preproduction. This may be the first time the director sees the script and budget. These documents become important elements in the remaining stages of preproduction.

Casting the teleplay (P 4). Following the choice of a director, casting the teleplay can be accomplished. The producer should involve the director in the choice of a cast.

Assisting in casting the teleplay (D 2). Because the first quality of a director is creativity, producers expect the assistance of the director during the choice of a cast for the teleplay.

Supervising a cast and crew interpretative reading of the script (P 5). After the teleplay is cast, it is a good and useful experience to have a joint reading of the script by the cast with the technical crew present. This might be followed by a discussion of interpretations of the teleplay. A discussion can answer many questions about the teleplay and can aid both the cast and crew in later creative choices to be made in characterization by actors and in production design by crew.

Reading the script and interpretation by cast and crew (T 1). The new cast should read the script, with each taking his or her own dialogue. Someone else present could read stage directions and settings. This reading will serve to give the cast, producer, and director a good sense of the teleplay and the direction to go with the remaining preproduction. After script reading a discussion and interpretation among all cast and crew serves to put many creative aspects of the teleplay into perspective and gives the cast some direction to use in further characterization of their respective roles.

Learning lines and developing characterization (T 2). The first preproduction requirement for actors is to learn their lines and develop characterization. Much information should have been gained from the interpretative reading conducted by the producer. Attention should shift to getting lines down well. A needless delay on location for crew members and cast is a missed or forgotten line.

Part of this preproduction requirement for the actors is characterization. Characterization means the concentrated effort to "become" the character of the teleplay. The better the characterization, the better the actor can tolerate the repeated takes for a scene required in single camera drama production and still be able to project a unified character.

One thing not required from single camera drama

preparation is blocking. Unlike acting preparation for the stage, video and film media do not expect blocking to be done until location production.

Fitting costumes and testing make-up (T 3). The other preproduction requirement for actors is costume fitting and make-up testing. This should be done before location shooting. There are demands of the video medium on color and design that should be known and tested before the shoot. Make-up should also be applied and critiqued before the location shoot. It would not be uncommon to actually light and videotape both costume and make-up tests to make certain of choices.

Doing a script breakdown (D 3). The first technical preproduction step for the director is a script breakdown. The breakdown is a systematic analysis of all nonstory elements of the script: script units, script pages per unit, interior or exterior setting, day or night time, approximate length of each unit (often calculated in terms of pages of script or portion of a page), and cast members needed for each unit. (See the script breakdown form.)

The script breakdown will determine the location scouting needs, the location shooting order, and ultimately the production schedule.

Directing location scouting and site survey (P 6). The task of location scouting is the next stage in preproduction. Location scouting requires searching out and visiting possible sites for the remote production videotaping.

The first production need from a location is that the requirements of the script must be met. The script breakdown should clearly indicate what the location demands are for producing the teleplay. Having described the script requirements, location scouting demands a thorough evaluation of a proposed site.

The producer and director may prefer to do their own location scouting. Other crew members could be used as location scouts. If other location scouts are used, they must then report back to the producer and director with summary notes on proposed sites, maps to the proposed location, diagrams of the location with compass points, and instant developing film pictures of all angles of the proposed site. (See the location site survey form.)

Supervising location scouting and site survey (D 4). The script breakdown should indicate the script requirements for production locations. Together with a producer, the director should supervise the scouting and surveying of potential location sites.

Some directors and producers prefer to do location scouting themselves. If they choose not to do the actual scouting, location scouts can do the actual traveling and survey. It would not be uncommon for camera operators, lighting directors, and audio directors to do or be a part of the location scouting crew also. In even a short teleplay, many locations may be required and many sites may be scouted before the right location is found. Location scouting is not always a fast and easy task. (See the location site survey form.)

Creating the master script: designing blocking plots (D 5). Once location sites are approved and location diagrams and photographs are in hand, the director's next responsibility to the preproduction process is blocking plots. Blocking plots for actors and camera placement are the first element to the director's master script. A master script contains (1) blocking plots of actor(s) on set diagrams, (2) storyboard frames of desired shots, (3) framing directions (and changes in framing) for each shot, and (4) the consecutive numbering of storyboard frames on pages inserted into the director's script opposite the respective script dialogue.

A blocking plot is a bird's eye view of the location environment with physical properties indicated (e.g., furniture), actors placed in opening positions for the shot, and actors' blocking movements indicated. Actors are usually symbolized by circles with a code letter and movements are symbolized by directed line segments.

Blocking plots assist the camera operator, lighting director, and the audio director in their preproduction tasks; thus, this stage of preproduction is important to the rest of the production crew. (See the blocking plot/storyboard form.)

Creating the master script: storyboarding (D 6). When blocking plots are completed, the director begins the work of storyboarding the script. Storyboard frames are the second step to creating the director's master script. Directors should find it advantageous to make blocking plots and storyboard frames a part of a master script. Pages containing these plots and frames can then be inserted into the director's script opposite the respective script units they illustrate. With the bird's eye view of the actor's blocking plot completed and a camera set-up position indicated, the director can then draw individual aspect ratio frames to the left of each blocking diagram. These aspect ratio frames are sketched to represent what the camera sees from each indicated camera position. The frames are then numbered consecutively. To coordinate storyboard frames with the script dialogue and scene directions, a slash and the number of the frame can be indicated in the dialogue where the cut will be made to that frame.

The director should then make note beneath the storyboard frame of the desired framing (e.g., CU, LS) of the actor(s) ("M" for Mary), any change of framing during the shot (e.g., MS > CU), and what camera motion may be called for (e.g., a zoom).

A vertical stroke alongside the script dialogue relates each aspect frame easily to the videotaped length of each particular shot. The blocking plot and storyboard should also contain the in-cue and out-cue for each shot. Having all this shot information readily available before the production shoot saves immeasurable time on location when all this detailed information will be needed constantly. (See the blocking plot/storyboard form.)

Developing the shot list (D 7). Once the master script is completed, the shot list can be developed. The shot list breaks the master script down into the order of shots to be videotaped by camera placement positions that will be needed and by the order of shooting each script unit. (See the shot list form.)

Creating the production schedule (P 7). When the producer and director make location site decisions, the producer can create the production schedule. The script breakdown and shot list from the director is necessary to create a production schedule.

The shooting order of the script and production schedule is usually determined by a variety of requirements. Location availability is often the first requirement. Not all chosen sites are advantageous simply because they are available (e.g., a shopping mall parking lot on weekends). Some requirements that determine scheduling are how open locations are to the general public, the day of the week a location is needed, the time of day the location is needed, cast of characters for a scene and actor availability, and the script units requiring that location.

Production schedules are calendars with production dates and alternate rain dates, time of day, specific

FIGURE 3–1
The director's master script. The director's master script is a loose-leaf notebook with the script pages on the left and the blocking plot/storyboard pages facing them on the right. Notation from the blocking plot/storyboard form are made on the script pages.

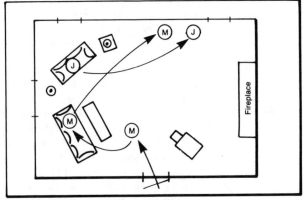

Bird's eye floor plan
Props/blocking/camera

FIGURE 3–2
Director's blocking plot. The director's blocking plot includes set properties and camera placement. Actors are indicated by an initial code within a circle; arrows show movement.

locations and contact personnel, required cast, script units to be videotaped, crew and cast call times, equipment set-up deadlines, and estimated strike time. Production schedules also list any large action props needed for each production unit (e.g., a horse and buggy). (See the production schedule form.)

Obtaining necessary insurance coverage (P 8). Once location sites are determined and approved and the production schedule is completed, the producer should obtain necessary insurance coverage for the crew and the cast, damage and loss of production equipment, and location property damage.

Academic programs generally have adequate coverage for students and faculty while on authorized school projects, on or off school property. It is important to note that faculty supervision is usually required for active coverage. Similar coverage probably can account for damage and loss of production equipment. A check should be made for extended coverage to location property. Any other production project producer should inquire from any reputable agent or agency for adequate rates and coverage for the production.

Choosing and meeting with the camera operator (D 8). Once location sites are determined, a director is at the stage of preproduction to choose and involve a camera operator. A camera operator is chosen for aesthetic capabilities in composing the view through the lens. Technical skills include the knowledge and experience with the remote video camera and its set-up and operation. The first requirement of the camera operator is to meet with the director and discuss the video camera needs of the production. The director should share the master script and shot list with the camera operator.

Meeting with the producer and director (CO 1). The first requirement of the new camera operator is to meet with the producer and the director to get a perspective on both the teleplay and its interpretation and the proposed production design. The camera operator plays an important role in achieving the creative goals of the production. The camera operator should receive a copy of the master script, the shot list, and the production schedule.

Working the master script and the shot list (CO 2). The next preproduction task for the camera operator is to become familiar with the master script (blocking plots with storyboard) and the shot list. The camera operator can begin checking the camera placement for each shot on the shot list.

Preparing camera equipment and accessories list (CO 3). After meeting with the director (and producer), the requirement of the camera operator is to prepare an equipment and accessories list of camera requirements. The list should include equipment/accessories available, the elements that need to be rented, and those that will have to be purchased. (See the equipment checklist.)

Choosing a lighting director (D 9). The choice of a lighting director by the director completes the crew members who are aesthetically involved with the video qualities in the design of drama production. A director should choose a lighting director who can create in lighting design the same mood, period, and style for the production for which the director was chosen. After meeting with the director, the lighting director should have a master script and begin a lighting assessment for the drama production.

Meeting with the director (LD 1). As with all creative crew members, the lighting director should meet with the director after assignment to the crew. The lighting director should have copies of the master script, the shot list, location site survey forms (with lighting and power analyses of the site), and the production schedule.

Working the master script and shot list (LD 2). The lighting director begins preproduction work by studying the master script and the shot list as a prelude to designing the placement of lights to create the mood and setting necessary for the production of the teleplay.

Designing lighting plots (LD 3). With the master script and the shot list, the lighting director's next stage in preproduction is to design the lighting plot for each video shot noted on the production schedule. The lighting director will need camera placement information (on the blocking plots) from the master script to know what lighting instruments are to be used in a shot, where to set up lighting instruments and stands, and the direction to aim lights. The master script will note any change of lighting needs during a shot (e.g., property light is turned on). The lighting director will have to make aesthetic decisions on the basis of the information contained in the master script. Much of that information from the master script will be transferred to the lighting plots by the lighting director. (See the lighting plot form.)

Preparing lighting equipment and accessories list (LD 4). After designing the lighting plots, the lighting director has to access the lighting equipment and lighting accessory needs of the production shoot on the basis of the lighting plots. (See the equipment checklist.)

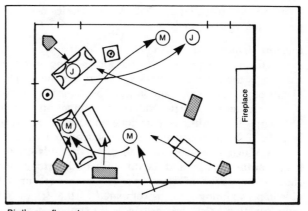

Bird's eye floor plan
Props / blocking / camera placement / lighting instruments

FIGURE 3–3
Lighting director's lighting plot. The lighting director designs lighting for a set by placing lighting instruments on the director's blocking plot. Lighting instruments are noted here by shading.

FIGURE 3-4
Lighting instruments for remote drama production. There are three basic and common lighting instruments for video drama production: (A) the hard light for key lighting, (B) the broad light for soft lighting, and (C) the portable soft light for soft lighting large set areas.

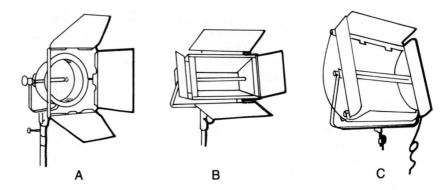

A   B   C

Choosing a videotape recorder operator and audio director and meeting with them (CO 4). Because the relationships between the camera operator and the videotape recorder operator and an audio director are close working relationships, the camera operator should choose the videotape recorder operator and audio director. The first requirement of the appointment is to meet together with them and share production information such as master script, shot list, and the production schedule.

Meeting with the camera operator (VTRO 1). The videotape recorder operator should meet with the camera operator and the audio director as a first stage of preproduction. Because the three crew members will have to establish a close working relationship, this meeting serves to open communication and exchange production notes and ideas. The videotape recorder operator should have a copy of the master script, shot list, and production schedule.

Meeting with the camera operator (AD 1). The audio director should meet with the camera operator and the videotape recorder operator as the first stage of audio recording preproduction. The audio director should have a copy of the master script, shot list, and the production schedule.

Preparing videotape recording equipment and accessories list (VTRO 2). After meeting with the camera operator and obtaining preproduction information, the videotape recorder operator's next responsibility is to determine the videotape recording equipment and accessories needs for production videotaping.

Ordering videotape stock (VTRO 3). One of the production necessities that requires lead time for ordering and purchasing is the videotape stock necessary for the project. The most probable videotape stock is the ¾ inch videotape size in the small cassette unit of 20 minutes in length. This varies if recording is to be done on a 1 inch videotape recorder or broadcast quality ½ inch videotape recorder.

How much videotape stock to order depends on the length of the teleplay and the difficulty of the production shoot. One gauge of videotape use is the 3:1 or 4:1 videotape shooting ratio as compared to the 8:1 or 9:1 ratio for film. This means single camera videotaping customarily requires 3 or 4 takes for each shot needed as compared to 8 or 9 for each shot in single camera film production.

Labeling and organizing videotape stock (VTRO 4). A preproduction requirement for the videotape recorder operator

is to select a numerical coding system for each videotape cassette that will facilitate handling and organizing videotape stock on location and in postproduction. Labeling involves identical coding on both the cassette itself and the videotape carrying case. Consecutive numbering will organize the videotapes for accurate and swift reordering after production. The coding system should also be shared with the continuity secretary for the coordination of videotapes and location takes on the continuity record for the shoot itself.

Working the master script and the shot list (AD 2). With the master script and the shot list the audio director can begin designing the audio perspective for the production. The audio perspective includes the choice of pick-up patterns necessary and types of microphones and microphone holders.

Designing audio plots (AD 3). The audio director is now ready to create audio plots for recording the sound of the drama production on location. Audio plots are calculated judgments on the choice of microphones—either a directional boom microphone on a fishpole or a wireless microphone—depending on the information available from the director's master script. Length of audio cables needed can also be judged from the location survey diagrams.

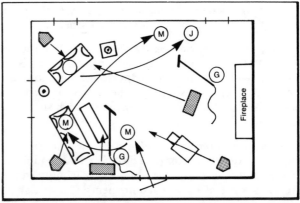

Bird's eye floor plan
Props / blocking / camera placement / lighting instruments

FIGURE 3-5
Audio director's audio plot. The audio director plans sound pick-up from a consideration of the director's blocking plot and the lighting director's lighting plot. Note the "G" for mike grip and the fishpole mike holder.

Preparing audio recording equipment and accessories list (AD 4). After meeting with the camera operator and sharing preproduction information, the audio director can begin accessing audio recording equipment and accessories needs for the production. (See the equipment checklist.) Location sound playback requirements will also have to be assessed (e.g., radio program, background music).

Choosing music and sound effects (AD 5). The audio design of the drama production includes creating and choosing music and effects for the final edited master tape. The sound requirements (e.g., music, effects) for the final edited drama production should be determined by the audio director. The list of requirements should be turned over to the producer for copyright clearance.

Obtaining clearances for copyrighted sound materials (P 9). It is the audio director who designs the music and sound effects for the final production and presents the choices to the producer and director. It is the producer's responsibility to obtain legal clearance for any copyrighted materials proposed for inclusion in the final drama production. Adequate lead time is required to obtain all necessary legal clearance for copyrighted recordings. Most legal clearance demands written requests by mail.

Choosing a continuity secretary (D 10). As a final crew decision, a director should choose a secretary who will be responsible for observing and recording continuity notes during production. The main skill requirement of a continuity secretary is attention to details.

Preparing continuity notes' sheets (CS 1). The continuity secretary is responsible to the director on location and during preproduction preparation. The continuity secretary should create shorthand codes for record taking and be familiar with crew and cast lists, production schedule, and the continuity notes recording form. (See the video continuity notes form.) Adequate copies of continuity record forms and a binder to hold them while recording them should also be prepared.

Coordinating with the videotape recorder operator (CS 2). The continuity secretary needs to coordinate continuity note records with the numerical coding and order of new videotape stock. The videotape recorder operator has the responsibility for the videotape stock. Together a simple mutually agreeable coding system should be used.

Notification of municipal police (P 10). The final preproduction responsibility of the producer is to notify the municipal police in the area of the location shoot that the production will be in that vicinity on the scheduled production dates. Notification of police serves two purposes. Some exterior location shoots will involve some form of traffic control. Traffic control entails halting traffic for a period of time during a take or requesting no parking restrictions alongside a shooting location. Also, the size of a remote production crew and the number of vehicles needed to transport crew, cast, and equipment to a location site can create a disturbance at any location. It assists the police to be informed of the production's presence in their area of jurisdiction for complaints and security.

THE PRODUCTION PROCESS

• Personnel

The remote camera video drama production is a strongly group task-oriented project. The knowledge and skills of many people must be directed to such a narrow range of goals that it distinguishes itself as a unique production experience. On location the production team must function similarly to an orchestra under the direction of one person, the conductor.

Producer (P). The producer plays a continuing support role on location. The producer is responsible for all location details from location access and utilization to the coordination of meal breaks and rapport with the drama ensemble.

Director (D). It is the director who conducts the skills of the cast and crew to videotape the drama units scheduled for any single shooting day. In addition to the actors and their support crew (make-up, wardrobe, and property master) the director looks to the production crew for the response necessary to make the shoot come together. The director's production responsibility includes the supervision of the camera operator, the lighting director, the audio director, the videotape recorder operator, the continuity secretary, the mike or boom grip, and the slate person. The director's drama ensemble responsibility includes the performance direction of the actors and action properties.

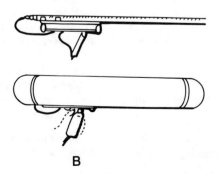

FIGURE 3–6
Audio equipment and technique for remote drama videotaping. (A) The handheld fishpole extended by the mike grip into the location set is the most common sound pick-up technique for drama. (B) The handheld shotgun mike is also a common sound pick-up technique.

A   B

Camera operator (CO). The camera operator is responsible for the acquisition of the video camera and camera support equipment and its availability during the location shoot. The camera operator performs the camera set-up and equipment check and prepares to receive and take direction from the director.

Lighting director (LD). The lighting director is responsible for creating the lighting design required for the production. The lighting director secures all lighting equipment and accessories and sets up and checks the necessary lighting equipment for each take. The lighting director is directly responsible to the director of the production.

Videotape recorder operator (VTRO). The responsibilities of the videotape recorder operator on location include the acquisition of videotape recording and monitoring equipment and their set-up and systems check. The utilization and security of videotape recording stock is also among the videotape recorder operator's obligations on location. The videotape recorder operator is first responsible to the camera operator and ultimately to the director on location.

Audio director (AD). The responsibilities of the audio director include the acquisition of all necessary audio recording equipment and accessories and their respective set-up and testing. The audio director is directly responsible to the camera operators, and as the lighting director, ultimately to the director while on location.

Continuity secretary (CS). The continuity secretary has the responsibility to be prepared to record all production details for the order and organization of each videotaped take on location. These details will facilitate the edit flow from one take to another. The continuity secretary should have copies of continuity recording forms and a binder, which holds them and allows making notes on them.

The continuity secretary is responsible to the director, and in turn has authority to make demands of crew and cast in the performance of continuity record taking. This entails calling for a freeze for actors, releasing crew to reset equipment, and reestablishing details before a subsequent take.

Slate person (SP). Someone among the crew is needed to keep the production slate for the videotape leader up-to-date during location production. The additional task of the slate person is to announce the content of the slate as it is videotaped on the leader of the videotape for each take.

Microphone boom grip/operator (MBG/O). Another necessary crew member on location is the microphone boom grip. The only efficient way to get a microphone into a set is to extend it at the end of a pole called a fishpole or a boom. This task demands someone who will not tire easily with outstretched arms and still function intelligently without getting the microphone or shadows in the field of view of the camera. The microphone boom/grip operator is responsible to the audio director during production.

Actors/talent (T). The actors/talent are directly responsible to the director on location during production. Actors should be ready with lines learned, characterizations firm, costumed, and in full make-up at the appointed time listed on the production schedule.

• Production Stages

Supervising crew call (P 1). The beginning of a remote production day is a crew call, which gathers and organizes the whole crew. Usually, the production crew needs an earlier and separate call than the drama ensemble. The technical needs and set-up demands consume more time than most actors and support staff can tolerate with patience. Experience shows that an hour or more is reasonable to separate technical and ensemble crew calls. Experience also teaches that a uniform departure site for the whole crew both allows an attendance count and ensures arrival at an unfamiliar location. Parking arrangements and unloading arrangements are the responsibility of the producer and should be called to the attention of the crew at crew call.

Holding a production meeting (D 1). One of the first requirements for every production day is a production meeting. With all the preproduction work that facilitates a drama production, there are still last minute changes and details that should be covered with the entire crew together. This is the opportunity for the director to make changes in the production schedule and solicit questions about videotaping details.

Meeting location hosts (P 2). A courtesy the producer can extend to a location host is adequate communication and pleasant reminders that their environment has been scheduled for a given day at a given hour. The producer should have followed location site approval (when permission is granted for a shoot) with a detailed letter outlining all the details of the request for using the location for a video shoot and remind the host of the details conveyed previously by word. The day before shooting, a telephone call as a courtesy reminder is also a good practice.

Unloading the amount of equipment needed by a remote video production requires special notice to the location host. In turn, the host may request that special directions (insurance or fire safety regulations) be followed, such as the use of loading docks, a particular entrance door, or the use of a freight elevator.

After equipment is unloaded at the location site, each member of the crew has tasks to perform in preparation for videotaping. It is at this point that the producer and the director have the responsibility to keep informed of the progress of each crew member as the crew members have the mutual responsibility to keep the producer and director informed of their progress in equipment set-up and operation check.

The producer should also know what demands the crew and cast have for security for both production equipment and personal valuables while on location and also for privacy for costume and make-up preparation as well as crew breaks and meals.

Handling location environment rearrangement (P 3). The producer handles the rearrangement of the location environment for the needs of the script units for any particular shoot as the first location requirement. Photographs taken during location site survey (or taking instant developing film pictures of the location before rearrangement) is beneficial. With a photographic record of the way a location appeared upon crew arrival, the location can be restored to the way it was after a strike. Often furniture must be removed to meet the blocking of a scene, or action properties, such as an automobile, may have to be positioned for a particular shot.

The producer should have cleared all major changes to a location environment with the location host during location site survey and repeated the requirement in a confirmation letter. Mention of environment changes might also be made in the courtesy reminder phone call. If unanticipated changes should have to be made, the producer should always check first with the location host or security for proper permission to make the changes.

Supervising location environment rearrangement (D 2). Whereas the producer handles the rearrangement of the location environment, it is the director who supervises the changes. The director should make the decisions on what is moved or removed in light of the master script, script interpretation, and production design.

Handling production crew and drama ensemble details (P 4). The ongoing task of the producer on location is the many details required of both crew and cast. Restroom facilities, meals, breaks, and lounging areas are needs for both crew and cast, and cast and crew need to be informed of them. The drama cast require additional room for changing into costumes, getting into make-up, and space for just waiting to be videotaped. Most of these details should have been worked out with the location host at the time of the site survey.

Arranging camera equipment and accessories pick-up/delivery (CO 1). Because camera equipment may be already available, rented, or purchased, the camera operator is responsible for arranging either pick-up or delivery to the location site. For some location sites there may be required equipment delivery areas and freight elevators that must be used.

Arranging lighting equipment and accessories pick-up/delivery (LD 1). Similar to other crew members responsible for equipment, the lighting director must arrange for the acquisition of available lighting equipment and accessories as well as the equipment that must be rented or purchased. Loading and carting lighting equipment should follow the requirements of the location as set for all equipment.

Arranging videotape recorder equipment and accessories pick-up/ delivery (VTRO 1). The videotape recorder operator is responsible for the pick-up and delivery of either available, rented, or purchased equipment for videotape recording. Loading of videotape recording equipment should follow the same requirements of all other equipment loading and carting.

Arranging audio equipment and accessories pick-up/delivery (AD 1). The responsibility of the audio director is to secure the pick-up and/or delivery of available, rented, or purchased audio recording equipment and accessories for the production shoot.

Standing in for purposes of lighting, sound, and video checks (T 2). Frequently, actors/talent are needed while the production crew makes checks on various aesthetic elements of recording equipment. It is a tedious task for actors but a necessary one. Although crew members use other location personnel to stand in when exact reproduction of height and color are not important, it does come to a point when the individual actor has to take the place of a stand-in.

Location camera set-up (CO 2). The camera operator should follow the blocking plots and begin camera equipment set-up. When set-up is complete, the camera operator can make an operational check by communicating with the videotape recorder operator who can read the vectorscope for light levels for the scene. Unacceptable levels may require adjustment of the f-stop of the lens or change of light intensity levels. When set-up and check are finished, the camera operator should communicate this fact to the director and the producer.

Location lighting set-up (LD 2). After the production meeting with the director and producer, the lighting director should follow the production schedule and lighting plots for the first take and begin location lighting set-up. The lighting director makes a lighting set-up check by viewing the actors or stand-ins both on the set and over the video monitor. The lighting director works closely with the camera operator and the videotape recorder operator. The lighting director will have to work with the videotape recorder operator who should be monitoring the vectorscope for the adequacy of the light levels. The lighting director should be observant of unwanted shadows from either actors or microphone booms on the location set.

Videotape recorder location set-up (VTRO 2). The videotape recorder operator should see to the proper set-up and operation of the videotape recorder after the production meeting. The mobility of the videotape recorder set-up should be facilitated for easy movement when the camera and lighting placements are changed with different takes. A table with wheels or a cart makes an excellent set-up platform for the videotape recorder and accessories.

The videotape recorder operator should request a check of the recording set-up by recording some video and audio with the camera and microphones before notifying the director and the producer that set-up is complete. Part of the videotape recorder set-up is the vectorscope to monitor video levels for broadcast quality and a headset for monitoring audio input.

Location audio set-up (AD 2). The audio director sets up the equipment for audio recording the remote drama production immediately following the production meeting. The audio set-up requires the cooperation of the videotape recorder operator because microphone connections and the audio monitoring headset connection are made into the videotape recorder.

The audio director should make a set-up check by having run cables, checking microphones for batteries, setting gain levels with actors or stand-ins, and listening carefully for ambience sound, which may be unacceptable or intolerable to the scene.

The audio levels for voice recording can be made by watching the VU meter for audio input level and monitoring the audio by headset. When everything checks out, the director and producer should be notified.

Supervising equipment set-up (D 3). When all equipment is set up and operating, the director should make a final check. Because remote production equipment ultimately creates the aesthetic experience to be achieved with drama production, the director has the responsibility to check the proper set-up and functioning of the camera, videotape recorder, audio recording equipment, and lighting design.

Getting into costumes, make-up (T 1). Preferences vary among directors for the preparation they expect from their actors. Some prefer that actors report to location in make-up and costume; others break for make-up and costuming after blocking and rehearsal. One determining factor is always the extent of make-up and costuming required. Long and detailed make-up, e.g., extensive aging, should be done early with adequate lead time. Basic make-up could be applied before blocking and final touches and powdering before the first take.

Blocking the actors (D 4). Once the director has determined that camera, recorder, audio, and lighting are ready, the actors can be summoned. Having already indicated to the camera operator where the first set-up position was for the camera, the director blocks the actor(s) from the master script without their line delivery. This step is best achieved by the director simply noting the phrase or point in the dialogue when and where an actor is to move and physically moving the actor(s), one at a time, on their cue(s).

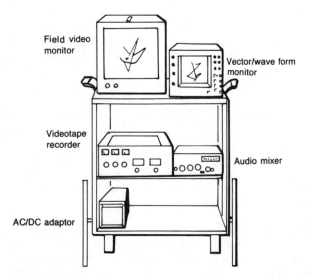

FIGURE 3–7
On-set video and audio recording/monitoring equipment.
On-set recording equipment needs easy mobility. The equipment cart facilitates camera changes during videotaping.

Following the director's requests and directions during blocking, rehearsals, and takes (T 3). The director is the first and final word on a location videotape shoot. For actors, apart from learning lines and developing characterizations, this is usually the first time on the set and blocking is new to everyone. Following the director's directions accurately and swiftly helps everyone in both cast and crew. Most directors will rehearse until actors feel comfortable with their lines and movements. Actors should not hesitate to ask for additional rehearsals before a take. Following a director's commands includes the director's calls to action, cut, freeze, and another take.

Rehearsing the actors (D 5). Once the actor(s) know the blocking for the scene, the next step involves allowing them to rehearse the blocking with their lines. During these two steps, blocking and rehearsing actors, the camera operator, microphone boom grip, audio director, and lighting director should be checking their response to the blocking as the director blocks and rehearses the actor(s).

Blocking the camera (D 6). Now the director can set camera shots with the camera operator. Setting camera shots means directing the composition of the take (who is in the field of view), the camera framing (the kind of shot, e.g., CU, LS), and movement of the camera (e.g., pan, tilt, zoom) during a video take. It is presumed that the camera operator has had a shot list of the shots required for the scene and has been observing the director block and rehearse the actors in the scene.

Setting camera shots can be done with the actors delivering lines or simply rehearsing the blocking. Some directors find that with the delivery of lines, it is difficult to spend quality time with the camera operator because the scene passes swiftly. Hence, many prefer that the actors simply rehearse blocking at this step. During this stage the mike boom grip should also participate and work out positions in the videotaping environment for covering dialogue audio for the scene without getting in the frame and not casting shadows.

Rehearsing the camera (CO 4). After blocking the camera position, composition, framing, and movement, the camera operator rehearses what the director blocked with the actors and their line delivery. The director may watch the camera performance on a monitor and offer the camera operator some criticism.

Observing blocking and rehearsals (MBG/O 1). The mike boom grip/operator has the responsibility to observe the director's blocking of actors and rehearsals with actors for the purpose of determining where and how far to project the microphone holder, e.g., the fishpole, into the location set. The mike boom grip/operator must look for the fall of shadows from a microphone or fishpole. When these shadows occur, then the position of both the microphone and fishpole and the boom grip/operator have to be changed and checked again.

Blocking the camera position with the actors (CO 3). In video drama production, the camera is treated as an actor; the camera must be blocked for position and movement and

FIGURE 3–8
Blocking actors and camera. The director has a five-stage technique for blocking the actors and camera for remote drama videotaping.

changes during a scene just as an actor. Camera operators find it convenient to observe the blocking of actors alone first and then take notes while the director blocks their camera.

Rehearsing both actors and camera (D 7).   The director should now call for a rehearsal of the actors with lines and with the camera operator performing all the shots called for. The director should observe the scene where both the real action and a video playback can both be seen. It is at this point that the mike grip should also have worked out the best position(s) for covering the scene adequately for sound pick-up. During this step the video monitor should be watched for boom or microphone shadows or catching the microphone itself on camera. The audio director should carefully monitor the sound reproduction for any abnormalities in covering the dialogue and setting gain levels. The videotape recorder operator or the camera operator should be checking video levels on the vectorscope and communicating to the lighting director any levels that may not be acceptable for broadcast quality video.

Observing CU and LS framing for microphone positions (MBG/O 2).   From the director's defined framing of shots, e.g., CU versus LS, during blocking and rehearsals, the mike boom grip/operator has to determine how close or low to actors the microphone can be tolerated without getting into the video picture frame. When the microphone gets in the picture, usually another take is required. Constant vigilance is required to avoid microphone boom shadows and microphones in shot.

Making changes and rehearsing again (D 8).   Having troubleshot any problems, the director calls for a rehearsal of the scene one more time to check for any remaining difficulties or that old ones have been corrected. This rehearsal might focus solely on audio coverage and microphone boom handling. This is a good opportunity for the director to check actors' make-up and costuming on camera under the lights and over the video monitor.

Calling for a take (D 9).   At this stage the director might call for a take. This means that the director is ready to videotape the scene. In turn, this means that actors should have make-up and costuming checks and attend to last minute prop details. This step requires that the continuity secretary make ready to record all the details necessary for accounting for the scene and any subsequent portions of the scene. There is no question of the importance of the continuity secretary and note taking. The smallest slip in detail between a previous take and a subsequent take to be cut into the earlier one will create impossible problems in editing.

There is also a need for the slate at this point in the production. The slate is readied with the appropriate information, which will label the leader video of the scene, enabling the postproduction editor later to best identify the following take without having to see the entire scene. The slate records at least the title of the teleplay, the director, the taping date, the script unit, and the take number. The continuity secretary might be responsible for the slate or another member of the crew

assigned to perform the task. In any case, both the continuity secretary and the person responsible for the slate should be coordinated because they both must share accurate information of scene numbers, units, and video takes. The correct standardized language for a director's control of a take is as follows:

Director: "Stand by for a take."

Director: "Ready to roll tape."

Videotape recorder operator: "Ready to roll tape."

Director: "Roll tape."

Videotape recorder operator: "Tape is rolling."

Director: "Slate it" or "Mark it."

Slate person (steps in front of the lens of the camera with the slate and reads aloud both the unit number and the take number): "Unit ___; take ___."

Director: "Ready to cue action." "Action!"

Actor(s) take a breath, a pause, and begin.

Director (records beyond planned edit point): "Cut!"

Actor(s) freeze.

Continuity secretary (makes necessary notes): "Okay" or "Hold it."

Director announces his intentions: "That's a take. Strike," "Master scene, unit ___," "Cut-ins, unit ___," "Take it again, unit ___," or "Take it from line ___."

Videotaping the take (CO 5).   When the last changes are made and no more rehearsal needed, the camera operator will be asked to keep the camera position, shot composition, shot framing, and any required movement for a videotaped take. The camera operator should carefully observe camera work, subject composition, framing, and movement and be ready to tell the director that some problem was encountered if there was one, some mistake made, or even to suggest a better shot before a wrap is called on that take.

Responding to the director's call to roll tape (VTRO 3).   The responsibility of the videotape recorder operator during production is to respond to the readiness call by the director and to indicate that the videotape is indeed rolling and that video and audio recording levels check out.

Monitoring audio input (AD 3).   During the videotaping the audio director has to monitor audio input. The audio director must watch audio levels on the VU meter of the videotape recorder and listen over a headset for dialogue and ambience sounds. Ambience sound can be acceptable background sounds for a scene or unacceptable noise, such as an airplane or automobile. At the end of a videotape take, the audio director should let the director know if the audio recording was correct and acceptable or whether an error was made necessitating a retake.

Monitoring vectorscope (VTRO 4).   The videotape recorder operator should monitor vectorscope levels during a videotape take. Bursts of light and reflections of light as

FIGURE 3–9
Remote drama production crew.

actors move and properties are used can push light levels for the camera to unacceptable levels. Should these light bursts be seen by the videotape recorder operator, the director should be notified after a cut is called.

Following the director's directions (AD 4). The audio director is directly responsible to the production director during a videotaping, as are all crew members.

Miking dialogue during takes (MBG/0 3). Once rehearsals are over and clearance of shadows and microphones is made, the mike boom grip/operator then booms the dialogue of actors during videotaping. During videotaping the mike boom grip/operator has to hold the fishpole steadily following safety distances rehearsed, and handle microphone extension cables at the fishpole and on the floor or ground of the location set. Some mike boom grips/operators prefer to monitor audio input with a headset from the videotape recorder during taping too.

One guideline for good audio perspective is that the wider the framing is for a video shot, the more distant the audio perception should appear; the closer the framing is for a video shot, the louder the audio perception should appear. Hence, during long shots, the microphone is held higher, giving a further audio perspective; on close-ups, the microphone can be closer to the actors, effecting a louder audio perspective.

Updating and slating videotape leader (SP 1). The slate person has the responsibility of constantly updating the information on the slate for recording on the leader of every videotape take. The slate person must be in coordination with the videotape recorder operator and the continuity

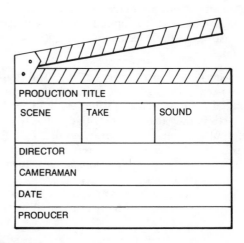

FIGURE 3–10
The video production slate. The slate, when filled in with relevant information, is videotaped on the leader of each take on location.

secretary. Information in script unit and number of take are important to accurate postproduction.

Coordinating the slate with the continuity secretary and videotape recorder operator (SP 2). The slate person needs to be in regular communication with both the continuity secretary who keeps record of all takes, and the videotape recorder operator who keeps record of videotape codes.

Following the director's directions (SP 3). The slate person is directly responsible to the call of the director for every videotape take. The director's call, "slate it," means that the slate person positions the slate in focus in front of the lens of the camera and audibly reads the script unit being taped and the take number into the microphone. If the take is interrupted by a minor error, e.g., a flubbed line of dialogue, a director may forego a slate at the front of a take, and instead call for an end board, slating the take at the end of the videotape.

Announcing intentions: retake, wrap, or strike (D 10). The primary determinant of the director's intentions after a take should always include a check of the video and audio recording by the videotape recorder operator and the audio director, preferably by the director. This is the advantage of video over film, i.e., the ability to see the take immediately after it is finished. It would be foolhardy not to view the scene before proceeding. If the take is satisfactory, a wrap is called and another scene or camera placement may be called for. Specific script units should be noted to reduce uncertainty about the new scene. If the take is unsatisfactory, another take may be called by the director. Reasons for the retake should be given so that crew and cast can avoid the same problem and make corrections. If all the takes for the day as listed on the production schedule are complete, a strike of the location may be called by the director.

Observing and recording continuity details (CS 1). The continuity secretary has the responsibility to observe all details of a videotaped take. This includes actors' dialogue, costuming, make-up, blocking, hand properties, and vehicle properties. The continuity notes form suggests what details to observe, but it is up to the continuity secretary to be sensitive to those details that might change from take to take.

Working with the continuity secretary (T 4). The continuity secretary needs to record more details of the actors than any other element of a take. It is important to good order and less stress that actors be sensitive to the requests of the continuity secretary to a freeze until all details are observed and noted, as well as be refreshed about details from the continuity secretary before a subsequent take. Actors can assist a continuity secretary by not changing detail elements, e.g., locks of hair askew, hand holding a purse, during a break, and by helping recall detail elements.

Releasing actors after a cut (CS 2). When a director calls for a cut in videotaping, the continuity secretary may call for a freeze among the actors (and even the production crew) until all elements of detail are correctly recorded.

Being available but out-of-the-way (T 5). Between takes actors should be available but out of the crew's way. More time is lost between takes on a location shoot when crew members have to fall over or go around actors who should vacate shooting space. The opposite problem is actors who disappear and cannot be found when a take is ready. Although crew and cast alike prefer to engage in idle talk, such behavior holds up a production and serves to distract actors from consistent characterization.

Reestablishing details before subsequent shot (CS 3). At the beginning of a subsequent shot to be edited to the previous shot, the continuity secretary has the obligation to redirect dialogue elements, costuming, make-up, and blocking to meet the same detail elements recorded from the previous cut.

Getting talent release forms signed (P 5). The end of the shooting day is the time for the producer to make certain that release forms are secured for any extras who may have been used from the location site for the shoot. It is not uncommon, for example, to recruit people standing around a location shoot for roles as extras in street scenes. Their release forms should be obtained for purposes of legal clearance. (See the talent release form.)

Striking camera equipment (CO 6). When the director indicates the final wrap and location strike, the camera operator is responsible for the breakdown of all camera equipment and accessories as part of the location strike. Repackaging and loading of equipment should proceed according to the requirements of unloading at the beginning of the shoot.

Striking lighting equipment (LD 3). When the director calls a strike for the production day, the lighting director is responsible for striking and repacking all lighting equipment and accessories. The lighting director should allow incandescent light bulbs to cool down before striking or moving lighting instruments. When incandescent bulbs are hot, the filament of the bulb is more sensitive to being jarred. Jarring a hot bulb can lessen the light life of the bulb.

Striking the videotape recorder equipment and accessories (VTRO 4). When the director calls a strike, the videotape recorder operator begins to break down the videotape recorder set-up. After the strike call it is important that the videotape operator remove the record button from all the source tapes used for the shoot to prevent accidental erasing or recording over.

Labeling videotape cassettes and carrying cases is also an important production detail for the videotape recorder operator. Any agreed upon coding is sufficient. Coordination with the continuity secretary facilitates reordering the videotapes for postproduction preparation.

Care should be exercised that any B-roll tapes be used for that purpose only. A B-roll tape may be designated by a director in anticipation of special editing effects such as a dissolve, in which two tapes will have to be rolled onto the master tape. Not anticipating a B-roll source tape requires another generation of the video needed for the special effect. B-rolling saves a second generation of a length of videotape.

Striking audio equipment (AD 5). When the director calls for a strike at the end of a production day, the audio director is responsible for the breakdown and repacking of audio equipment and accessories.

THE POSTPRODUCTION PROCESS

The postproduction process for single camera video drama production is dependent on the quality of video editing equipment at any facility. It is probably obvious that the better the editing facility, the better the final process and the techniques involved in a master edit. However, editing can be done with the simplest "cuts only" equipment. Because the content of the dramatic genre suggests the need of more refined editing techniques than the cut, the capability of dissolving and fading with capability of matting titles and credits will be assumed.

• Personnel

Producer (P). The responsibilities of the producer continue into the postproduction stage by handling details of the editing process: scheduling, facilities, postproduction preparation, titling, and credits.

Director (D). The director of a drama production may also be the editor in postproduction. If the director does not do the actual editing, supervision of editing sessions is still a responsibility.

Camera operator (CO). The only remaining responsibility of the camera operator to postproduction tasks is the need to secure the return of all remote camera equipment and any accessories for the camera. Part of the proper return of camera equipment is to report all lost, damaged, or malfunctioning equipment. Report should also be made of any new purchases or any addition to available equipment.

Lighting director (LD). The lighting director must also complete responsibilities by returning lighting equipment and lighting accessories used for the shoot. Any lighting equipment loss, damage, or malfunction should be reported to equipment supervisory/maintenance personnel. Also any new purchases for lighting purposes should be accounted for.

Videotape recorder operator (VTRO). The videotape recorder operator continues with the project into postproduction and assumes the responsibility the operator had for videotapes during production. There is also the responsibility to secure the return of all videotape recording equipment and accessories, to report any loss, damage, or malfunction, and to properly account for new equipment or accessories purchases.

Audio director (AD). The audio director has a similar responsibility to other crew members and should also secure the return of all location audio reproduction and recording equipment. The audio director is also accountable to report any lost, damaged, or malfunctioning audio equipment. Accountability should also cover any new purchases made for this production.

Continuity secretary (CS). The continuity secretary also continues into postproduction with the responsibility for taking continuity notes recorded on location.

Technical director/editor (TD/E). The only new crew member in postproduction for the video drama production might be a technical director or editor. Some editing facilities require a technical director/editor who knows the postproduction facility.

• Postproduction Stages

Arranging postproduction schedule and facilities (P 1). The producer has the responsibility to make arrangements for editing suite scheduling. Editing should not begin until all preparation elements are complete.

A high quality videotape should be secured for the master tape and striped with time code to permit accurate editing of the teleplay from the source tapes. If the SMPTE time code is going to be used in editing, the source tapes will also have to be striped. Source tapes can be striped during the location videotaping if desired. If source tape striping is done in preparation for editing, be careful to stripe the correct audio track. Location audio could be erased if the wrong track is striped. If the time code is not being used, remember that the master tape must have at least a control track before editing begins on it. The source tapes are automatically striped with a time code when they are recorded with a video signal during the location shooting.

Supervising postproduction preparation (P 2). The producer has the responsibility for three elements in the preparation of the project for postproduction: the master script, the source tapes, and the continuity notes. The master script will have to be reordered in sequential order and edited if changes were made during production. The director should see to this reordering and editing. The source tapes will have to be reordered in the order of the master script. They should be properly labeled both on the cassette and on the carrying case. This is the responsibility of the videotape recorder operator. The continuity notes sheets will also have to be ordered according to the master script. This is the responsibility of the continuity secretary.

Postproduction preparation: the master script (D 1). The director has the postproduction preparation responsibility of reordering the master script and editing it for changes that may have been made during location production. It is not uncommon that short scenes were dropped or takes not preplanned were videotaped. These additions as well as deletions will have to be made. The master script, whether edited by the director or a technical director/editor, becomes the only point of reference for the master tape edition.

Preparing the source videotapes (VTRO 1). The videotape recorder operator has the responsibility of handing the

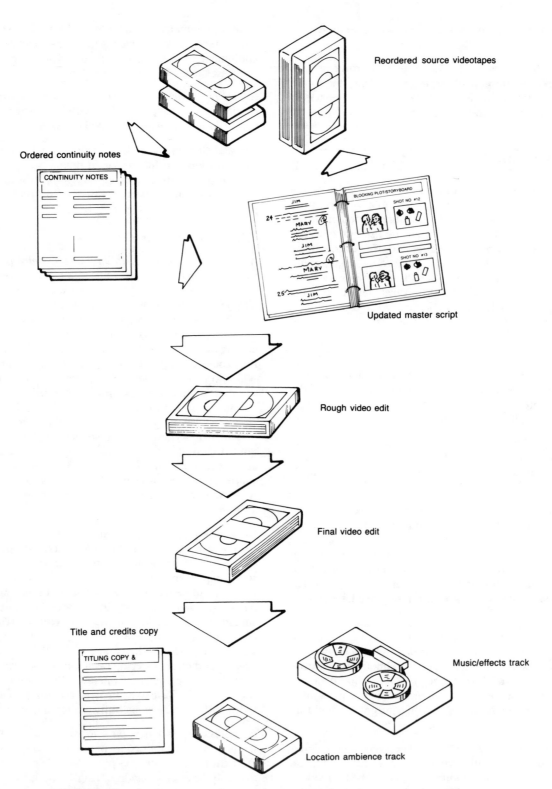

Reordered source videotapes

Ordered continuity notes

Updated master script

Rough video edit

Final video edit

Title and credits copy

Music/effects track

Location ambience track

FIGURE 3–11
Video drama postproduction preparation. The stages of drama postproduction from reordering
the source videotapes, continuity notes, and master script through the rough edit and final edit
to mixing of music and effects and ambience and titling.

source videotapes to the director or the producer. The preparation of the source tapes means to remove record buttons so that the video signal will not be erased or recorded over accidentally. Proper labeling of both video-cassettes and carrying cases must also be complete so that any source videotape may be found with little trouble.

The final preparatory work on the source tapes is to have them all striped with SMPTE time code, which facilitates more accurate editing of the master tape than simple control track editing. Because SMPTE assigns a consecutive number to every frame of the videotape, matching numbered frames from the source tape to the master tape creates a controlled edit. SMPTE code on the master tape will also allow the audio track to be removed later for sweetening and mixing and re-laying it to exact synchronization.

Reordering source videotapes (VTRO 2).   The videotape recorder operator should finally reorder all the source videotapes according to the units of the master script.

Reordering continuity notes sheets (CS 1).   Because the continuity secretary has been recording all pertinent details of each location video take on the continuity forms, they are in need of reordering according to the order of the master script. The continuity notes sheets were defined as a kind of location log, which would replace the tedious job of having to view all source tapes after videotaping and before editing could begin. If the continuity notes sheets were well recorded, more than enough information is contained on them to allow postproduction to proceed rapidly and smoothly. Continuity notes serve as the editing work sheets of other postproduction processes.

Making editing decisions (D 2).   The director alone should make editing decisions. The control of the production by a director is such that all creative energy is channeled through the director and videotaping decisions affect editing decisions. In many ways they are the same. Directors often look to others, i.e., the producer or technical director, for advice, but ultimately the decision should be that of the director.

Observing the editing process with the director (P 3).   The producer is a valuable resource person in the editing suite during editing sessions. The experience with the project at all stages becomes helpful when particular points of the project, the drama performance, and the editing arise.

Editing a rough edit (D 3).   From single camera film production comes the practice of editing a rough version of the whole teleplay first. A rough edit is created by simply cutting blindly, following the master script and the continuity sheets. Remember that the continuity sheets indicate which take was good or bad. The rough edit can move along swiftly if members of the editing team use a fast search playback deck and monitor system to find the good takes while an editor or technical director does the "cuts-only" editing with simple insert edits.

The reasons for making a rough edit first instead of channeling efforts into a final version may not be immediately evident. First, a cuts-only version allows for an early glance at the whole project. It serves to anticipate problems in a polished final edition. These problems can range from continuity (e.g., edits do not match) to pacing (e.g., the overall flow of the video does not reflect the script).

Second, the rough edit allows the drama ensemble to see their performance while they may still be together as a group. If the project is working with academic objectives, the ability to see a performance early allows criticizing to occur, which is a necessary ingredient to the professional growth of amateurs, but even professionals like to see their own performances. Third, a rough edit can point to less-than-the-best video quality or location problems that might still be redone because the rough edit is not far removed from the shooting dates, and the cast and crew may still be available.

Overseeing audio quality and mixing of the edited master (AD 1).   The audio director has the final responsibility for sound quality of the edited master. The audio director has not only had the experience of the audio input on location, but has also planned the music and sound effects to be edited into the master tape. Assuming that all copyright clearances for copyrighted music and effects have been obtained, final audio editing can begin. The audio director serves as a resource person during audio editing. After the video and audio edits are completed with the use of SMPTE time code with more advanced postproduction audio capabilities, the audio track can be removed from the master tape to be mixed and sweetened. Here mixing of music and other sound effects are introduced.

If this level of postproduction work is not available, acceptable audio mixing can occur on the second audio track of the master tape itself. With proper preparation, music and ambience track can be premixed and placed on the auxiliary audio track under the dialogue track with little or no problem.

Reviewing the rough edit (D 4).   The best use of the rough edit version is to scrutinize the video and audio for polishing a final version. There are many advantages to having this edition. Now is the time to sense the pacing of the final teleplay. Does the flow of video images complement the dialogue and the dramatic tension? Perhaps having seen the flow of images as preplanned, the pacing may be violated and some originally planned video edits should not be used. Only by seeing the entire drama at this stage can decisions like these be intelligently and aesthetically made and implemented in the final editing.

Preparing titles and credits for matting (P 3).   The producer should have the complete lists of cast and crew and their assigned roles in the production. If the lists are correct and complete, preparing titles and credits copy is not difficult. Correct spelling of all proper names and exact production position is the difficult task.

The final stage of the production involves matting titles and credits to the master tape. This can be done with a character generator in a postproduction editing suite or by running the master tape through a production switcher and character generator in a control room of a television studio facility. There seems to be no standardized order for title and credits in the industry. It is not uncommon to allow the creative beginning of a movie or teleplay to dictate the proper way of introducing the title, main characters, and above-the-line video personnel. In a general way, the following might be considered an approach to titling and crediting the master tape of a teleplay:

OPENING
    Frame #1: _____Teleproductions presents
    Frame #2: Arthur P. Jone's
    Frame #3: A Day in the Life
    Frame #4: Starring
    _____ as Billy
    _____ as Suzanne
    Frame #5: Produced by
    _____
    Frame #6: Directed by
    _____

CLOSING
    First set of frames: technical credits in descending order of importance—executive producer to grip;
    Second set of frames: drama credits in descending order of importance—executive director to last extra;
    Last set of frames: trades and thank yous followed by the copyright notation, the year of production, and the owner of the copyright.

Making the final edit (D 5). With adequate review of the rough edit, final editing can begin. Here all the shortcomings perceived in the rough edit can be repaired and improved. It is at this stage that SMPTE code is best employed. Now transitions other than a cut can be carefully chosen and executed. As part of this stage, titles and credits can be added to the master tape.

Music, effects, ambience added; audio mixing and sweetening (AD 2). After all the video is edited to the satisfaction of the director, the audio director can add the music, effects, and/or the ambience called for by the master script.

During the process of mixing the two audio channels used to this point for dialogue (one channel) and music and effects (the other channel) to one channel, audio sweetening can be done. Sweetening allows the audio track to be filtered and cleared of unwanted noises and hums and synchronized back to the master tape with the video track.

Labeling the final edited master (D 6). The final edited master tape should be clearly labeled on both video cassette and cartridge. The record button should also be removed. It is a good practice to make a dub immediately as a safety measure against losing all the work that has gone into the final edited version.

VIDEO PRODUCTION ORGANIZING FORMS

• Production Budget Form

Production process: Video drama preproduction

Responsibility: Producer

Purpose: To realistically estimate all possible costs of the production of the proposed video drama production from preproduction to postproduction.

Objective: The budget form is a blank model of a budget for the production of a video drama. The form is meant to organize all facets of single camera drama production into estimated expenses and actual expenses. It serves to suggest possible cost items across the whole spectrum of video production, personnel, equipment, labor, and materials. The form should be used to suggest expenses and to call attention to possible hidden costs.

Notes on use: The form should be studied for line items that might pertain to a proposed single camera video drama shoot. Only applicable line items for the proposed teleplay need to be considered. Use the suggestion of line items to weigh possible costs for the project. Note that all sections of the budget are summarized on the front page of the form. The subtotal of costs from the individual sections are brought forward to be listed in the summary. Some costs are calculated by the number of days employed, the hourly rate of pay, and overtime hours. Other costs are calculated by the number of items or people by allotted amount of money per day for the item. The cost of materials is calculated by the amount of material(s) by the cost of a unit. Most cost entry columns of this budget form are labeled "Days, Rate, O/T (overtime) Hrs, Total"; for those line items that do not involve day and rate, the total column alone should be used. Projected costs to be applied to the budget can be found from a number of sources. One source of equipment rental and production costs is the rate card of a local video production facility. Salary estimates and talent fees can be estimated from the going rates of relevant services of equivalent professionals or from their agencies. Phone calls to providers of services and materials will also produce cost quotes. Travel costs can be obtained by a phone call to travel agencies or airline companies. There is no question that preparing a good budget involves a lot of time and research.

Glossary

No. Preproduction Days Estimate the number of days to complete the necessary preproduction stages for the teleplay. This estimate includes quality time on all preproduction stages (e.g., budget, site survey, production schedule, script breakdown, casting, master script, shot list, equipment lists) for all production crew members involved in the preproduction of the teleplay (e.g., producer, director, camera operator, lighting director, videotape recorder operator, audio director, continuity secretary, actors).

No. Studio Shoot Days/Hours Estimate the number of days and hours for which a studio or control room facilities may be needed. This time estimate accounts for any in-studio videotaping (e.g., talent on a set) or the use of control room switcher or character generator for postproduction effects.

No. Location Days/Hours Estimate the number of shooting days and hours that may be required on location.

No. Postproduction Days/Hours Estimate the number of days and hours that will be spent in postproduction in completing the video drama master edit.

First Shooting Date Indicate the first date proposed to begin videotaping the drama.

Completion Date Indicate the projected completion of the video drama project. This date should include all postproduction tasks.

Location Sites List the proposed location shooting sites at which the previous days and hours were estimated.

Summary of Production Costs This summary area brings forward the subtotals of costs from the respective sections within the budget form. Note that lines 1 through 21 are found as section heads within the budget form. When the individual sections are completed within the budget, the subtotal is listed in the summary table.

Contingency This term refers to the practice of adding a contingency percentage to the subtotal of subtotals as a padding against the difference in actual final costs from the estimated costs of all line items. The customary contingency percentage is 15%. Multiply the subtotal in line 22 by 0.15 to determine the contingency figure. That result added to line 22 becomes the grand total of the drama production budget costs.

Story Rights, Other Rights, and Clearances This section accounts for the cost that might be incurred in obtaining necessary copyright clearances for music or script.

Estimated The estimated category refers to costs that can only be projected before the production. Rarely are the estimated costs the final costs to be incurred because of the number of variables that cannot be anticipated. Every attempt should be made to ensure real estimated cost figures and to ensure the consideration of as many variables to the cost as possible. The challenge of estimated budget costs is to project as close as possible to actual costs when they are known.

Actual The actual category of a budget will record the costs that are finally incurred for the respective line items during or after the video drama production is completed. The actual costs are those costs that will really be paid out for the production. The ideal budget seeks to have actual costs come as close as possible— either at or preferably under—to the estimated costs for the production.

Script This section suggests some of the possible costs that might be incurred with the writing or rewriting of the script for the teleplay. On some storylines searches may have to be made for legal purposes, e.g., authenticity or libel.

Producing Staff This section of the budget accounts for the producer of the teleplay and other personnel who may be involved with producing responsibilities. The role of producer is divided into the three areas of a video production: responsibilities that occur before, during, and after production.

Directing Staff The next section covers the director and personnel associated with the directing responsibilities of the teleplay. As with most budgets, some line items/personnel are listed for purposes of suggesting enlarged staffs and additional roles during single camera drama production. They are not necessary to all remote productions.

Talent The expenses of any talent associated with the production of the teleplay are accounted for in this section. Some talent may be hired by contract and may be subject to other fees, e.g., Screen Actors Guild (SAG). Other talent may be freelancers.

Benefits Depending on the arrangements made with talent, some production budgets may have to account for benefits accruing to talent and crew members (e.g., health benefits, pensions). Insurance coverage should be accounted for in this section as well as state and federal taxes applicable to any salaries of talent and crew members.

Production Staff This section accounts for production staff and crew members.

Crew This unit lists some extra production crew personnel and miscellaneous and duplication costs.

Camera The personnel and expenses that function with the maintenance and use of the video camera are accounted for in this section. This section also records the equipment items that are purchased and rented.

Set Design and Construction Because any dramatic production involves the use of sets of some sort, either existing location sites or constructed sets with artwork, some consideration should be made for set art and set construction. This section of the budget suggests some art and construction personnel and costs.

Set Operations Similar to the dramatic need for art and set construction, the care and development of sets should also be accounted for. Under set operations fall the personnel and equipment needed with location sets, e.g., video camera mounts.

Lighting-Electrical The dramatic need to create mood and setting on location sets accounts for the personnel and equipment for set lighting.

Set Decoration Most drama sets, location site included, require dressing and care. This section of the budget accounts for personnel and equipment for set decoration and care.

Props, Animals, Vehicles One advantage to doing remote location video drama production is the opportunity to use vehicles and animals. This section of the budget suggests and accounts for personnel and action properties and their care and handling for the production.

Wardrobe Drama production requires costumes. The personnel, materials, production, and care of costumes are accounted for in this section.

Make-up and Hairdressing Make-up and hair preparation are also necessary to drama production. This section of the budget suggests some line items to be accounted for when make-up, hair, and wigs are used.

Sound Production Sound production and recording are essential to video drama production. This section suggests personnel and equipment rental and purchase line items for the production.

Location Expenses Location site costs from scouting and insurance to services in the location environment are accounted for in this section of the budget.

Transportation Because location shoots usually require travel, whether local or distant, this section suggests personnel, services, and fuel costs accounting.

Videotape Stock   The provision of necessary videotape stock in required sizes is accounted for in this section.

Postproduction Editing   The personnel, facilities, and materials for postproduction needs during editing are accounted for in this section of the budget.

Music   Because most drama production involves music, original or recorded, this section of the budget suggests some of the potential costs and personnel involved in the music for a drama production.

• **Script Breakdown Form**

Production process: Video drama preproduction

Responsibility: Director

Purpose: To break the drama script down into production units usually according to common location or talent requirements.

Objective: The script breakdown form organizes the drama script into a video production shooting order according to differing common criteria for the shoots, e.g., location similarity, talent, time of day. The script breakdown form helps organize the shooting units by script pages or number of script lines criteria for scheduling and managing the remote production.

Glossary

Length   This entry records the estimated length of the final video drama production.

Script Length   The length of the drama script in number of script pages is recorded here.

Script Unit   Script unit is a common way of organizing video drama scripts by writers. Script units replace the classic theatrical division of a stage script into acts and scenes. Teleplays convert acts and scenes into consecutively numbered units. The script unit being analyzed should be listed in this column.

Script Pages/Lines   The number of pages and/or lines of script copy for a unit of the script determines the length of a shooting unit. The page count can be made in whole page and portion of page numbers. The line count should be every line of talent copy in the unit.

Int/Ext   These abbreviations stand for interior/exterior, referring to the script demands for shooting indoors or outdoors. Whether the shoot is an interior or an exterior shoot can also be a determinant for the script breakdown and shooting unit.

Time   The time of day or night that the location and interior/exterior setting requires should be recorded here.

Setting   Setting means the specific area of a required location site, e.g., the parents' bedroom for the Smith's home location site.

Location   The location column records the remote location environment at which the setting is to be found. For example, the Smith's home is the location site for the parents' bedroom.

Cast   This entry records by name the specific cast characters who are required in the setting at the location for a particular unit.

Shooting Order   When the entire script is broken down into shooting units, then the producer can determine the units for individual shoots and determine the consecutive shooting order for the entire remote project.

• **Location Site Survey Form**

Production process: Video drama preproduction

Responsibility: Director

Purpose: To organize and facilitate the survey of possible remote video drama production location environments.

Objective: The location site survey form is designed to assist the director or location scouts who have to search out and describe potential remote environments for drama production purposes. Because many sites may have to be evaluated for any particular shoot, details of each site will have to be recorded to be evaluated and approved at a later time, usually away from the site by the director and producer. The form is designed to raise all possible production needs and location details for a successful remote video production. The form serves to organize and record location site details for later evaluation away from the site.

Glossary

Location Scout(s)   This entry should list those other than the director who have been recruited to help scout potential locations for the production of the video drama production.

Script Page(s)   This entry should coordinate the location being scouted with the pages from the drama script that call for the use of the location.

Script Unit(s)   Some television scripts are divided into shooting units for production location purposes. These script units are numbered consecutively. This entry records the script unit number(s) that will be videotaped at the scouted location.

Location   This entry should record the actual environment called for by the script, for example, "Bob's bedroom."

Site Identification   This entry should correspond with a city map (e.g., H-3) or name of the location environment (e.g., Town Point Park).

Local Contact Person   This is the name of the responsible owner, manager, or supervisory officer of a proposed location. This person is the individual who is the location scout(s)' contact person at the highest level of authority over a proposed location site. This person is the use-granting authority for the location. The name, title, address, city, state, and phone number of the contact person should all be accurately recorded. All this information, including the proper title, will be needed for mail correspondence purposes. The "comments" space allows for any notes about the contact person (e.g., executive secretary's name) that might be relevant.

Facilities Personnel   The facilities personnel information is a record of the person who is the individual with whom the producer and production crew will work on the location. For example, the maintenance engineer, office manager, and janitor are the individuals responsible for the everyday operation of the proposed location. The name, position, title, address, city, state, and phone number of each should be recorded. This information becomes the most practical to the production crew and the producer. This is the information most utilized once the location is chosen for use. The "comments" space should be used for any other relevant information about the facilities personnel. For example, the directions to the facilities personnel office at the location site, or maintenance workshop should be recorded here.

Lighting Problems Defined This area of the form focuses attention on the details of the proposed location that can affect lighting of the environment for videotape production.

Light Contrast Ratios Scouts should note any extreme light areas of the environment. A light meter can read and record should be made of the extreme lighting intensity of any existing areas of the environment. For example, one end of a proposed location site may have no windows and no ceiling lights. The light reading for this end of the room will be very low to nonexistent. The other end of the room may be flooded with light from a number of windows. The light reading at this end of the room will be very high. These readings form the contrast ratio between the most existing light and least existing light for this room.

Lighting Intensity This entry records the highest light level reading in the proposed location environment. This information will inform the producer that some controls will have to be used on the light source or other light will have to be created to balance this light intensity.

Ceiling Height The height of an existing ceiling is important. For example, ceiling height indicates the available height for lighting stands for lighting instruments to be used. A low ceiling allows light to be bounced, or a high ceiling means that light will be absorbed, and that fact has to be taken into account. High ceilings also demand a lot of light if the ceiling needs to be lit.

Windows/Compass Direction Knowing the number of windows opening to the exterior of the location is an important location consideration. Many windows may demand correcting incandescent lights with filters or the need to gel the windows. Another important fact about a location environment with windows is the compass direction they face. East facing windows can expect a flood of strong morning sunlight that can push the lighting intensity in the location environment. West facing windows will create the same problem in the afternoon. When working remote locations the strongest source of light is the sun, and the sun is a constantly moving light source. Knowing the direction of that moving light source is important. Shadows and reflections change constantly. It is a good practice to have a compass when scouting locations and to take an accurate reading of due east.

Existing Light Control A question to ask facilities personnel during location scouting is about the control of existing lighting. For example, in an all fluorescent lighting environment, there may be one master switch. It would be important to know where it is. Simple wall switches for other light control should also be noted.

Lighting Use Notation should be made of how some existing lighting is used. For example, lighted display cases in the environment, parking lot lights, and night lights are conditions of lighting use in the location environment. Much such light use cannot be controlled.

Floor Description The description of the type of flooring in a proposed location environment can have consequences for set lighting design. For example, a highly polished floor covering reflects light; a dark carpet absorbs light or reflects unwanted hues.

Special Consideration Use this space to record any other specific location detail that might affect lighting design in the environment for the production. For example, a pool of water could reflect light or a mirror on a wall.

Power Problems Defined This area of the form focuses attention and records those details that have to do with electrical power sources. Video production equipment relies heavily on available power sources.

Number of Power Outlets Count should be made of the number of electrical power outlets in the immediate environment of the proposed shoot. An additional count should be made of the outlets that can be accessed by power cable runs.

Number of Separate Circuits It is important to know how many separate electrical circuits are represented by the power outlets. This is a question for the facilities personnel/maintenance engineer. The power outlets and separate circuits should be noted on a location diagram.

Types of Fuses One liability of heavy electrical needs for video production equipment is the frequent blown fuse. In some facilities restoring power is not a matter of resetting a circuit, but replacing a fuse. A good example of the need for fuses is the older private home location environment. Fuses come in many sizes and wattages. It is important to know both size and wattage for the proposed location.

Number of Outlet Prongs There are at least two common types of electrical outlets: the two-prong and the three-prong. Many older environments have only the two-prong outlets. Almost all video production equipment utilizes the three-prong plug. Hence, adapters will have to be used on all two-prong outlets. The number of two-prong outlets will have to be known during location scouting so that adapters can be provided.

Location of Circuit Breakers Given the common occurrence of overloading electrical circuits with video production equipment needs, the location of fuse boxes and circuit breakers should be known. Often crew members will have to reset breakers and replace blown fuses.

Portable Generator Need It may happen that there is no power source available in a proposed location environment. The only possible source of electricity may be that generated by the production crew itself with a portable power generator. Power generators can be easily rented if needed. Caution must be exercised with the use of a power generator. They are a source of unwanted noise in the environment which can be difficult to control.

Audio Problems Defined   This area of the form focuses on details that affect the production of audio recording in the proposed location environment.

Interior Environmental Sounds   This entry should contain all perceived sound that is audible in the interior of the proposed location environment. This means careful listening for hums and buzzes from air conditioning, refrigerators, freezers, sound speakers, copying machines, and fluorescent lights. All sounds should be noted. Note should also be made of the ability to control or turn off the sounds.

Ceiling Composition   The composition of a ceiling can determine the quality of sound recordings made in the proposed location environment. For example, a hard composition ceiling reflects sound; sound proofing materials on a ceiling absorb sound. Both can make a difference in the quality of sound recorded in an environment.

Wall Composition   The composition of the walls of a proposed location environment also makes a difference in the quality of sound recorded in that environment. For example, cork, carpet or cloth, and sound proofing absorb sound; tile, mirror, and plaster reflect sound.

Exterior Environmental Sounds   Location scouts must listen carefully to both interior and exterior sounds in an environment. Exterior sounds affect both an exterior and an interior shoot. For example, some common exterior sounds that can affect an interior shoot are airplanes, emergency vehicles, a school playground, busy highway, and a noisy manufacturing plant. Make note of every perceivable sound.

Floor Covering Composition   The composition of a floor also has an effect on sound recording in an environment. For example, a polished hardwood or tile floor reflects sound as well as creates sound (e.g., footsteps). Deep pile carpeting absorbs sound.

Cast and Crew Needs   This area of the form reminds location scouts that care and consideration of cast and crew needs will have to be accounted for during a location shoot.

Restroom Facilities   Restroom facilities for men and women will have to provided. Part of the location site survey is to note, perhaps on the diagram of the location, where the restroom facilities are closest to the shooting area.

Green Room Availability   A green room is a theater term for a waiting area for actors. Some such waiting area may also be required for the cast for a video production. This should be a room close to the shooting area, but separate from the shooting area, where cast can relax and await their blocking and videotaping calls.

Parking Arrangements   A remote video production crew and cast can create a parking space demand on a neighborhood or public parking area. During scouting the question of special parking should be addressed. This may occasion some parking privileges or special directions or restrictions.

Freight Elevator   In some location environments, the number of crew, cast, and equipment involved in video production may require the use of a freight elevator in a facility. The location of the freight elevator should be part of a location environment diagram giving directions from the freight elevator to the shooting area.

Eating Facilities   When the length of a shooting day requires a meal on location, some eating facility, special room, or vending machines should be noted. Some facilities may prohibit any eating on premises. Notation then will have to be made of restaurants in the vicinity of the proposed location.

Make-up Facilities   If the video production requires that cast or talent appear in make-up, some facility will have to be provided for the application of the make-up. Ideally, make-up application demands mirrors, adequate lighting, and sinks. Restroom facilities make decent make-up preparation accommodations. If nothing else is available, a double set of restrooms can be designated for make-up and costuming.

Loading/Unloading Restrictions   The amount of equipment needed for a remote video production may require special unloading and loading requirements at a location site, e.g., an outside loading dock area. Such an unloading dock may also be close to a freight elevator. Location personnel should always be made aware of the great amount of equipment video production requires. They should be the judge of any special circumstances that might be required for so much equipment.

Hardware Store   Because remote video production demands so much hardware equipment, there is often the need to purchase supplies or replace broken, lost, or forgotten supplies. Facilities representatives may be able to provide information regarding where the closest hardware store is in the vicinity of the proposed location environment.

Civil Emergency Services   This area of the form lists essential civil services in the service of both the production cast and crew and the location site.

Police Station   The address and phone number of the police station that services the proposed location site is important contact information. With the number of individuals a remote video production crew involves, the amount of equipment and the use of an environment warrants the sensitivity to police presence and availability.

Fire Station   The same holds true for the fire protection station within the environmental area of the proposed location shoot site. The heavy use of electrical power for a remote video production shoot should alert both producer and production crew to the potential dangers of so much power use. This holds especially true for an older facility such as a private home used as a location site. The address and phone number of the fire station should be entered here.

Location Security and Equipment Safety   This area of the form records important information on general personal and property security and safety.

Facility Security   This entry records the general security of crew and cast and equipment during the production shoot. Some proposed locations in highly public areas, such as a shopping mall, present a security risk;

confined production sites, such as a private home, would be more secure. Note should be made of apparent security in general for all production elements.

Personnel Values Security Record should be made of the arrangements made with facilities personnel for the safety and security of personal belongings while crew and cast are involved in production; this includes wallets and purses especially. Facilities personnel can often provide a locked and secure room for the deposit of personal valuables during production.

Equipment Safe Storage Arrangements should be made for the security of unused equipment and accessories that should be safely stored until needed or stored after use until the location strike. The facilities personnel can often provide a locked and secure room for equipment storage.

Overnight Storage/Security Often remote location shoots take place over the period of more than one day. This entails the safe and secure overnight storage of equipment. Complete breakdown of all location equipment and loading, transport, and unloading a second day can result in the loss of valuable time and energy. Facilities personnel can often provide adequate overnight storage that is both safe and secure.

Other Relevant Information This area of the form records other important information that falls outside the other areas of location details.

Public Area Power Source Often in open public areas, such as a city park, the local power company may already provide a power box with an electrical outlet for private use. This service has to be requested from the power company and a deposit made to secure power costs at the end of the production shoot. Location scouts should search a public area for some sign of power source facility. It may serve the site survey to make a call to the local power company and request a listing of outdoor power sources.

Clearance/Insurance Personal security for the crew and talent and property damage insurance coverage should be secured before video production. Academic programs have personal insurance coverage for students and property damage and loss coverage for school equipment that is active when the shoot is a valid academic project with a supervising faculty present. Other remote video production projects can easily receive coverage by contacting a reliable insurance agent. Some potential location facilities personnel require verification of insurance coverage before approval of their location for a shoot. Anticipating insurance notification before facilities personnel require it is a sign of professional competence.

Photographs Taken When more than one location environment is being scouted for a shoot, and a decision may be made away from a potential site, a producer will have to judge from the location scout's report. An important part of a location site survey is photographs of the proposed location. Instant developing film is most convenient. When adequate photographs of a location site are part of a survey, these photographs help a producer and camera operator plan a shoot and assist a crew after a location strike in replacing a location environment to the arrangement and condition it was before the production crew arrived. The photographs taken should be listed. The photographer's camera position and direction of the lens of the photographed site should be noted on the location diagram as an aid in designing the video camera shots and lens framing for the production.

Location Environment Drawing/Map Another important product of location scouting is a drawing or map of the proposed location site. This entails a rough pacing off of all environments (both interior and exterior) that are being considered as a video setting. Windows should be placed, compass direction indicated, power outlets and circuits noted, and existing furniture and other properties sketched. Everything should be included that may enter into the use of the location from the needs of the production and the adaptability of the location environment.

Traffic Control At some exterior location environments, the extent of a video production crew, talent, and equipment will necessitate some control of vehicular traffic. For example, parking restriction may be required along the area of a shooting set, moving traffic may have to be redirected during a shoot, or a street may have to be closed off entirely from traffic. Most police departments are cooperative to such requests, but they need adequate advance time notification. In some instances the approval of a city or town council may be required. This also needs adequate lead time to process the request and get it to the council in good time for the shoot or a change of plans if the request is denied.

Exterior Compass Direction If the remote location site is an exterior shoot, an accurate assessment of the compass directions of the area should be made with respect to the proposed shooting site. The sun is the principal light source to an exterior shoot, and that source is in constant movement. Knowing the direction the sun takes from east to west on a proposed location environment is a most important variable to designing an outdoor video shoot. A compass is a necessity to scouting a location site. Many location personnel are not accurate about their recollection of east and west directions and are not reliable sources of information, given the importance that the sun's direction has on a remote video shoot.

Other Comments/Observations This area should record any other details not covered in the form to this point. It is important to record all impressions of a proposed location site. Sometimes the smallest detail missed or the smallest detail included can become either an obstacle or an asset to the production later. When in doubt about including a detail, include it.

- **Master Script: Blocking Plot/Storyboard Form**

Production process: Video drama preproduction

Responsibility: Director

Purpose: To create the director's master script, the location document from which the actors, dialogue, properties, camera operator, and camera framing will be directed.

Objective: This essential preproduction stage prepares the director for all details for directing the cast and crew while on location. From the location survey and photographs the director can design all production elements for location videotaping. The master script: blocking plot/storyboard serves to record the blocking of actors and sets and to record the storyboard sketch of every video frame proposed for production.

Notes on use: Many copies of the blocking plot/storyboard form will be needed. Two storyboard frames are contained on each page.

There is a lead page for the series and a secondary page for the remainder. Each page of the blocking plot/storyboard form is designed to be inserted into the director's copy of the teleplay script facing the respective page of script dialogue. The director should complete the bird's eye floor plan first for each shot. After the camera is placed in the floor plan in the position to frame the actor(s) and/or the set, then the director should sketch the storyboard frame of the shot. Each separate storyboard frame is drawn adjacent to a bird's eye floor plan. The floor plan need not be redrawn each time the storyboard framing changes if no major changes occur to the floor plan and nothing is to be added.

Glossary

Script Page Every blocking plot and/or storyboard frame should be related to its respective place in the script. The script page number should be recorded here.

Script Unit The blocking plot and storyboard should also be related to the script unit to which it refers. The script unit should be recorded here.

Shot No. After the design of the master script, the director creates a shot list from the storyboard frames. The shot list number for each storyboard frame is recorded here. Shot enumeration is location specific, i.e., a remote shot can be counted as though starting over for a new location site. This shot number should be entered at the corresponding in-cue on the script dialogue or scene directions on the script pages opposite the blocking plot/storyboard form page. It is these numbered shots for each location that the director eventually takes from the blocking plot/storyboard and lists on the shot list form.

3:4 Video Frame This is the storyboard video aspect ratio frame. The sketch of the desired content and camera framing of the shot should be drawn in this frame.

Framing The choice of framing (XCU, CU, MS, LS, XLS) should be checked here. This will facilitate calling out directions to the camera operator on location.

Change to If camera framing is to change during the shot, that camera framing change can be checked here.

Camera Motion The camera motion that will be required as part of the shot or the change of framing during the shot indicated in the storyboard frame can be checked here.

Lighting The director can check the kind of lighting required for the shot in this area of the form.

Sound The audio requirements for videotaping this shot can be checked here. Synchronous means that both audio and video will be recorded; silent means that the shot will not require any sound; wild means that the video need not be recorded, sound alone needs to be recorded.

Bird's Eye Floor Plan The director should reproduce in reduced form the location environment for the set. This should include the properties on the location set. The director should then place the actors (using circles with the initial letter of the character for each actor) in the set and block them (using arrows and repeating the actor's circle). The director should then draw the camera in place to achieve the shot that will be sketched in the storyboard frame for the shot.

Description of Take/Unit This area of the form allows for some notation of special directions for the particular take. This may involve the actor(s), some blocking movement, or the use of some prop.

In-cue This entry can be the first words of dialogue of the shot or some indication from scene directions for the beginning of the proposed shot.

Out-cue This entry can be the final words of dialogue of the shot or some indication from scene directions for the ending of the proposed shot.

- **Shot List Form**

Production process: Video drama preproduction

Responsibility: Director

Purpose: To translate the proposed storyboard frames from the master script into location videotape recording shots or camera takes.

Objective: The shot list form organizes each proposed storyboard frame into videotaping shots. Each shot should generate the necessary video to create the proposed edits as designed on the preproduction script. Each numbered shot is then entered on the dialogue of the script at the spot where the proposed shot is to be edited. This preproduction task facilitates the "what's next" syndrome during location productions. The shot list should exactly define every camera set-up, lens framing, and video shot needed to achieve that video.

The shot list form will translate each proposed shot from the master script to a simpler list for the advantage of the camera operator, videotape recorder operator, audio director, and lighting director.

Glossary

Location Every planned location site camera set-up and change of location site camera set-up should be noted in this column.

Shot No. From the master script, every proposed shot needed to create the storyboard frame of the teleplay script should be numbered consecutively. The respective number should be recorded here. Because shot numbers are location-specific, the shot numbers can begin at the count of one for each separate location.

Master Shot If a proposed shot is a master shot or

establishing shot (e.g., XLS) for a scene, it should be noted here. For example, a master shot might be an XLS of a couple walking toward the camera during dialogue.

Cut-in Shot   If a proposed shot is a cut-in (from a master shot), it should be noted in this column. For example, a cut-in would be a CU shot of one of the couple in the master shot.

Cut-away Shot   Unlike the cut-in (to a master shot), the cut-away shot is a relevant but extraneous to (usually away from) the master scene shot. An example of a cut-away would be generic footage of a city street.

Shot Framing   Shot framing directions for every proposed shot should make use of the symbols for the basic camera shot framing: XLS, LS, MS, CU, XCU. This would communicate to the camera operator the lens framing for the proposed shot. The framing choice for the shot should be checked on the master script by the director. That framing direction should be recorded here.

Shot Motion   Shot motion directions should indicate the kind of movement desired in the proposed shot. Movement in a shot can be either primary movement (on the part of the talent in front of the camera) which is the blocking of the talent; or secondary movement (on the part of the camera itself) which can be the pan, tilt, arc, truck, dolly, pedestal, or zoom. This direction also should have been checked by the director on the master script. That motion direction should be repeated here.

Content Notes   Any particular details of any shot that are not covered in the previous directions can be noted here. Content notes may be found in the description of the take directions from the master script. What is considered important to production crew members should be repeated here.

- **Production Schedule Form**

Production process: Video drama preproduction

Responsibility: Producer

Purpose: To organize and schedule the videotape production of individual script and location units of the video drama production.

Objective: The production schedule form organizes the elements of each remote location into production days and dates for videotaping. The form serves to notify the production crew and talent of specific location addresses, dates, times, script units, and pages of scheduling the videotape production of the teleplay. The schedule also sets alternate dates, projected equipment set-up, location strike times, and approximate times for completing the shoot.

Glossary

Shooting Day 1   This area of the form sets a specific date (weekday, month, and day) for the first shooting day. The production schedule form also firms up an alternate rain date. Full teleplays are lengthy productions generally. A half hour teleplay will generally take

5 full work days to videotape. A two-hour teleplay will take 4 weeks or 20 work days to complete.

Location Site   The remote environment/place approved for the shoot after site survey was completed should be noted here. This names the building, geographic area, etc., where the videotaping is to take place. The street address of the location site should also be recorded here.

Location Map No.   This notation relates the location site and address to a municipal map of the geographic area (e.g., H-3).

Location Host   The name of the location personnel responsible for the facility/area where the shoot is to occur should be recorded here. This is the everyday contact person with whom the producer will cooperate on details of the location and the shoot. A contact telephone number where the location host can be reached should be included.

Crew Call   The time and place of the production crew starting crew call should be entered here.

Cast Call   The time and place for the arrival call for the cast is also listed. Because the cast does not need the lead time for equipment set-up as the production crew do, the cast call can be up to an hour later than the production crew call. Time should be allotted for make-up if make-up is being required for the cast.

Set-up   This entry is a range of time including a deadline for the production crew to complete all equipment set-up and checks of the equipment.

Projected Strike Time   This time sets an approximate termination hour for completing the shoot and striking the location.

Shoot Order Units   The individual units of the teleplay that will be shot on the scheduled shooting day and the order in which they will be shot are recorded in this column.

Script Pages   This column records the script pages for the units that will be produced during the shoot.

Setting   The specific setting within the location where the videotaping will occur is listed here.

Approx. Time   A range of hours and minutes approximating the time needed to complete the script units proposed for production during that shooting day.

Cast   The cast members who will be a part of the videotaping are listed here.

Action Properties   On many location shoots, some action properties are required, e.g., an automobile, an animal. Those action properties required for the respective script units are recorded here.

Comments   The comments section allows the producer the opportunity to make any additional notes to be called to the attention of the crew and cast.

- **Audio Plot Form**

Production process: Video drama preproduction

Responsibility: Audio director

Purpose: To facilitate and encourage the design of sound perspective and recording on the remote location video drama production.

Objective: The audio plot form is designed to prompt the audio director to weight the location environment and sound production values in the planning for audio equipment and quality microphone pick-up and recording during remote drama videotaping.

Notes on use: The audio plot form is intended to encourage preproduction by the audio director. One plot for every location set is probably adequate, although multiple forms might be required in a detailed and complicated sound recording take.

Glossary

Script Page The audio director will require an orientation to the respective page(s) of a script for every location set to be miked.

Script Unit The script unit being videotaped is also another orientation to the script to benefit the audio director.

Shot No. The number of the shot being videotaped from the shot list is a good determination for the audio director of whether there is need for any significant changes in sound design during a shoot. The shot number from the master script should be recorded here.

Location This notation is a reminder of the location environment in which the videotaping is to occur.

Lighting This area of the plot notes the basic facts for sound perspective design: inside or outside, day or night.

Sound This choice of sound recording needs indicates what would be required on the set by the audio director. Synchronous sound indicates that both audio and video will be recorded during a take; silent means that video only is required; wild means that a sound track will be recorded with or without video. This is required when a location ambience track is called for in production design during editing.

Microphone The audio director can make a choice of microphones to be used during videotaping the proposed shot.

3:4 Video Frame Insofar as the audio design of a shot is affected and in return affects what the shot shows, occasionally the composition of the framing will dictate the sound perspective needs. The audio director may sketch from the master script elements of the storyboard frame as an aid to sound recording design for specific shots of the production.

Framing The extent of the framing of subjects will also determine sound perspective design. The composition of framing is indicated by checking the appropriate symbols for frame composition as checked on the master script for the shot.

Sound Perspective When a change in framing is indicated, it could require a change in sound perspective or that the change in framing be calculated in the basic sound design. The new framing composition is indicated by checking the appropriate symbols for new framing. Quality sound perspective creates the auditory sense that when an actor is framed closely, sound levels

should be higher; when an actor is framed at a distance, sound levels should be lower. Close or distant framing will also indicate to an audio director that careful use of a microphone mount will have to be controlled to avoid catching the mike in the camera shot or the presence of mike or boom shadows in the shot.

Bird's Eye Floor Plan The best preproduction information for the audio director is the floor plan for the location with actor(s) blocking and movement indicated. This should be sketched in this box from the master script. Where the camera is to be placed is also important to the audio director, sound design, and microphone and mike grip placement during production.

Description of Take/Unit Any director's notes on the elements of the take that will affect sound design and recording should be noted here. For example, excessive movement of actors or properties and expressive gestures could affect sound recording and control on a location. The fact that some sound playback may be required during a take would be noted here.

In-cue The in-cue, either from script dialogue or action, can affect the sound design of a take. That in-cue should be noted here.

Out-cue The out-cue or final words of dialogue or action can affect sound design. Notation of that cue should be made here.

- **Lighting Plot Form**

Production process: Video drama preproduction

Responsibility: Lighting director

Purpose: To prepare and organize the lighting design of the video drama remote location production shoot.

Objective: The lighting plot form is designed to facilitate the lighting design for the lighting director for every different location set. The plot serves to preplan the placement of lighting instruments, kind of lighting, lighting control, and lighting design. When lighting is preplanned, lighting equipment needs are easily realized and provided.

Notes on use: The lighting plot form is created to encourage preplanning for lighting design and production. Hence, the more lighting needs and aesthetics that can be anticipated, the better the lighting production tasks.

At the minimum, every different location set lighting design should be created in advance of the location production. Lighting design can begin after the master script is complete. The essentials to planning lighting design are the bird's eye floor plan, the actor(s) blocking, the time of day, and the mood of the script.

A different plot is not required for every shot on the shot list. Base lighting design need not change as camera placement changes, but changes of location will require all new lighting set-up and design. It is these changes that the lighting director needs to be aware of.

Glossary

Script Page The lighting director will require an orientation to the respective page(s) of a script for every location set to be lighted.

Script Unit The script unit being videotaped is also another orientation to the script to benefit the lighting director.

Shot No. The number of the shot being videotaped from the shot list is a good determination for the lighting director of whether there is need for any significant changes in lighting design during a shoot. The shot number from the master script should be recorded here.

Location This notation is a reminder of the location environment in which the videotaping is to occur.

Lighting This area of the plot notes the basic facts for lighting design: inside or outside, day or night.

Light Change It is important to lighting design and lighting control to know if the script or the director plans any change of lighting during the shot being videotaped. This notation alerts the lighting director to that need.

Mood One of the functions of lighting design is to create mood. An indication of the mood to be created in the shot is noted here.

3:4 Video Frame Insofar as the lighting design of a shot is affected and in return affects what the shot shows, occasionally the composition of the framing will dictate the lighting needs. The lighting director may sketch from the master script elements of the storyboard frame as an aid to lighting design for specific shots of the production.

Framing The extent of the framing of subjects will also determine lighting design. The composition of framing is indicated by checking the appropriate symbols for frame composition as checked on the master script for the shot.

Change When a change in framing is indicated, it could trigger a change in lighting or that the change in framing be calculated in the basic lighting design. The new framing composition is indicated by checking the appropriate symbols for new framing.

Bird's Eye Floor Plan The best preproduction information for the lighting director is the floor plan for the location with actors' blocking and movement indicated. This should be sketched in this box from the master script. Where the camera is to be placed is also important to the lighting director and lighting design.

Description of Take/Unit Any director's notes on the elements of the take that will affect lighting design should be noted here.

Lighting Instruments/Lighting Accessories/Filters/Property Lights/Windows These lists in the plot form are designed to assist the lighting director in considering all elements of lighting design and materials in the preparation of the lighting plot. A lighting director can make notation in the proper space in planning for the particular design of each set.

In-cue A lighting director may find it convenient to make note of the in-cue from the script when (on what action or dialogue) the lighting design is to begin.

Out-cue The same notation on an out-cue of action or dialogue for the end of a shot or a change of lighting may be advantageous to the lighting director.

- **Equipment Checklist Form**

Production process: Video drama preproduction

Responsibility: Camera operator, videotape recorder operator, lighting director, audio director

Purpose: To suggest and account for all possible equipment and accessories necessary for a successful remote video drama shoot.

Objective: The equipment checklist form is an all-inclusive checklist for equipment and accessories hardware that may be used or needed on a video production location site. The checklist notes first the equipment available to the production crew, usually the equipment owned by the production facility. Second, the list notes the equipment that may have to be purchased for the shoot. Third, the checklist allows for notation for any equipment that may have to be rented for the shoot. There are blank lines in equipment groups to personalize the checklist for an individual production or facility.

Glossary

Location(s) The location(s) for which the equipment will be needed should be noted here.

Avl This abbreviation stands for available equipment that may be owned by the production facility. A check in this column indicates that the equipment or accessory is available to the production crew and free to be used on the scheduled production day.

Pch This abbreviation stands for purchase and indicates that the needed equipment or accessory will have to be purchased for the production project. Items checked as needed to be purchased will probably require some other requisition step and approval. The checklist also does not imply when the purchasing will be done or by whom. This is the responsibility of the production crew member.

Rnt This abbreviation stands for rent and indicates that the needed equipment or accessory is not available, perhaps too expensive to purchase for the shoot, and will have to be rented from a supplier. Similar to items checked in the purchase column, additional steps may be required in the process of obtaining the rented equipment. Some requisition may have to be made, approval received, and rental details made.

Camera/Recorder/Tripod/Test Equipment/Audio/Power Supplies/Lighting/Cables These areas of the form listed are an attempt to anticipate all possible equipment and accessories needs for a remote video production. Many items may be superfluous. They are listed as an attempt to suggest all possible production needs and equally to suggest the use of some hardware that could be needed during a remote location shoot. One way to use this checklist is to permit it to suggest hardware elements to make the experience of a remote video shoot smooth and productive.

Miscellaneous This area of the form is the result of years of remote video production experience and represents many production disasters during which these elements could have made a difference. Some items are redundant; some may suggest some use not before anticipated. Most items are helpful to the good order and task facilitation on location.

• **Video Continuity Notes Form**

Production process: Video drama production

Responsibility: Continuity secretary

Purpose: To record during remote videotaping the details of all elements of the production as an aid to reestablishing details for sequential takes. The need is to facilitate a continuity of production details so that editing across takes is continuous.

Objective: The video continuity form is a record of all possible video production details (e.g., location, talent, properties, dialogue) that must carry over from take to take and across edits in postproduction. The nature of single camera production is the fact that although videotaped takes are separate in production, the final video editing of various takes must look continuous. The continuity form records specific details at all facets of production and records them to reestablish the detail in subsequent videotaping.

Notes on use: The form is designed to be used for each separate shot being taken in single camera remote field production. This means that for any single shot with many takes, one continuity notes page should be used. In preparing for a lengthy remote shoot involving many shots to be achieved and many camera and lighting set-ups, many copies of this form will have to be made.

The person keeping continuity notes should be observant. The role demands attention to the slightest detail of the production that may have to be reestablished in another camera take. The role needs a crew person with 100% of the time spent on note taking.

Admittedly, the immediacy of replaying video on a playback monitor on location is a fast check on any detail in a previous videotaped take. Although playback is fast, it is time-consuming and is not a habit that a director should have. Careful continuity notes are still a requirement in remote single camera video drama production.

Glossary

Slate No. A production slate may have a number attached to it. That number is recorded here.

Continuity Secretary The continuity secretary's name should be recorded here. The extent of detail necessary in the production of remote single camera video drama is so great that a full time continuity secretary is a necessity. Continuity note taking is not a hit or miss task in remote production.

Set-up/Location A description or sketch of the location or the set-up of the environment is required here. Note

should be taken of things that were moved (e.g., action properties) to be replaced.

Interior/Exterior These choices allow the notation as to whether the shoot is indoor or outdoor.

Day/Night These choices allow the notation of time of day.

Sync Cam 1/2 This alternative is the indication that the shoot is video and audio synchronous recording and indicates which audio channel is being used for recording the audio signal, channel 1 or channel 2.

Silent This choice indicates that the camera is taking video without recording any audio signal.

Wildtrack Wildtrack means that audio signals are being recorded without video. For example, to record a portion of location ambience for later audio mixing would not require video signals also.

WT with Cam This alternative, wildtrack with camera, indicates that a wildtrack is being recorded with a video signal also.

Sequence No. Some remote production video units are parts of a numbered sequence. This entry is used to record the sequence number being videotaped.

Shot No. When a shot list is being followed on location, the sequential number of the shot being videotaped is recorded here.

Script Page No. For a script being produced with numbered pages, the page number of the script being videotaped is recorded in this space.

Shot List Page No. When a lengthy shot list is being videotaped, the page number of the shot list being videotaped is recorded here.

Costume/Make-up/Properties Notes The area should be used to verbally record all details noticed during production that may have to be reestablished for a subsequent shot. Note should be taken of any costume use (e.g., a tie off-centered, a pocket flap tucked in), make-up detail (e.g., smudged lipstick, position of a wound), or property use (e.g., half-smoked cigarette in the right hand between the index and middle finger or fresh ice cream cone in the left hand).

Tape No. This should be a record of the numerically coded videotape being recorded for this shot. This record should coordinate this shot with a particular videocassette.

Circle Takes (1–10) This area of the form facilitates record of each subsequent take of a shot or scene. The best use of these boxes is to circle each number representing the take in progress until the take is satisfactorily videotaped.

End Board The normal practice of indicating on the videotape leader what take of a shot is being recorded is to use the slate. If a particular take is flubbed or messed up for a minor problem (e.g., an actor missing a line), a producer might simply indicate that instead of stopping the taping and beginning from scratch. The crew keeps going by starting over without stopping. Because the slate then was not used to record at the beginning of the retake, an end board is used—the slate is recorded on tape at the end of the take instead of at the beginning. This note will alert the postproduction crew not to look for a slate at the beginning of that take but at the end.

Timer/Counter This area of the form should be used to record either a consecutive stopwatch time or the consecutive videotape recorder digital counter number. Both of these times should be a record of the length into the videotape where this take is recorded. Therefore, the stopwatch or the counter should be at zero when the tape is rewound to its beginning at the start of the tape. It is a good practice for the videotape recorder operator to have the habit of calling the counter numbers aloud to the continuity note taker at the beginning of every take.

Reason for Use/Not Good The benefit of the continuity notes is to save the tedium of reviewing all takes after a shoot to make a determination of the quality of each take. If conscientious notes are taken here, a judgmental notation on the quality of each take is recorded and one postproduction chore is complete. Usually, a producer makes a judgment on location anyway in determining whether to retake a shot or to move on to a new shot. The continuity secretary should note whether the take is good or not, and the reason for that judgment.

Action Continuity details on any action during the take should be noted here. For example, the direction talent takes when turning or the hand used to open a door should be listed.

Dialogue An area of continuity interest can be the dialogue of the script. Here notation should be made of any quirk of dialogue used in a take that may have to be repeated in a take intended for a matched edit.

- **Talent Release Form**

Production process: Video drama production

Responsibility: Producer

Purpose: To give the producer legal rights over the video and audio recording of individual talent.

Objective: The talent release form is a legal document, which when filled out and signed by talent, gives to the producer and the producing organization the legal right to use both video and audio recording of an individual for publication. This form is especially necessary in the case of talent when profit may be gained from the eventual sale of the video product. If talent contracts were completed and signed, talent releases were probably included. When talent volunteer their services or perform for only a nominal fee or other gratuity, a signed talent release is recommended. Generally, any talent being featured in video and audio taping should sign a talent release before the final video production is aired.

Glossary

Talent Name This entry should contain the name of the individual talent recorded on video or audio.

Recording Location The location site of the video or audio recording should be entered here.

Producer The name of the supervising producer should be entered here.

Producing Organization The incorporated name of the video producing organization should be entered here.

Note: The expression, "For value received," may imply that some remuneration, even a token remuneration, is required for the form to be legally binding. When there is any doubt about the legal nature of the document, consult a lawyer.

PRODUCTION BUDGET

VIDEO DRAMA PRODUCTION

Producer: Production Title:
Director: Author:
                                   Length: :

No. Preproduction Days: ☐ Hours: ☐ First Shooting Date: /   /
No. Studio Shoot Days: ☐ Hours: ☐ Completion Date: /   /
No. Location Days: ☐ Hours: ☐ Location Sites:
No. Post Production Days: ☐ Hours: ☐

SUMMARY OF PRODUCTION COSTS		ESTIMATED	ACTUAL
1. Story, Other Rights and Clearances			
2. Script			
3. Producing Staff			
4. Directing Staff			
5. Talent			
6. Benefits			
7. Production Staff			
8. Camera and VTR			
9. Set Design and Construction			
10. Set Operations			
11. Lighting/Electrical			
12. Set Decorating			
13. Props, Animals, Vehicles			
14. Wardrobe			
15. Make-up and Hairdressing			
16. Sound			
17. Location Expenses			
18. Transportation			
19. Videotape Stock			
20. Post Production Editing			
21. Music			
22.	Sub Total		
23. Contingency			
	Grand Total		

COMMENTS

STORY RIGHTS, OTHER RIGHTS AND CLEARANCES	ESTIMATED	ACTUAL
1. Story Rights Purchased		
2.		
3. Other Rights		
4. Music Clearances		
5.		
Sub Total		

SCRIPT	ESTIMATED	ACTUAL
6. Writer(s) Salaries: No. ( ) @ ( )		
7.		
8. Secretary: No. ( ) @ ( )		
9. Secretary: No. ( ) @ ( )		
10.		
11. Story Editor(s): No. ( ) @ ( )		
12.		
13. Office Supplies		
14.		
15. Searches (authenticity, libel avoidance, etc.)		
16. Travel Expenses		
17. Photocopying		
18. Telephone		
19. Postage		
20. Miscellaneous		
21.		
Sub Total		

PRODUCING STAFF								
CREW	ESTIMATED				ACTUAL			
	Days	Rate	O/T Hrs	Total	Days	Rate	O/T Hrs	Total
22. Producer: Preproduction								
23. Production								
24. Post Prod								
25. Prod Mgr: Preproduction								
26. Production								
27. Post Prod								
28.								
29.								
30.								
31. Secretary: No. ( )								
32.								
33. Producer Supplies								
34.								
35. Travel Expenses								
36. Per Diem								
37. Miscellaneous								
38.								
Sub Total								

DIRECTING STAFF

CREW	ESTIMATED				ACTUAL			
	Days	Rate	O/T Hrs	Total	Days	Rate	O/T Hrs	Total
39. Director: Preproduction								
40. Production								
41. Post Prod								
42. Asst Dir: Preproduction								
43. Production								
44. Post Prod								
45.								
46.								
47.								
48. Dialogue Coach								
49. Secretary: No. ( )								
50.								
51. Choreographer(s)								
52. Director's Supplies								
53. Expenses								
54. Miscellaneous								
55.								
Sub Total								

TALENT

	ESTIMATED				ACTUAL			
	Days	Rate	O/T Hrs	Total	Days	Rate	O/T Hrs	Total
56. Talent (Contract)								
57.								
58. Talent (Freelance)								
59.								
60. Specialty Acts								
61.								
62. Stunts								
63. Casting Service Fee								
64. Extra Talent								
65.								
Sub Total								

BENEFITS

	TOTAL
66. Health and Welfare - Pension Plan	
WGA @ %	
DGA @ %	
PGA @ %	
SAG @ %	
IA @ %	
67. Employer Share of Taxes (FICA, etc.)	
Writers	
Producers	

BENEFITS (Con't)

	TOTAL
Directors	
Talent	
IATSE	
Sub Total	

PRODUCTION STAFF
CREW

	ESTIMATED				ACTUAL			
	Days	Rate	O/T Hrs	Total	Days	Rate	O/T Hrs	Total
68. Unit Manager								
69. Preproduction								
70. Production								
71. Post Production								
72.								
73.								
74. Script Supervisor								
75. Technical Advisor								
76. Production Secretary								
77.								
78.								
79. Miscellaneous								
80.								
81. Photocopying								
82.								
Sub Total								

CAMERA

	ESTIMATED				ACTUAL			
	Days	Rate	O/T Hrs	Total	Days	Rate	O/T Hrs	Total
83. Camera Operator								
84.								
85.								
86.								
87. VTR Operator								
88.								
89. Equipment Rental								
90.								
91. Equipment Purchases								
92.								
93. Maintenance/Repair								
94.								
95. Miscellaneous								
96.								
Sub Total								

SET DESIGN AND CONSTRUCTION

	ESTIMATED				ACTUAL			
	Days	Rate	O/T Hrs	Total	Days	Rate	O/T Hrs	Total
97. Art Director								
98. Artist(s)/Draftsman								
99. Construction Labor								
100.								
101. Location Striking								
102. Construction Materials								
103.								
104. Miscellaneous								
105.								
Sub Total								

SET OPERATIONS

	ESTIMATED				ACTUAL			
	Days	Rate	O/T Hrs	Total	Days	Rate	O/T Hrs	Total
106. Grip(s)								
109.								
110. Crane/Dolly Crew								
111.								
112. Craft Service(s)								
113.								
114. Special Effects								
115. Hospitality								
116. Fireman/Police								
117. Dressing Rooms								
118. Effects Purchases								
119. Materials/Purchases								
120. Effects Rentals								
121. Rentals								
Crane								
Mobile Unit(s)								
Camera Plane/Chopper								
Camera Car(s)								
Camera Boat(s)								
Travel Time Allow								
122. Rentals - Other								
123.								
124. Miscellaneous								
125.								
Sub Total								

LIGHTING/ELECTRICAL

	ESTIMATED				ACTUAL			
	Days	Rate	O/T Hrs	Total	Days	Rate	O/T Hrs	Total
126. Lighting Director								
127. Preproduct								
128. Production								
129. Post Prod								
130. Generator Operator(s)								
131. Special Operator(s)								
132.								
133. Expendables (gels,etc)								
134. Equipment Rentals								
135.								
136. Equipment Purchases								
137.								
138. Generator Rental/Fuel								
140. Miscellaneous								
141.								
Sub Total								

SET DECORATION

	ESTIMATED				ACTUAL			
	Days	Rate	O/T Hrs	Total	Days	Rate	O/T Hrs	Total
141. Set Decorator:Preprod								
142. Product								
143.								
144. Set Dressing Labor								
145.								
146. Set Dressing Props								
147. Cleaning/Loss/Damage								
148. Purchases								
149. Rentals								
150.								
151. Miscellaneous								
152.								
Sub Total								

PROPS, ANIMALS, VEHICLES

	ESTIMATED				ACTUAL			
	Days	Rate	O/T Hrs	Total	Days	Rate	O/T Hrs	Total
153. Property Master								
154. Asst Prop Master								
155.								
156. Property Labor								
157. Vehicle(s)								
158.								
159. Livestock								
160.								
161. Animal Handler(s)								

PROPS, ANIMALS, VEHICLES (Con't)

	ESTIMATED				ACTUAL			
	Days	Rate	O/T Hrs	Total	Days	Rate	O/T Hrs	Total
162. Feed/Stabling								
163. SPCA								
164. Action Props Rentals								
165. Action Props Purchased								
166. Cleaning/Loss/Damage								
167. Food								
168. Miscellaneous								
169.								
Sub Total								

WARDROBE

	ESTIMATED				ACTUAL			
	Days	Rate	O/T Hrs	Total	Days	Rate	O/T Hrs	Total
170. Wardrobe Master								
171. Preproduction								
172. Production								
173. Post Production								
174. Wardrobe Labor								
175. Wardrobe Rentals								
176.								
177. Wardrobe Purchases								
178.								
179. Loss/Damage								
180.								
181. Dyeing/Cleaning								
182. Location Load/Unload								
183. Wardrobe Manufacture								
184.								
185. Miscellaneous								
186.								
Sub Total								

MAKE-UP AND HAIRDRESSING

	ESTIMATED				ACTUAL			
	Days	Rate	O/T Hrs	Total	Days	Rate	O/T Hrs	Total
187. Make-up Artist(s)								
188.								
189. Body Make-up								
190. Hairstylist								
191.								
192. Make-up Supplies								
193.								
194. Wig Rentals								
195. Wig Purchases								
196. Hairdressing Supplies								

MAKE-UP AND HAIRDRESSING (Con't)

	ESTIMATED				ACTUAL			
	Days	Rate	O/T Hrs	Total	Days	Rate	O/T Hrs	Total
197. Miscellaneous								
198.								
Sub Total								

SOUND

	ESTIMATED				ACTUAL			
	Days	Rate	O/T Hrs	Total	Days	Rate	O/T Hrs	Total
199. Audio Director								
200. Preproduction								
201. Production								
202. Post Product								
203. Grip/Boom Operator(s)								
204.								
205. Miscellaneous Labor								
206. Equipment Rentals								
207. Equipment Purchases								
208. Miscellaneous								
209.								
Sub Total								

LOCATION EXPENSES

	ESTIMATED				ACTUAL			
	Days	Rate	O/T Hrs	Total	Days	Rate	O/T Hrs	Total
210. Site Rentals/Fees								
211.								
212. Scouting								
Travel								
Car Rental								
Housing								
Per Diem								
213. Shipping								
214. Telephone/Postage								
215. Entertainment/Tips								
216. Location Police/Fire								
217. First Aid/Medical								
218. Rentals: Rooms, etc.								
219. Baggage/Equip Shipping								
210. Miscellaneous								
211.								
Sub Total								

TRANSPORTATION

	ESTIMATED				ACTUAL			
	Days	Rate	O/T Hrs	Total	Days	Rate	O/T Hrs	Total
212. Transportation Captain								
213. Driver(s)								
214.								
215. Vehicle(s)								
216.								
217. Mileage Allowance								
218. Gasoline and Oil								
219. Repair and Maintenance								
220. Miscellaneous								
221.								
Sub Total								

VIDEOTAPE STOCK

	ESTIMATED				ACTUAL			
	Days	Rate	O/T Hrs	Total	Days	Rate	O/T Hrs	Total
222. Videotape:								
1" (:) x ($)								
3/4" (S :20) x ($)								
3/4" (:30) x ($)								
3/4" (:60) x ($)								
223.								
224.								
Sub Total								

POST PRODUCTION EDITING

	ESTIMATED				ACTUAL			
	Days	Rate	O/T Hrs	Total	Days	Rate	O/T Hrs	Total
225. Editor(s)								
226.								
227. Technical Director(s)								
228.								
229. Continuity Expenses								
230. Editing Suite Rental								
231.								
232. SMPTE Coding								
233. Stock Video Footage								
234. Sound Effects								
235. Dupes ( ) x ($)per								
236. Miscellaneous								
237.								
Sub Total								

MUSIC	ESTIMATED				ACTUAL			
	Days	Rate	O/T Hrs	Total	Days	Rate	O/T Hrs	Total
238. Music Purchases								
239. Music Royalities								
240. Song Writer(s) Salary								
241.								
242. Arranger(s)								
243. Copyist(s)								
244. Composer(s)								
245. Recording Facility								
246. Recording Crew								
247. Vocalist(s)								
278. Conductor								
249. Audio Recording Tape								
250.								
251. Miscellaneous								
252.								
	Sub Total							

COMMENTS

SCRIPT BREAKDOWN

VIDEO DRAMA PRODUCTION

Producer:

Director:

Production Title:
Author:
Length: :
Script Length: pages
Page   of
Date: /   /

SCRIPT UNIT	SCRIPT PAGES/ LINES	INT/ EXT	TIME	SETTING	LOCATION	CAST	SHOOT-ING ORDER

VIDEO DRAMA PRODUCTION SCRIPT BREAKDOWN					Page	of	
SCRIPT UNIT	SCRIPT PAGES/ LINES	INT/ EXT	TIME	SETTING	LOCATION	CAST	SHOOT- ING ORDER

LOCATION SITE SURVEY

VIDEO DRAMA PRODUCTION

Producer:	Production Title:
Director:	Author:
Location Scout(s):	Script Unit(s):
	Script Page(s):
Approval:	Date: / /

Location: Site Identification:
Local Contact Person: Comments:
  Name:
  Title:
  Address:
  City: State:
  Phone No.: (   )   -
Facilities Personnel: Comments:
  Name:
  Position Title:
  Address:
  City: State:
  Phone No.: (   )   -

LIGHTING PROBLEMS DEFINED

Light contrast ratios   Existing light control

Lighting intensity   Lighting use

Ceiling height   Floor description

Windows/Compass direction   Special consideration

POWER PROBLEMS DEFINED

Number of power outlets	Number of outlet prongs
Number of separate circuits	Location of circuit breakers
Types of fuses	Portable generator need

AUDIO PROBLEMS DEFINED

Interior environmental sounds	Exterior environmental sounds
Ceiling composition	Floor covering composition
Wall composition	

CAST AND CREW NEEDS

Restroom facilities	Eating facilities
Green room availability	Make-up facilities
Parking arrangements	Loading/unloading restrictions
Freight elevator	Hardware store

CIVIL EMERGENCY SERVICES

Police station   Fire station

LOCATION SECURITY AND EQUIPMENT SAFETY

Facility security   Equipment safe storage

Personnel values security   Overnight storage/security

OTHER RELEVANT INFORMATION

Public area power source   Traffic control

Clearance/Insurance needed   Exterior compass direction

Photographs taken   Location environment drawing/map

Other information:

OTHER COMMENTS/OBSERVATIONS

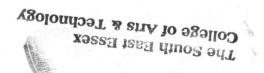

BLOCKING PLOT/STORYBOARD

MASTER SCRIPT

VIDEO DRAMA PRODUCTION

Teleplay Title: _____ Director: _____ Date: / /

Script Page [ ] Script Unit [ ] Shot No. [ ]

3:4 Video Frame

Lighting
☐ Interior
☐ Exterior
☐ Day
☐ Night

Sound
☐ Synchronous
☐ Silent
☐ Wild

Shot
☐ Master
☐ Cut-in
☐ Cut-away

Bird's Eye Floor Plan
Properties/Blocking/Camera

Framing: ☐ XCU ☐ CU ☐ MS ☐ LS ☐ XLS   Change to: ☐ XCU ☐ CU ☐ MS ☐ LS ☐ XLS
Camera Motion: Pan ☐ Tilt ☐ Zoom ☐ Dolly ☐ Truck ☐ Arc ☐ Pedestal ☐ Defocus ☐

Description of Take/Unit   Actors/Movement/Properties

In-Cue   Action/Dialog   Out-Cue   Action/Dialog

Script Page [ ] Script Unit [ ] Shot No. [ ]

3:4 Video Frame

Lighting
☐ Interior
☐ Exterior
☐ Day
☐ Night

Sound
☐ Synchronous
☐ Silent
☐ Wild

Shot
☐ Master
☐ Cut-in
☐ Cut-away

Bird's Eye Floor Plan
Properties/Blocking/Camera

Framing: ☐ XCU ☐ CU ☐ MS ☐ LS ☐ XLS   Change to: ☐ XCU ☐ CU ☐ MS ☐ LS ☐ XLS
Camera Motion: Pan ☐ Tilt ☐ Zoom ☐ Dolly ☐ Truck ☐ Arc ☐ Pedestal ☐ Defocus ☐

Description of Take/Unit   Actors/Movement/Properties

In-Cue   Action/Dialog   Out-Cue   Action/Dialog

| VIDEO DRAMA PRODUCTION BLOCKING PLOT/STORYBOARD | Page | of |

Script Page ☐ Script Unit ☐ Shot No. ☐

Lighting
☐ Interior
☐ Exterior
☐ Day
☐ Night

Sound
☐ Synchronous
☐ Silent
☐ Wild

Shot
☐ Master
☐ Cut-in
☐ Cut-away

Bird's Eye Floor Plan
Properties/Blocking/Camera

3:4 Video Frame

Framing: ☐ XCU ☐ CU ☐ MS ☐ LS ☐ XLS   Change to: ☐ XCU ☐ CU ☐ MS ☐ LS ☐ XLS

Camera Motion: Pan☐ Tilt☐ Zoom☐ Dolly☐ Truck☐ Arc☐ Pedestal☐ Defocus☐

Description of Take/Unit   Actors/Movement/Properties

| In-Cue | Action/Dialog | Out-Cue | Action/Dialog |

Script Page ☐ Script Unit ☐ Shot No. ☐

Lighting
☐ Interior
☐ Exterior
☐ Day
☐ Night

Sound
☐ Synchronous
☐ Silent
☐ Wild

Shot
☐ Master
☐ Cut-in
☐ Cut-away

Bird's Eye Floor Plan
Properties/Blocking/Camera

3:4 Video Frame

Framing: ☐ XCU ☐ CU ☐ MS ☐ LS ☐ XLS   Change to: ☐ XCU ☐ CU ☐ MS ☐ LS ☐ XLS

Camera Motion: Pan☐ Tilt☐ Zoom☐ Dolly☐ Truck☐ Arc☐ Pedestal☐ Defocus☐

Description of Take/Unit   Actors/Movement/Properties

| In-Cue | Action/Dialog | Out-Cue | Action/Dialog |

SHOT LIST

VIDEO DRAMA PRODUCTION

Producer:
Director:
Camera Operator:

Production Title:

Date: / /
Page of

| LOCATION | SHOT | | | | | | CONTENT NOTES |
	NO.	MASTER	CUT-IN	CUT-AWAY	FRAMING	MOTION	

LOCATION	SHOT						CONTENT NOTES
	NO.	MASTER	CUT-IN	CUT-AWAY	FRAMING	MOTION	

VIDEO DRAMA PRODUCTION SHOT LIST   Page   of

PRODUCTION SCHEDULE

VIDEO DRAMA PRODUCTION

Producer: Production Title:

Director: Date: / /
                                   Page   of

SHOOTING DAY 1   RAIN DATE
                                                  __/__/__
_____, _____, ____
   (Weekday)   (Month)   (Day)

Location Site:_____   Location Map No._____

Address:_____
        City_____   State _____

Location Host:_____
Phone No.: (__)___-_____

Crew call:__:___AM/PM
    Address:_____

Cast call:__:___AM/PM
    Address:_____

Set-up:__:___ to ___:___   Projected Strike Time:___:___

SHOOT ORDER UNITS	SCRIPT PAGES	SETTING	APPROX. TIME	CAST	ACTION PROPERTIES
			: to :		
			: to :		
			: to :		
			: to :		
			: to :		

Comments:

SHOOTING DAY 2

_____, _____, _____
(Weekday)   (Month)   (Day)

RAIN DATE
___/___/___

Location Site:_____ Location Map No. _____

Address: _____
      City_____ State _____

Location Host:_____
Phone No.: (___)___-_____

Crew call:___:___AM/PM
    Address:_____

Cast call:___:___AM/PM
    Address:_____

Set-up:___:___ to ___:___   Projected Strike Time:____:___

SHOOT ORDER UNITS	SCRIPT PAGES	SETTING	APPROX. TIME	CAST	ACTION PROPERTIES
			: to :		
			: to :		
			: to :		
			: to :		
			: to :		

SHOOTING DAY 3

_____, _____, _____
(Weekday)   (Month)   (Day)

RAIN DATE
___/___/___

Location Site:_____ Location Map No. _____

Address: _____
      City_____ State _____

Location Host:_____
Phone No.: (___)___-_____

Crew call:___:___AM/PM
    Address:_____

Cast call:___:___AM/PM
    Address:_____

Set-up:___:___ to ___:___   Projected Strike Time:____:___

SHOOT ORDER UNITS	SCRIPT PAGES	SETTING	APPROX. TIME	CAST	ACTION PROPERTIES
			: to :		
			: to :		
			: to :		
			: to :		
			: to :		

SHOOTING DAY 4   RAIN DATE

_____, _____, _____   __/__/__
　　(Weekday)　　　　(Month)　　　(Day)

Location Site:_____ Location Map No. _____

Address: _____

　　　　　City_____ State _____

Location Host: _____
Phone No.: (___)___-_____

Crew call:___:___AM/PM
　　Address:_____

Cast call:___:___AM/PM
　　Address:_____

Set-up:___:___ to ___:___   Projected Strike Time: ___:___

SHOOT ORDER UNITS	SCRIPT PAGES	SETTING	APPROX. TIME	CAST	ACTION PROPERTIES
			: to :		
			: to :		
			: to :		
			: to :		
			: to :		

SHOOTING DAY 5   RAIN DATE

_____, _____, _____   __/__/__
　　(Weekday)　　　　(Month)　　　(Day)

SHOOT ORDER UNITS	SCRIPT PAGES	SETTING	APPROX. TIME	CAST	ACTION PROPERTIES
			: to :		
			: to :		
			: to :		
			: to :		
			: to :		

SHOOTING DAY 6   RAIN DATE
                                                        __/__/__

_____, _____, _____
   (Weekday)   (Month)   (Day)

Location Site:_____ Location Map No._____

Address:_____
        City_____ State _____

Location Host:_____
Phone No.: (__)___-_____

Crew call:__:___AM/PM
    Address:_____

Cast call:__:___AM/PM
    Address:_____

Set-up:__:___ to ___:___   Projected Strike Time:___:____

SHOOT ORDER UNITS	SCRIPT PAGES	SETTING	APPROX. TIME	CAST	ACTION PROPERTIES
			: to :		
			: to :		
			: to :		
			: to :		
			: to :		

AUDIO PLOT

VIDEO DRAMA PRODUCTION

Teleplay Title:	Audio Director:	Date: / /

Script Page:	Script Unit:	Shot No.:	Location:

Lighting
☐ Interior
☐ Exterior
☐ Day
☐ Night

Sound
☐ Synchronous
☐ Silent
☐ Wild

Microphone
☐ Directional
☐ Wireless
☐ _____

Bird's Eye Floor Plan
Properties/Blocking/Camera/Lights
Mic Grip/Mic Holder/Cable Run

3:4 Video Frame
Framing: ☐ XCU ☐ CU ☐ MS ☐ LS ☐ XLS

Sound Perspective: ☐ close ☐ distant

Description of Take/Unit

Actors/Movement/Properties
Location Playback Requirement

In-Cue	Action/Dialog	Out-Cue	Action/Dialog

Comments:

LIGHTING PLOT

VIDEO DRAMA PRODUCTION

Teleplay Title: Lighting Director: Date: /   /

Script Page ☐   Script Unit ☐   Shot No. ☐   Location:

Lighting
- ☐ Interior
- ☐ Exterior
- ☐ Day
- ☐ Night

Light Change
- ☐ Yes
- ☐ No

Mood
_____
_____

3:4 Video Frame
Framing: ☐ XCU ☐ CU ☐ MS ☐ LS ☐ XLS

Bird's Eye Floor Plan
Props/Blocking/Camera Placement
Lighting Instruments

Change to: ☐ XCU ☐ CU ☐ MS ☐ LS ☐ XLS

Description of Take/Unit   Actors/Movement/Properties

Lighting Instruments
Key Lights:

Fill Lights:

Soft Lights:

Lighting Accessories
Barn Doors:

Flags:

Gobo:

Filters
Spun Glass:

Gels:

Screens:

Scrims:

Neutral Density:

Property Lights
Lamps:

Ceiling:

Other:

Windows   N
Compass Directions: W   E
     S
Blacked:

Gels:

In-Cue   Action/Dialog

Out-Cue   Action/Dialog

Comments:

EQUIPMENT CHECKLIST

VIDEO DRAMA PRODUCTION

Director:

Camera Operator:

Videotape Recorder Operator:

Audio Director:

Lighting Director:

Production Title:

Date: / /

First Shooting Date: / /

Location(s):

Avl Pch Rnt

CAMERA

- Video Camera
- Lenses
- Filters
- AC/DC Monitor
- Lg Screen Monitor
- _____

RECORDER

- Videotape Recorder
- _____
- _____

TRIPOD

- Tripod w/Head
- Camera Head Adapter
- Dolly
- _____

TEST EQUIPMENT

- Waveform Monitor
- Vectorscope
- Grey Scale
- Registration Chart
- White Card
- Headphones
- _____

AUDIO

- Shot gun Microphone
- Lavaliere Microphone
- Hand-held Microphone
- Fishpole
- Wind screens

Avl Pch Rnt

AUDIO (continued)

- Mixer
- Adapter plugs
- Earphone
- Headphones
- _____

POWER SUPPLIES

- Batteries for Camera
- Batteries for Recorder
- Batteries for Monitor
- AC Power Converter
- Microphone Batteries

LIGHTING

- Light Kit
- Soft Light Kit
- Barn Doors
- Spun Glass Filters
- Blue Gels
- Orange Gels
- Screens
- Scrims
- ND Filters
- Aluminum Foil
- Wooden Clothes Pins
- Light Meter
- Reflector
- Spare Bulbs
- Flags
- _____

Avl Pch Rnt

CABLES

- ☐ ☐ ☐ Multi-pin Cable Camera to Recorder
- ☐ ☐ ☐ Video Cable Camera to Recorder
- ☐ ☐ ☐ Video Cable Camera to Waveform Monitor/ Scope
- ☐ ☐ ☐ Video Cable Scope to Monitor
- ☐ ☐ ☐ Audio Mixer Cable to Recorder
- ☐ ☐ ☐ Audio Extension Cables
- ☐ ☐ ☐ _____

MISCELLANEOUS

- ☐ ☐ ☐ Video tape
- ☐ ☐ ☐ Teleprompter
- ☐ ☐ ☐ Teleprompter Script
- ☐ ☐ ☐ Cue Card Paper
- ☐ ☐ ☐ Duct Tape
- ☐ ☐ ☐ Masking Tape
- ☐ ☐ ☐ Spare Fuses
- ☐ ☐ ☐ Tool Kit
- ☐ ☐ ☐ Stopwatch
- ☐ ☐ ☐ Slate
- ☐ ☐ ☐ Chalk
- ☐ ☐ ☐ Eraser
- ☐ ☐ ☐ Bullhorn
- ☐ ☐ ☐ Walkie-Talkie
- ☐ ☐ ☐ Dulling Spray
- ☐ ☐ ☐ Talent Release Forms
- ☐ ☐ ☐ Step Ladder
- ☐ ☐ ☐ Lens Cleaner and Tissue

Avl Pch Rnt

- ☐ ☐ ☐ Sewing Kit
- ☐ ☐ ☐ Paper, Pens, Felt Markers
- ☐ ☐ ☐ Rope
- ☐ ☐ ☐ Barrier Cones
- ☐ ☐ ☐ Poster Board
- ☐ ☐ ☐ Flashlight
- ☐ ☐ ☐ Scissors
- ☐ ☐ ☐ 100' Power Cords
- ☐ ☐ ☐ Staple Gun and Staples
- ☐ ☐ ☐ Power Outlet Boxes
- ☐ ☐ ☐ _____
- ☐ ☐ ☐ _____
- ☐ ☐ ☐ _____
- ☐ ☐ ☐ _____
- ☐ ☐ ☐ _____
- ☐ ☐ ☐ _____
- ☐ ☐ ☐ _____
- ☐ ☐ ☐ _____
- ☐ ☐ ☐ _____
- ☐ ☐ ☐ _____
- ☐ ☐ ☐ _____
- ☐ ☐ ☐ _____
- ☐ ☐ ☐ _____

VIDEO CONTINUITY NOTES

VIDEO DRAMA PRODUCTION

PRODUCTION TITLE:				SLATE NO.
DIRECTOR:	CONTINUITY SEC'Y			DATE / /
SET-UP/LOCATION	INTERIOR	DAY	SYNC Cam 1/2 SILENT	SEQUENCE NO.
	EXTERIOR	NIGHT	WILDTRACK WT with Cam	SHOT NO.
	SCRIPT PAGE NO.		SHOT LIST PAGE NO.	

COSTUME/MAKE-UP/PROPERTIES NOTES

TAPE NO.										
CIRCLE TAKES	1	2	3	4	5	6	7	8	9	10
END BOARD										
TIMER										
COUNTER										
REASON FOR USE/ NOT GOOD										

ACTION   DIALOGUE

TALENT RELEASE FORM
VIDEO DRAMA PRODUCTION

Talent Name: _____
(Please Print)

Project Title: _____

For value received and without further consideration, I hereby consent to the use of all photographs, videotapes or film, taken of me and/or recordings made of my voice and/or written extraction, in whole or in part, of such recordings or musical performance

at _____ on _____ 19___
   (Recording Location)   *(Month)*   *(Day)*   *(Year)*

by_____ for_____
   (Producer)   *(Producing Organization)*

and/or others with its consent, for the purposes of illustration, advertising, or publication in any manner.

Talent Name_____
              (Signature)

Address_____ City_____

State _____ Zip Code _____

Date:____/___/____

If the subject is a minor under the laws of the state where modeling, acting, or performing is done:

Guardian _____ Guardian _____
         (Signature)   *(Please Print)*

Address _____ City _____

State _____ Zip Code _____

Date:____/____/____

Chapter 4

Television Commercial Production

INTRODUCTION

• The Television Commercial

There is probably no other television genre that has been the subject of more study and development than the television commercial. There is little doubt that the genre of the 10-, 20-, 30- or 60-second commercial is an art form. In a commercial all the elements necessary for the judgment of art, i.e., unifying themes, intense interest, and complex plots, can be found in any evening's commercial television viewing.

No other video genre has such a rich history of achieving persuasive effects from controlled manipulation of perceptive hooks as the commercial. The orchestrated devices of attention getting and interest holding are paramount among commercial production techniques. Advertisers weigh such persuasive techniques as credibility, logic and reasonability of advertising copy, and the psychological profile of the target audience in the interest of selling a product or service.

A dramatized commercial can present all the elements of quality drama from character presentation and development, plot development, crisis, and resolution in 30 seconds. Commercial content today runs the gamut from serious drama to high comedy, from clever salesmanship to serious art.

• Film Versus Video

There are many advantages to either film or video as the recording medium for the production of the television commercial. Each producer or director has weighed the pros and cons of each technology. Film and video have their defenders and detractors. The all-video production

of the television commercial is gaining in popularity. Much of that popularity is the growing dissatisfaction of professionals with the cost of film stock, and with the slow process of developing and printing.

Video gains in popularity with the speed of production, the immediacy with which a videotaped take may be viewed, and the acknowledgment that whatever the recording medium, it is still viewed through the medium of the small screen in competition with the multichannel receiver for the attention of the audience.

The limited life of a television commercial on the medium is also reason for choosing video. The time, cost, and effort in film production does not pay for the short contract life of an advertised campaign to promote a product or service.

THE PREPRODUCTION PROCESS

Unlike other video production genres, the television commercial has a well-developed organization and hierarchy of personnel. Many commercials are the products of established advertising agencies with equally well-established processes for the creative development of all forms of advertising. Although many agencies have their directories of producers and directors who work for them in a contractual or salaried capacity, just as many agencies are open to accepting bids from the independent freelance producers or directors.

Even for the amateur producer or director, beginning the production of a television commercial entails seeking out a client. In some academic forums, it is not uncommon for the student producer to seek out a client or product

FLOWCHART AND CHECKLIST FOR TELEVISION COMMERCIAL PRODUCTION

PREPRODUCTION	PRODUCTION	POSTPRODUCTION
PRODUCER (P)		
□ (1) Contacts client	□ (1) Supervises crew call	□ (1) Arranges postproduction schedule and facilities
□ (2) Researches/reviews marketing problem	□ (2) Meets location host	□ (2) Supervises postproduction preparation
□ (3) Writes script (television script form)	□ (3) Supervises location rearrangement	□ (3) Observes editing with director
□ (4) Designs storyboard (storyboard form)	□ (4) Handles production crew and cast ensemble details	
□ (5) Prepares budget (budget form)	□ (5) Prepares production of stills, graphics, product shot, etc.	
□ (6) Chooses and meets with director	□ (6) Secures talent release form signatures (talent release form)	
□ (7) Casts script		
□ (8) Obtains legal clearances		
□ (9) Supervises location scouting (location site survey form)		
□ (10) Designs production schedule (production schedule form)		
□ (11) Obtains insurance; notifies police		
DIRECTOR (D)		
□ (1) Meets with producer	□ (1) Holds production meeting	□ (1) Directs postproduction preparation: script and storyboard
□ (2) Assists in casting script	□ (2) Directs location rearrangement	□ (2) Makes editing decisions
□ (3) Does script breakdown (script breakdown form)	□ (3) Supervises equipment set-ups	□ (3) Edits rough edit
□ (4) Directs location scouting and site survey (location site survey form)	□ (4) Blocks actors without lines	□ (4) Reviews rough edit
□ (5) Designs blocking plots (blocking plot form)	□ (5) Rehearses actors with lines	□ (5) Makes final edit
□ (6) Develops shot list (shot list form)	□ (6) Blocks camera	□ (6) Oversees final audio mixing and sweetening
□ (7) Chooses and meets with CO	□ (7) Rehearses both camera and actors	□ (7) Labels master edit
□ (8) Chooses and meets with LD	□ (8) Makes changes/rehearses	
□ (9) Chooses CS	□ (9) Calls for take	If the director does not edit:
	□ (10) Oversees production of stills, graphics, product shot, etc.	**TECHNICAL DIRECTOR/EDITOR (TD/E)**
	□ (11) Announces intentions/strike	□ (1) Edits from editing cue sheet under supervision of producer
		□ (2) Edits rough edit
		□ (3) Makes final edit
CAMERA OPERATOR (CO)		
□ (1) Meets with director and producer	□ (1) Arranges camera equipment/accessories pick-up/delivery	□ (1) Returns remote camera equipment and accessories
□ (2) Works storyboard, blocking plots, and shot list	□ (2) Sets up location camera and performs check	□ (2) Reports damaged, lost, malfunctioning equipment or accessories
□ (3) Prepares camera equipment/accessories list (equipment checklist form)	□ (3) Blocks camera position	
□ (4) Chooses/meets with VTRO	□ (4) Rehearses camera	
□ (5) Chooses/meets with AD	□ (5) Videotapes take	
	□ (6) Strikes camera equipment	
LIGHTING DIRECTOR (LD)		
□ (1) Meets with director	□ (1) Arranges lighting equipment/accessories pick-up/delivery	□ (1) Returns remote lighting equipment and accessories
□ (2) Works storyboard, shot list, and blocking plots	□ (2) Sets up location lighting and performs check	□ (2) Reports damaged, lost, malfunctioning equipment or accessories
□ (3) Designs lighting plots (lighting plot form)	□ (3) Strikes lighting equipment	
□ (4) Prepares equipment/accessories list (equipment checklist form)		

VIDEOTAPE RECORDER OPERATOR (VTRO)

- [ ] (1) Meets with CO
- [ ] (2) Works script and shot list
- [ ] (3) Orders videotape stock
- [ ] (4) Prepares videotape recording equipment/accessories list (equipment checklist form)
- [ ] (5) Labels and organizes tape stock

- [ ] (1) Arranges videotape recording equipment/accessories pick-up/delivery
- [ ] (2) Sets up location videotape recording and performs check
- [ ] (3) Responds to director's call for roll tape
- [ ] (4) Monitors vectorscope
- [ ] (5) Strikes videotape recording equipment

- [ ] (1) Removes record buttons and labels both videocassettes and cases
- [ ] (2) Reorders source tapes to master storyboard and script
- [ ] (3) Returns remote videotape recording equipment and accessories
- [ ] (4) Reports damaged, lost, malfunctioning equipment or accessories

AUDIO DIRECTOR (AD)

- [ ] (1) Meets with VTRO
- [ ] (2) Works storyboard, blocking plots, and shot list
- [ ] (3) Designs audio plot (audio plot form)
- [ ] (4) Prepares audio recording equipment/accessories list (equipment checklist form)

- [ ] (1) Arranges audio recording equipment/accessories pick-up/delivery
- [ ] (2) Sets up location audio recording and performs check
- [ ] (3) Monitors audio input: dialogue and noise, mike in frame
- [ ] (4) Responds to director's directions
- [ ] (5) Strikes audio recording equipment/accessories

- [ ] (1) Returns remote videotape and sound recording equipment and accessories
- [ ] (2) Reports damaged, lost, malfunctioning equipment or accessories
- [ ] (3) Oversees audio quality of rough edit and final edited master
- [ ] (4) Performs final audio mixing and sweetening

CONTINUITY SECRETARY (CS)

- [ ] (1) Prepares continuity sheets (continuity notes form)
- [ ] (2) Coordinates with VTRO

- [ ] (1) Observes and records continuity details
- [ ] (2) Releases actors after cut
- [ ] (3) Establishes details before take

- [ ] (1) Reorders continuity sheets to master storyboard

SLATE PERSON (SP)

- [ ] (1) Handles and updates slate
- [ ] (2) Coordinates with CS and VTRO
- [ ] (3) Follows director/slates video leader

MICROPHONE BOOM GRIP/OPERATOR (MBG/O)

- [ ] (1) Observes blocking/rehearsals/lighting instruments/shadows
- [ ] (2) Observes CU/LS framing/shadows
- [ ] (3) Booms and mikes dialogue during shot

ACTORS/TALENT (T)

- [ ] (1) Learns lines, develops characterizations
- [ ] (2) Fits costumes, tests make-up

- [ ] (1) Prepares for costuming and make-up
- [ ] (2) Stands in location set for lighting, sound, and video checks
- [ ] (3) Follows director: blocking, rehearsal, action, cut, freeze, take
- [ ] (4) Checks with CS
- [ ] (5) Is available/out-of-the-way

from the marketplace as a way to best approximate the real world of television advertising.

• **Personnel**

Producer (P). The producer, either attached to an advertising agency or freelancing, is the catalyst in beginning the preproduction process of commercial production. The producer searches out the client, chooses the director, writes the script, prepares the budget, and oversees all details of preproduction.

Director (D). The director is generally chosen by the producer, usually for the creative experience needed in the production of the commercial. Although the creative abilities of the director are much in demand, the director may have little creative input into the production of the commercial. In many advertising agencies, the director is expected to oversee the production of the commercial from the storyboard (usually the product of a creative department or a producer) to the television screen without any input, control, or change. Some directors insist on the right to do their own storyboard or at least the right to change the existing one.

Assuming that the director is either in charge of or participates in the development of the storyboard, the director's responsibilities include the script breakdown, choosing the camera operator, designing blocking plots, and the shot list. Given that many directors see the overall look of a commercial to be a trademark of their style of production, they also choose a lighting director for the production who will give their look in the lighting design for the commercial.

Camera operator (CO). The first responsibility of the camera operator is to prepare camera equipment and accessories lists, indicating what equipment is available and what has to be rented or purchased. The camera operator is expected to work over the script and the shot list before the shoot, and choose a videotape operator with whom to work.

Lighting director (LD). Once a director has completed the storyboard and blocking plot for the shoot, a lighting director is chosen to begin preproduction work on lighting. Lighting designs have to be drawn up as a measure of needed equipment. Equipment from lamps and cables to generators and gels will have to be made available, rented, or purchased.

Videotape recorder operator (VTRO). The preproduction responsibilities of the videotape recorder operator begin with equipment inventory and include listing what is available and what needs to be rented or purchased. The remaining preproduction responsibility of the videotape recorder operator is to order the supply of videotape stock needed for the shoot. This entails purchasing videotape cassettes. These cassettes will then need to be organized and labeled. The videotape recorder operator should design some enumeration or code system to facilitate an ordered recording of tapes during the shoot and an equal reordering of tapes after the shoot as a preparation to postproduction editing.

Audio director (AD). The audio director begins preproduction responsibilities for the commercial by planning audio production and recording from the script. Preproduction audio planning entails checking location site survey forms and knowing the audio requirements of the script. Audio recording planning requires an equipment and accessories check list.

Continuity secretary (CS). The continuity secretary is responsible for the proper and detailed note taking necessary to record all production details of the location shoot. Preproduction responsibility entails organizing a structured approach to record notes of the production. The continuity secretary will need some set of codes, lists of crew and actors, and a videotape stock code.

• **Preproduction Stages**

Contacting a client (P 1). The starting point for the producer is the client with a product or service and a marketing problem. The worst client for a producer is one who thinks he knows what to do and only wants a yea-sayer producer. The best client for a producer is one who respects the craft and skills of a producer and is willing to turn the commercial project over to a professional. The client who makes few demands can also be the client who respects the medium and those who work in it. The most a client should ask from a producer is that the product or service be featured alone for a few video frames within the commercial, i.e., the product shot. The client has the right to pass on the copy and the storyboard before production begins.

Determining the marketing problem (P 2). The reason for creating a commercial is to solve a marketing problem. Problems range from how to get a product or service known to the public to the challenge of positioning a product or service within the marketplace to win a target audience. The best place for a producer to begin is to set narrow goals and objectives for the commercial spot, and to define the target audience. Once commercial goals and objectives are set, a production statement can be created. Together with goals and objectives, a target audience, and the production statement, video production values and techniques can be intelligently chosen to orchestrate the final commercial to the goals, audience, and statement.

Writing the script (P 3). The next stage in the preproduction process for the producer is crucial because it involves the choice of words, phrases, and logic, which serve to hook the audience and influence them favorably toward the product or service being advertised.

Bearing in mind that the audience has only a single pass at hearing the copy of the commercial, the producer has to write for the ear (not the eye, as for print advertising). The guide for writing for the ear is the most common form of communication experienced—conversation. A good commercial writer writes as one speaks—conversationally—often in incomplete sentences and just as often with only a word.

There is justification for writing the voice copy before

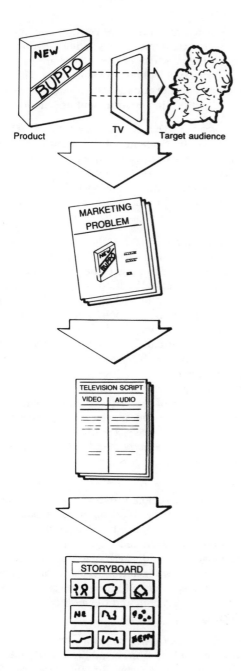

FIGURE 4–1
Developmental stages for the television commercial.

imaging. One picture, as the proverb goes, is worth a thousand words. There will be less visual imaging than there will be audio copy. Realistically, one sense does not really come before the other because they are considered simultaneous in creative development. (See the television script form.)

Designing the storyboard (P 4). The storyboard probably has its origin in commercial production. There is no other video genre so refined, so orchestrated that the whole commercial concept is designed, sketched or photographed, and presented to the client for approval before production begins. The extent of the thoroughness and neatness of a storyboard is at the heart of the preproduc-

tion process. The commercial storyboard has no standardized form. It can be constructed with small aspect ratio frames on 8 1/2″ x 11″ paper or on large aspect ratio frames each equal to the size of a sheet of paper. All storyboards should include the imaging of the major video cuts to be contained in the final edited commercial coordinated with the voice-over/dialogue copy to be heard while that video frame is being seen by the audience. The aspect ratio frames should be drawn or photographed exactly as they will be seen in the final commercial. This includes framing details, location details, as well as talent and the colors of clothes and objects within the frame. The completed storyboard with the script and proposed music or sound effects is then presented by the producer to the client for changes and approval. (See the storyboard form.)

Preparing the budget (P 5). The next preproduction step for the producer is tedious yet important. Before any further commitments are made to anyone in the production of the commercial, a budget must be prepared and approved by the client. The client will want to know what the total cost of the production of the commercial being proposed will be. The producer has to prepare the budget accounting for all the elements to be financed as the commercial goes from preproduction to postproduction.

There are many model budget forms available to the producer as a guide to creating an estimated budget before production. Any budget form can serve as a reminder of the many elements to be considered in estimating costs of video commercial production. (See the commercial budget form.) The final budget must also be presented to the client for approval before production can begin.

Choosing and meeting with a director (P 6). With the approval of the budget by the client, the producer can choose and make a commitment to a director. A director is a critical choice by a producer. A director expects complete production control and sometimes creative control. A director is chosen on the basis of both production skills and creative qualities. The first step for the new director is a meeting with the producer. Here script and storyboard are discussed.

Meeting with the producer (D 1). Once the appointment of a director is made, the producer and director should meet. This meeting affords the opportunity to exchange production values and design concepts. The director should have the script, budget, and storyboard after this meeting.

Casting the commercial (P 7). The producer and the director have the responsibility for casting the talent for the commercial. In addition to the demands of the script copy and the goals and objectives of the commercial, the profile of the target audience become guidelines for choosing the right talent. Talent for commercials can be obtained by advertising open casting calls and having all actors responding read for the part.

Assisting in casting the commercial (D 2). Because one of the first qualities of a director is creativity, producers expect the assistance of the director during the choice of cast for the commercial.

Obtaining necessary clearances (P 8). With approval of a budget, legal clearances can be sought. The clearances for which the producer is responsible are some of the legal work in which any producer must be involved. Clearances fall under two main areas: music or other copyrighted material being used in the commercial, and claims about the product or service being advertised that may be made as part of the commercial itself.

An important part of both the script and storyboard is the music to be used. The choice of music can make or break what mood or setting the audio and video portions of the commercial have created. The producer is legally responsible for obtaining all rights for any copyrighted material being used in the commercial, especially music. Three options are usually open to a producer: (1) use original music, (2) obtain synchronization rights for some previously published (and copyrighted) music, or (3) use stock/library music for the cost per drop of the music used in the commercial.

The clearances necessary for claims that are made of a product or service in a commercial demand legal counsel. This counsel should rule that the laboratory or scientific data available for the product or service demonstrates the validity of the claims made in the commercial.

Script/storyboard breakdown (D 3). The director usually has access to the script and storyboard as soon as the producer and the director have met. The director's first preproduction responsibility is to do a breakdown of the script and the storyboard. The breakdown is an analysis of the script and the storyboard into locations, talent, time of day, and interior or exterior setting. (See the script breakdown form.) This stage in preproduction paves the way for location scouting.

Supervising location scouting (P 9). The next stage in the process of preproduction follows upon the completed script and storyboard. Once a producer knows what environments are needed to create the whole mood and feeling of the commercial, and the director has completed the breakdown, location scouting can begin.

Although some producers may wish to actively engage in actual scouting, that task can be left to other crew members and the director. The final approval of the choice of a location may be reserved by the producer. It is a decision that can be made by both the producer and the director. The judgment of a location site is usually made with the use of instant developing film pictures, diagrams drawn to scale of the site itself, and maps to the proposed location site together with the availability of the site for the time and days needed for the shoot. This information should come from the location scouts. (See the location site survey form.)

When a location site has met with the approval of both the producer and the director, the producer should mail a confirmation letter to the host location personnel detailing the approval of the their location environment as a site for videotaping the video drama. Included in the letter should be a listing of previously discussed requirements for the shoot and the terms of the host's involvement. Size of crew and cast should be noted, as well as

production dates and times. A copy of the production schedule when complete is a good addendum to the confirmation letter. A day or two before production on a location, a courtesy telephone call is in order. This gesture is a reminder that the production crew and cast will be on time at their location environment as scheduled.

Directing location scouting and site survey (D 4). Once the director knows the demands of the script/storyboard for locations, location scouting and site survey can begin. The director may do the actual scouting or send other crew members. (See the location scouting and site survey form.) The director and the producer should approve the location sites.

Designing the production schedule (P 10). When the decisions of location sites are made, the next stage in the producer's preproduction responsibilities is the production schedule. After weighing all input, location demands and availability, and cast and crew timetables, the producer can plan the calendar for the actual shooting of the commercial.

Given that the time length of a commercial is so brief, and judging the lack of difficulty of a shoot, it is not unrealistic to plan one full shooting day as a guideline for a single commercial.

When shooting does not extend beyond a single day, the use of the hours of that day should be orchestrated in detail. Exact crew call times, actors' calls, make-up calls, rehearsal calls, meal breaks, equipment set-ups, strikes, and moves should all be accounted for. (See the production schedule form.)

Designing blocking plots (D 5). A responsibility of the director to facilitate remote production for crew members and cast is preproduction blocking plots. A blocking plot is a bird's eye view of the location environment with physical properties indicated (e.g., furniture) and actors and their movements indicated. Actors are symbolized by circles with a code letter and movements are symbolized by directed line segments. Blocking plots assist the camera operator, lighting director, and the audio director in their preproduction tasks.

Insurance coverage and police notification (P 11). When the production schedule is firm, insurance (bodily injury and property) should be covered by the producer for all production crew and cast, and for all location sites. When some location sites include exteriors, local police need to be notified and when necessary, arrangements have to be made in advance for closing streets or regulating traffic. Even if the production does not need exterior locations of public places, the size of a production crew can be so large when invading a neighborhood that it is a good practice to notify police that you are there and with authorization.

Developing the shot list (D 6). Once the director has completed blocking plots, attention should turn to camera shot lists. A camera shot list breaks down the blocking plots by actor(s), props, and locations to the order in which camera shots will be needed during the location shoot. The videotape recorder operator, audio director, and lighting director will use the shot list in performing their production tasks. The shot list contains the numbered order of proposed shots, the framing of each shot (e.g., CU), the composition of the shot (e.g., husband and child), and any motion directions required (e.g., zoom from an MS to a CU). (See the shot list form.) A good shot list saves a lot of time and questions on location. It allows the production crew on location a chance to be prepared for succeeding shots throughout the shoot.

Choosing and meeting with the camera operator (D 7). Once location sites are determined, a director is at the stage of commercial preproduction to choose and involve a camera operator. A camera operator is chosen for aesthetic capabilities in composing the view through the lens. Technical skills include the knowledge and experience with the remote video camera. The first requirement of the camera operator is to meet with the director and discuss the video camera needs of the production. The director should share the storyboard, blocking plots, and shot list with the camera operator.

Meeting with the producer and director (CO 1). The first requirement of the new camera operator is to meet with the producer and the director to get a perspective on both the commercial and its creative concept and proposed production design. The camera operator plays an important role in achieving the creative goals of the production. The camera operator should receive a copy of the storyboard, the blocking plots, and the shot list.

Working the storyboard, blocking plots, and the shot list (CO 2). The remaining preproduction task for the camera operator is to become familiar with the storyboard, blocking plots, and shot list.

Preparing camera equipment and accessories list (CO 3). After meeting with the director (and producer), the next requirement of the camera operator is to prepare an equipment and accessories list of camera requirements. The list should include equipment and accessories available and the elements that need to be rented or purchased. (See equipment checklist.)

Choosing and meeting with the lighting director (D 8). The choice of a lighting director by the director completes the crew members who are aesthetically involved with the video qualities in the design of drama production. A director should choose a lighting director who can create, in lighting design, the same mood, period, and style for the production for which the director was chosen. After meeting with the director, the lighting director should have a master script and blocking plots and begin preproduction.

Meeting with the director (LD 1). The first thing a lighting director should do is meet with the director. The director should share production values, designs, goals, and objectives of the commercial. With the storyboard, the blocking plots, and the location site survey plans, the lighting director is ready to begin preproduction.

Working the script/storyboard and the location survey plans (LD 2). The lighting director should spend time with the preproduction documents, i.e., script/storyboard, location survey plans, and blocking plots, to create the setting and mood necessary for the production of the commercial.

Choosing a videotape recorder operator and audio director and holding a meeting (CO 4). Because the relationship between the camera operator and the videotape recorder operator and an audio director are close working relationships, the camera operator should choose the videotape recorder operator and audio director. The first requirement of the appointment of the videotape recorder operator and the audio director is to meet together with them and share production information, such as the script and shot list.

Meeting with the camera operator (VTRO 1). The videotape recorder operator should meet with the camera operator and the audio director as a first stage of preproduction. Because the three crew members will have to establish a close working relationship, this meeting serves to open communication and exchange production notes and ideas. The videotape recorder operator should have a copy of the script, shot list, and production schedule.

Meeting with the camera operator (AD 1). The audio director should meet with the camera operator and the videotape recorder operator as the first stage of audio recording preproduction. The audio director should have a copy of the script, the shot list, and the production schedule.

Working with the script and shot list (VTRO 2). The videotape recorder operator has the obligation of working with the preproduction documents (script and shot list) necessary to help determine videotape recording equipment and other video recording accessories.

Ordering videotape stock (VTRO 3). One of the production necessities that requires lead time for ordering and purchasing is the videotape stock necessary for the project. The most probable videotape stock is the ¾ inch videotape size and the small cassette unit 20 minutes in length. This varies if the recording is to be done on 1 inch or ½ inch videotape.

Designing the lighting plots (LD 3). The lighting director should begin designing the lighting for the shoot. The actors' blocking plots mark actors, props, and camera positions. The lighting director will add lighting instruments to the location diagrams with actors' blocking. The lighting plots create the lighting designs necessary not only to light the location, actors, and props, but also to create the mood and emotion for the scene.

Preparing lighting equipment and accessories list (LD 4). Once the lighting director has designed the lighting plots, the assessment of the lighting equipment and accessory needs of the production shoot should be apparent. (See the equipment checklist.)

Preparing videotape recording equipment and accessories list (VTRO 4). After meeting with the camera operator and sharing preproduction information, the videotape recorder operator's next responsibility is to determine the video-tape recording equipment and accessories needs for production videotaping.

Labeling and organizing videotape stock (VTRO 5). A preproduction requirement for the videotape recorder operator is to select a coding system that facilitates handling and organizing videotape stock on location and in postproduction. Labeling involves identical coding on both the cassette itself and the videotape carrying case. Consecutive numbering organizes the videotapes for accurate and swift reordering after production. The coding system should also be shared with the continuity secretary for the coordination of videotapes and location takes on the continuity record for the shoot itself.

Working the script, blocking plots, and shot list (AD 2). With the script, blocking plots, and shot list, the audio director can begin designing the audio perspective for the production. The audio perspective includes the choice of pick-up patterns necessary, types of microphones, and microphone holders. The audio perspective also includes creating and choosing music and effects for the final edited master tape.

Designing audio plots (AD 3). The audio director is now able to create audio plots for the production. Audio plots are calculated judgments for the choice of microphone—either a boom microphone on a fishpole, or perhaps a wireless microphone—depending on the information available from the director's preproduction work. Length of needed audio cables can also be judged from the location diagrams. (See the audio plot form.)

Preparing the audio recording equipment and accessories list (AD 4). After completing audio plot design, the audio director can begin accessing audio recording equipment and accessories needs for the production. (See the equipment checklist form.)

Choosing a continuity secretary (D 9). As a final crew decision, a director should choose a secretary who will be responsible for observing and recording continuity notes during production. The skill requirement of a continuity secretary is attention to details.

Preparing continuity notes sheets (CS 1). The continuity secretary is responsible to the director on location and during preproduction preparation. The continuity secretary should create codes for record taking and be familiar with crew and cast lists, production schedule, and the continuity notes recording form. (See the continuity notes form.) Adequate copies of continuity record forms and a binder to hold them while writing should also be prepared.

Coordinating with the videotape recorder operator (CS 2). The continuity secretary needs to coordinate continuity note records with the coding and order of new videotape stock. The videotape recorder operator has the responsibility for videotape stock. Together, a simple, mutually agreeable coding should be used.

THE PRODUCTION PROCESS

The video production process for the television commercial is identical to almost all stages of remote drama production. The commercial is a video drama production.

• Personnel

Producer (P). The producer plays a continuing support role on location. The producer is responsible for all location details from location access and utilization to the coordination of meal breaks and rapport with the drama ensemble.

Director (D). It is the director who conducts the skills of the cast and crew to videotape the drama units scheduled for any single shooting day. In addition to the actors and their support crew (make-up, wardrobe, and property master), the director looks to the production crew for the response necessary to make the shoot come together. The director's production crew responsibility includes the supervision of the camera operator, the lighting director, the audio director, the videotape operator, the continuity secretary, the mike or boom grip, and slate person. The director's drama ensemble responsibility includes the performance direction of the actors and action properties.

Camera operator (CO). The camera operator is responsible for the acquisition of the video camera and camera support equipment and its availability during the location shoot. The camera operator performs the camera set-up and equipment check and prepares to receive and take direction from the director.

Lighting director (LD). The lighting director is responsible for creating the lighting design required for the production. The lighting director secures all lighting equipment and accessories and sets up and checks the necessary equipment for each take. The lighting director is directly responsible to the director of the production.

Videotape recorder operator (VTRO). The responsibilities of the videotape recorder operator on location include the acquisition of videotape recording and monitoring equipment and their set-up and systems check. The utilization and security of videotape recording stock is also among the videotape operator's obligations on location. The videotape recorder operator is first responsible to the camera operator and ultimately to the director on location.

Audio director (AD). The responsibilities of the audio director include the acquisition of all necessary audio recording equipment and accessories and their respective set-up and testing. The audio director is directly responsible to the camera operator, and as the lighting director, ultimately to the director while on location.

Continuity secretary (CS). The continuity secretary has the responsibility to be prepared to record all production details for the order and organization of each videotaped take on location. These details facilitate the edit flow from one take to another. The continuity secretary should have copies of continuity recording forms and a binder that holds them and allows making notes on them.

The continuity secretary is responsible to the director and in turn has authority to make demands of crew and cast in the performance of continuity record taking. This entails calling for a freeze for actors, releasing crew to reset equipment, and reestablishing details before a subsequent take.

Slate person (SP). Someone among the crew is needed to keep the production slate for the videotape leader up-to-date during location production. The additional task of the slate person is to announce the content of the slate as it is videotaped on the leader of the videotape for each take.

Microphone boom grip/operator (MBG/O). Another necessary crew member on location is the microphone boom grip. The only efficient way to get a microphone into a set is to extend it at the end of a pole (a fishpole) or a boom. This task demands someone who will not tire easily with outstretched arms and still function intelligently without getting the microphone or shadows in the field of the camera. The microphone boom/grip operator is responsible to the audio director during production.

Actors/talent (T). The actors/talent are directly responsible to the director on location. Actors should be ready with lines learned, characterizations firm, costumed, and in full make-up at the appointed time listed on the production schedule.

Other crew. Given the size of a production and the amount of the budget, other crew members may be involved. A production manager would take a lot of responsibilities from both the producer and the director while on location. An assistant director could be of service to the director during the details of blocking and rehearsing actors. Any number of grips might be of assistance during camera and lighting set-up changes.

• **Production Stages**

The single camera remote production of the television commercial is similar to the production of drama. Most commercials are dramatized vignettes with all the same production elements and values.

Supervising crew call (P 1). The beginning to a remote production day is a crew call that collects and organizes the whole crew. Usually, the production crew needs an earlier and separate call from the drama ensemble. The technical needs and set-up demands consume more time than most actors and support staff can tolerate with patience. Experience shows that an hour or more is reasonable to separate technical and ensemble crew calls. A uniform departure site for the entire crew allows both an attendance count and assures arrival at an unfamiliar location together. Parking arrangements and unloading arrangements are the responsibility of the producer.

Holding a production meeting (D 1). One of the first requirements for every production day is a production meeting. Even with all the preproduction work that facilitates a video commercial production, there are still last minute changes and details that should be covered with the entire crew together. This is the opportunity for the director to make changes in the production schedule and solicit questions about videotaping details.

Meeting location hosts (P 2). A courtesy the producer can extend to a willing location host is adequate communication and pleasant reminders that their environment has been scheduled for a given day and hour. It is a good practice for the producer to have followed location scouting (when permission is granted for a shoot) with a detailed letter outlining all the details of the request for using the host location for a video shoot and remind the host of the details conveyed previously by word. The day before shooting, a telephone call as a courtesy reminder is also beneficial.

Unloading the amount of equipment a remote video production needs requires special notice to the location host. In turn, the host may request that special directions (e.g., insurance or fire safety regulations) be followed, such as the use of loading docks, a particular entrance door, and the use of a freight elevator.

After the equipment is unloaded at the location site, each member of the crew has tasks to perform in preparation for videotaping. It is at this point that the producer and the director have the responsibility to keep informed of the progress of each crew member as the crew members have the mutual responsibility to keep the producer and director informed of their progress in equipment set-up and operation check.

The producer should also know what demands the crew and cast have for security for both production equipment and personal valuables while on location and also for privacy for costume and make-up preparation as well as crew breaks and meals.

Supervising location environment rearrangement (P 3). The producer handles the rearrangement of the location environment for the needs of the script units for any particular shoot as the first location requirement. Instant developing film pictures taken during location site survey (or taking instant developing pictures of the location before rearrangement) is a good practice. With a photographic record of the way a location appeared upon crew arrival, the environment can be restored to the way it was. Often furniture will have to be removed to meet the blocking of a scene, or action properties, such as an automobile, may have to be positioned for a particular shot.

The producer should have cleared all major changes to a location environment with the location host during the location site survey. If unanticipated changes should have to be made, the producer should always check with the location host or security for proper permission to make the changes.

Directing location environment rearrangement (D 2). Whereas the producer handles the rearrangement of the location environment, it is the director who directs the changes. The director should make the decisions on what is moved or removed in light of the storyboard, creative concept and production design.

Handling production crew and cast details (P 4). The ongoing task of the producer on location is the many details required of both crew and cast. Toilet facilities, meals, breaks, and lounging areas are needs for both crew and cast, who need to be informed of them. The drama cast require additional room for changing into costumes, getting into make-up, and space for just waiting to be videotaped. Most of these details should have been worked out with the location host at the time of the site survey.

Arranging camera equipment and accessories pick-up/delivery (CO 1). Because camera equipment may either be already available, rented, or purchased, the camera operator is responsible for arranging either pick-up or delivery to the location site. For some location sites, there may be required equipment delivery areas and freight elevators that must be used.

Arranging lighting equipment and accessories pick-up/delivery (LD 1). Similar to other crew members responsible for equipment, the lighting director must arrange for the acquisition of available lighting equipment and accessories as well as the equipment that must be rented or purchased. Loading and carting lighting equipment should follow the requirements of the location as set for all equipment.

Arranging videotape recording equipment and accessories pick-up/delivery (VTRO 1). The videotape recorder operator is responsible for the pick-up and delivery of either available, rented, or purchased equipment for videotape recording. Loading of videotape recording equipment should follow the same requirements of all other equipment loading and carting.

Arranging audio recording equipment and accessories pick-up/delivery (AD 1). The responsibility of the audio director is to secure the pick-up and delivery of available, rented, or purchased audio recording equipment and accessories for the production shoot.

Getting into costumes and make-up (T 1). Preferences vary among directors for the preparation they expect from their actors. Some prefer that actors report to location in make-up and costume; others break for make-up and costuming after blocking and rehearsal. One determining factor is always the extent of make-up and costuming required. Long and detailed make-up, e.g., extensive aging, should be done early with adequate lead time. Basic make-up could be applied before blocking and final touches and powdering before the first take.

Location camera set-up and check (CO 2). The camera operator should follow the blocking plots and begin camera equipment set-up. When set-up is complete, the camera operator can make an operational check by communicating with the videotape operator who can read the vectorscope for light levels for the scene. Unacceptable levels may mean

that the f-stop of the lens needs to be adjusted or light intensity levels need to be changed. When set-up and check are finished, the camera operator should communicate this fact to the director and the producer.

Location lighting set-up and check (LD 2). After the production meeting with the director and producer, the lighting director should follow the production schedule and lighting plots for the first take and begin location lighting set-up. The lighting director makes a lighting set-up check by viewing the actors or stand-ins both on the set and over the video monitor. The lighting director works closely with the camera operator and the videotape operator. The lighting director will have to work with the videotape recorder operator who should be monitoring the vectorscope for the adequacy of light levels. The lighting director should be observant of unwanted shadows from either actors or microphone booms on the location set.

Videotape recorder location set-up and check (VTRO 2). The videotape recorder operator should see to the proper set-up and operation of the videotape recorder after the production meeting. The mobility of the videotape recorder set-up should be facilitated for easy movement when the camera and lighting placements are changed with different takes. The videotape recorder operator should request a check of the recording set-up by laying some video and audio from the camera and microphones before notifying the director and the producer that set-up is complete. Part of the videotape recorder set-up is the vectorscope to monitor video levels for broadcast quality and a headset for monitoring audio input.

Location audio set-up and check (AD 2). The audio director sets up the equipment for audio recording the video commercial production immediately following the production meeting. The audio set-up requires the cooperation of the videotape recorder operator because microphone connections and the audio monitoring headset connection are made into the videotape recorder.

The audio director should make a set-up check by checking run cables, checking microphones for batteries, setting gain levels with actors or stand-ins, and listening carefully for ambience sounds that may be unacceptable or intolerable to the scene. The audio levels for voice recording can be made by watching the VU meter for audio input level and monitoring the audio by headset. When everything checks out, the director and producer should be notified.

Supervising equipment set-ups and checks (D 3). When all equipment is set up and operating, the director should make a final check. Because remote production equipment ultimately creates the aesthetic experience to be achieved with video commercial production, the director has the responsibility to check the proper set-up and functioning of the camera, videotape recorder, audio recording equipment, and lighting design.

The director should call for videotaping some video and audio as the best check of equipment and location set-ups. There is no better criterion for location video and audio recording equipment than to see and hear what the audience will see and hear, the video and audio product of the shoot.

Standing in for purposes of lighting, sound, and video checks (T 2). Frequently, actors are needed while the production crew makes checks on various aesthetic elements of recording equipment. It is a tedious task for actors but a necessary one. While crew members will use other location personnel to stand in when exact reproduction of height and color are not important, it does come to a point when the individual actor has to take the place of a stand-in.

Blocking the actors (D 4). Once the director has determined that camera, recorder, audio, and lighting are ready, the actors can be summoned. Assuming that the camera is in place for the first shot of the day, the director blocks the actors from the storyboard and blocking plot and script without the actors' line delivery. This step is best achieved by the director simply noting the phrase or point in the script dialogue or action when and where an actor is to move and physically moving the actors, one at a time, on their cues.

Following the director's requests and directions during blocking, rehearsals, and takes (T 3). The director is the first and final word on a location videotape shoot. For actors, apart from learning lines and developing characterizations, this is usually the first time on the set and blocking is new to everyone. Following the director's directions accurately and swiftly helps everyone in both cast and crew. Most directors rehearse until actors feel comfortable with their lines and movements. Actors should not hesitate to ask for additional rehearsals before a take. Following a director's commands includes the director's calls to action, cut, freeze, and another take.

Rehearsing the actors (D 5). Once the actors know the blocking for the scene, the next step involves allowing them to rehearse the blocking with their lines. During these two steps, blocking and rehearsing actors, the camera operator, microphone boom grip, audio director, and lighting director should be checking their production response to the blocking as the director blocks and rehearses the actor(s).

Blocking the camera (D 6). At this point the director can set camera shots with the camera operator. Setting camera shots means directing the composition of the take (who is in the field of view), the camera framing (the kind of shot, e.g., CU, LS), and movement of the camera (e.g., pan, tilt, zoom) during a video take. It is presumed that the camera operator has had a shot list of the shots required for the scene and has been observing the director block and rehearse the actors in the scene.

Setting camera shots can be done with the actors delivering lines or simply rehearsing the blocking. Some directors find that with the delivery of lines, it is difficult to spend quality time with the camera operator because the scene passes swiftly. Hence, many prefer that the actors simply rehearse blocking at this step. During this stage the mike boom grip should also participate and work out positions in the videotaping environment for

covering dialogue audio for the scene without getting in the frame and without casting shadows.

Blocking the camera position with the actors (CO 3). In video commercial production, the camera is treated as an actor; the camera must be blocked for position and movement and changes during a scene just as an actor. Camera operators find it convenient to observe the blocking of actors alone first, and then take notes while the director blocks their camera.

Observing blocking and rehearsals (MBG/O 1). The microphone boom grip/operator has the responsibility of observing the director's blocking of actors and rehearsals with actors for the purpose of determining where and how far to project the microphone holder, i.e., the fishpole, into the location set. The mike boom grip/operator must look for the fall of shadows from a microphone or fishpole. When these shadows occur, then the position of both the microphone and fishpole and the mike boom grip/operator have to be changed and checked again.

Rehearsing the camera (CO 4). After blocking the camera position, composition, framing, and movement, the camera operator rehearses what the director blocked with the actors and their line delivery. The director may watch the camera performance on a playback monitor and offer the camera operator some criticism.

Rehearsing both actors and camera (D 7). The director should now call for a rehearsal of the actors with lines and the camera operator effecting all the shots called for. The director should observe the scene where both the real action and a video playback can both be seen.

It is at this point that the mike grip should also have worked out the best positions for covering the scene adequately for sound pick-up. During this step the video monitor should be watched for boom or microphone shadows or catching the microphone itself on camera.

The audio director should carefully monitor the sound reproduction for any abnormalities in covering the dialogue and setting gain levels. The video recorder operator or the camera operator should check video levels on the vectorscope and communicate to the lighting director any levels that may not be acceptable for broadcast quality video.

Observing CU and LS framing for microphone positions (MBG/O 2). From the director's defined framing of shots, e.g., CU versus LS, during blocking and rehearsals, the mike boom grip/operator has to determine how close or low to actors the microphone can be tolerated without getting into the video picture frame. When the microphone gets in the picture, usually another take is required. Constant vigilance is required to avoid microphone boom shadows and microphones in shot.

Making changes and rehearsing again (D 8). Having troubleshot any problems, the director calls for a rehearsal of the scene one more time to check for any remaining difficulties or that old ones have been corrected. This rehearsal might focus solely on audio coverage and microphone boom handling. This is a good opportunity for the director to check actors' make-up and costuming on camera under the lights and over the video monitor.

Calling for a take (D 9).   At this stage the director might call for a take. This means that the director is ready to videotape the scene. In turn this means that actors should have make-up and costuming checks and attend to last minute prop details.

This step requires that the continuity secretary be ready to record all the details necessary for accounting for the scene and any subsequent portions of the scene. There is no question of the importance of the continuity secretary and note taking. The smallest slip in detail between a previous take and a subsequent take to be cut into the earlier one will create impossible problems in editing.

There is also a need for the slate at this point in the production. The slate is readied with the appropriate information that will label the leader video of the scene enabling the video editor later to best identify the following take without having to see the entire scene. The slate records at least the title of the commercial, the director, the taping date, the script unit, and the take number. The continuity secretary might be responsible for the slate or another member of the crew assigned to perform the task. In any case, both the continuity secretary and the person responsible for the slate should be coordinated because they both must share accurate information of scene numbers, units, and video takes.

The correct standardized language for director's control of a take is as follows:

Director: "Stand by for a take."

Director: "Ready to roll tape."

Videotape operator: "Ready to roll tape."

Director: "Roll tape."

Videotape operator: "Tape is rolling."

Director: "Slate it (or mark it)."

Slate person (steps in front of the lens of the camera with the slate and reads aloud both the unit number and the take number): "Unit ___; take ___."

Director: "Ready to cue action." "Action!"

Actors take a breath, a pause, and begin.

Director (records beyond planned edit point): "Cut!"

Actors freeze.

Continuity secretary (makes necessary notes): "Okay" or "Hold it."

Director (announces his intentions): "That's a wrap. Next shot." "Master scene, unit ___." "Cut-ins, unit ___." "Take it again, unit ___." "Take it from line ___." "That's a wrap. Strike the location."

Videotaping the take (CO 5).   When all last minute changes are made and no more rehearsals are needed, the camera operator will be asked to keep the camera position, shot composition, shot framing, and any required movement for a videotaped take. The camera operator should care-fully observe camera work during each take, subject composition, framing, and movement and be ready to tell the director that some problem was encountered. If there was a problem observed, some mistake made, or even a better shot that could be suggested, it should be called to the director's attention before a wrap is called on that take.

Responding to the director's call to roll tape (VTRO 3).   The responsibility of the videotape recorder operator during production is to respond to the readiness call by the director, with the roll tape response that the videotape is indeed rolling, and that the video and audio recording levels check out.

Monitoring audio input (AD 3).   During videotaping the audio director has to monitor audio input. The audio director must watch audio levels on the VU meter of the videotape recorder and listen over a headset for dialogue and ambience sounds. Ambience sound can be acceptable background sound for a scene or unacceptable noise such as an airplane or automobile. At the end of a videotaped take, the audio director should let the director know if the audio recording was correct and acceptable or whether an error was made, necessitating a retake.

Monitoring vectorscope (VTRO 4).   The videotape recorder operator should monitor vectorscope levels during a videotape take. Bursts of light and reflections of light as actors move and props are used can push light levels for the camera to unacceptable levels. Should these bursts be seen by the videotape recorder operator, the director should be notified after the cut is called.

Following the director's directions (AD 4).   The audio director is directly responsible to the production director during a videotaping, as are all crew members.

Booming and miking dialogue during takes (MBG/O 3).   Once rehearsals are over and clearance of shadows and microphones is made, the mike boom grip/operator then booms the dialogue of actors during videotaping. During videotaping the mike boom grip/operator has to hold the fishpole steadily following safety distances rehearsed, and handle microphone extension cables at the fishpole and on the floor or ground of the location set. Some mike boom grips/operators prefer to monitor audio input with a headset from the videotape recorder during taping too.

A major guideline for good audio perspective is that the wider the framing is for a video shot, the more distant the audio perception should appear; the closer the framing is for a video shot, the louder the audio perception should appear. Hence, during long shots the microphone is held higher giving a further audio perspective; on close-ups the microphone can be closer to the actors, effecting a louder audio perspective.

Updating and slating videotape leader (SP 1).   The slate person has the responsibility of constantly updating the information on the slate for recording on the leader of every videotape take. The slate person must be in coordination with the videotape recorder operator and the continuity secretary. Information in script unit and number of take are important to accurate postproduction.

Coordinating the slate with the continuity secretary and videotape recorder operator (SP 2). The slate person needs to be in regular communication with the continuity secretary who keeps record of all takes and the videotape recorder operator who keeps record of videotape codes and is responsible for and knowedgeable of the videotape cassette being recorded at the time.

Following the director's directions (SP 3). The slate person is directly responsible to the call of the director for every videotape take. The director's call, "slate it!," means that the slate person positions the slate in focus in front of the lens of the camera and audibly reads the script unit being taped and the take number into the microphone. If a take is interrupted by a minor error, e.g., a flubbed line of dialogue, a director may forego a slate at the front of a take, and instead call for an end board, slating the take at the end of the videotape.

Announcing intentions: retake, wrap, or strike (D 10). The primary determinant of the director's intentions after a take should always include a check of the video and audio recording by the videotape operator and the audio director, preferably by the director. This is an advantage of video over film: the ability to see the take immediately after it is finished. It would be foolhardy not to view the scene before proceeding. If the take is satisfactory, a wrap is called and another scene or camera placement may be called for. Specific script units should be noted to reduce uncertainty about the new scene. If the take is unsatisfactory, another take may be called by the director. Reasons for the retake should be given so that crew and cast can avoid the same problem and make corrections. If all the takes for the day as listed on the production schedule are complete, a strike of the location may be called by the director.

Observing and recording continuity details (CS 1). The continuity secretary has the responsibility to observe all details of a videotaped take. This includes actors' dialogue, costuming, make-up, blocking, hand properties, and vehicle properties. Continuity notes forms suggest what details to observe, but it is up to the continuity secretary to be sensitive to the details that might change from take to take.

Working with the continuity secretary (T 4). The continuity secretary will need to record more details of the actors than any other element of a take. It is important to good order and less stress that actors be sensitive to the requests of the continuity secretary for a freeze until all details are observed and noted, as well as be refreshed about details from the continuity secretary before a subsequent take. Actors can assist a continuity secretary by not changing detail elements, e.g., locks of hair askew, hand holding a purse, during a break, and by helping recall detail elements.

Releasing actors after a cut (CS 2). When the director calls for a cut in videotaping, the continuity secretary may call for a freeze among the actors (and even the production crew) until all elements of detail are correctly recorded.

Being available but out-of-the-way (T 5). Between takes actors should be available but out of the crew's way. More time is lost between takes when crew members have to fall over or go around actors who should vacate shooting space. The opposite problem is actors who disappear and cannot be found when a take is ready. Although crew and cast alike prefer to engage in idle talk, such behavior holds up a production and serves to distract actors from consistent characterization.

Reestablishing details before subsequent shots (CS 3). At the beginning of a subsequent shot to be edited to the previous take, the continuity secretary has the obligation to redirect dialogue elements, costuming, make-up, and blocking to meet the same detail elements recorded from the previous cut.

Preparing the videotape production of stills, graphics, and product shot (P 5). A final video production stage for the producer is the preparation and videotaping of product shots (stills) and pages of text and graphics (e.g., logo) to be edited into the final version of the commercial. Some of this graphic preparation will not be done on location but in a studio. What is to be videoptaped on location should be done before a strike is called.

Getting talent release forms signed (P 6). The end of the shooting day is the time for the producer to make certain that release forms are secured for any extras who may have been used from the location site for the shoot. It is not uncommon, for example, to recruit people standing around a location shoot for roles as extras in street scenes. Their release forms should be obtained for purposes of legal clearance. (See the talent release form.)

Striking camera equipment (CO 6). When the director indicates the final wrap and location strike, the camera operator is responsible for the breakdown of all camera equipment and accessories as part of the location strike.

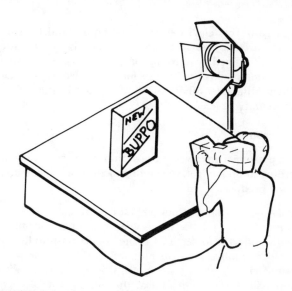

FIGURE 4–2
Videotaping stills. Still images may have to be videotaped as part of the final commercial. For example, a static shot of the product is always part of a commercial.

Repackaging and loading of equipment should proceed according to the requirements of unloading at the beginning of the shoot.

Striking lighting equipment (LD 3). When the director calls a strike for the production day, the lighting director is responsible for striking and repacking all lighting equipment and accessories.

Striking the videotape recording equipment and accessories (VTRO 4). When the director calls a strike, the videotape recorder operator begins to break down the videotape recorder set-up. After the strike call it is important for the videotape operator to remove the record button from all the source tapes used for the shoot to prevent accidental erasing or recording over.

Labeling videotape cassettes and carrying cases is also an important production detail for the videotape recorder operator. Any agreed upon coding is sufficient. Coordination with the continuity secretary facilitates reordering the videotapes for postproduction preparation.

Care should be exercised that any B-roll tapes be used for that purpose only. A B-roll tape may be designated by a director in anticipation of special editing effects, such as a dissolve, in which two tapes will have to be rolled onto the master tape. Not anticipating a B-roll source tape requires another generation of the video needed for the special effect. B-rolling saves a second generation of a length of videotape.

Striking audio equipment (AD 5). When the director calls for a strike at the end of a production day, the audio director is responsible for the breakdown and repacking of audio equipment and accessories.

THE POSTPRODUCTION PROCESS

Because of the television broadcasting demand for split-second accuracy for television commercials, the requirements of refined postproduction editing is greater. Apart from timing, postproduction for the video commercial differs little from other genres in postproduction except for accuracy in length.

• Personnel

The personnel involved in postproduction may vary according to the budget, the editing facility, or the demands of the producer.

Producer (P). Some producers edit or oversee the entire editing process themselves. However, it is not uncommon for the director to serve as editor. Some postproduction facilities require either the producer or the director of the commercial to work with a technical director or editor who will actually function at the editing console. The producer or the director would still make the editing decisions in such a case.

Director (D). The director of the location production may assume the role of postproduction editor also. However,

if the director's preproduction tasks were thorough and accurate, the master storyboard and script with the continuity sheets should be sufficient for another editor or technical director to effect what the producer or director designed.

Camera operator (C/VTRO). With the production of the video commercial completed, there are only summary tasks remaining for the camera operator. The return and accountability of remote camera and location lighting equipment and accessories remain the final responsibility of the camera/videotape recorder operator.

Videotape recorder operator (VTRO). Similar to the camera operator, the only remaining tasks of the videotape recorder operator are to return videotape recording and sound recording equipment and note any loss, damage, or malfunctioning equipment or accessories.

Lighting director (LD). The lighting director has the added postproduction responsibility to ensure the return of all lighting equipment, noting damage, loss, and malfunction.

Audio director (AD). The final responsibility of the audio director is the return of audio recording equipment. This involves the reporting damage, loss, and malfunction of any equipment or accessory. It is not uncommon for the audio director to exercise sound quality recording in the final mixing and sweetening of audio tracks for the edited master.

Technical director/editor (TD/E). Some postproduction facilities require their own personnel to operate the editing consoles in the editing suites. In such a case, the producer or director would serve in a decision-making capacity during editing sessions. It should be expected that an editor could complete editing from the storyboard and script with the continuity sheets.

• Postproduction Stages

Arranging postproduction schedule and facilities (P 1). The producer has the responsibility to make arrangements for editing suite scheduling. Editing should not begin until all preparation elements are complete. A high quality videotape should be secured for the master tape and striped with SMPTE time code to permit accurate editing of the teleplay from the source tapes. If time code is not used, remember that the master tape must have at least a control track before editing begins on it.

Supervising postproduction preparation (P 2). The producer has responsibility for three elements in the preparation of the project for postproduction: the commercial script, the source tapes, and the continuity notes. The source tapes have to be reordered in the order of the script and storyboard. They should be properly labeled both on the cassette and on the carrying case. This is the responsibility of the videotape recorder operator. The continuity notes sheets also have to be ordered according to the script and storyboard. This is the first responsibility of the continuity secretary.

Postproduction preparation: the script/storyboard (D 1). The director has the postproduction responsibility of reordering the script/storyboard and editing it for changes that may have been made during location production. It is not uncommon that short units were dropped or takes not preplanned were videotaped. These additions as well as deletions have to be made. The script/storyboard, whether the director edits the master tape or a technical director/editor does so, becomes the only point of reference for the master tape edition.

Preparing the source videotapes (VTRO 1). The videotape recorder operator has the responsibility of turning over the source videotapes to the director. The preparation of the source videotapes means that the videotape recorder operator has to remove record buttons from every videocassette recorded on location so that the video signal will not be erased or recorded over. Proper labeling of both videocassettes and carrying cases must also be complete so that any source videotape may be found with little trouble.

The final preparatory work on the source tapes is to have them all striped with SMPTE time code, which facilitates more accurate editing of the master tape than simple control track editing. Because SMPTE assigns a consecutive number to every frame of the videotape, matching number frames from the source tape to the master tape creates a controlled edit. SMPTE code on the master tape will later allow the audio track to be removed for sweetening and mixing and re-laying it to exact synchronization.

Reordering source videotapes (VTRO 2). The videotape recorder operator should reorder all the source videotapes according to the units of the script/storyboard if the videotape recorder operator did not.

Reordering continuity notes sheets (CS 1). Because the continuity secretary has been recording all pertinent details of each location video take on the continuity forms, they are now in need of reordering according to the order of the master script. This is the final responsibility of the continuity secretary.

The continuity notes sheets were defined as a kind of location log that would replace the tedious job of having to view all source tapes after videotaping and before editing could begin. If the continuity notes sheets were well recorded, more than enough information is contained on them to allow postproduction to proceed rapidly and smoothly. Continuity notes serve as the editing work sheets of other postproduction processes.

Returning remote video and lighting equipment and accessories (CO 1). It is the responsibility of the camera operator to return to maintenance/storage facilities all the camera and lighting equipment used during the remote location shoot. Rented equipment must be returned to the equipment rental agency. Equipment purchased for the shoot should be reported separately to maintenance/storage personnel.

Reporting damaged, lost, or malfunctioning equipment (CO 2). As a final obligation to the video documentary shoot, the camera operator should report any equipment or accessory that may have been damaged during the location shoot. This report should also include any loss of equipment or accessories. Most equipment maintenance/storage

personnel also appreciate a written report of any equipment or accessory that may have malfunctioned during the location shoot. It is a good practice to report any repair or replacement made to equipment during the shoot.

Returning videotape recording equipment and accessories (VTRO 3). It is the responsibility of the videotape recorder operator to return to maintenance/storage facilities all the videotape recording equipment used during the remote location shoot. Rented equipment must be returned to the equipment rental agency. Equipment purchased for the shoot should be reported separately to maintenance/storage personnel.

Reporting damaged, lost, or malfunctioning equipment (VTRO 4). As a final obligation to the video documentary shoot, the videotape recorder operator should report any equipment or accessory that may have been damaged during the location shoot. This report should also include any loss of equipment or accessories. Most equipment maintenance/storage personnel also appreciate a written report of any equipment or accessory that may have malfunctioned during the location shoot. It is a good practice to report any repair or replacement made to equipment during the shoot.

Returning remote lighting equipment and accessories (LD 1). It is the responsibility of the lighting director to return to maintenance/storage facilities all the lighting equipment used during the remote location shoot. Rented equipment must be returned to the equipment rental agency. Equipment purchased for the shoot should be reported separately to maintenance/storage personnel.

Reporting damaged, lost, or malfunctioning equipment (LD 2). As a final obligation to the video drama shoot, the lighting director should report any equipment or accessory that may have been damaged during the location shoot. This report should also include any loss of equipment or accessories.

Most equipment maintenance/storage personnel also appreciate a written report of any equipment or accessory that may have malfunctioned during the location shoot. It is a good practice to report any repair or replacement made to equipment during the shoot.

Returning sound recording equipment and accessories (AD 1). It is the responsibility of the audio director to return to maintenance/storage facilities all the sound recording equipment used during the remote location shoot. Rented equipment should be returned to the equipment rental agency. Equipment purchased for the shoot should be reported separately to maintenance/storage personnel.

Reporting damaged, lost, or malfunctioning equipment (AD 2). As a final obligation to the video drama shoot, the audio director should report any equipment or accessory that may have been damaged during the location shoot. This report should also include any loss of equipment or accessories.

Most equipment maintenance/storage personnel also appreciate a written report of any equipment or accessory that may have malfunctioned during the location shoot.

It is a good practice to report any repair or replacement made to equipment during the shoot.

Observing the editing process with the director (P 3). The producer is a valuable resource person in the editing suite during editing sessions. The experience with the project at all stages becomes helpful as particular points of the project, the drama performance, and the editing arise.

Overseeing the sound quality of the edited master (AD 3). With the close association of the audio director to the sound recording on location, the audio director is an invaluable assistant in the editing suite. The audio director is qualified to make suggestions on possible improvement of a sound bite in sweetening. The audio director should take notes during videotape editing in preparation for audio mixing and sweetening.

Editing a rough edit (D 3). A rough edit is created by simply cutting blindly following the script/storyboard and the continuity sheets. Remember that the continuity sheets indicate which take on every recorded videocassette was good or which was bad. The rough edit can move along swiftly if members of the editing team use a fast search playback deck and monitor system to find the good takes while an editor or technical director does the cuts-only editing with simple insert edits.

The reasons for making a rough edit first instead of channeling efforts into a final version may not be immediately evident. First, a cuts-only version allows for an early glance at the whole project. It serves to anticipate problems in a polished final commercial. These problems can range from continuity (e.g., insert edits do not match) to pacing (e.g., the overall flow of the video does not reflect the script). Second, the rough edit allows the actors to see their performance while they may still be together as a group. If the project is working with academic objectives, the ability to see a performance early allows criticizing to occur, which is a necessary ingredient to the professional growth of amateurs, but even professionals like to see their own performances. Third, a rough edit can point to less-than-the-best video quality or location problems that might still be redone because the rough edit is not far removed from the shooting dates and the cast and crew may still be available.

Reviewing the rough edit (D 4). The best use of the rough edit version is to scrutinize the video and audio for final version polishing. There are so many advantages to having this edition. Now is the time to sense the pacing of the final teleplay. Does the flow of video images complement the dialogue and the dramatic tension? Perhaps having seen the flow of images as preplanned, the pacing may be violated and some originally planned video inserts should not be used. Only by seeing the whole drama at this stage can such decisions be intelligently and aesthetically made and implemented in the final editing.

Making the final edit (D 5). With adequate review of the rough edit, final editing can begin. Here all the shortcomings perceived in the rough edit can be repaired and improved. It is at this stage that SMPTE code will best be employed. Transitions other than a cut can be carefully chosen and executed. As part of this stage, titles and credits can be added to the master tape.

Music, effects, ambience added; audio mixing; and sweetening (AD 4). After all the video is edited to the satisfaction of the director, the audio director can add the music, effects, and the ambience called for by the master script. During the process of mixing the two audio channels used to this point for dialogue and music and effects to one channel, audio sweetening can be done. Sweetening allows the audio track to be filtered and cleared of unwanted noises and hums and synchronized back to the master tape with the video track.

After the video and audio edits are completed with the use of SMPTE time code, now with more advanced postproduction audio capabilities, the audio track can be removed from the master tape to be mixed and sweetened. Here mixing of music and other sound effects are introduced. If this level of postproduction work is not available, acceptable audio mixing can occur on the second audio track of the master tape itself. With proper planning, music and ambience track can be premixed and placed on the auxiliary audio track under the dialogue track with no problem.

Overseeing the audio mixing and sweetening (D 6). The final responsibility for the director is to oversee the audio mixing and sweetening with the audio director for the production. The director had the initial aesthetic concept for the video drama, and after effecting the final video editing, the audio mixing and sweetening is a final production task.

VIDEO PRODUCTION ORGANIZING FORMS

• Television Script Form

Production process: Video commercial preproduction

Responsibility: Producer

Purpose: To coordinate in side-by-side columns audio copy and a verbal description of the video imaging of the video commercial.

Objective: The preproduction script is the proposed audio copy and the verbal description of the proposed video commercial. The audio copy of a video commercial is an important step in the production of the commercial. Rational and emotional appeals and claims have to weighed carefully. The audio copy is usually written first. In the simple two-column television script, a verbal description of proposed video is adequate at this stage of preproduction.

Glossary

Commercial Title Commercials are usually titled and the title is used throughout the production of the commercial.

Client   Because all commercials are usually marketing the product or services of some client, the client for the proposed commercial is listed here.

Length   Commercials are distinguished by their length. The length of the proposed commercials should be listed here.

Video   The video column should contain an abbreviated verbal description of the video elements of the video commercial. This column should contain image content descriptions and framing (e.g., XLS of New York City Skyline), editing transitions (e.g., dissolve, cut, fade), and special effects (e.g., DVE rotation), cut-ins, cut-aways, and character generator copy. For example,

VIDEO

XLS New York City Skyline;
Diss to MS house front;
Cut to CU Mrs. Betty Kasper

Super LT   Mrs. Betty Kasper
                    Artist

Audio   The audio column should contain the full verbal copy to accompany the video described in the VIDEO column. Audio copy is written first in the development of a script. Audio copy should be typed in all caps. All talent and production directions should be typed in upper and lower caps. All audio copy should be introduced with the label of the talent intended to deliver the copy. The AUDIO column should also record the use of sound effects, music, ambience. For example,

SFX: City street traffic sounds.

ANN: NOT EVERYONE LIVING IN NEW YORK CITY SUFFERS FROM THE IMPERSONALIZATION OF THE BIG APPLE.

• **Storyboard Form**

Production process: Video commercial preproduction

Responsibility: Producer

Purpose: To assist in the imaging, flow, and pacing of a proposed video commercial.

Objective: The storyboard form coordinates in aspect ratio form each change of screen image and audio copy in sequential manner. The storyboard facilitates the communication of concept and image of a video commercial to the client, the director, camera operators, and video editors. A storyboard encourages a producer and a director to make a commitment to video elements of screen content, framing, and picturization.

Notes on use: Each aspect ratio frame should be sketched with basic form or design of proposed video content of the commercial. The basic form or design should approximate the desired video framing expected by the camera. A new frame should be sketched for every significant proposed image change. Transitions between frame other than the cut can be indicated in an in-between frame.

Frames should be numbered consecutively in the circles provided for that purpose for easy reference during other preproduction and later production stages. Below each frame corresponding audio copy should be recorded.

• **Video Script/Storyboard Form**

Production process: Video commercial preproduction

Responsibility: Producer

Purpose: To coordinate a verbal description of the proposed video commercial and the proposed audio copy with corresponding storyboard frames.

Objective: The video script and storyboard combination form is an alternative script form in which each corresponding storyboard frame is coordinated with the verbal visual description and audio copy.

Glossary

Video   This column is used similarly to the video column in the two-column script form. It should contain a simplified verbal description of the video content, camera framing, edit transition, and character generator copy of the proposed video commercial.

Storyboard Frame   The storyboard frames should be used that coordinate with the entry in the video column. Not all frames are used or needed. Simply skip those frames that do not match video and audio entries. See the directions for using storyboard aspect ratio frames on the storyboard form.

Audio   This column is used similarly to the audio column in the two-column script form. It contains all audio copy for the proposed video package. As with any television script, audio copy should be written first; then the video descriptions opposite the respective audio cue should be created. On this form the storyboard frame should then be sketched corresponding to the first line of each new VIDEO column entry description.

• **Production Budget Form**

Production process: Video commercial preproduction

Responsibility: Producer

Purpose: To realistically estimate all possible costs of the production of the proposed video commercial production from preproduction to postproduction.

Objective: The budget form is a blank model of a budget for the production of a video commercial. The form is meant to organize all facets of single camera commercial production into estimated expenses and actual expenses. It serves to suggest possible cost items across the entire spectrum of video production, personnel, equipment, labor, and materials. The form should be used to suggest expenses and to call attention to possible hidden costs.

Notes on use: The form should be studied for line items that might pertain to a proposed single camera video commercial shoot. Only applicable line items for the proposed commercial need to be considered. Use the suggestion of line items to weigh possible costs for the project. Note that all sections of the budget are summarized on the front page of the form. The subtotal of costs from the individual sections are brought forward to be listed in the summary. Some costs are calculated by the number of days employed, the hourly rate of pay, and overtime hours. Other costs are calculated by the number of items or people by allotted amount of money per day for the item. The cost of materials is calculated by the amount of materials by the cost of a unit. Many cost entry columns of this budget form are labeled "Days, Rate, O/T (overtime) Hrs, Total"; for those line items that do not involve day and rate, the total column alone should be used. Projected costs to be applied to the budget can be found from a number of sources. One source of equipment rental and production costs is the rate card of a local video production facility. Salary estimates and talent fees can be estimated from the going rates of relevant services of equivalent professionals or from their agencies. Phone calls to providers of services and materials also produce cost quotes. Travel costs can be obtained by a phone call to travel agencies or airline companies. There is no question that preparing a good budget involves a lot of time and research.

Glossary

No. Preproduction Days Estimate the number of days to complete the necessary preproduction stages for the commercial. This estimate includes quality time on all preproduction stages (budget, site survey, production schedule, script breakdown, casting, script, shot list, and equipment lists) for all production crew members involved in the preproduction of the commercial (producer, director, camera operator, lighting director, videotape recorder operator, audio director, continuity secretary, and actors).

No. Studio Shoot Days/Hours Estimate the number of days and hours for which a studio or control room facilities may be needed. This time estimate accounts for any in-studio videotaping (e.g., talent on a set) or the use of a control room switcher or character generator for postproduction effects.

No. Location Days/Hours Estimate the number of shooting days and hours that may be required on location.

Location Sites List the proposed location shooting sites at which the previous days and hours were estimated.

No. Post Production Days/Hours Estimate the number of days and hours that will be spent in postproduction in completing the video commercial master edit.

First Shooting Date Indicate the first date proposed to begin videotaping the commercial.

Completion Date Indicate the projected completion of the video commercial. This date should include all postproduction tasks.

Summary of Production Costs This summary area brings forward the subtotals of costs from the respective sections within the budget form. Note that each line unit 1 through 16 is found as section heads within the

budget form. When the individual units are completed within the budget, the subtotal is listed in the summary table.

Contingency This term refers to the practice of adding a contingency percentage to the subtotal of subtotals as a padding against the difference in actual final costs from the estimated costs of all line items. The customary contingency percentage is 15%. Multiply the subtotal after line 20 by 0.15 to determine the contingency figure. That result added to line 21 becomes the grand total of the budget costs.

Preproduction/Wrap Crew This section of the budget lists production crew members who may be involved in preproduction tasks for the commercial and those who will be involved in wrapping up the production, i.e., some postproduction tasks.

Estimated The estimated category refers to costs that can only be projected before the production. Rarely are the estimated costs the final costs to be incurred because of the number of variables that cannot be anticipated. Every attempt should be made to ensure real estimated cost figures and to ensure the consideration of as many variables to the cost as possible. The challenge of estimated budget costs is to project as close as possible to actual costs when they are known.

Actual The actual category of a budget records the costs that are finally incurred for the respective line items during or after the video drama production is completed. The actual costs are those costs that will really be paid out for the production. The ideal budget seeks to have actual costs come as close as possible (either at or preferably under) to the estimated costs for the production.

Shoot Crew This section treats the production crew and costs incurred during production of the commercial or the shoot.

Director Creative Fees Because the director plays the key role in the production of a video commercial, this section of the budget attempts to cover the preproduction, production, and postproduction costs to be incurred for the director fees.

Production and Wrap Materials and Expenses This section of the budget accounts for the cost items that cover materials and expenses incurred during the shoot and wrap for the production.

Location Expenses Location site costs from scouting and insurance to services in the location environment are accounted for in this section of the budget.

Props and Wardrobe and Animals This section of the budget accounts for the purchase and rental of properties and costumes and the use of action props and animals.

Studio and Hall Rental and Expenses It is often necessary to use a studio or interior shooting space for the production of a commercial. This section accounts for costs incurred in the use of a studio.

Set Construction Because many commercials involve a set in the production of the video, this section itemizes possible expenses incurred in building and completing the construction of a set.

Set Construction Materials The costs of materials in the construction of a set are itemized in this section.

Equipment Rental This section of the budget accounts for the rental of equipment in video commercial production.

Videotape Stock The provision of necessary videotape stock in required sizes are accounted for in this section.

Miscellaneous Costs This section permits accounting the production cost items that do not fall under other categories of the budget but are essential to the production at all stages.

Talent The expenses of any talent associated with the production of the commercial are accounted for in this section. Actors and extras have to be accounted for. Some talent may be hired from agencies; others may be freelancers. Creative fees must be paid to professional agencies if agency actors are used.

Talent Expenses Talent may require per diem expenses and other costs including travel; these costs are included in this section of the budget.

Postproduction Facilities and materials for postproduction needs during editing are accounted for in this section of the budget.

Sound All sound requirements in the postproduction of the commercial are accounted for in this section. This includes the cost of copyright clearance for copyrighted music.

Labor This section accounts for the personnel involved in postproduction.

Animation Animation, very common in commercials and other art work in the production of the commercial, are accounted for in this section.

• **Script Breakdown Form**

Production process: Video commercial preproduction

Responsibility: Director

Purpose: To break the preproduction script down into production units usually according to common location or talent requirements.

Objective: The script breakdown form organizes the preproduction script from proposed edited order of a final video commercial to a shooting order according to differing common criteria for single camera shoots, e.g., location similarity, talent. The breakdown form helps organize the shooting units by script pages, script units, or number of script lines criteria for managing the remote production.

Glossary

Length This entry records the estimated length of the video commercial.

Script Length The length of the preproduction script in number of script pages is recorded here.

Storyboard Frames The total number of storyboard frames proposed as the visualization for the commercial is recorded here. In this column of breakdown analysis, the particular frame representing a unit of the commercial should be recorded.

No. of Script Lines The number of lines of script copy is another determinant of length of a shooting unit. The count should be every line of talent copy to be recorded during the unit shoot.

Int/Ext These abbreviations stand for interior/exterior, referring to the script demands for shooting indoors or outdoors. Whether the shoot is an interior or an exterior shoot can also be a determinant for the script breakdown and shooting unit.

Time The time of day or night the location and interior/exterior setting require should be recorded here.

Setting Setting means the specific area of a required location site, e.g., the parents' bedroom for the Smith's home location site.

Location The location column records the remote location environment at which the setting is to be found. For example, the Smith's home is the location site for the parents' bedroom.

Cast This entry records by name the specific actors who are required in the setting at the location for a particular shoot.

Shooting Order When the entire script is broken down into shooting units, then the producer can determine the units for individual shoots and determine the consecutive shooting order for the entire remote project.

• **Location Site Survey Form**

Production process: Video commercial preproduction

Responsibility: Producer/director/location scout(s)

Purpose: To organize and facilitate the survey of possible remote video commercial production location environments.

Objective: The location site survey form is designed to assist the director or location scout(s) who have to search out and describe potential remote environments for video production purposes. Because many sites may have to be evaluated for any particular shoot, details of each site will have to be recorded to be evaluated and approved at a later time, usually away from the site by the producer and the director. The form is designed to raise all possible production needs and location details for a successful remote video production. The form serves to organize and record location site details for later evaluation away from the site.

Glossary

Location Scout(s) This entry should list those other than the producer who have been recruited to help scout potential locations for the production of the soft news video package.

Script Unit(s) Some television scripts are divided into shooting units for production location purposes. These script units are numbered consecutively. This entry records the script unit numbers that will be videotaped at the scouted location.

Storyboard Frames Because the basis for commercial production is the production storyboard, the storyboard frames representing the location being scouted should be recorded here.

Location The entry should record the actual environment called for in the script, for example, "Bob's bedroom."

Site Identification This entry should correspond with a city map (e.g., H-3) or name of the location environment (e.g., Town Point Park).

Local Contact Person The name of the responsible owner, manager, or supervisory officer of a proposed location. This person is the individual who is the location scout's contact person at the highest level of authority over a proposed location site. This person is the use-granting authority for the location. The name, title, address, city, state, and phone number of the contact person should all be accurately recorded. All this information, including the proper title, is needed for mail correspondence purposes. The "comments" space allows for any notes about the contact person (e.g., executive secretary's name) that might be relevant.

Facilities Personnel The facilities personnel information is a record of the person who is the individual with whom the producer and production crew will work on the location. For example, the maintenance engineer, office manager, and janitor are the individuals responsible for the everyday operation of the proposed location. The name, position title, address, city, state, and phone number of each should be recorded. This information becomes most practical to the production crew and the producer. This is the information most utilized once the location is chosen for use. The "comments" space should be used for any other relevant information about the facilities personnel. For example, the directions to the facilities personnel office at the location site, or maintenance workshop, should be recorded here.

Lighting Problems Defined This area of the form focuses attention on the details of the proposed location that can affect lighting of the environment for videotape production.

Light Contrast Ratios Scouts should note any extreme light areas of the environment. A light meter can read (and record should be made of) the extreme lighting intensity of any existing areas of the environment. For example, one end of the proposed location site may have no windows and no ceiling lights. The light reading for this end of the room will be very low to nonexistent. The other end of the room may be flooded with light from a number of windows. The light reading at this end of the room will be very high. These readings form the contrast ratio between the most existing light and least existing light for this room.

Lighting Intensity This entry records the highest light level reading in the proposed location environment. This information informs the producer that some controls will have to be used on the light source or other light will have to be created to balance this light intensity.

Ceiling Height The height of an existing ceiling is important. For example, ceiling height indicates the available height for lighting stands for lighting instruments to be used. A low ceiling allows light to be bounced, or a high ceiling means that light is absorbed,

and that fact has to be taken into account. High ceilings also demand a lot of light if the ceiling needs to be lit.

Windows/Compass Direction Knowing the number of windows opening to the exterior of the location is an important location consideration. Many windows may demand correcting incandescent lights with filters or the need to gel the windows. Another important fact to know about a location environment with windows is the compass direction they face. East facing windows can expect a flood of strong morning sunlight that can push the lighting intensity in the location environment. West facing windows create the same problem in the afternoon. When working remote locations the strongest source of light is the sun, and the sun is a constantly moving light source. Knowing the direction of that moving light source is important. Shadows and reflections change constantly. It is a good practice to have a compass when scouting locations and to take an accurate reading of due east.

Existing Light Control A question to ask facilities personnel during location scouting is the control of existing lighting. For example, in an all fluorescent lighting environment, there may be one master switch. It would be important to know where it is. Simple wall switches for other light control should also be noted.

Lighting Use Notation should be made of how some existing lighting is used. For example, lighted display cases in the environment, parking lot lights, and night lights are conditions of lighting use in the location environment. Much such light use cannot be controlled.

Floor Description The description of the type of flooring in a proposed location environment can have consequences for set lighting design. For example, a highly polished floor covering reflects light; a dark carpet absorbs light or reflects unwanted hues.

Special Consideration Use this space to record for any other specific location detail that might affect lighting design in the environment for the production. For example, a pool of water or a mirror on a wall could reflect light.

Power Problems Defined This area of the form focuses attention and records the details that pertain to electrical power sources. Video production equipment relies heavily on available power sources.

Number of Power Outlets Count should be made of the number of electrical power outlets in the immediate environment of the proposed shoot. Additional count should be made also of the outlets that can be accessed by power cable runs.

Number of Separate Circuits It is important to know how many separate electrical circuits are represented by the power outlets. This is a question for the facilities personnel/maintenance engineer. The power outlets and separate circuits should be noted on a location diagram.

Types of Fuses One liability of heavy electrical needs for video production equipment is the frequent blown fuse. In some facilities restoring power is not a matter of resetting a circuit but replacing a fuse. A good example of the need for fuses is the older private home location environment. Fuses come in many sizes and wattages. It is important to know both size and wattage for the proposed location.

Number of Outlet Prongs There are at least two common types of electrical outlets: the two-prong and the three-prong. Many older environments have only the two-prong outlets. Almost all video production equipment utilize the three-prong plug. Hence, adapters will have to be used on all two-prong outlets. The number of two-prong outlets will have to be known during location scouting so that adapters can be provided.

Location of Circuit Breakers Given the common occurrence of overloading electrical circuits with video production equipment needs, the location of fuse boxes and circuit breakers should be known. Often crew members have to reset breakers and replace blown fuses.

Portable Generator Need It may happen that there is no power source available in a proposed location environment. The only possible source of electricity may be that generated by the production crew itself with a portable power generator. Power generators can be easily rented if needed. Caution must be exercised with the use of a power generator. They are a source of unwanted noise in the environment and can be difficult to control.

Audio Problems Defined This area of the form focuses on details that affect the production of audio recording in the proposed location environment.

Interior Environmental Sounds This entry should contain all perceived sound that is audible in the interior of the proposed location environment. This means careful listening for hums and buzzes from air conditioning, refrigerators, freezers, sound speakers, copying machines, and fluorescent lights. All sounds should be noted. Note should also be made on the ability to control or turn off the sounds.

Ceiling Composition The composition of a ceiling can determine the quality of sound recordings made in the proposed location environment. For example, a hard composition ceiling reflects sound; sound proofing materials on a ceiling absorb sound. Both can make a difference in the quality of sound recorded in an environment.

Wall Composition The composition on the walls of a proposed location environment also make a difference in the quality of sound recorded in that environment. For example, cork, carpet or cloth, and sound proofing absorb sound; tile, mirror, and plaster reflect sound.

Exterior Environmental Sounds Location scouts must listen carefully to both interior and exterior sounds in an environment. Exterior sounds affect both an exterior and an interior shoot. For example, some common exterior sounds that can affect an interior shoot are airplanes, emergency vehicles, a school playground, busy highway, or a noisy manufacturing plant. Make note of every perceivable sound.

Floor Covering Composition The composition of a floor also has an effect on sound recording in an environment. For example, a polished hardwood or tile floor reflects as well as creates sound (e.g., footsteps). Deep pile carpeting absorbs sound.

Cast and Crew Needs This area of the form reminds location scouts that care and consideration of cast and crew needs must be accounted for during a location shoot.

Restroom Facilities Restroom facilities for men and women will have to be provided. Part of the location site survey is to note, perhaps on the diagram of the location, where the restroom facilities are closest to the shooting area.

Green Room Availability A green room is a theater term for a waiting area for actors. Some such waiting area may also be required for the cast for a video production. This should be a room close to the shooting area, but separate from the shooting area where cast can relax and await their blocking and videotaping calls.

Parking Arrangements A remote video production crew and cast can create a parking space demand on a neighborhood or public parking area. During scouting the question of special parking should be addressed. This may occasion some parking privileges or special directions or restrictions.

Freight Elevator In some location environments, the number of crew, cast, and equipment involved in video production may require the use of a freight elevator in a facility. The location of the freight elevator should be part of a location environment diagram giving directions from the freight elevator to the shooting area.

Eating Facilities When the length of a shooting day will require a meal on location, some eating facility, special room, or vending machines should be noted. Some facilities may prohibit any eating on the premises. Notation then will have to be made of restaurants in the vicinity of the proposed location.

Make-up Facilities If the video production requires that cast or talent appear in make-up, some facility will have to be provided for the application of the make-up. Ideally, make-up application requires mirrors, adequate lighting, and sinks. Restroom facilities make decent make-up preparation accommodations. If nothing else is available, a double set of restrooms can be designated for make-up and costuming.

Loading/Unloading Restrictions The amount of equipment needed for a remote video production may require special unloading and loading requirements at a location site, e.g., an outside loading dock area. Such an unloading dock may also be close to a freight elevator. Location personnel should always be made aware of the great amount of equipment video production requires. They should be the judge of any special circumstances that might be required for so much equipment.

Hardware Store Because remote video production demands so much hardware equipment, there is often the need to purchase supplies or replace broken, lost, or forgotten supplies. Facilities representatives may be the persons to know where the closest hardware store is in the vicinity of the proposed location environment.

Civil Emergency Services This area of the form lists essential civil services in the service of both the production cast and crew and the location site.

Police Station The address and phone number of the

police station that services the proposed location site is important contact information. With the number of individuals a remote video production crew involves, the amount of equipment and the use of an environment warrants the sensitivity to police presence and availability.

Fire Station The same holds true for the fire protection station within the environmental area of the proposed location shoot site. The heavy use of electrical power for a remote video production shoot should alert both producer and production crew to the potential dangers of so much power use. This holds especially true for an older facility, such as a private home used as a location site. The address and phone number of the fire station should be entered here.

Location Security and Equipment Safety This area of the form records important information on general personal and property security and safety.

Facility Security This entry records the general security of crew, cast, and equipment during the production shoot. Some proposed locations in highly public areas, such as a shopping mall, present a security risk; confined production sites, such as a private home, are more secure. Note should be made of apparent security in general for all production elements.

Personnel Values Security Record should be made of the arrangements made with facilities personnel for the safety and security of personal belongings while crew and cast are involved in production. This includes wallets and purses especially. Facilities personnel can often provide a locked and secure room for the deposit of personal valuables during production.

Equipment Safe Storage Arrangements should be made for the security of unused equipment and accessories that should be safely stored until needed or stored after use until the location strike. The facilities personnel can often provide a locked and secure room for equipment storage.

Overnight Storage/Security Often remote location shoots take place over the period of more than one day. This entails the safe and secure overnight storage of equipment. Complete breakdown of all location equipment and loading, transport, and unloading a second day can result in the loss of valuable time and energy. Facilities personnel can often provide adequate overnight storage that is both safe and secure.

Other Relevant Information This area of the form records other important information that falls outside the other areas of location details.

Public Area Power Source Often in open public areas, such as a city park, the local power company may already provide a power box with electrical outlets for private use. This service has to be requested from the power company and a deposit made to secure power costs at the end of the production shoot. Location scouts should search a public area for some sign of power source facility. It may serve the site survey to make a call to the local power company and request a listing of outdoor power sources.

Clearance/Insurance Personal security for the crew and talent and property damage insurance coverage should be secured before video production. Academic programs have personal insurance coverage for students and property damage and loss coverage for school equipment, which is active when the shoot is a valid academic project with a supervising faculty present. Other remote video production projects can easily receive coverage by contacting a reliable insurance agent. Some potential location facilities personnel require verification of insurance coverage before approval of their location for a shoot. Anticipating insurance notification before facilities personnel require it is a sign of professional competence.

Photographs Taken When more than one location environment is being scouted for a shoot, a decision may be made away from a potential site. A producer must judge from the location scout's report. An important part of a location site survey is photographs of the proposed location. Instant developing film is most convenient. When adequate photographs of a location site are part of a survey, these photographs help a producer and camera operator plan a shoot and assist a crew after a location strike in replacing a location environment to the arrangement and condition it was in before the production crew arrived. The photographs taken should be listed. The photographer's camera position and direction of the lens of the photographed site should be noted on the location diagram as an aid in designing the video camera shots and lens framing for the production.

Location Environment Drawing/Map Another important product of location scouting is a drawing or map of the proposed location site. This entails a rough pacing off of all environments, both interior and exterior, that are being considered as a video setting. Windows should be placed, compass direction indicated, power outlets and circuits noted, and existing furniture and other properties sketched. Everything should be included that may enter into the use of the location from the needs of the production and the adaptability of the location environment.

Traffic Control At some exterior location environments, the extent of a video production crew, talent, and equipment necessitate some control of vehicular traffic. For example, parking restriction may be required along the area of a shooting set, moving traffic may have to be redirected during a shoot, or a street may have to be closed off entirely from traffic. Most police departments are cooperative to such requests, but they need adequate advance time notification. In some instances the approval of a city or town council may be required. This too requires adequate lead time to process the request and get it to the council in good time for the shoot or a change of plans if the request should be denied.

Exterior Compass Direction If the remote location site is an exterior shoot, an accurate assessment of the compass directions of the area should be made with respect to the proposed shooting site. The sun is the principal light source to an exterior shoot, and that source is in constant movement. Knowing the direction the sun takes from east to west on a proposed location environment is a most important variable to designing an outdoor video shoot. A compass is a necessity to scouting a location site. Many location personnel are not accurate about their recollection of east and west directions and are not reliable sources of information, given the importance that the sun's direction has on a remote video shoot.

Other Comments/Observations This area should record any other details not covered in the form to this point. It is important to record all impressions of a proposed location site. Sometimes the smallest detail missed or the smallest detail included can become either an obstacle or an asset to the production later. When in doubt about including a detail, include it.

• Blocking Plot Form

Production process: Video commercial preproduction

Responsibility: Director

Purpose: To create the director's location script, the location document from which the actors, dialogue, properties, camera operator, and camera framing will be directed.

Objective: This essential preproduction stage prepares the director for all details for directing the cast and crew while on location. From the location survey and photographs the director can design all production elements for location videotaping. The blocking plot serves to record the blocking of actors and sets and to record the storyboard sketch of every video frame proposed for production.

Notes on use: Many copies of the blocking plot form may be needed. Two blocking frames and storyboard frames are contained on each page. There is a lead page for the series and a secondary page for the remainder. Each page of the blocking plot form is designed to be inserted into the director's copy of the commercial script facing the respective page of script dialogue. The director should sketch the storyboard frame from the production storyboard approved by the client of the commercial. Then from the location site survey form and site survey photographs the bird's eye floor plan can be drawn. The director should then position the actors in the floor plan and indicate the blocking for the actor(s). Then the camera should be sketched in place to achieve the shot(s) as proposed in the storyboard frame. Each separate bird's eye floor plan is drawn adjacent to a storyboard frame. Neither the floor plan nor storyboard frame need to be redrawn each time if no major changes occur to the storyboard or floor plan and nothing is to be added.

Glossary

Script Page Every blocking plot and storyboard frame should be related to its respective place in the script. The script page number should be recorded here.

Script Unit The blocking plot and storyboard should also be related to the script unit to which it refers. The script unit should be recorded here.

Storyboard Frame The production basis for the video commercial is an approved storyboard. The blocking plot for each storyboard frame should be related to the respective frame of the production storyboard. The number of each frame should be recorded here.

Shot No. After the design of the master script, the director will create a shot list from the storyboard frames. The shot list number for each storyboard frame is recorded here. This shot number should be entered at the corresponding in-cue on the script dialogue or scene directions on the script pages opposite the blocking plot form page.

3:4 Video Frame This is the storyboard video aspect ratio frame. The sketch of the approved shot from the production storyboard should be drawn in this frame.

Framing The choice of framing (e.g., XCU, CU, MS, LS, XLS) should be checked here. This will facilitate calling out directions to the camera operator on location.

Change to If camera framing is to change during the shot, that camera framing change can be checked here.

Camera Motion The camera motion that will be required as part of the shot or the change of framing during the shot indicated in the storyboard frame can be checked here.

Lighting The director can check the kind of lighting required for the shot in this area of the form.

Sound The audio requirements for videotaping this shot can be checked here. Synchronous means that both audio and video will be recorded; silent means that the shot will not require any sound; wild means that the video need not be recorded—sound alone needs to be recorded.

Bird's Eye Floor Plan The director should reproduce in reduced images the location environment for the set. This should include the properties on the location set. The director should then place the actors (using circles with the initial letter of the character for each actor) in the set and block them (using arrows and repeating the actor's circle). The director should then draw the camera in place to achieve the shot sketched in the storyboard frame for the shot.

Description of Take/Unit This area of the form allows for some notation of special directions for the particular take. This may involve the actors, some blocking movement, or the use of some prop.

In-cue This entry can be the first words of dialogue of the shot or some indication from scene directions for the beginning of the proposed shot.

Out-cue This entry can be the final words of dialogue of the shot or some indication from scene directions for the ending of the proposed shot.

• Shot List Form

Production process: Video commercial preproduction

Responsibility: Director

Purpose: To translate the proposed storyboard frames from the blocking plot into location videotape recording shots or camera takes.

Objective: The shot list form organizes each proposed storyboard frame and blocking plot into videotaping shots. Each shot should generate the necessary video to create the proposed edits as designed on the production story-board and script. Each numbered shot is then entered on the dialogue of the script at the spot where the proposed shot is to be edited. This preproduction task facilitates the "what's next" syndrome during location productions. The shot list should exactly define every camera set-up, lens framing, and video shot needed to achieve that video. The shot list form will translate each proposed shot from the blocking plot to a simpler list for the advantage of the camera operator, videotape recorder operator, audio director, and lighting director.

Glossary

Location Every planned location site camera set-up and change of location site camera set-up should be noted in this column.

Shot No. From the blocking plot form, every proposed shot needed to create the storyboard frame of the commercial script should be numbered consecutively. The respective number should be recorded here. The shot numbers are location-specific. Each different location shot list can begin with the count of one.

Master Shot If a proposed shot is a master shot or establishing shot (e.g., XLS) for a scene it should be noted here. For example, a master shot might be an XLS of a couple walking toward the camera during dialogue.

Cut-in Shot If a proposed shot is a cut-in (from a master shot), it should be noted in this column. For example, a cut-in would be a CU shot of one of the couple in the master shot.

Cut-away Shot Unlike the cut-in (to a master shot), the cut-away shot is relevant but extraneous to (usually away from) the master scene shot. An example of a cut-away would be generic footage of a city street.

Shot Framing Shot framing directions for every proposed shot should make use of the symbols for the basic camera shot framing: XLS, LS, MS, CU, and XCU. This would communicate to the camera operator the lens framing for the proposed shot. The framing choice for the shot should be checked on the blocking plot by the director. That framing direction should be recorded here.

Shot Motion Shot motion directions should indicate the kind of movement desired in the proposed shot. Movement in a shot can be either primary movement (on the part of the talent in front of the camera) which is the blocking of the talent, or secondary movement (on the part of the camera itself) which can be the pan, tilt, arc, truck, dolly, pedestal, or zoom. This direction too should have been checked by the director on the blocking plot form. That motion direction should be repeated here.

Content Notes Any particular details of any shot that are not covered in the previous directions can be noted here. Content notes may be found in the description of the take directions from the blocking plot form. What is considered important to production crew members should be repeated here.

• **Production Schedule Form**

Production process: Video commercial preproduction

Responsibility: Producer

Purpose: To organize and schedule the videotape production of the individual script and location units of the video commercial.

Objective: The production schedule form organizes the elements of each remote location into a production day and date for videotaping. The form serves to notify the production crew and talent of specific location address, date, time, and script pages of scheduling the videotape production of the commercial. Because the commercial video genre is a short genre, rarely is more than a single production day needed. The schedule also sets an alternate date, projected equipment set-up and location strike time, and approximate times for completing each stage of the shoot.

Glossary

Shooting Day This area of the form sets the specific date (weekday, month, and day) for the shooting day. The production schedule form also firms up an alternate rain date.

Location Site The remote environment/place approved for the shoot after site survey was completed should be noted here. This names the building and geographic area where the videotaping is to take place.

Location Map No. This notation relates the location site and address to a municipal map of the geographic area (e.g., H-3).

Location Host The name of the location personnel responsible for the facility/area where the shoot is to occur should be recorded here. This is the everyday contact person with whom the producer will cooperate on details of the location and the shoot. A contact telephone number where the location host can be reached should be included.

Crew Call The time and place of the production crew starting crew call should be entered here.

Cast Call The time and place for the arrival call for cast is also listed. Because the cast do not need the lead time for equipment set-up as the production crew do, the cast call can be up to an hour later than the production crew call. Time should be allotted for make-up if make-up is being required for the cast.

Set-up This entry is a range of time including a deadline for the production crew to complete all equipment set-up and checks of the equipment.

Projected Strike Time This time sets an approximate termination hour for completing the shoot and striking the location.

Shoot Order Units If the production script was arranged in script units, this column records the order in which the script units will be shot.

Script Pages This column coordinates and records the script pages that will be produced at each stage of the shoot.

Setting The specific setting within the location where the videotaping will occur is listed here.

Approx. Time A range of hours and minutes approximating the time needed to complete the script units or script pages proposed for production during the shooting day.

Cast The cast who will be a part of the videotaping are listed here.

Action Properties On many location shoots, some action properties are required, e.g., an automobile, an animal. The action properties required for the respective script units/pages are recorded here.

Comments The comments section allows the producer the opportunity to make any additional notes to be called to the attention of the crew and talent.

• Audio Plot Form

Production process: Video commercial preproduction

Responsibility: Audio director

Purpose: To facilitate and encourage the design of sound perspective and recording on the remote location video commercial production.

Objective: The audio plot form is designed to prompt the audio director to weigh the location environment and sound production values in the planning for audio equipment and quality microphone pick-up and recording during remote commercial videotaping.

Notes on use: The audio plot form is intended to encourage preproduction by the audio director. One plot for every location set is probably adequate, although multiple forms might be required in a very detailed and complicated sound recording take.

Glossary

Script Page The audio director requires an orientation to the respective pages of a script for every location set to be miked.

Script Unit The script unit being videotaped is also another orientation to the script to benefit the audio director.

Storyboard Frame Given the close reliance of commercial production to an approved storyboard, it is appropriate that the respective storyboard frames for which sound recording is required be recorded here.

Shot No. The number of the shot being videotaped from the shot list is a good determination for the audio director of the need for significant changes in sound design during a shoot. The shot number from the blocking plot should be recorded here.

Location This notation is a reminder of the location environment in which the videotaping is to occur.

Lighting This area of the plot notes the basic facts for sound perspective design: inside or outside, day or night.

Sound This choice of sound recording needs indicates what would be required on the set by the audio director. Synchronous sound indicates that both audio and video are recorded during a take; silent means that video only is required; wild means that a sound track will be recorded with or without video. This is required when a location ambience track is called for in production design during editing.

Microphone The audio director can make a choice of microphones to be used during videotaping the proposed shot.

3:4 Video Frame Insofar as the audio design of a shot is affected and in return affects what the shot shows, occasionally the composition of the framing dictates the sound perspective needs. The audio director may sketch from the blocking plot elements of the storyboard frame as an aid to sound recording design for specific shots of the production.

Framing The extent of the framing of subjects also determines sound perspective design. The composition of framing is indicated by checking the appropriate symbols for frame composition as checked on the blocking plot for the shot.

Sound Perspective When a change in framing is indicated, it could require a change in sound perspective or that the change in framing be calculated in the basic sound design. The new framing composition is indicated by checking the appropriate symbols for new framing. Quality sound perspective creates the auditory sense that when an actor is framed closely, sound levels should be higher; when an actor is framed at a distance, sound levels should be lower. Close or distant framing will also indicate to an audio director that careful use of a microphone mount will have to be controlled to avoid catching the mike in the camera shot or the presence of mike or boom shadows in the shot.

Bird's Eye Floor Plan The best preproduction information for the audio director is the floor plan for the location with actors' blocking and movement indicated. This should be sketched in this box from the blocking plot. Where the camera is to be placed is also important to the audio director, sound design, and microphone and mike grip placement during production.

Description of Take/Unit Any director's notes on the elements of the take that will affect sound design and recording should be noted here. For example, excessive movement of actors or properties and expressive gestures could affect sound recording and control on a location. The fact that some sound playback may be required during a take would be noted here.

In-Cue The in-cue, either from script dialogue or action, can affect the sound design of a take. That in-cue should be noted here.

Out-cue The out-cue or final words of dialogue or action can affect sound design. Notation of that cue should be made here.

• Lighting Plot Form

Production process: Video commercial preproduction

Responsibility: Lighting director

Purpose: To prepare and organize the lighting design of the video commercial remote location production shoot.

Objective: The lighting plot form is designed to facilitate the lighting design for the lighting director for every different location set. The plot serves to preplan the placement of lighting instruments, kind of lighting, lighting control, and lighting design. When lighting is preplanned, lighting equipment needs are easily realized and provided.

Notes on use: The lighting plot form is created to encourage preplanning for lighting design and production. Hence, the more lighting needs and aesthetics that can be anticipated, the better the lighting production tasks.

At the minimum, every different location set lighting design should be created in advance of the location production. Lighting design can begin after the director's script is complete. The basics to planning lighting design are the bird's eye floor plan, the actors' blocking, the time of day, and the mood of the script. This information will be available from the director after blocking plots are completed. A different plot is not required for every shot on the shot list. Base lighting design need not change completely as camera placement changes, but changes of location require all new lighting set-up and design. It is these changes that the lighting director needs to be aware of.

Glossary

Script Page The lighting director requires an orientation to the respective pages of a script for every location set to be lighted.

Script Unit The script unit being videotaped is also another orientation to the script to benefit the lighting director.

Storyboard Frame Because the basic orientation to the production of the commercial is the approved storyboard, the corresponding storyboard frame(s) for which the lighting is being designed should be recorded here.

Shot No. The number of the shot being videotaped from the shot list is a good determination for the lighting director of any need for significant changes in lighting design during a shoot. The shot number from the shot list or blocking plot should be recorded here.

Location This notation is a reminder of the location environment in which the videotaping is to occur.

Lighting This area of the plot notes the basic facts for lighting design: inside or outside, day or night.

Light Change It is important to lighting design and lighting control to know if the script or the director plans any change of lighting during the shot being videotaped. This notation alerts the lighting director to that need.

Mood One of the functions of lighting design is to create mood. An indication of the mood to be created in the shot is noted here.

3:4 Video Frame Insofar as the lighting design of a shot is affected and in return affects what the shot shows, occasionally the composition of the framing will dictate the lighting needs. The lighting director may sketch from the script elements of the storyboard frame as an aid to lighting design for specific shots of the production.

Framing The extent of the framing of subjects will also determine lighting design. The composition of framing is indicated by checking the appropriate symbols for frame composition as checked on the script for the shot.

Change When a change in framing is indicated, it could require a change in lighting or that the change in framing be calculated in the basic lighting design. The new framing composition is indicated by checking the appropriate symbols for new framing.

Bird's Eye Floor Plan The best preproduction information for the lighting director is the floor plan for the location with actors' blocking and movement indicated. This should be sketched in this box from the blocking plot. Where the camera is to be placed is also important to the lighting director and lighting design.

Description of Take/Unit Any director's notes on the elements of the take that will affect lighting design should be noted here.

Lighting Instruments/Lighting Accessories/Filters/Property Lights/Windows These lists in the plot form are designed to assist the lighting director in considering all elements of lighting design and materials in the preparation of the lighting plot. A lighting director can make notation in the proper space in planning for the particular design of each set.

In-cue A lighting director may find it convenient to make note of the in-cue from the script when (on what action or dialogue) the lighting control is to begin or change.

Out-cue The same notation on an out-cue of action or dialogue for the end of a shot or a change of lighting may be advantageous to the lighting director.

• **Equipment Checklist Form**

Production process: Video commercial preproduction

Responsibility: Camera operator, videotape recorder operator, lighting director, audio director

Purpose: To suggest and account for all possible equipment and accessories necessary for a successful remote video commercial shoot.

Objective: The equipment checklist form is an all-inclusive checklist for equipment and accessories hardware that may be used or needed on a video production location site. The checklist notes first the equipment available to the production crew, usually the equipment owned by the production facility. Second, the list notes that equipment that may have to be purchased for the shoot. Third, the checklist allows for notation for any equipment that may have to be rented for the shoot. There are blank lines in equipment groups to personalize the checklist for an individual production or facility.

Glossary

Location(s) The location(s) for which the equipment will be needed should be noted here.

Avl This abbreviation stands for available equipment that may be owned by the production facility itself. A check in this column indicates that the equipment or accessory is available to the production crew and free to be used on the scheduled production day.

Pch This abbreviation stands for purchase and indicates that the needed equipment or accessory will have to be purchased for the production project. Items checked as needing to be purchased will probably require some other requisition step and approval. The checklist also does not imply when the purchasing will be done or by whom. This is the responsibility of the production crew member.

Rnt This abbreviation stands for rent and indicates that the needed equipment or accessory is not available, perhaps too expensive to purchase for the shoot, and will have to be rented from a supplier. Similar to items checked in the purchase column, additional steps may be required in the process of obtaining the rented equipment. Some requisition may have to be made, approval received, and rental details made.

Camera/Recorder/Tripod/Test Equipment/Audio/Power Supplies/Lighting/Cables These areas of the form listed are an attempt to anticipate all possible equipment and accessories needs for a remote video production. Many items may be superfluous. They are listed as an attempt to suggest all possible production needs and equally to suggest the use of some hardware that could be needed during a remote location shoot. One way to use this checklist is to permit it to suggest hardware elements to make the experience of a remote video shoot smooth and productive.

Miscellaneous This area of the form is the result of years of remote video production experience and represents many production disasters during which these elements could have made a difference. Some items are redundant; some may suggest some use not before anticipated. Most items are helpful to the good order and task facilitation on location.

• **Continuity Notes Form**

Production process: Video commercial production

Responsibility: Continuity secretary

Purpose: To record during remote videotaping the details of all elements of the production as an aid to reestablishing details for sequential shots. The need is to facilitate a continuity of production details so that editing across shots is continuous.

Objective: The video continuity form is a record of all possible video production details (e.g., location, talent, properties, dialogue) that must carry over from shot to shot and across edits in postproduction. The nature of single camera production is the fact that whereas videotaped shots are separate in production, the final video editing of various shots must look continuous. The continuity form records specific details at all facets of production and records them to reestablish the details in subsequent videotaping.

Notes on use: The form is designed to be used for each separate shot being taken in single camera remote field production. This means that for any single shot with many takes, one continuity notes page should be used. In preparing for a lengthy remote shoot involving many shots to be achieved and many camera and lighting set-ups, many copies of this form will have to be made.

The person keeping continuity notes should be observant. The role demands attention to the slightest detail of the production that may have to be reestablished in another camera take. The role needs a crew person with 100% of the time spent on note taking.

Admittedly, the immediacy of replaying video on a playback monitor on location is a fast check on any detail in a previous videotaped take. Although playback is fast, it is time-consuming and it is not a habit that a director should have. Careful continuity notes are still a requirement in remote single camera video commercial production.

Glossary

Slate No. A production slate may have a consecutive number attached to it. That number is recorded here.

Continuity Secretary The continuity secretary's name should be recorded here. The extent of detail necessary in the production of remote single camera video commercials is so great that a full-time continuity secretary is a necessity. Continuity note taking is not a hit or miss task in remote production.

Set-up/Location A description or sketch of the location or the set-up of the environment is required here. Note should be taken of things that were moved (e.g., action properties) to be replaced.

Interior/Exterior These choices allow the notation of whether the shoot is indoor or outdoor.

Day/Night These choices allow the notation of time of day.

Sync Cam 1/2 This alternative is the indication that the shoot is video and audio synchronous recording and indicates which audio channel is being used for recording the audio signal, channel 1 or channel 2.

Silent This choice indicates that the camera is taking video without recording any audio signal.

Wildtrack Wildtrack means that audio signals are being recorded without video. For example, to record a portion of location ambience for later audio mixing would not require video signals also.

WT with Cam This alternative, wildtrack with camera, indicates that a wildtrack is being recorded with a video signal also.

Sequence No. Some remote production video units are parts of a numbered sequence. This entry is used to record the sequence number being videotaped.

Shot No. When a shot list is being followed on location, the sequential number of the shot being videotaped is recorded here.

Script Page No. For a script being produced with numbered pages, the page number of the script page being videotaped is recorded in this space.

Storyboard Frame No. Similar to most commercial production stages, an orientation to the storyboard frame being videotaped is crucial. The respective frame number is recorded here.

Costume/Make-up/Properties Notes This area should be used to record all details noticed during production that may have to be reestablished for a subsequent shot. Note should be taken of any costume use (e.g., a tie off-centered, a pocket flap tucked in), make-up detail (e.g., smudged lipstick, position of a wound), or property use (e.g., half-smoked cigarette in the right hand between index and middle finger or fresh ice cream cone in the left hand).

Tape No. This should be a record of the numerically coded videotape being recorded for this shot. This record should coordinate this shot with a particular videocassette. The videotape recorder operator has the correct videotape number of the tape being recorded.

Circle Takes (1–10) This area of the form facilitates record of each subsequent take of a shot or scene. The best use of these boxes is to circle each number representing the take in progress until the take is satisfactorily videotaped.

End Board The normal practice of indicating on the videotape leader what take of a shot is being recorded is to use the slate. If a particular take is flubbed or messed up for a minor problem (e.g., an actor missing a line), a producer might simply indicate that instead of stopping the taping and beginning from scratch. The crew keeps going by starting over without stopping. Because the slate then was not used to record at the beginning of the retake, an end board is used; the slate is recorded on tape at the end of the take instead of at the beginning. This note alerts the postproduction crew not to look for a slate at the beginning of that take but at the end.

Timer/Counter This area of the form should be used to record either a consecutive stopwatch time or the consecutive videotape recorder digital counter number. Both of these times should be a record of the length into the videotape where this take is recorded. Therefore, the stopwatch or the counter should be at zero when the tape is rewound to its beginning at the start of the tape. It is a good practice for the videotape recorder operator to call the counter numbers aloud to the continuity note taker at the beginning of every take.

Reason for Use/Not Good The benefit of the continuity notes is to save the tedium of reviewing all takes after a shoot to make a determination of the quality of each take. If conscientious notes are taken here, a judgmental notation on the quality of each take is recorded, and one postproduction chore is complete. Usually, a producer makes a judgment on location anyway in determining whether to retake a shot or move on to a new shot. The continuity secretary should note whether the take is good or not, and the reason for that judgment.

Action Continuity details on any action during the take should be noted here. For example, the direction talent takes when turning, or the hand used to open a door should be recorded.

Dialogue An area of continuity interest can be the dialogue of the script. Here notation should be made of any quirk of dialogue used in a take that may have to be repeated in a take intended for a matched edit.

• **Talent Release Form**

Production process: Video commercial production

Responsibility: Producer

Purpose: To give the producer and the production company legal rights over the video and audio recording of individual talent.

Objective: The talent release form is a legal document, which when filled out and signed by talent, gives to the producer and the producing organization the legal right to use both video and audio recording of an individual for publication. This form is especially necessary in the case of talent when profit may be gained from the eventual sale of the video product. If talent contracts were completed and signed, talent releases were probably included. When talent volunteer their services or perform for only a nominal fee or other gratuity, a signed talent release is recommended. Generally, any talent being featured in video and audio taping should sign a talent release before the final video production is aired.

Glossary

Talent Name This entry should contain the name of the individual talent recorded on video or audio.

Commercial Title The title of the commercial being produced becomes a reference point for the talent and the release forms.

Recording Location The location site of the video or audio recording should be entered here.

Producer The name of the supervising producer should be entered here.

Producing Organization The incorporated name of the video producing organization should be entered here.

Note: The expression, "For value received," may imply that some remuneration, even a token remuneration, be required for the form to be legally binding. When there is any doubt about the legal nature of the document, consult a lawyer.

TELEVISION SCRIPT

VIDEO COMMERCIAL PRODUCTION

Producer:	Commercial Title:
	Client:
Director:	Length: :
	Date: / /
	Page of

VIDEO	AUDIO

VIDEO COMMERCIAL PRODUCTION TELEVISION SCRIPT	Page	of
VIDEO	**AUDIO**	

STORYBOARD

VIDEO COMMERCIAL PRODUCTION

Producer:

Director:

Commercial Title:
Client:
Length: :
Page   of

VIDEO SCRIPT/STORYBOARD
VIDEO COMMERCIAL PRODUCTION

Producer:

Director:

Commercial Title:
Client:
Length: :
Date: /   /
Page   of

VIDEO	AUDIO

VIDEO	AUDIO

PRODUCTION BUDGET
VIDEO COMMERCIAL PRODUCTION

Producer:

Director:

Commercial Title:
Client:
Length: :

No. Preproduction Days: [ ] Hours: [ ] First Shooting Date: /   /
No. Studio Shoot Days: [ ] Hours: [ ] Completion Date: /   /
No. Location Days: [ ] Hours: [ ] Location Sites:
No. Post Production Days: [ ] Hours: [ ]

SUMMARY OF PRODUCTION COSTS	ESTIMATED	ACTUAL
1. Preproduction costs		
2. Production crew		
3. Director		
4. Production materials and expenses		
5. Location expenses		
6. Properties, wardrobe, animals		
7. Studio rental and expenses		
8. Set design and construction		
9. Set construction materials		
10. Equipment rental		
11. Videotape stock		
12. Miscellaneous		
13. Talent		
14. Talent expenses		
15. Sub Total		
16. Post production costs/editing		
17. Sound		
18. Personnel		
19. Art work		
20. Sub Total		
21. Contingency		
22. Grand Total		

COMMENTS

PREPRODUCTION COSTS

CREW	ESTIMATED				ACTUAL			
	Days	Rate	O/T Hrs	Total	Days	Rate	O/T Hrs	Total
1. Producer								
2. Asst Director								
3.								
4. Camera Operator								
5. Videotape Operator								
6. Audio Director								
7. Boom Operator								
8. Lighting Director								
9. Electrician								
10.								
11. Grip								
12. Continuity Secretary								
13.								
14. Make-Up								
15. Hair Stylist								
16. Costuming								
17.								
18. Location Scout(s)								
19. Storyboard Artist								
20.								
	Sub Total							

PRODUCTION COSTS

CREW	ESTIMATED				ACTUAL			
	Days	Rate	O/T Hrs	Total	Days	Rate	O/T Hrs	Total
21. Producer								
22. Asst Director								
23.								
24. Camera Operator								
25. Videotape Operator								
26. Audio Director								
27. Boom Operator								
28. Lighting Director								
29. Electrician								
30.								
31. Grip								
32. Continuity Secretary								
33.								
34. Make-Up								
33. Hair Stylist								
36. Costuming								
37.								
38. Location Scout(s)								
39. Storyboard Artist								
40.								

CREW (Con't)	ESTIMATED				ACTUAL			
	Days	Rate	O/T Hrs	Total	Days	Rate	O/T Hrs	Total
41. Slate Person								
42.								
Sub Total								

DIRECTOR	ESTIMATED				ACTUAL			
	Days	Rate	O/T Hrs	Total	Days	Rate	O/T Hrs	Total
43. Preproduction Fees								
44. Travel								
45. Per Diem								
46. Production Days Fees								
47. Post Production Fees								
48.								
49. Miscellaneous								
50.								
Sub Total								

PRODUCTION MATERIALS AND EXPENSES	ESTIMATED	ACTUAL
51. Auto Rentals: No. of Cars		
52. Air Fares: No. of People ( ) x Amt per Day ( )		
53. Per Diems: No. of People ( ) x Amt per Day ( )		
54. Trucking		
55. Deliveries and Taxis		
56.		
57. Casting: Prep Days Casting Days Call back		
58. Casting Facilities		
59. Working Meals		
60.		
Sub-Total		

LOCATION EXPENSES	ESTIMATED	ACTUAL
61. Location Fees		
62. Permits		
63. Insurance		
64. Vehicle Rental		
65. Parking, Tolls, and Gas		
66. Shipping/Trucking		
67. Scouting		
Travel		
Car Rental		
Housing		
Per Diem		
68. Taxis/Other Transportation		
69. Location Police/Firemen		
70. Gratuities		

LOCATION EXPENSES (Con't)	ESTIMATED	ACTUAL
71. Miscellaneous		
72.		
Sub Total		

PROPERTIES, WARDROBE AND ANIMALS	ESTIMATED	ACTUAL
73. Prop Rental		
74. Prop Purchase		
75. Wardrobe Rental		
76. Wardrobe Purchase		
77. Picture Vehicles		
78. Animals and Handlers		
79. Miscellaneous		
80.		
Sub Total		

STUDIO RENTAL AND EXPENSES	ESTIMATED				ACTUAL			
	Days	Rate	O/T Hrs	Total	Days	Rate	O/T Hrs	Total
81. Rental: Preproduction								
82. Rental: Production								
83. Rental: Post Product								
84. Generator/Operator								
85. Electrical Power								
86. Studio Charges								
87. Meals: Crew/Talent								
88. Security								
89. Miscellaneous								
90.								
Sub Total								

SET DESIGN AND CONSTRUCTION	ESTIMATED				ACTUAL			
	Days	Rate	O/T Hrs	Total	Days	Rate	O/T Hrs	Total
91. Set Designer								
92. Carpenter(s)								
93. Grip(s)								
94. Outside Props								
95. Inside Props								
96. Scenics								
97. Electrician(s)								
98. Strike Personnel								
99.								
100. Miscellaneous								
101								
Sub Total								

SET CONSTRUCTION MATERIALS	ESTIMATED	ACTUAL
102. Set Dressing Rentals		
103. Set Dressing Purchases		
104. Lumber		
105. Paint		
106. Hardware		
107. Special Effects		
108. Trucking		
109. Miscellaneous		
110.		
Sub Total		

EQUIPMENT RENTAL	ESTIMATED	ACTUAL
111. Camera Rental		
112. Videotape Recorder Rental		
113. Audio Rental		
114. Lighting Rental		
115. Generator Rental		
116. Crane/Cherry Picker Rental		
117. Walkie Talkies/Bull Horn(s)		
118. Dolly Rental		
119. Mobile Unit Rental		
120. Camera Plane/Chopper Rental		
121. Camera Car(s) Rental		
122. Camera Boat(s) Rental		
123. Production Supplies		
124. Miscellaneous		
125.		
126.		
Sub Total		

VIDEOTAPE STOCK	ESTIMATED	ACTUAL
127. Videotape:		
1" (:) x ($)		
3/4" (S :20) x ($)		
3/4" (:30) x ($)		
3/4" (:60) x ($)		
128.		
129. Miscellaneous		
Sub Total		

MISCELLANEOUS COSTS	ESTIMATED	ACTUAL
130. Petty Cash		
131. Air Shipping/Special Carriers		
132. Telephones/Cables		
133. Billing Costs		
134. Special Insurance		
135. Miscellaneous		
Sub Total		

TALENT	ESTIMATED				ACTUAL			
	Days	Rate	O/T Hrs	Total	Days	Rate	O/T Hrs	Total
136. Actor(s)								
137. Actor(s)								
138. Extra(s)								
139. Extra(s)								
140.								
141.								
142. Rehearsal Fees								
143. Audition Fees								
144. Miscellaneous								
145.								
	Sub Total							

TALENT EXPENSES	ESTIMATED	ACTUAL
146. Per Diems: No. of Days ( ) x Amt per Day ( )		
147. Air Fare: No. of People ( ) x Amt per Fare ( )		
148. Taxis/Other Transportation		
149. Talent Handling		
150. Miscellaneous		
151.		
Sub Total		

POST PRODUCTION COSTS

EDITING	ESTIMATED				ACTUAL			
	Days	Rate	O/T Hrs	Total	Days	Rate	O/T Hrs	Total
152. Time Coding								
153. On-Line Editing								
154.								
155. DVE Special Effects								
156. Tape-to-tape Duping								
157. Audio Mixing								
158. Audio Sweetening								
159. Sound Effects								
160. Character Generator								
161. Master(s)								
162. Dub(s)								
163. Tape Stock and Reels								
164. Paint Box								
165.								
166. Miscellaneous								
167.								
	Sub Total							

SOUND	ESTIMATED				ACTUAL			
	Days	Rate	O/T Hrs	Total	Days	Rate	O/T Hrs	Total
168. Narration Recording								
169. Sound Effects								
170. Stock Music Search								
171. Stock Music Fee								
172. Mixing								
173.								
174. Miscellaneous								
Sub Total								

PERSONNEL	ESTIMATED				ACTUAL			
	Days	Rate	O/T Hrs	Total	Days	Rate	O/T Hrs	Total
175. Editor								
176. Asst Editor								
177.								
178. Miscellaneous								
Sub Total								

ART WORK	ESTIMATED				ACTUAL			
	Days	Rate	O/T Hrs	Total	Days	Rate	O/T Hrs	Total
179. Art Work								
180. Animator(s)								
181.								
182. Animation Materials								
183. Animation Photography								
184. Miscellaneous								
185.								
Sub Total								

COMMENTS

SCRIPT BREAKDOWN

VIDEO COMMERCIAL PRODUCTION

Producer:

Director:

Commercial Title:
Client:
Length: :
Script Length: pages
Storyboard Frames:
Page   of
Date: /   /

STORY-BOARD FRMS	NO. OF SCRIPT LINES	INT/EXT	TIME	SETTING	LOCATION	CAST	SHOOT-ING ORDER

VIDEO COMMERCIAL PRODUCTION SCRIPT BREAKDOWN						Page	of
STORY-BOARD FRMS	NO. OF SCRIPT LINES	INT/EXT	TIME	SETTING	LOCATION	CAST	SHOOT-ING ORDER

LOCATION SITE SURVEY

VIDEO COMMERCIAL PRODUCTION

Producer:	Commercial Title:
Director:	Client:
Approval:	Script Unit(s):
Location Scouts:	Storyboard Frame(s):
	Date: / /

Location: Site Identification:
Local Contact Person: Comments:
  Name:
  Title:
  Address:
  City: State:
  Phone No.: (   )   -
Facilities Personnel: Comments:
  Name:
  Position Title:
  Address:
  City: State:
  Phone No.: (   )   -

LIGHTING PROBLEMS DEFINED

Light contrast ratios   Existing light control

Lighting intensity   Lighting use

Ceiling height   Floor description

Windows/Compass direction   Special considerations

POWER PROBLEMS DEFINED

Number of power outlets	Number of outlet prongs
Number of separate circuits	Location of circuit breakers
Types of fuses	Portable generator need

AUDIO PROBLEMS DEFINED

Interior environmental sounds	Exterior environmental sounds
Ceiling composition	Floor covering composition
Wall composition	

CAST AND CREW NEEDS

Restroom facilities	Eating facilities
Green room availability	Make-up facilities
Parking arrangements	Loading/unloading restrictions
Freight elevator	Hardware store

CIVIL EMERGENCY SERVICES

Police station   Fire station

LOCATION SECURITY AND EQUIPMENT SAFETY

Facility security   Equipment safe storage

Personnel values security   Overnight storage/security

OTHER RELEVANT INFORMATION

Public area power source   Traffic control

Clearance/Insurance needed   Exterior compass direction

Photographs taken   Location environment drawing/map

Other information:

OTHER COMMENTS/OBSERVATIONS

BLOCKING PLOT

VIDEO COMMERCIAL PRODUCTION

Commercial Title:	Director:	Date: / /

Script Page [ ]   Script Unit [ ]   Storyboard Frame [ ]   Shot No. [ ]

Lighting
- ☐ Interior
- ☐ Exterior
- ☐ Day
- ☐ Night

Sound
- ☐ Synchronous
- ☐ Silent
- ☐ Wild

Shot
- ☐ Master
- ☐ Cut-in
- ☐ Cut-away

Bird's Eye Floor Plan
Properties/Blocking/Camera

3:4 Video Frame

Framing: ☐ XCU ☐ CU ☐ MS ☐ LS ☐ XLS   Change to: ☐ XCU ☐ CU ☐ MS ☐ LS ☐ XLS
Camera Motion: Pan ☐ Tilt ☐ Zoom ☐ Dolly ☐ Truck ☐ Arc ☐ Pedestal ☐ Defocus ☐

Description of Take/Unit	Actors/Movement/Properties

In-Cue	Action/Dialog	Out-Cue	Action/Dialog

Script Page [ ]   Script Unit [ ]   Storyboard Frame [ ]   Shot No. [ ]

Lighting
- ☐ Interior
- ☐ Exterior
- ☐ Day
- ☐ Night

Sound
- ☐ Synchronous
- ☐ Silent
- ☐ Wild

Shot
- ☐ Master
- ☐ Cut-in
- ☐ Cut-away

Bird's Eye Floor Plan
Properties/Blocking/Camera

3:4 Video Frame

Framing: ☐ XCU ☐ CU ☐ MS ☐ LS ☐ XLS   Change to: ☐ XCU ☐ CU ☐ MS ☐ LS ☐ XLS
Camera Motion: Pan ☐ Tilt ☐ Zoom ☐ Dolly ☐ Truck ☐ Arc ☐ Pedestal ☐ Defocus ☐

Description of Take/Unit	Actors/Movement/Properties

In-Cue	Action/Dialog	Out-Cue	Action/Dialog

VIDEO COMMERCIAL PRODUCTION BLOCKING PLOT	Page	of

Script Page [ ]   Script Unit [ ]   Storyboard Frame [ ]   Shot No. [ ]

Lighting
☐ Interior
☐ Exterior
☐ Day
☐ Night

Sound
☐ Synchronous
☐ Silent
☐ Wild

Shot
☐ Master
☐ Cut-in
☐ Cut-away

Bird's Eye Floor Plan
Properties/Blocking/Camera

3:4 Video Frame

Framing: ☐ XCU ☐ CU ☐ MS ☐ LS ☐ XLS   Change to: ☐ XCU ☐ CU ☐ MS ☐ LS ☐ XLS

Camera Motion: Pan ☐ Tilt ☐ Zoom ☐ Dolly ☐ Truck ☐ Arc ☐ Pedestal ☐ Defocus ☐

Description of Take/Unit   Actors/Movement/Properties

In-Cue   Action/Dialog   Out-Cue   Action/Dialog

Script Page [ ]   Script Unit [ ]   Storyboard Frame [ ]   Shot No. [ ]

Lighting
☐ Interior
☐ Exterior
☐ Day
☐ Night

Sound
☐ Synchronous
☐ Silent
☐ Wild

Shot
☐ Master
☐ Cut-in
☐ Cut-away

Bird's Eye Floor Plan
Properties/Blocking/Camera

3:4 Video Frame

Framing: ☐ XCU ☐ CU ☐ MS ☐ LS ☐ XLS   Change to: ☐ XCU ☐ CU ☐ MS ☐ LS ☐ XLS

Camera Motion: Pan ☐ Tilt ☐ Zoom ☐ Dolly ☐ Truck ☐ Arc ☐ Pedestal ☐ Defocus ☐

Description of Take/Unit   Actors/Movement/Properties

In-Cue   Action/Dialog   Out-Cue   Action/Dialog

SHOT LIST

VIDEO COMMERCIAL PRODUCTION

Producer:

Director:

Commercial Title:
Length: :
Date: /   /
Page   of

LOCATION	SHOT						CONTENT NOTES
	NO.	MASTER	CUT-IN	CUT-AWAY	FRAMING	MOTION	

LOCATION	SHOT						CONTENT NOTES
	NO.	MASTER	CUT-IN	CUT-AWAY	FRAMING	MOTION	

VIDEO COMMERCIAL PRODUCTION SHOT LIST   Page   of

PRODUCTION SCHEDULE

VIDEO COMMERCIAL PRODUCTION

Producer:

Director:

Commercial Title:
Client: Length: :
Date: /   /
Page   of

SHOOTING DAY   RAIN DATE
                                                    ___/___/___
_____, _____, _____
      (Weekday)   (Month)   (Day)

Location Site:_____ Location Map No. _____

Address: _____
         City_____ State _____

Location Host:_____
Phone No.: (___)___-_____

Crew call:___:___ AM/PM
    Address:_____

Cast call:___:___ AM/PM
    Address:_____

Set-up:___:___ to ___:___   Projected Strike Time: ____:____

SHOOT ORDER UNITS	SCRIPT PAGES	SETTING	APPROX. TIME	CAST	ACTION PROPERTIES
			: to :		
			: to :		
			: to :		
			: to :		
			: to :		
			: to :		
			: to :		

Comments:

AUDIO PLOT

VIDEO COMMERCIAL PRODUCTION

Commercial Title: Audio Director: Date: /   /

Script Page ☐   Script Unit ☐   Storyboard Frame ☐   Shot No. ☐

Lighting
☐ Interior
☐ Exterior
☐ Day
☐ Night

Sound
☐ Synchronous
☐ Silent
☐ Wild

Microphone
☐ Directional
☐ Wireless
☐ _____

3:4 Video Frame

Framing: ☐ XCU ☐ CU ☐ MS ☐ LS ☐ XLS

Bird's Eye Floor Plan
Properties/Blocking/Camera/Lights
Mic Grip/Mic Holder/Cable Run

Sound Perspective: ☐ close ☐ distant

Description of Take/Unit   Actors/Movement/Properties
Location Playback Requirement

In-Cue   Action/Dialog   Out-Cue   Action/Dialog

Comments:

LIGHTING PLOT

VIDEO COMMERCIAL PRODUCTION

Commercial Title:	Lighting Director:	Date: / /

Script Page	Script Unit	Storyboard Frame	Shot No.

Lighting
- ☐ Interior
- ☐ Exterior
- ☐ Day
- ☐ Night

Light Change
- ☐ Yes
- ☐ No

Mood
_____
_____

3:4 Video Frame

Bird's Eye Floor Plan
Props/Blocking/Camera Placement
Lighting Instruments

Framing: ☐ XCU ☐ CU ☐ MS ☐ LS ☐ XLS   Change to: ☐ XCU ☐ CU ☐ MS ☐ LS ☐ XLS

Description of Take/Unit	Actors/Movement/Properties

Lighting Instruments
Key Lights:

Fill Lights:

Soft Lights:

Lighting Accessories
Barn Doors:

Flags:

Gobo:

Filters
Spun Glass:

Gels:

Screens:

Scrims:

Neutral Density:

Property Lights
Lamps:

Ceiling:

Other:

Windows   N
Compass Directions: W   E
                              S

Blacked:

Gels:

In-Cue	Action/Dialog	Out-Cue	Action/Dialog

Comments:

EQUIPMENT CHECKLIST
VIDEO COMMERCIAL PRODUCTION

Producer:

Camera Operator:

Videotape Recorder Operator:

Audio Director:

Lighting Director:

Commercial Title:

Client:

Length: :

Date: /   /

Location(s):

Avl Pch Rnt

CAMERA
- ☐ ☐ ☐ Video Camera
- ☐ ☐ ☐ Lenses
- ☐ ☐ ☐ Filters
- ☐ ☐ ☐ AC/DC Monitor
- ☐ ☐ ☐ Lg Screen Monitor
- ☐ ☐ ☐ _____

RECORDER
- ☐ ☐ ☐ Videotape Recorder
- ☐ ☐ ☐ _____
- ☐ ☐ ☐ _____

TRIPOD
- ☐ ☐ ☐ Tripod w/Head
- ☐ ☐ ☐ Camera Head Adapter
- ☐ ☐ ☐ Dolly
- ☐ ☐ ☐ _____

TEST EQUIPMENT
- ☐ ☐ ☐ Waveform Monitor
- ☐ ☐ ☐ Vectorscope
- ☐ ☐ ☐ Grey Scale
- ☐ ☐ ☐ Registration Chart
- ☐ ☐ ☐ White Card
- ☐ ☐ ☐ Headphones
- ☐ ☐ ☐ _____

AUDIO
- ☐ ☐ ☐ Shot gun Microphone
- ☐ ☐ ☐ Lavaliere Microphone
- ☐ ☐ ☐ Hand-held Microphone
- ☐ ☐ ☐ Fishpole
- ☐ ☐ ☐ Wind screens

Avl Pch Rnt

AUDIO (continued)
- ☐ ☐ ☐ Mixer
- ☐ ☐ ☐ Adapter plugs
- ☐ ☐ ☐ Earphone
- ☐ ☐ ☐ Headphones
- ☐ ☐ ☐ _____

POWER SUPPLIES
- ☐ ☐ ☐ Batteries for Camera
- ☐ ☐ ☐ Batteries for Recorder
- ☐ ☐ ☐ Batteries for Monitor
- ☐ ☐ ☐ AC Power Converter
- ☐ ☐ ☐ Microphone Batteries

LIGHTING
- ☐ ☐ ☐ Light Kit
- ☐ ☐ ☐ Soft Light Kit
- ☐ ☐ ☐ Barn Doors
- ☐ ☐ ☐ Spun Glass Filters
- ☐ ☐ ☐ Blue Gels
- ☐ ☐ ☐ Orange Gels
- ☐ ☐ ☐ Screens
- ☐ ☐ ☐ Scrims
- ☐ ☐ ☐ ND Filters
- ☐ ☐ ☐ Aluminum Foil
- ☐ ☐ ☐ Wooden Clothes Pins
- ☐ ☐ ☐ Light Meter
- ☐ ☐ ☐ Reflector
- ☐ ☐ ☐ Spare Bulbs
- ☐ ☐ ☐ Flags
- ☐ ☐ ☐ _____

Avl Pch Rnt   Avl Pch Rnt

☐ ☐ ☐ **CABLES**
        Multi-pin Cable Camera   ☐ ☐ ☐ Sewing Kit
            to Recorder   ☐ ☐ ☐ Paper, Pens, Felt Markers
☐ ☐ ☐   Video Cable Camera   ☐ ☐ ☐ Rope
            to Recorder   ☐ ☐ ☐ Barrier Cones
☐ ☐ ☐   Video Cable Camera   ☐ ☐ ☐ Poster Board
            to Waveform Monitor/   ☐ ☐ ☐ Flashlight
            Scope   ☐ ☐ ☐ Scissors
☐ ☐ ☐   Video Cable Scope to   ☐ ☐ ☐ 100' Power Cords
            Monitor   ☐ ☐ ☐ Staple Gun and Staples
☐ ☐ ☐   Audio Mixer Cable to   ☐ ☐ ☐ Power Outlet Boxes
            Recorder   ☐ ☐ ☐
☐ ☐ ☐   Audio Extension Cables   ☐ ☐ ☐ _____
☐ ☐ ☐   _____   ☐ ☐ ☐ _____
                                   ☐ ☐ ☐ _____
        MISCELLANEOUS   ☐ ☐ ☐ _____
☐ ☐ ☐   Video tape   ☐ ☐ ☐ _____
☐ ☐ ☐   Teleprompter   ☐ ☐ ☐ _____
☐ ☐ ☐   Teleprompter Script   ☐ ☐ ☐ _____
☐ ☐ ☐   Cue Card Paper   ☐ ☐ ☐ _____
☐ ☐ ☐   Duct Tape   ☐ ☐ ☐ _____
☐ ☐ ☐   Masking Tape   ☐ ☐ ☐ _____
☐ ☐ ☐   Spare Fuses   ☐ ☐ ☐ _____
☐ ☐ ☐   Tool Kit   ☐ ☐ ☐ _____
☐ ☐ ☐   Stopwatch   ☐ ☐ ☐ _____
☐ ☐ ☐   Slate   ☐ ☐ ☐ _____
☐ ☐ ☐   Chalk   ☐ ☐ ☐ _____
☐ ☐ ☐   Eraser
☐ ☐ ☐   Bullhorn
☐ ☐ ☐   Walkie-Talkie
☐ ☐ ☐   Dulling Spray
☐ ☐ ☐   Talent Release Forms
☐ ☐ ☐   Step Ladder
☐ ☐ ☐   Lens Cleaner and Tissue

CONTINUITY NOTES

VIDEO COMMERCIAL PRODUCTION

COMMERCIAL TITLE:				SLATE NO.

DIRECTOR:	CONTINUITY SEC'Y:	DATE / /

SET-UP/LOCATION	INTERIOR	DAY	SYNC Cam 1/2 SILENT	SEQUENCE NO.
	EXTERIOR	NIGHT	WILDTRACK WT with Cam	SHOT NO.
	SCRIPT PAGE NO.		STORYBOARD FRAME NO.	

COSTUME/MAKE-UP/PROPERTIES NOTES

TAPE NO.										
CIRCLE TAKES	1	2	3	4	5	6	7	8	9	10
END BOARD										
TIMER										
COUNTER										
REASON FOR USE/ NOT GOOD										

ACTION   DIALOGUE

TALENT RELEASE FORM

VIDEO COMMERCIAL PRODUCTION

Talent Name: _____
(Please Print)

Commercial Title: _____

For value received and without further consideration, I hereby consent to the use of all photographs, videotapes or film, taken of me and/or recordings made of my voice and/or written extraction, in whole or in part, of such recordings or musical performance

at _____ on _____ 19___
  (Recording Location)   _(Month)_   _(Day)_   _(Year)_

by_____ for_____
  (Producer)   _(Producing Organization)_

and/or others with its consent, for the purposes of illustration, advertising, or publication in any manner.

Talent Name_____
          (Signature)

Address_____ City_____

State _____ Zip Code _____

Date:____/____/____

If the subject is a minor under the laws of the state where modeling, acting, or performing is done:

Guardian _____ Guardian _____
        (Signature)   _(Please Print)_

Address _____ City _____

State _____ Zip Code _____

Date:____/____/____

261

Chapter 5

Music
Video
Production

INTRODUCTION

• Origin of the Music Video

The 1980s will go down in the history of television as the decade of the music video. The phenomenon of the music video had its roots in movie house sing-a-longs, in television commercials, and in the big film musicals. In 1981 the music video found a niche for itself in television. In June 1981 USA Cable Network premiered "Night Flight," featuring music videos. Then in August 1981 Warner-Amex introduced the 24-hour MTV channel.

There is perhaps no other video genre for which the television medium is the reason for its success. Television, the free forum (albeit a cable pay channel in some markets), presented the free video performance (no charge to the telecaster) of music groups and artists on film and videotape and immediately found an accepting audience. The rest is history.

It is important to realize that the great majority of music videos are shot on film, transferred to video, and edited. As seen in remote video drama production, the advantages (cheaper, faster) of video from start to finish are beginning to outweigh the disadvantages (film look missing), and more producers are tuning to video for the whole production.

• From Commercials to Music Videos

The closest format in the television medium to the music video is the television commercial. The commercial is a short video genre, often involving music, and often enough, conceptual and creative in content. It is no small wonder that many producers and directors of music videos started in commercial production. The form, content, and processes are similar.

THE PREPRODUCTION PROCESS

The preproduction process of music videos began as a free form process. With the formation and organization of the Music Video Producer's Association, there has been a real attempt to standardize some elements of the process of music video production.

• Personnel

The crew positions in music video production are small in number considering the extent of the production process. However, given the developing genre of the music video, it should not be surprising to find a small preproduction team. Perhaps the presence of many former commercial production personnel in early music video production has created from their commercial production experience a better and more creatively satisfying replacement to the preproduction organization of commercials.

Producer (P). The process of music video production begins with an independent producer. The producer initiates the preproduction process by writing the concept (analogous to a treatment) for a music track from a new release album. The producer, as in other video genres, is responsible for all preproduction details.

Director (D). The director is chosen by the producer. The director continues with the rest of the preproduction tasks and oversees the other crew assignments.

Camera operator(s) (CO). Once the director has begun preproduction stages, camera operator(s) are assigned. Music video productions usually work with professional artists who lip sync their own music. Directors of music videos work with two or more isolated cameras to elimi-

FLOWCHART AND CHECKLIST FOR MUSIC VIDEO PRODUCTION

PRODUCER (P)

PREPRODUCTION
- (1) Scans trade magazines for album producing groups
- (2) Secures music track cut
- (3) Writes a concept for a music video (music video concept form)
- (4) Obtains clearances: copyright and synchronization rights
- (5) Creates a storyboard (music video storyboard form)
- (6) Constructs a budget (production budget form)
- (7) Chooses and meets with director
- (8) Casts additional talent
- (9) Supervises location scouting (location site survey form)
- (10) Designs production schedule (production schedule form)
- (11) Obtains insurance coverage; notifies police

PRODUCTION
- (1) Supervises crew call
- (2) Meets location host
- (3) Supervises location rearrangement
- (4) Handles crew and artists/musicians' details
- (5) Secures talent release signatures (talent release form)

POSTPRODUCTION
- (1) Arranges postproduction schedule and facilities
- (2) Supervises postproduction preparation: master track, source tapes, storyboard, continuity notes
- (3) Observes editing with director
- (4) Reviews rough edit
- (5) Approves final edit

DIRECTOR (D)

PREPRODUCTION
- (1) Meets with producer
- (2) Assists in casting additional talent
- (3) Does concept/storyboard breakdown (storyboard breakdown form)
- (4) Directs location scouting (location site survey form)
- (5) Designs blocking plots (blocking plot form)
- (6) Develops shot list (shot list form)
- (7) Chooses and meets with CO
- (8) Chooses and meets with LD
- (9) Chooses and meets with AD
- (10) Chooses CS

PRODUCTION
- (1) Holds production meeting
- (2) Directs location rearrangement
- (3) Supervises equipment set-ups
- (4) Rehearses playback system
- (5) Blocks artists/musicians alone
- (6) Rehearses artists/musicians alone
- (7) Blocks camera(s) alone
- (8) Rehearses camera(s) alone
- (9) Rehearses both artists/musicians and crew
- (10) Makes changes/rehearses
- (11) Calls for take
- (12) Announces intentions: take/wrap/strike

POSTPRODUCTION
- (1) Supervises postproduction preparation: edits storyboard
- (2) Transfers master music track to master videotape
- (3) Creates rough editing
- (4) Reviews rough edit
- (5) Makes final edit

If the director does not edit:

TECHNICAL DIRECTOR/EDITOR (TD/E)
- (1) Edits from storyboard and continuity notes under supervision of director
- (2) Transfers master music track to master videotape
- (3) Edits rough edit
- (4) Rough edit reviewed by producer and director
- (5) Makes final edit
- (6) Submits final edit for producer's approval

CAMERA OPERATOR(S) (CO)

PREPRODUCTION
- (1) Meets with director and producer
- (2) Works with concept/storyboard and blocking plots
- (3) Prepares camera equipment/accessories list (equipment checklist)
- (4) Chooses and meets with VTRO
- (5) Chooses and meets with AD

PRODUCTION
- (1) Arranges camera equipment/accessories pick-up/delivery
- (2) Sets up and checks location camera
- (3) Blocks camera position
- (4) Rehearses camera blocking
- (5) Rehearses camera and artists/musicians
- (6) Makes changes/rehearses again
- (7) Videotapes take
- (8) Strikes camera equipment/accessories

POSTPRODUCTION
- (1) Returns remote camera equipment and accessories
- (2) Reports damaged, lost, malfunctioning equipment or accessories

LIGHTING DIRECTOR (LD)

☐ (1) Meets with director
☐ (2) Works storyboard, blocking plots, location survey, and shot list
☐ (3) Designs lighting plots (lighting plot form)
☐ (4) Prepares lighting equipment/accessories list (equipment checklist form)

☐ (1) Arranges lighting equipment/accessories pick-up/delivery
☐ (2) Sets up and checks location lighting
☐ (3) Strikes lighting equipment/accessories

☐ (1) Returns remote lighting equipment and accessories
☐ (2) Reports damaged, lost, malfunctioning equipment or accessories

VIDEOTAPE RECORDER OPERATOR(S) (VTRO)

☐ (1) Meets with CO
☐ (2) Works shot list
☐ (3) Orders videotape stock
☐ (4) Prepares equipment/accessories list (equipment checklist form)
☐ (5) Labels and organizes tape stock

☐ (1) Arranges videotape recording equipment/accessories pick-up/delivery
☐ (2) Sets up and checks location videotape recording equipment
☐ (3) Responds to director's call for rolling tape
☐ (4) Monitors vectorscope during videotaping
☐ (5) Strikes videotape recording equipment/accessories

☐ (1) Removes record buttons/labels source videotapes/stripes source videotapes
☐ (2) Reorders source tapes to final storyboard
☐ (3) Returns remote camera and lighting equipment and accessories
☐ (4) Reports damaged, lost, malfunctioning equipment or accessories

AUDIO DIRECTOR (AD)

☐ (1) Meets with director
☐ (2) Works with master track, location survey form, and blocking plots
☐ (3) Prepares audio playback equipment/accessories list (equipment checklist form)

☐ (1) Arranges audio playback equipment/accessories pick-up/delivery
☐ (2) Sets up and checks location audio playback system
☐ (3) Monitors audio playback
☐ (4) Follows director: playback for rehearsals and take(s)
☐ (5) Strikes audio playback equipment/accessories

☐ (1) Returns audio playback equipment and accessories
☐ (2) Reports damaged, lost, malfunctioning equipment or accessories

CONTINUITY SECRETARY (CS)

☐ (1) Prepares continuity notes sheets (continuity notes form)
☐ (2) Coordinates with VTRO

☐ (1) Observes and records continuity details
☐ (2) Releases actors after cut
☐ (3) Reestablishes details before subsequent shot

☐ (1) Reorders continuity notes sheets to the final storyboard

SLATE PERSON (SP)

☐ (1) Handles and updates slate
☐ (2) Coordinates with CS and VTRO
☐ (3) Follows director; slates video leader

MUSICIANS/ARTISTS/TALENT (T)

☐ (1) Rehearses lip synchronizing of music
☐ (2) Fits costumes, tests make-up

☐ (1) Stands in for lighting, audio, video checks
☐ (2) Prepares for costuming, make-up
☐ (3) Follows director: blocking, rehearsal, action, cut, freeze, take
☐ (4) Checks with CS
☐ (5) Is available/out-of-the-way

nate the tedium and time consumption of the single camera and at the same time get all the video footage desired from as few video takes as possible. Hence, for purposes of this text, at least two camera operators will be considered for production.

Lighting director (LD). The only other significant preproduction crew member who could gain from preproduction planning is a lighting director. The director hires or appoints the lighting director. Once the director of the production has storyboarded the concept and blocked the actors/artists and movement, the lighting director can begin lighting designs.

Audio director (AD). The audio director is chosen by the director and begins preproduction responsibilities by planning audio playback reproduction for accurate lip syncing by the musicians and artists. Preproduction audio planning entails checking location sites and knowing the audio playback requirements of the storyboard. Audio playback planning requires an equipment and accessories checklist.

Continuity secretary (CS). The continuity secretary is responsible for the proper and detailed note taking necessary to record all production details of the location shoot. The director chooses the continuity secretary. Preproduction responsibility entails organizing a structured approach to record notes of production details. The continuity secretary needs a set of codes, lists of crew, artists, and musicians, and a videotape stock code.

• Preproduction Stages

The first stage of preproduction is to select a prerecorded music track. Almost 100% of music videos are imaged to already recorded music. Music videos are usually produced for a cut or two from an artist or musician's recent release album and have become an almost necessary counterpart to every album recorded today.

Scanning trade magazines for new albums being produced (P 1). The professional producer reads the trade papers, especially *Variety,* for any notice of a musical group in recording sessions for a new release album. The producer needs to obtain a copy of the cut of a song or songs, and from a transcription of the lyrics or a test pressing of the album, writes a conceptual treatment (the concept) for a music video.

Securing a music track cut (P 2). To get a handle on the possibility of producing a music video, a producer has to get a hearing of the music tracks from a new release album. Then a transcription of the lyrics, some sense or knowledge of the style of music, and a history of the recording artist serve to help evaluate a new song and suggest some direction to the possible video images that might be used in the creation of the music video.

Writing the concept (P 3). New to the development of the music video is the idea of a concept. Having decided on a music track, the producer writes a concept of the proposed music video. A concept is synonymous with a

FIGURE 5–1
Getting started on a music video concept. Reading the trade magazines is a way to get started on a music video concept. The producer gets a copy of the song, then writes a concept and sends it to the musicians.

treatment required of other video genres (e.g., the documentary), but it focuses more on the creative design of the proposed music video. Using highly kinetic imagery in the description, a producer describes what will be a verbal description of the final music video.

Generally concepts express the performance of the group or artist(s) playing their song, an entirely narrative imaging apart from the group's performance, or even a mixture of both . . . or neither. There are also purely surrealistic music videos with no apparent relation to the music or lyrics of the song. It is on the strength of a concept that a recording artist contracts with a producer. (See the music video concept form.)

Obtaining legal clearances (P 4).   The producer must also obtain copyright clearance and synchronization rights from the owner of the copyright of the music for which the music video will be created. It is not uncommon for the recording artist(s) not to hold the copyright for the music they perform. Recording companies, who also seek to have music videos created for cuts of albums they publish, may also not be the owners of the copyright of the music. Besides copyright clearance, the right to add images to the music is called synchronization, and clearance rights to that must also be obtained apart from copyright clearance.

Creating a storyboard (P 5).   Preferences differ among producers (and directors) over the choice to create and to work from a storyboard (in lieu of a master script as in drama). Many directors, usually those with much experience, find it just as satisfying to work from a shot list. However, for beginning producers, the time spent in the preproduction design of a storyboard is never lost time. Preproduction tasks progress faster, producers and directors better communicate their ideas to others, and often productions progress less expensively with quality preproduction in the form of the storyboard. The producer who spends a thorough job preplanning the music video on a storyboard will commit location production work from the storyboard rather than from creative intuition at the moment.

The music video storyboard includes aspect ratio frames, music bars and measures, and the lyrics of the song. This way, exact beat and timing (pacing) can be achieved in a tangible way before production begins. Proposed images are graphically represented and an overall sense of the whole is achieved. (See the music video storyboard form.)

Constructing a budget (P 6).   With the concept and storyboard complete, the producer needs one more document for the artist's approval before continuing with preproduction and production—the budget. The budget is critical to building a production staff and crew. A model budget form can help a producer consider the many details that need funding. (See the production budget form.)

Choosing and meeting with the director (P 7).   The choice of a director for the music video production follows the approval of a budget. A producer chooses a director for

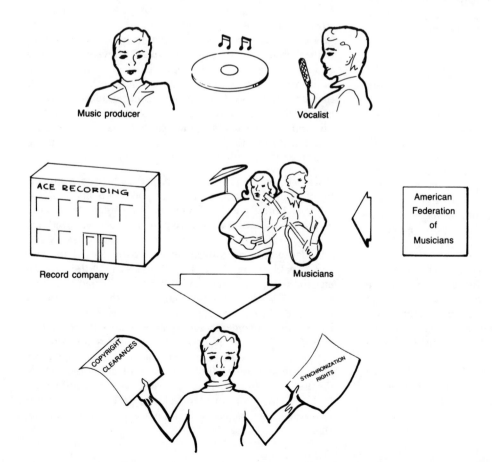

FIGURE 5–2
Getting clearances. The producer must obtain copyright clearance and synchronization rights from the song's copyright owners.

creative abilities and production management skills. The choice of a music track may suggest the type of director to be chosen. The period, mood, and style of the music could determine the qualities in a director suited for the production. During a preproduction meeting the producer should share the music track, concept, storyboard, and budget with the director.

Meeting with the producer (D 1).   The director should meet with the producer as the first step in preproduction. This may be the first time the director hears the music track, reads the concept and storyboard, and sees the budget. These documents become important elements to the director in the remaining stages of preproduction.

Casting the music video (P 8).   Following the choice of a director, casting the music video can be accomplished. The producer should involve the director in the choice of a cast. Besides the music artist(s) and/or group, there may be other roles to cast in imaging the music track. The artist(s) and/or group may have to act roles in imaging the video that may require some casting.

Assisting in casting the music video (D 2).   Because an important quality of a director of music videos is creativity, producers expect the assistance of the director during the choice of cast for the music video.

Practicing lip synchronizing to the music (T 1).   After casting the director may have to work with the artists on the technique of lip synchronizing to their music. Because music videos are produced to the recorded track from an album, any on-camera performance of the artists requires lip syncing. This is not easy to do without some prompting and practice.

Costume fitting and make-up testing (T 2).   The other preproduction requirement for the artists is costume fitting and make-up testing. It is possible that the creative design of the concept for the music video requires a period setting and costuming. Also, the artists may have to wear make-up unlike their preparation for a concert. Checking the fit of costumes should be done before location shooting. There are demands of the video medium on color and design, which should be known and tested before the shoot. Make-up should also be applied and critiqued before the location shoot. It would not be uncommon to actually light and videotape both costume and make-up tests to make certain of choices before production.

Doing a concept/storyboard breakdown (D 3).   The first preproduction task of the director of the music video is a breakdown of the concept/storyboard (similar to a script breakdown in drama production). The concept/storyboard breakdown is song-content-neutral and focuses on the analysis of production design in the concept/storyboard imaging of the video, which must be weighed before a production schedule can be designed. The breakdown makes note of what locations are necessary, whether the locations are interiors and exteriors, whether the time is day or night, what cast (recording group and/or actors) will be needed, what kind of sets will be needed on location, what hand or action properties are needed, and whether costumes are needed. (See the concept/storyboard breakdown form.)

Supervising location scouting and site survey (P 9).   The task of location scouting is the next stage in music video preproduction. Location scouting requires searching out and visiting possible sites for the remote production videotaping. The first production need from a location is that the requirements of the concept/storyboard must be met. Having met the concept/storyboard requirements, location scouting demands a thorough evaluation of a proposed site.

The producer and director may prefer to do their own location scouting. Other crew members might be used as location scouts. Location scouts should report back to the producer and director with summary notes on proposed sites, maps to the proposed location, diagrams of the location with compass points, and instant developing film pictures of all angles of the proposed site. (See the location site survey form.)

The producer should follow final location site approval with confirmation letters to the host location personnel. This confirmation should include all details of the production as previously discussed with the location host, confirmation of shooting date and time, as well as some notification of the extent of the production crew, cast, and equipment required. Closer to the shooting day, a courtesy reminder letter or telephone call should also be placed to the location host of the production and last minute details.

Directing location scouting and site survey (D 4).   The concept/storyboard breakdown and the shot list indicate the production requirements for remote locations. Together with a producer, the director should direct the scouting and surveying of potential location sites. Some directors, as producers, prefer to do location scouting themselves. If they choose not to do the actual scouting, location scouts can do the actual traveling and survey. It would not be uncommon for camera operators, lighting directors, and audio directors to do or be a part of location scouting also. (See the location site survey form.)

Designing blocking plots (D 5).   A preproduction responsibility of the director to the preproduction tasks of the other technical crew members is blocking plots. Once a director has approved the remote production locations, attention can turn to blocking plots for camera shots and the placement and movement of artists, musicians, and actors. A blocking plot is a bird's eye view of the location environment with physical properties indicated (e.g., set, furniture) and artists/musicians and their movements indicated. Artists are symbolized by circles with a code letter, and movements are symbolized by directed line segments. Blocking plots assist the camera operators to plan camera placements and videotape recorder operators for equipment set-up and placement. Blocking plots allow the lighting director to begin necessary preproduction. Lighting directors can plan lighting designs and account for needed lighting equipment before getting to a location site.

Developing the shot list (D 6). Once the blocking plots are completed, the shot list can be developed. The shot list creates the order of shots to be videotaped by camera placement positions that will be needed and the order of shooting each storyboard unit. (See the shot list form.)

Designing the production schedule (P 10). After the producer and director make location site decisions, the producer can create the production schedule. The concept/storyboard breakdown and shot list from the director are necessary to create a production schedule.

The production schedule is a calendar with dates, hours of the day, locations, cast, storyboard units to be produced, and crew call times. Production schedules also contain larger action props needed that day for production (e.g., a horse and buggy). Alternate shooting dates are also included in a production schedule, especially for exterior shoots. (See the production schedule form.)

It is not unusual to be able to shoot a music video in one day. If much more time is involved for such a short video piece, the costs become more prohibitive. Most songs average only three to five minutes in length. Hence, there is just so much video to be created. The producer must take into account the availability of the recording artists, which can be a difficult task in light of the travel and concert schedules of musicians and artists.

Similar to the drama production schedule, location sites, crew call times, cast, staggered for different stages of the music video, and action props all become elements in the production schedule.

The shooting order of the music video for purposes of the production schedule is determined by a variety of requirements. Location availability is often the first requirement. Not all chosen sites are advantageous simply because they are available (e.g., a shopping mall parking lot on weekends). Some requirements that determine scheduling are how open locations are to the general public, the day of the week a location is needed, the time of day the location is needed, cast of characters for a scene, and script units requiring that location.

Choosing and meeting with the camera operator(s) (D 7). Once location sites are determined and the shot list completed, a director is at the stage of preproduction to choose and involve the camera operator(s).

It is customary for professional directors to film or videotape the performance video of a group or artist(s) with multiple cameras, at least two. This is the process of isolated cameras. This multiple camera operation serves at least two purposes. With professional artists and musicians on location, less of their valuable time is spent if multiple cameras record their lip synchronization to amplified playback of the music track being imaged. Also, it is easier to match edits from multiple camera images from one and the same performance shoot than to take the time necessary to control continuity and try to match images from single camera videotape recordings.

Camera operators are chosen for their aesthetic capabilities in composing the view through the lens of the camera. Technical skills necessary for the camera operators

include the knowledge and experience with the remote video camera. The first requirement of the camera operator is to meet with the director and discuss the video camera needs of the production. The director should share the concept/storyboard, shot list, production schedule, and blocking plots with the camera operator. The location site survey forms may also be of interest.

Meeting with the producer and director (CO 1). The first requirement of the camera operator is to meet with the producer and the director to get a perspective on the music video, its creative concept, and the proposed production design. The camera operator plays an important role in achieving the creative goals of the production. The camera operator should receive a copy of the concept/storyboard, the shot list, the production schedule, and blocking plots.

Obtaining insurance and notifying police (P 11). When the music video production schedule is firm, insurance (equipment, bodily injury, and property) should be covered by the producer for all location sites, cast, and crew. When some location sites include exteriors, local police need to be notified and, when necessary, arrangements have to be made in advance for closing streets and regulating traffic. Even if the production does not need exterior locations of public places, the size of a production crew can be so large when invading a neighborhood or other public place that it is a good practice to notify police that a production crew is there and that it has the authorization of the owners and facilities personnel.

Working the storyboard, blocking plots, and shot list (CO 2). The next preproduction task for the camera operator is to become familiar with the storyboard, blocking plots, and shot list. These preproduction documents will become the bases for determining equipment needs for the production.

Preparing camera equipment and accessories list (CO 3). After meeting with the director and producer, the requirement of the camera operator is to prepare an equipment and accessories list of camera requirements. The list should include equipment/accessories available, those that need to be rented and those that will have to be purchased. (See the equipment checklist form.)

Choosing and meeting with a lighting director (D 8). The choice of a lighting director by the director completes the crew members who are aesthetically involved with the video qualities in the design of the music video production. A director should choose a lighting director who can create, in lighting design, the same mood, period, and style for the music video for which the director was chosen. After meeting with the director, the lighting director should have the storyboard, shot list, blocking plots, and production schedule.

Meeting with the director (AD 1). The audio playback director should meet with the director as a step to orchestrating the playback music tracks on location during production. The audio playback director should have a master copy of the music track to be produced and a copy of the storyboard and the shot list as documents to planning adequate location playback during production.

Working with the master track, the location survey forms, and the blocking plots (AD 2). After a meeting with the director the audio director for the location production should have the master track recording of the music to be produced, the location site survey forms, and the blocking plots. The master track should have backup copies made for safety and security purposes and work copies for testing purposes. The location survey forms will permit the audio director the opportunity to examine the location environment for adequate playback sound quality for lip syncing purposes during remote production. Blocking plots will alert the audio director to the placement of talent and will assist in determining playback speaker needs and placement.

Choosing and meeting with an audio playback operator (P 9). The director should choose an audio playback operator. The first requirement of the appointment is for the director to meet with the audio director and share production information, such as music track, the storyboard, and the shot list.

Meeting with the director (LD 1). As with all creative crew members, the lighting director should meet with the director after assignment to the crew. The lighting director should have copies of the storyboard, the shot list, blocking plots, and production schedule. A copy of the location site survey forms is advantageous.

Working the storyboard, shot list, blocking plots, and location survey forms (LD 2). The lighting director begins preproduction work by studying the storyboard, the shot list, blocking plots, and location site survey forms as a prelude to designing the placement of lights in creating the mood and setting necessary for the production of the music video. The lighting director will have to determine lighting design and equipment needs from these preproduction documents.

Designing lighting plots (LD 3). With the storyboard, shot list, blocking plots, and location site survey forms, the lighting director's next stage in preproduction is to design the lighting plot for each videotape take noted on the production schedule. The lighting director will need camera placement plots from the camera operator to know where to set-up lighting instruments and the direction to aim lights. (See the lighting plot form.)

Preparing lighting equipment and accessories list (LD 4). After designing lighting plots, the lighting director can assess the lighting equipment/accessory needs of the production shoot. Some lighting equipment may be available; some may have to be rented or purchased. (See the equipment checklist form.)

Choosing a videotape recorder operator(s) and holding a meeting (CO 4). Because there is a close working relationship between the camera operator and the videotape recorder operator, the camera operator should choose the videotape

recorder operator. The first requirement of the appointment is to meet together with them and share production information such as storyboard, shot list, and blocking plots.

Meeting with the camera operator(s) (VTRO 1). The videotape recorder operator should meet with the camera operator as a first stage of preproduction. Because the crew members will have to establish a close working relationship, this meeting serves to open communication and exchange production notes and ideas. The videotape recorder operator(s) should have a copy of the storyboard, shot list, blocking plots, and production schedule.

Working with the shot list (VTRO 2). The videotape recorder operator should determine from the shot list some estimate of the amount of videotape stock needed for the music video shoot. Keeping in mind the multiple videotape recorders being planned, the amount of videotape to be recorded will have to be multiplied. A common videotape shooting ratio in the determination of videotape stock is 3:1 or 4:1. Videotape shoots record 3 or 4 times the amount of videotape actually needed.

Ordering videotape stock (VTRO 3). One of the production necessities that may require lead time for ordering and purchasing is the videotape stock necessary for the project. The most common videotape stock is the ¾ inch videotape size in the small cassette unit 20 minutes in length. This varies if recording is to be done on 1 inch or ½ inch videotape recording equipment.

Preparing videotape recording equipment and accessories list (VTRO 4). After meeting with the camera operator and sharing preproduction information, the videotape recorder operator's next responsibility is to determine the videotape recording equipment and accessories needs for production videotaping. This equipment list will indicate what equipment is available and what will have to be rented or purchased. (See the equipment checklist form.)

Labeling and organizing videotape stock (VTRO 5). A preproduction requirement for the videotape recorder operator is to select a coding system that will facilitate handling and organizing videotape stock on location and in postproduction. Labeling involves identical coding on the cassette and on the videotape carrying case. Consecutive numbering organizes the videotapes for accurate and swift reordering after production. Coding and labeling can be complicated with multiple isolated cameras in production. Care in proper coding and labeling should be taken to avoid confusion during postproduction. A code for each camera must be added to other codes if necessary. The coding system should also be shared with the continuity secretary for the coordination of videotapes and location takes on the continuity record for the shoot itself.

Preparing audio playback equipment and accessories list (AD 3). After meeting with the director and working the preproduction documents exchanged, the audio director can begin accessing audio playback equipment and accessories needs for the production.

The need for audio on music video remote production

is solely for prerecorded music track playback. Playback facilitates the lip syncing necessary for videotaping the music video on location.

The audio playback needs include the correct audio fidelity reproduction equipment and adequate speakers for accurate sound reproduction on location. Quality playback equipment is essential on location to assure equivalent reproduction in playback to the quality of the master track. (See the equipment checklist form.)

Choosing a continuity secretary (D 10). As a final crew decision, a director should choose a secretary who will be responsible for observing and recording continuity notes during production. The skill requirement of a continuity secretary is attention to details. This skill should also include the interpersonal tact necessary when having to work with and control music recording artists and musicians on location. The continuity secretary will need to call freezes and reestablish many personal details of talent during production.

Preparing continuity notes sheets (CS 1). The continuity secretary is responsible to the director on location and during preproduction preparation. The continuity secretary should create codes for record taking and be familiar with crew and cast lists, production schedule, and the continuity notes recording form. Adequate copies of continuity record forms and a binder to hold them while writing should also be prepared. (See the video continuity notes form.)

Coordinating with the videotape recorder operator(s) (CS 2). The continuity secretary needs to coordinate continuity note records with the coding and order of new videotape stock. This task is complicated with multiple videotape recorders and operators. The complication can arise with double videotape stock and the codes necessary to account for different videotape stock in different videotape recorders. The videotape recorder operator has the responsibility for the videotape stock and the coding.

THE PRODUCTION PROCESS

The production process of the music video is similar to the production process of drama, with the exception that audio recording is not necessary on music video production location. Audio recording is replaced by audio playback; the master track has to be played back on location for the purpose of lip synchronization by the artist or musician being videotaped. Another difference of music video remote production from remote drama production is the use of multiple isolated video cameras.

• Personnel

Producer (P). The producer takes charge of all production details on location. All rapport and arrangements with the location personnel are the responsibilities of the producer. Arrangements, control, and care of artists and actors are other responsibilities.

Director (D). The director has complete creative control of the production on location. The blocking of cast and crew and calling for takes, wraps, and strikes are also the responsibility of the director.

Camera operator(s) (CO). It has become common practice in music video production to utilize two or more isolated cameras. Isolated cameras, each videotaping the scene at the same time, facilitate postproduction editing when lip synchronization is so essential to the production of the music video.

Videotape operator(s) (VTRO). With the probability of more than one isolated camera videotaping the shoot, as many camera operators will be needed. For each camera set-up and camera operator, another videotape recorder is needed and another videotape recorder operator will be needed. The videotape operators should be responsible for the videotape stock by the day of shooting. Cassettes should be labeled and numbered accordingly. There should be an adequate amount of tape stock especially when more than one isolated camera will be used. Each isolated camera will need its own vectorscope to monitor light levels entering the lenses of the cameras.

Audio playback director (AD). There is no need for an audio recording director because generally all music videos use prerecorded audio tracks. There is also little use for location ambience or audio effects. There is need for a crew member with audio technical skills to handle the music track playback used for lip and instrument synchronization by the artists or musicians during videotaping.

Continuity secretary (CS). Similar to the remote production of drama, there is need on location to record in detail all elements of continuity of cast, property, and location. Although isolated cameras diminish the need for many single camera takes necessitating extreme continuity care, many units of music videos are dramatic and narrative in style, thus requiring continuity observation. Recording field continuity notes also means little or no need to view and log source tapes before postproduction editing begins. Good continuity notes include a judgment of good or bad takes on the many different takes videotaped on location.

• Production Stages

The production stages of music video production are little different from the production stages of the remote drama production or the commercial production. The only addition to the production of music videos is the multiple isolated camera operation while artists or musicians lip sync the music track being imaged.

Supervising crew call (P 1). The beginning to a remote production day is a crew call, which serves to collect and organize the technical production crew. Usually, the production crew needs an earlier and separate call from the artists and musicians. The technical needs and set-up demands of the production crew consume more time than most artists, musicians, and support staff can tolerate with patience. Experience shows that an hour or more is reasonable to separate technical and talent crew calls. Experience also teaches that a uniform departure site for the production crew allows an attendance count and assures arrival at a unfamiliar location together. Parking arrangements and unloading arrangements are the responsibility of the producer.

Holding a production meeting (D 1).   One of the first requirements for the director on every production day is a production meeting. Even with all the preproduction work that facilitates the production of a music video, there are still last minute changes and details that should be covered with the entire crew together. This is the opportunity for the director to make changes in the production schedule and solicit questions regarding videotaping details.

Meeting location hosts (P 2).   The producer should extend a courtesy reminder to the location hosts, a telephone call, through, that their environment is scheduled for the production day and include the time of arrival and scheduled departure of the crew and cast. It is a good practice for the producer to have followed location site scouting (when permission is granted for a shoot) with a detailed letter outlining all the details of the request for using the host location for a video shoot and reminding the host of the details conveyed previously by word.

Unloading the amount of equipment needed by a remote video production requires special notice to the location host. In turn, the host may request that special directions (insurance or fire safety regulations) be followed, e.g., the use of loading docks, a particular entrance door, or the use of a freight elevator.

After equipment is unloaded at the location site, each member of the crew has tasks to perform in preparation for videotaping. It is at this point that the producer and the director have the responsibility to keep informed of the progress of each crew member as the crew members have the mutual responsibility to keep the producer and director informed of their progress in equipment set-up and operation check.

The producer should also know what demands the crew and cast have for security for both production equipment and personal valuables while on location and also for privacy for costume and make-up preparation as well as crew breaks and meals.

Supervising location environment rearrangement (P 3).   The producer supervises the rearrangement of the location environment for the needs of the music video storyboard units for any particular shoot as a location responsibility. Instant developing film pictures taken during location site survey (or taking instant developing film pictures of the location before rearrangement) is a good practice. With a photographic record of the way a location appeared upon crew arrival, the location can be restored to the way it was at the end of the shoot. Often furniture will have to be removed to meet the blocking of a scene or action properties, such as an automobile, may have to be positioned for a particular shot.

The producer should have cleared all major changes to a location environment with the location host during location site survey. If unanticipated changes should have

to be made, the producer should always check with the location host or security for proper permission to make the changes.

Directing location environment rearrangement (D 2).   Whereas the producer supervises the rearrangement of the location environment, it is the director who directs the changes. The director should make the decisions on what is moved or removed in light of the storyboard, creative concept, and production design.

Handling production crew and artist(s)/musician(s) details (P 4).   The ongoing task of the producer on location is the many details required of both crew and artist(s)/musician(s). Restroom facilities, meals, breaks, and lounging areas are needs for both crew and artists, and artists and crew need to be informed of them. The talent require additional room for changing into costumes, getting into make-up, and space for just waiting to be videotaped. Most of these details should have been worked out with the location host at the time of the site scouting.

Arranging camera equipment and accessories pick-up/delivery (CO 1).   Because camera equipment may be already available, rented, or purchased, the camera operators are responsible for arranging either pick-up or delivery to the location site. For some location sites, there may be required equipment delivery areas and freight elevators that must be used.

Arranging lighting equipment and accessories pick-up/delivery (LD 1).   Similar to other crew members responsible for equipment, the lighting director must arrange for the acquisition of available lighting equipment and accessories as well as the equipment that must be rented or purchased. Loading and carting lighting equipment should follow the requirements of the location as set for all equipment.

Arranging videotape recorder equipment and accessories pick-up/ delivery (VTRO 1).   The videotape recorder operators are responsible for the pick-up and delivery of available, rented, or purchased equipment for videotape recording. Loading of videotape recording equipment should follow the same requirements of all other equipment loading and carting.

Arranging audio playback equipment and accessories pick-up/ delivery (AD 1).   The responsibility of the audio playback director is to secure the pick-up and delivery of available, rented, or purchased audio playback equipment and accessories for the production shoot.

Standing in for purposes of lighting, sound, and video checks (T 1).   Frequently, artists and musicians are needed while the production crew makes checks on various aesthetic elements of recording and playback equipment. It is a tedious task for artists and musicians but a necessary one. Although crew members will use other location personnel to stand in when exact reproduction of height and color are not important, the point of time does come when the individual artist or musician has to take the place of a stand-in.

Setting up and checking location camera (CO 2). The camera operators should follow the blocking plots and begin camera equipment set-ups. When set-up is complete, the camera operators can make an operational check by communicating with the videotape recorder operators who can read the vectorscope for light levels for the scene. Unacceptable levels may mean the f-stop of the lens should be adjusted or light intensity levels need to be changed. When set-up and check are finished, the camera operators should communicate this fact to the director and the producer.

Setting up and checking location lighting (LD 2). The lighting director should follow the production schedule and lighting plots for the first take and begin location lighting equipment set-up. The lighting director makes a lighting set-up check by viewing the artist/musicians or stand-ins both on the set and over the video monitor. The lighting director works closely with the camera operators and the videotape recorder operators. The lighting director will have to work with the videotape recorder operators who should be monitoring the vectorscope for the adequacy of light levels. The lighting director should be observant of unwanted shadows from artist/musicians and props on the location set.

Setting up and checking videotape recorder location (VTRO 2). The videotape recorder operators should ensure the proper set-up and operation of the videotape recorders after the production meeting. The mobility of the videotape recorder set-ups should be facilitated for easy movement when the cameras and lighting placements are changed for different takes. The videotape recorder operators should request a check of the recording set-up by recording some video from the cameras before notifying the director and the producer that set-ups are complete. Part of the videotape recorder set-up is the vectorscope to monitor video levels for broadcast quality.

Setting up and checking location audio playback (AD 2). The audio director sets up the equipment for audio playback during the remote music video production immediately following the production meeting.

Supervising equipment set-up (D 3). When all equipment is set up and operating, the director should make a final check. Because remote production equipment ultimately creates the aesthetic experience to be achieved with music video production, the director has the responsibility to check the proper set-up and functioning of the camera, videotape recorder, audio playback equipment, and lighting design. Some test videotaping and playback are still the best way to check all equipment set-up; seeing what the audience will eventually see is the best judge.

Getting into costumes and make-up (T 2). Preferences vary among directors for the amount of preparation they expect from their talent. Some prefer that talent report to location in make-up and costume; others break for make-up and costuming after blocking and rehearsal. One determining factor is the extent of make-up and costuming required. Long and detailed make-up, e.g., extensive aging, should be done early with adequate lead time. Basic make-up could be applied before blocking and final touches and powdering before the first take.

Rehearsing the music track playback system (D 4). An important element of preparation for production is a rehearsal of the playback of the music track for lip syncing. The director needs the assurance that the artists and musicians can hear and lip sync properly.

Monitoring audio playback (AD 3). The audio playback set-up requires the placement of the playback machines and the placement of speakers so that all talent and crew can hear the music track being synchronized with the video imaging. The audio director should make a set-up check by having run cables, checking all speakers, and setting gain levels with artist/musicians.

Blocking the artists/musicians (D 5). Once the director has determined that cameras, recorders, audio playback, and lighting are ready, the talent can be summoned. Having already indicated to the camera operators where the first set-up positions were for the cameras, the director blocks the artist/musicians from the storyboard without lip syncing. This step is best achieved by the director simply noting the phrase or point in the music or lyrics when an artist/musician is to move and to where and physically moving the artists/musicians one at a time on their cues.

Following the director's requests and directions during blocking, rehearsals, and takes (T 3). The director has the first and final word on a location videotape shoot. For artists/musicians this is usually the first time on the set and blocking is new to everyone. Following the director's directions accurately and swiftly helps everyone—both talent and crew. Most directors will rehearse until talent feel comfortable with their movements. Talent should not hesitate to ask for additional rehearsals before a take. Following a director's commands includes the director's calls to action, cut, freeze, or another take or wrap.

Rehearsing the artists/musicians (D 6). Once the talent know the blocking for the scene, the next step involves allowing them to rehearse the blocking with their music track playback. During these two steps, blocking and rehearsing talent, the camera operators, audio playback director, and lighting director should be checking their responses to the blocking as the director blocks and rehearses the talent.

Blocking the cameras (D 7). Now the director should set camera shots with the camera operators. Setting camera shots means directing the composition of the take (who is in the field of view), the camera framing (the kind of shot, e.g., CU, LS), and the movement of the camera (e.g., pan, tilt, zoom) during a video take. It is presumed that the camera operators have had a shot list of the shots required for the scene and have been observing the director block and rehearse the talent in the scene. Setting camera shots can be done with the artists/musicians lip syncing or simply rehearsing the blocking. Some directors find that with lip syncing, it is difficult to spend quality time with the camera operators because the song passes swiftly. Hence, many prefer that the talent simply rehearse blocking at this step.

Rehearsing the cameras (D 8).   After blocking the cameras the director will observe the positions, lens composition, lens framing, and movement during a rehearsal of the cameras only.

Rehearsing the cameras (CO 4).   After blocking the camera positions, composition, framing, and movement, the camera operators rehearse what the director blocked. The director may watch the camera performance on the video monitors and offer the camera operators some criticism.

Blocking the camera positions with the artists/musicians (CO 3).   In music video production as in drama production, the cameras are treated as talent; cameras must be blocked for positions, movements, and changes during a scene just as talent. Camera operators find it convenient to observe the blocking of talent alone first, and then take notes while the director blocks the cameras.

Rehearsing artists, musicians, actors, and cameras (D 9).   The director should now call for a rehearsal of the talent with lip syncing and the camera operators effecting all the shots called for. The director should observe the scene where both the real action and a video monitor can both be seen. The audio playback director should carefully monitor the sound reproduction and check gain levels. The videotape recorder operators or the camera operators should be checking video levels on the vectorscopes and communicating to the lighting director any levels that may not be acceptable for broadcast quality video.

Rehearsing cameras with talent (CO 5).   After talent and cameras have been blocked and rehearsed separately, they are all now rehearsed together. This is the first total coordination of cameras, talent, and audio playback. The director may prefer to observe this rehearsal on a playback monitor.

Making changes and rehearsing again (D 10).   Having troubleshot all problems, the director again calls for a rehearsal of the scene to check for any remaining difficulties or that old ones have been corrected. This rehearsal might focus solely on audio playback and lip syncing among the talent. This is a good opportunity for the director to check talent make-up and costuming on camera under the lights and over the video monitor.

Rehearsing cameras again with talent (CO 6).   After any changes are made to camera work, cameras, talent, and audio playback are rehearsed once again.

Calling for a take (D 11).   At this stage the director might call for a take. This means that the director is ready to videotape the storyboard unit. In turn, this means that talent should have make-up and costuming checks and attend to last minute prop details.

This step requires that the continuity secretary be prepared to record all the details necessary for accounting for the storyboard unit and any subsequent portions of the unit. There is no question of the importance of the continuity secretary and note taking. The smallest slip in detail between a previous take and a subsequent one to be cut into the earlier one will create impossible problems in editing.

There is also a need for the slate at this point in the production. The slate is readied with the appropriate information that labels the leader video of the scene, enabling the video editor later to best identify the following take without having to see the entire scene. The slate records at least the title of the music cut, the director, the taping date, the storyboard unit, and the take number. The continuity secretary might be responsible for the slate or another member of the crew is assigned to perform the task. In any case, both the continuity secretary and the person responsible for the slate should be coordinated because they both must share accurate information of storyboard units and video takes. Some attempt at standardizing directorial language in controlling a location shoot is as follows:

Director: "Stand by to roll tape."

Director: "Ready to roll tape."

Videotape operator: "Ready to roll tape."

Director: "Ready to cue playback."

Audio director: "Ready to cue playback."

Director: "Roll tape."

Video operator: "Tape is rolling."

Director: "Slate it" or "Mark it."

Slate person steps in front of the camera lens with the slate and reads aloud both the take number and the storyboard unit number or shot list number: "Unit _____; take _____."

Director: "Cue playback."

Director: "Action."

Director (records beyond planned edit point): "Cut!"

Continuity secretary (makes necessary notes): "Okay" or "Hold it."

Director (announces his intentions): "That's a wrap," "Strike," "Storyboard, unit _____," "Cut-ins, unit _____," "Take it again, unit _____," or "Take it from _____."

Videotaping the take (CO 7).   When last minute changes are made and no more rehearsals are needed, the camera operators will be asked to keep the camera positions, shot composition, shot framing, and any required movement for a videotaped take. The camera operators should carefully observe camera work, subject composition, framing, and movement and be ready to tell the director that some problem was encountered if there was one, some mistake made, or even to suggest a better shot before a wrap is called on that take.

Responding to the director's call to roll tape (VTRO 3).   The responsibility of the videotape recorder operators during production is to respond to the readiness call for rolling videotape by the director, the rolling tape response that the videotapes are indeed rolling, and that video recording levels check out.

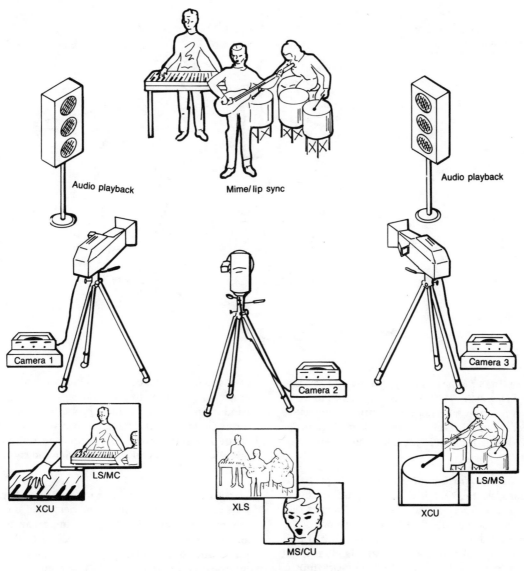

Audio playback

Mime/ lip sync

Audio playback

Camera 1

Camera 2

Camera 3

XCU

LS/MC

XLS

MS/CU

XCU

LS/MS

Music video performance footage
Multiple isolated cameras

FIGURE 5–3
Music video performance. Videotaping a music video is often performed with multiple isolated cameras. Because music videos are performed by lip synching to prerecorded music, adequate audio playback is required.

Monitoring the vectorscope(s) (VTRO 4). The videotape recorder operators should monitor vectorscope levels during a videotape take. Bursts of light and reflections of light as actors move and props are used can push light levels for the camera to unacceptable levels. Should these bursts be seen by the videotape recorder operators, the director should be notified after the cut is called.

Following the director's directions (AD 4). The audio playback director is directly responsible to the production director during a videotaping, as are all crew members. The call to be ready and to roll playback by the director should be responded to quickly. The audio playback director should be sensitive to the need and call to forward or rewind the master track, as well as to play. Having noted the playback

counter numbers for significant lyrics or music measures will facilitate all commands as swiftly as possible. It is advantageous to have a back-up copy of the master track in case of audio tape problems.

Updating and slating videotape leader (SP 1). The slate person has the responsibility of constantly updating the information on the slate for recording the leader of every videotape take. The slate person must be in coordination with the videotape recorder operators and the continuity secretary. Information on storyboard unit and number of take are important to accurate postproduction. In a multiple isolated camera operation, the videotape leader of each camera/videotape recorder must be slated identically except for the different camera code.

FIGURE 5–4
The roving camera. A camera technique that adds excitement to music video production is the "roving" video camera.

Coordinating the slate with the continuity secretary and videotape recorder operator(s) (SP 2). The slate person needs to be in regular communication with both the continuity secretary who keeps record of all takes, and the videotape recorder operator who keeps record of videotapes and their numbering codes.

Following the director's directions (SP 3). The slate person is directly responsible to the call of the director for every videotape take. The director's call, "slate it!," means that the slate person positions the slate in focus in front of the lens of the camera and audibly reads the storyboard unit being taped and the take number. If a take is interrupted by a minor error, e.g., a false start with playback music, a director may forego a slate at the front of a take and instead call for an end board, slating the take at the end of the videotaped take.

Announcing intentions: retake, wrap, or strike (D 12). The primary determinant of the director's intentions after a take should always include a check of the video recordings by the videotape operator—preferably by the director. This is an advantage of video over film: the ability to see the take immediately after it is finished. It would be foolhardy not to view the scene before proceeding. If the take is satisfactory, a wrap is called and another storyboard unit or camera placement may be called for. Specific storyboard units should be noted to reduce uncertainty about the new take. If the take is unsatisfactory, another take may be called by the director. Reasons for the retake should be given so that crew and cast can avoid the same problem and make corrections. If all the takes for the day as listed on the production schedule are complete, a strike of the location may be called by the director.

Observing and recording continuity details (CS 1). The continuity secretary has the responsibility to observe all details

of a videotaped take. This includes talent's lip syncing, musician performance, costuming, make-up, blocking, hand properties, and vehicle properties. Continuity notes forms suggest what details to observe, but it is up to the continuity secretary to be sensitive to those details that might change from take to take. (See the continuity notes form.)

Working with the continuity secretary (T 4). The continuity secretary needs to record more details of the talent than any other element of a take. It is important to good order and less stress that talent be sensitive to the requests of the continuity secretary to a freeze until all details are observed and noted, as well as be reminded about details from the continuity secretary before a subsequent take. Talent can assist a continuity secretary by not changing detail elements, e.g., locks of hair askew, hand holding a property, during a break, and by helping recall detail elements.

Releasing talent after a cut (CS 2). When a director calls for a cut in videotaping, the continuity secretary may call for a freeze among the talent (and even the production crew) until all elements of detail are correctly recorded.

Being available but out-of-the-way (T 5). Between takes talent should be available but out of the crew's way. More time is lost between takes when crew members have to fall over or go around talent who should vacate shooting space. The opposite problem is talent who disappear and cannot be found when a take is ready. Although crew and talent prefer to engage in idle talk, such behavior holds up a production and serves to distract large groups from the business at hand.

Reestablishing details before subsequent shots (CS 3). At the beginning of a subsequent shot to be edited to a previous shot, the continuity secretary has the obligation to remind talent of lip sync elements, costuming, make-up, and blocking to meet the same detail elements recorded from the previous cut.

Getting talent release forms signed (P 5). The end of the shooting day is the time for the producer to make certain that release forms are secured for any talent or extras who may have been used from the location site for the shoot. It is not uncommon, for example, to recruit people standing around a location shoot for roles, e.g., as extras in street scenes. Their release forms should be obtained for purposes of legal clearance. (See the talent release form.)

Striking camera equipment (CO 8). When the director indicates the final wrap and location strike, the camera operators are responsible for the breakdown of all camera equipment and accessories as part of the location strike. Repackaging and loading of equipment should proceed according to the requirements of unloading at the beginning of the shoot.

Striking lighting equipment (LD 3). When the director calls a strike for the production day, the lighting director is responsible for striking and repacking all lighting equipment and accessories.

Striking the videotape recorder equipment and accessories (VTRO 5). When the director calls a strike, the videotape recorder operators begin to breakdown the videotape recorder set-ups. After the strike call it is important for the videotape recorder operators to remove the record button from all the source tapes used for the shoot to prevent accidental erasing or recording over. Labeling videotape cassettes and carrying cases is also an important production detail for the videotape recorder operators. Any agreed upon coding is sufficient. Coordination with the continuity secretary facilitates reordering the videotapes for postproduction preparation. Care should be exercised that any B-roll tapes be used for that purpose only. A B-roll tape may be designated by a director in anticipation of special editing effects, such as a dissolve, in which two tapes will have to be rolled onto the master tape. Not anticipating a B-roll source tape requires another generation of the video needed for the special effect. B-rolling saves a generation of a length of videotape.

Striking audio playback equipment (AD 5). When the director calls for a strike at the end of a production day, the audio playback director is responsible for the breakdown and repacking of audio playback equipment and accessories.

THE POSTPRODUCTION PROCESS

The postproduction process for editing music videos differs slightly from that of other single camera genres. The important difference is that there is no audio editing with which to be concerned. Also, for a performance music video, the entire music track is the audio track.

- **Personnel**

Producer (P). All producers should oversee the entire editing process. Some producers might serve as editors. However, it is not uncommon for the director to serve as editor. Many postproduction facilities require either the producer or the director of the commercial to work with a technical director/editor who will actually function at the editing console. The producer or the director would still make the editing decisions in such a case. The producer is responsible to oversee all preproduction preparation work: reordering source tapes, editing final storyboard, reordering continuity notes sheets, and striping SMPTE time code on source and master tape.

Director (D). The director of the location production may assume the role of postproduction editor. However, if the director's preproduction tasks were thorough and accurate, the production storyboard with the continuity note forms should be sufficient for another editor or technical director to effect what the producer or director designed. The director's first postproduction role is editing the final storyboard.

Camera operator(s) (C/VTRO). With the production of the music video completed, there are only summary tasks remaining for the camera operators. The return and accountability of remote camera and location lighting equipment and accessories remain the final responsibility of the camera/videotape recorder operator.

Videotape recorder operator(s) (VTRO). Similar to the camera operators, the only remaining tasks of the videotape recorder operators are to return videotape recording equipment and to note any losses, damage, or malfunctioning equipment or accessories.

Lighting director (LD). The lighting director has the added postproduction responsibility of ensuring the return of all lighting equipment, noting damage, loss, and malfunction.

Audio director (AD). The final responsibility of the audio director is the return of audio playback equipment. This involves reporting damage, loss, and malfunction of any equipment or accessory.

Technical director/editor (TD/E). Some postproduction facilities require that their own personnel operate the editing consoles in the editing suites. In such a case the producer or director would serve in a decision-making capacity during editing sessions. An editor could complete editing from the storyboard and the continuity notes forms.

- **Postproduction Stages**

Arranging postproduction schedule and facilities (P 1). The producer has the first postproduction responsibility to make arrangements for editing suite scheduling. Editing should not begin until all preparation elements are complete. A high quality videotape should be secured for the master tape and striped with SMPTE time code to permit accurate editing of the music video from the source tapes. The source tapes themselves will have to be striped with

SMPTE code also. If time code is not being used, the master tape must have at least a control track before editing can begin on it. The source tapes received a control track when they were recorded in the field.

Supervising postproduction preparation (P 2). The producer has responsibility for four elements in the preparation of the project for postproduction: the master music track, the storyboard, the source tapes, and the continuity notes. The producer should have possession of the master music track of the cut imaged for the music video. The source tapes will have to be reordered in the order of final edited storyboard. They should be properly labeled on the cassette and on the carrying case. These tasks are the responsibility of the videotape recorder operators. The continuity notes forms will also have to be ordered according to the edited storyboard. The continuity secretary should ensure the reordering of continuity notes forms. The storyboard will have to be edited if changes were made during production. This is the responsibility of the director.

Postproduction preparation: the storyboard (D 1). The director has the postproduction responsibility to edit the storyboard for changes that may have been made during location production. It is not uncommon that short units were dropped, or shots not preplanned were videotaped. These additions as well as deletions will have to be made. The storyboard, whether the director or a technical director/editor edits the master tape, becomes an important point of reference for the master tape edition.

Preparing the source videotapes (VTRO 1). The videotape recorder operators have the responsibility of turning over the source videotapes to the director. The preparation of the source tapes means that the videotape recorder operators have to remove record buttons from every videocassette recorded on location so that the video signal will not be erased or recorded over. Proper labeling of videocassettes and carrying cases must also be complete so that any source videotape may be found with little trouble.

The final preparatory work on the source tapes is to have them all striped with SMPTE time code, which facilitates more accurate editing of the master tape than simple control track editing. Because SMPTE assigns a consecutive number to every frame of the videotape, matching numbered frames from the source tape to the master tape creates a controlled edit. SMPTE code on the master tape will later allow the audio track to be removed for sweetening and mixing and re-laying it to exact synchronization.

Reordering source videotapes (VTRO 2). The videotape recorder operators should reorder all the source videotapes according to the storyboard. The reordered videotapes should be turned over to the director.

Reordering continuity notes sheets (CS 1). Because the continuity secretary has been recording all pertinent details of each location video take on the continuity forms, they are now in need of reordering according to the order of the storyboard. This is the final responsibility of the continuity secretary. The continuity notes sheets were defined as a kind of location log, which would replace the tedious job of having to view all source tapes after videotaping and before editing could begin. If the continuity notes sheets were well recorded, more than enough information is contained on them to allow postproduction to proceed rapidly and smoothly. Continuity notes serve as the editing work sheets of other postproduction processes.

Returning remote video equipment and accessories (CO 1). It is the responsibility of the camera operators to return to maintenance/storage facilities all the camera and lighting equipment used during the remote location shoot. Rented equipment would have to be returned to the equipment rental agency. Equipment purchased for the shoot should be reported separately to maintenance/storage personnel.

Reporting damaged, lost, or malfunctioning equipment (CO 2). As a final obligation to the music video shoot, the camera operators should report any equipment or accessory that may have been damaged during the location shoot. This report should also include any loss of equipment or accessories. Most equipment maintenance/storage personnel also appreciate a written report of any equipment or accessory that may have malfunctioned during the location shoot. It is a good practice to report any repair or replacement made to equipment during the shoot.

Returning videotape recording equipment and accessories (VTRO 3). It is the responsibility of the videotape recorder operators to return to maintenance/storage facilities all the videotape recording equipment used during the remote location shoot. Rented equipment would have to be returned to the equipment rental agency. Equipment purchased for the shoot should be reported separately to maintenance/storage personnel.

Reporting damaged, lost, or malfunctioning equipment (VTRO 4). As a final obligation to the music video shoot, the videotape recorder operators should report any equipment or accessory that may have been damaged during the location shoot. This report should also include any loss of equipment or accessories. Most equipment maintenance/storage personnel also appreciate a written report of any equipment or accessory that may have malfunctioned during the location shoot. It is a good practice to report any repair or replacement made to equipment during the shoot.

Returning remote lighting equipment and accessories (LD 1). It is the responsibility of the lighting director to return to maintenance/storage facilities all the lighting equipment used during the remote location shoot. Rented equipment must be returned to the equipment rental agency. Equipment purchased for the shoot should be reported separately to maintenance/storage personnel.

Reporting damaged, lost, or malfunctioning equipment (LD 2). As a final obligation to the music video shoot, the lighting director should report any equipment or accessory that may have been damaged during the location shoot. This report should also include any loss of equipment or accessories. Most equipment maintenance/storage personnel also appreciate a written report of any equipment or accessory that may have malfunctioned during the location shoot. It is a good practice to report any repair or replacement made to equipment during the shoot.

Returning audio playback equipment and accessories (AD 1). It is the responsibility of the audio director to return to maintenance/storage facilities all the audio playback equipment used during the remote location shoot. Rented equipment must be returned to the equipment rental agency. Equipment purchased for the shoot should be reported separately to maintenance/storage personnel.

Reporting damaged, lost, or malfunctioning equipment (AD 2). As a final obligation to the music video shoot, the audio director should report any equipment or accessory that may have been damaged during the location shoot. This report should also include any loss of equipment or accessories. Most equipment maintenance/storage personnel also appreciate a written report of any equipment or accessory that may have malfunctioned during the location shoot. It is a good practice to report any repair or replacement made to equipment during the shoot.

Observing the editing process with the director (P 3). The producer is a valuable resource person in the editing suite during editing sessions. The experience with the music video project at all stages becomes helpful as particular points of the project, the music track, and the editing arise.

Laying the music track on the master video tape (D 2). Unlike almost every other video genre, in the editing of a music video, the prerecorded music track is recorded onto the master videotape first. The music cut is a closed unit, i.e., the track is complete and timed. Video imaging is then added to the audio track.

Creating a rough edit (D 3). A rough edit is created by simply cutting blindly following the edited storyboard and the continuity notes forms. The continuity notes indicate which takes were good and which were bad. The rough edit can move along swiftly if a member of the editing team uses a fast search playback deck and monitor system to find the good takes while an editor or technical director does the cuts-only editing with simple insert edits.

The reasons for making a rough edit first instead of channeling efforts into a final version may not be immediately evident. First, a cuts-only version allows for an early glance at the entire project. It serves to anticipate problems in a polished final music video. These problems can range from continuity (e.g., insert edits do not match) to pacing (e.g., the overall flow of the video does not reflect the music track). Second, the rough edit allows the artists and musicians to see their performance while they may still be around. If the project is working with academic objectives, the ability to see a performance early allows criticizing to occur, which is a necessary ingredient to the professional growth of amateurs, but even professionals like to see their own performances. Third, a rough edit can point to less-than-the-best video quality or

location problems that might still be redone because the rough edit is not far removed from the shooting dates, and the talent and crew may still be available.

Reviewing the rough edit (P 4). The producer should have the first review of the rough edit. It was the producer who created the concept for the music video and storyboarded the concept. The producer should be the primary reviewer of the rough edit.

Reviewing the rough edit (D 4). The best use of the rough edit version is to scrutinize the video and audio for polishing a final version. There are so many advantages to having this rough edition. Now is the time to sense the pacing of the final music video. Does the flow of video images complement the music cut? Perhaps having seen the flow of images as preplanned, the pacing may be violated and some originally planned video inserts should not be used. Only after seeing the whole music video at this stage can such decisions be intelligently and aesthetically made and implemented in the final editing.

Making the final edit (D 5). With adequate review of the rough edit, final editing can begin. Here all the shortcomings perceived in the rough edit can be repaired and improved. It is at this stage that SMPTE code is best employed. Now transitions other than a cut can be carefully chosen and executed.

Approving the final edited music video (P 5). The producer who began the production process of the music video should have the final approval of the edited master tape of the video.

VIDEO PRODUCTION ORGANIZING FORMS

• Music Video Concept Form

Production process: Music video preproduction

Responsibility: Producer

Purpose: To propose the creative imaging interpretation to an already produced music song track to the artists and musicians or to a music publishing company.

Objective: The music video concept form is meant to organize from the beginning to the end of a prerecorded song the verbal aesthetic description of the imaging of the proposed music video. The concept is considered to be the same as a treatment in other video genres except that the concept is expected to be a thorough and exact description of the proposed imaging of the music video. It is on the basis of the proposed concept that the producer will receive the authorization and funding to produce the music video.

Glossary

Album Title Because most recorded music is currently presented in multiple song collections on record, cassette, and compact disc albums, the album title should be recorded here.

Cut Title The separate songs of an album are called cuts of that album. The cut title is the proposed song title to be imaged in the music video.

Cut Length Albums usually list the title of all cuts on the album and the respective time length of each cut. The length of the proposed song cut should be indicated here in minutes and seconds. The average length of music videos is 3 to 5 minutes.

Recording Artists Most albums feature the artist or musician who performs the music on the album. The names or titles of the artists or musicians should be recorded here.

- **Music Video Concept Model***

Producer: Frank Management, Inc.
Director: Neil Tardio
Original Concept Written by: Neil Tardio
Album Title: Billy Joel: The Video Album, Vol. I. CBS/Fox
Cut Title: "While the Night Is Still Young"
Cut Length: 3:58
Recording Artist: Billy Joel
Dates: 9/15/86

Bright light and long shadows strike across a surface. The eye fetches along the shadows and moves up to the silhouette of a man leaning against a doorway and resting a guitar on the ground. The scene moves in on the distant figure. Suddenly, the figure is pulled out of sight, like a cut-out on a string.

An extreme CU reveals a wooden match being lit in the cup of a man's hands. He raises the flickering light past his concentrated face and exposes it for an instant before the wind blows it out.

A helmsman violently turns a ship's wheel.

A bow of a giant ship swings starboard.

Silhouette (night, telephoto) crewmen race through the fittings on a wet tanker deck.

A shark swims dangerously close (left to right) through the frame.

Fingers rip a template off a black surface revealing the words (in white) "While the Night."

Underlit and windblown in the door of a plane, a bride and groom bail out. They fall into space, tumbling. Slowly they gain control of their fall. They move toward each other, hands reach for hands. They touch. They hold. They pull each other together. They embrace. They hug and kiss and rotate through space.

Beautiful children holding candles are looking up, watching.

Again the children are watching.

Now increasingly underlit, the couple descend through the flies of a theater and arrive on a stage amidst the candle lit children and a rock band—to wild applause.

The scene becomes a black and white still in a darkroom pan and is slid from the shimmering liquid solution revealing a hot, open road. A man with a suitcase walks along. Soon a truck appears but passes him by. The driver studies the image of his face in the vibrating side mirror. The truck disappears over a hill. The man with the suitcase walks alone. The driver stops the truck and pulls the horn. The man hears the horn; he begins to run back toward the hill. The driver watches the crest of the hill through the mirror; the man hasn't appeared yet, so he pulls the horn again.

Factory workers stream out of a steel mill.

The sun moves tangent to the horizon.

A child sits on a piano bench, intimidated by the keys. The scene moves away from the child, passing through the detail of a warm sunlit middle-class Brooklyn apartment. A

tired suitcase is there, a guitar, a loose bunch of wild flowers. A seaman's cap and winter jacket. A warm light comes from the open door to the roof. A hand lights a wooden match and cups the flame against the twilight breeze. The cup of light underglows the face of a woman whose goodness and strength remark her beauty. She smiles.

Gently she parts the fingers that shield the flame. It flickers out. They embrace. The city lights begin to move like a carousel, faster and faster. They stream in a glow around them. She buries her face in his body; she knows he will never leave her again. He holds her protectively and looks up and closes his eyes.

The child's finger plays a note.

- **Production Budget Form**

Production process: Music video preproduction

Responsibility: Producer

Purpose: To realistically estimate all possible costs of the production of the proposed music video production from preproduction to postproduction.

Objective: The budget form is a blank model of a budget for the production of a music video. The form is meant to organize all facets of single camera music video production into estimated expenses and actual expenses. It serves to suggest possible cost items across the entire spectrum of video production, personnel, equipment, labor, and materials. The form should be used to suggest expenses and to call attention to possible hidden costs.

Notes on use: The form should be studied for line items that might pertain to a proposed single camera music video shoot. Only applicable line items for the proposed music video need to be considered. Use the suggestion of line items to weigh possible costs for the project. Note that all sections of the budget are summarized on the front page of the form. The subtotal of costs from the individual sections are brought forward to be listed in the summary. Some costs are calculated by the number of days employed, the hourly rate of pay, and overtime hours. Other costs are calculated by the number of items or people by allotted amount of money per day for the item. The cost of materials is calculated by the amount of materials by the cost of a unit. Most cost entry columns of this budget form are labeled "Days, Rate, O/T (overtime) Hrs, Total"; for the line items that do not involve day and rate, the total column alone should be used. Projected costs to be applied to the budget can be found from a number of sources. One source of equipment rental and production costs is the rate card of a local video production facility. Salary estimates and talent fees can be estimated from the going rates of relevant services of equivalent professionals or from their agencies. Phone calls to providers of services and materials will also produce cost quotes. Travel costs can be obtained by a phone call to travel agencies or airline companies. There is no question that preparing a good budget is going to involve a lot of time and research.

Glossary

No. Preproduction Days Estimate the number of days to complete the necessary preproduction stages for the

---

*Permission to reproduce this concept granted by Neil Tardio, Neil Tardio Productions, New York, New York.

music video. This estimate includes quality time on all preproduction stages (budget, site survey, production schedule, storyboard breakdown, casting, shot list, equipment lists) for all production crew members involved in the preproduction of the music video (producer, director, camera operator(s), lighting director, videotape recorder operator(s), audio director, continuity secretary, artists/musicians, actors).

No. Studio Shoot Days/Hours Estimate the number of days and hours for which a studio or control room facilities may be needed. This time estimate accounts for any in-studio videotaping (e.g., talent on a set) or the use of control room switcher or character generator for postproduction effects.

No. Location Days/Hours Estimate the number of shooting days and hours that may be required on location. Most music videos attempt to shoot in a single day. More than one day can push expenses beyond what is affordable.

Location Sites List the proposed location shooting sites at which the previous days and hours were estimated.

No. Postproduction Days/Hours Estimate the number of days and hours that will be spent in postproduction in completing the music video master edit.

Shooting Date Indicate the date proposed to begin videotaping the music video. Again, most music videos should be shot in one day.

Completion Date Indicate the projected completion of the music video project. This date should include all postproduction tasks.

Summary of Production Costs This summary area brings forward the subtotals of costs from the respective units within the budget form. Note that each line unit 1 through 21 is found as unit heads within the budget form. When the individual units are completed within the budget, the subtotal is listed in the summary table.

Contingency This term refers to the practice of adding a contingency percentage to the subtotal of subtotals as a padding against the difference in actual final costs from the estimated costs of all line items. The customary contingency percentage is 15%. Multiply the subtotal on line 20 by 0.15 to determine the contingency figure. That result added to line 21 becomes the grand total of the budget costs.

Preproduction Costs This section of the budget summarizes the estimated (and eventually records the actual) costs of all preproduction expenses for the music video.

Estimated The estimated category refers to costs that can only be projected before the production. Rarely are the estimated costs the final costs to be incurred because of the number of variables that cannot be anticipated. Every attempt should be made to ensure real estimated cost figures and the consideration of as many variables to the cost as possible. The challenge of estimated budget costs is to project as close as possible to actual costs when they are known.

Actual The actual category of a budget records the costs that are finally incurred for the respective line items during or after the video drama production is completed. The actual costs are those costs that will really be paid

out for the production. The ideal budget seeks to have actual costs come as close as possible (either at or preferably under) to the estimated costs for the production.

Crew This unit of the preproduction expenses section accounts for the music video preproduction crew, director excluded. This list suggests the minimum crew personnel and some extra roles. Crew size is dictated by budget funding and the extent of the proposed music video production.

Production Costs This section of the budget accounts for expenses, estimated and actual, incurred during the actual production shooting of the music video.

Crew Similar to the preproduction section of the budget, the shoot section accounts for possible crew members needed for the production of the music video.

Production Materials Expenses The next unit under the shoot section of the budget accounts for materials and expenses that are projected to be incurred during the production of the music video. Notice that most of these expenses involve vehicular use and travel as well as casting the music video and meals for crew and talent during shooting.

Location Expenses Other production costs to be estimated are those involving the location site for the production. These suggested line items should help estimate potential costs that should be considered for the production.

Props, Costumes, Animals Much music video production is similar to drama production and should account for the purchase or rental use of properties, costumes, and animals in the production of the video.

Studio and Hall Rental and Expenses Because some location sites are large interior spaces, budget accounting should consider the rental and expenses incurred with the utilization of a studio or hall for videotaping purposes.

Set Construction The similarity to drama production includes the design and creation of a set in which the music video may be recorded. Those possible expenses are suggested here.

Set Construction Materials Given the need for a set in which to record the music video, construction costs should be accounted for. This unit of the budget suggests some of those costs.

Equipment Rental The equipment checklist form suggests much of the equipment that may be needed for the production of the music video. Rental items are listed here. Other larger rental items are also suggested here.

Videotape Stock This unit accounts for the videotape stock needed for the production. Accounting should be made for the multiple isolated cameras that may be proposed and the same number of videotape recorders. Tape size is determined by the type of videotape recorder; not all tape sizes fit the remote videotape recording decks. The most common tape cassette size is the small size, ¾ inch 20 minute (S :20) units.

Miscellaneous Costs All budgets have to account for items not covered elsewhere in the budget.

Director Fees Given the role of the director in music

video production, director costs are covered separately in the music video production budget.

Talent This unit of the production section of the budget attempts to account for all talent involved on camera for the production of the music video. This includes artists and musicians, extras, and dancers. Some suggested line items include accounting for fees incurred in audition and rehearsal of talent. Depending on the arrangements made with talent, some production budgets may have to account for benefits accruing to talent and crew members (e.g., health benefits, pensions). Insurance coverage should be accounted for in the section as well as state and federal taxes, which are due to any salaries to talent and crew members.

Talent Expenses Other remaining expenses involving talent are included in this unit of the budget. Per diem account is made for cash monies for talent to get their own meals during production. The other suggested expenses generally involve travel costs.

Postproduction This section of the budget attempts to account for the expenses and personnel involved in the postproduction editing phase of the music video.

Editing This unit of the postproduction section of the budget accounts for expenses involving the editing of the music video. Primarily, this includes editing facility costs and special equipment utilized in completing the master tape. Editing supplies are included here also.

Sound This unit deals with expenses incurred with the music of the music video. Copyright clearance costs are included here as well as final mixing of the music track to the video.

Personnel This unit covers the personnel involved in the postproduction editing of the music video.

Art Work This final unit of the budget suggests the costs that may be incurred in the art involved with the production of the music video, including animation.

• **Music Video Storyboard Form**

Production process: Music video preproduction

Responsibility: Producer

Purpose: To create a storyboard with the music and lyrics of the proposed video to image the proposed music video.

Objective: The music video storyboard form provides the five line music staff with room to measure the music beat, transcribe lyrics, draw storyboard frames, and sketch the proposed imaging for each shot. This form becomes the production script for producing the music video.

Directions: In approaching the creation of the storyboard, the producer should have a copy of the song to be imaged, a copy of the lyrics of the song as they are produced, and a template of the aspect ratio frame as reproduced on the form.

Step 1: The producer must first determine the meter of the music. The meter is the basic recurrent rhythmic pattern of note values, accents, and beats per measure in the music. A measure is defined as a group of beats.

All music has meter, which is usually determined in sheet music at the beginning of the music staff. Following the clef symbol on the staff of music, two numbers give the meter of the music. For example, 4/3 indicates that there are four beats per measure; three indicates which typical note within a measure receives the beat. The most common meter in music is 4/4. Rock music is usually 4/4; ballads are usually 4/4.

Step 2: The producer must next determine the structure or form of the song. The structure or form of a song are the clearly defined sections of the song. For example, an introduction, a verse section, a chorus, and a bridge section are sections of a song which, in various combinations, create the structure of the song. A simple common structure to a song is as follows:

| Introduction | Verse₁ | Chorus | Verse₂ | Chorus | Bridge | | Verse₃ | Chorus | Chorus |

Expect variations, for example, an instrumental solo in place of a verse or over a bridge section. Change of key or different music can constitute a bridge.

Step 3: Knowing the structure or form of the song, copy out the actual measures under the blank staff. The lyrics should be added at this step and be allowed to "stretch" the measures. Usually, there are only four measures per staff line in music notation. For purposes of the music video storyboard and the importance of using lyrics and measures as cues to editing images, allow the lyrics to stretch the measures as they are blocked out. Once the lyrics are typed under the staff lines, and adequate space accounted for music measures with no lyrics, then draw bar lines at the beginning and end of each measure.

Step 4: Within each measure, indicate beats per measure over the respective word or syllable of the lyrics with a small "x" on a line of the music staff. For each measure, listen for the accent or strong part of the measure. This can be marked with a heavier "x" mark.

Step 5: With measures marked with bars, beats marked over lyrics with x's, and the accented beat indicated,

FIGURE 5–5
Preparing the music video storyboard. Step 1 entails determining the beat per measure and the accented beat within a measure. (A) An example of a 4/3 measure of music. (B) An example of a 4/4 measure of music.

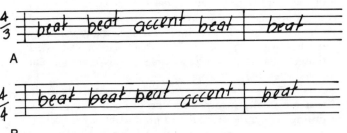

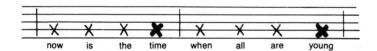

FIGURE 5–6
Step 3 in preparing the music video storyboard. After determining the beat and the structure of the song, lyrics are added to the storyboard staffs.

FIGURE 5–7
Step 4 in preparing the music video storyboard. Over the lyrics and the respective syllable, beats within each measure are indicated with x's. The accented beats are drawn darker.

the completed storyboard. Cross dissolves can be indicated as shown in Figure 5.10.

Zooms can be indicated as shown in Figure 5.11.

Finally, each aspect frame should be consecutively numbered, and each music measure should be consecutively numbered. It is suggested that in initial enumeration of both aspect frames a number be skipped every ten numbers to allow the addition of a frame at some later stage of design or production.

• Storyboard Breakdown Form

Production process: Music video preproduction

Responsibility: Director

Purpose: To break the preproduction storyboard down into production units usually according to common location or talent requirements.

Objective: The storyboard breakdown form organizes the preproduction storyboard from proposed edited order of a proposed final music video to a shooting order according to differing common criteria for single camera shoots, e.g., location similarity, talent. The breakdown form helps organize the shooting units by storyboard frames or music measures for managing the remote production.

Glossary

Music Measures The total number of music measures as enumerated on the storyboard should be recorded here.

Storyboard Frames The total number of storyboard frames proposed as the visualization for the music video is recorded here. Allow for dropping any number in enumeration of the frames.

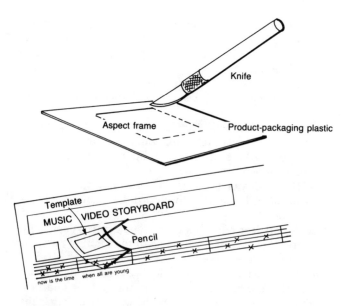

FIGURE 5–8
Making a template. The aspect ratio frame is copied and a template is cut for reproducing the frames on the music video storyboard.

storyboard frames can be drawn with the template at the point in the music and/or the lyrics where image changes are proposed to occur.

One guideline for placing the aspect frame over the staff is to position the lower left corner over the proposed edit point. Experience has taught that taping all pages of storyboard together assists in using the many pages that may be involved. An average storyboard length is five pages. Music staffs of successive pages of the form are designed to match up to each other for ease of reading

FIGURE 5–9
Final step in preparing the music video storyboard. Aspect ratio frames are drawn above the respective beat to indicate the change of video image for the music video.

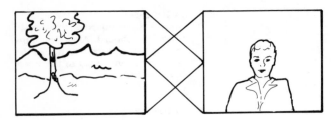

FIGURE 5–10
Technique for indicating a lap dissolve on a music video storyboard.

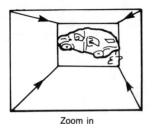 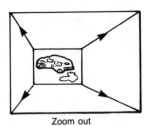

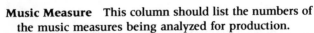

FIGURE 5–11
Technique for indicating a zoom on a music video storyboard.

Music Measure   This column should list the numbers of the music measures being analyzed for production.

Storyboard Frames   In this column of breakdown analysis the particular aspect frame representing a unit of the music video should be recorded.

Int/Ext   These abbreviations stand for interior/exterior and refer to the script demands for shooting indoors or outdoors. Whether the shoot is an interior or an exterior shoot can also be a determinant for the script breakdown and shooting unit.

Time   The time of day or night that the location and interior/exterior setting requires should be recorded here.

Setting   Setting means the specific area of a required location site, e.g., the parents' bedroom for the Smith's home location site.

Location   The location column records the remote location environment at which the setting is to be found. For example, the Smith's home is the location site for the parents' bedroom.

Artist(s)/Musician(s)/Actor(s)   This entry records by name the specific artists, musicians, and actors who are required in the setting at the location for a particular shoot.

Shooting Order   When the entire storyboard is broken down into shooting units, then the producer can determine the units for individual shoots and the consecutive shooting order for the entire remote project.

- **Location Site Survey Form**

Production process: Music video preproduction

Responsibility: Director

Purpose: To organize and facilitate the survey of possible remote music video production location environments.

Objective: The location site survey form is designed to assist the director or location scouts who have to search out and describe potential remote environments for video production purposes. Because many sites may have to be evaluated for any particular shoot, details of each site will have to be recorded to be evaluated and approved at a later time, usually away from the site by the director and producer. The form is designed to raise all possible production needs and location details for a successful remote video production. The form serves to organize and record location site details for later evaluation away from the site.

Glossary

Location Scouts(s)   This entry should list those persons other than the director who have been recruited to help scout potential locations for the production of the video drama production.

Music Measures   The total number of music measures as enumerated on the storyboard should be recorded here.

Storyboard Frames   The total number of storyboard frames proposed as the visualization for the music video is recorded here. Allow for dropping any number in enumeration of the frames.

Location   This entry should record the actual environment called for on the storyboard, for example, "Bob's bedroom."

Site Identification   This entry should correspond with a city map (e.g., H-3) or name of the location environment (e.g., Town Point Park).

Local Contact Person   This is the name of the responsible owner, manager, or supervisory officer of a proposed location. This person is the individual who is the location scout's contact person at the highest level of authority over a proposed location site. This person is the use-granting authority for the location. The name, title, address, city, state, and phone number of the contact person should all be accurately recorded. All this information, including the proper title, will be needed for mail correspondence purposes. The "comments" space allows for any notes about the contact person (e.g., executive secretary's name) that might be relevant.

Facilities Personnel   The facilities personnel information is a record of the people with whom the producer and production crew will work on the location. For example the maintenance engineer, office manager, and janitor are the individuals responsible for the everyday operation of the proposed location. The name, position title, address, city, state, and phone number of each should be recorded. This information becomes most practical to the production crew and the producer. This is the information most utilized once the location is chosen for use. The "comments" space should be used for any other relevant information about the facilities personnel. For example, the directions to the facilities personnel office at the location site or maintenance workshop should be recorded here.

Lighting Problems Defined   This area of the form focuses attention on the details of the proposed location that can affect lighting of the environment for videotape production.

Light Contrast Ratios Scouts should note any extreme light areas of the environment. A light meter can read (and record should be made of) the extreme lighting intensity of any existing areas of the environment. For example, one end of proposed location site may have no windows and no ceiling lights. The light reading for this end of the room will be very low to nonexistent. The other end of the room may be flooded with light from a number of windows. The light reading at this end of the room will be very high. These readings form the contrast ratio between the most existing light and least existing light for this room.

Lighting Intensity This entry records the highest light level reading in the proposed location environment. This information informs the producer that some controls will have to be used on the light source or other light will have to be created to balance this light intensity.

Ceiling Height The height of an existing ceiling is important. For example, ceiling height indicates the available height for lighting stands for lighting instruments to be used. A low ceiling allows light to be bounced, or a high ceiling means that light is absorbed, and that fact has to be taken into account. High ceilings also demand a lot of light if the ceiling needs to be lit.

Windows/Compass Direction Knowing the number of windows opening to the exterior of the location is an important location consideration. Many windows may demand correcting incandescent lights with filters or the need to gel the windows. Another important fact about a location environment with windows is the compass direction they face. East facing windows can expect a flood of strong morning sunlight that can push up the lighting intensity in the location environment. West facing windows create the same problem in the afternoon. When working remote locations the strongest source of light is the sun, and the sun is a constantly moving light source. Knowing the direction of that moving light source is important. Shadows and reflections change constantly. It is a good practice to have a compass when scouting locations and to take an accurate reading of due east.

Existing Light Control A question to ask facilities personnel about during location scouting is the control of existing lighting. For example, in an all fluorescent lighting environment, there may be one master switch. It would be important to know where it is. Simple wall switches for other light control should also be noted.

Lighting Use Notation should be made of how some existing lighting is used. For example, lighted display cases in the environment, parking lot lights, and night lights are conditions of lighting use in the location environment. Much such light use cannot be controlled.

Floor Description The description of the type of flooring in a proposed location environment can have consequences for set lighting design. For example, a highly polished floor covering reflects light; a dark carpet absorbs light or reflects unwanted hues.

Special Consideration Use this space to record for any other location-specific detail that might affect lighting design in the environment for the production. For example, a pool of water or a mirror on a wall could reflect light.

Power Problems Defined This area of the form focuses attention on and records the details regarding electrical power sources. Video production equipment relies heavily on available power sources.

Number of Power Outlets Count should be made of the number of electrical power outlets in the immediate environment of the proposed shoot. Additional count should also be made of the outlets that can be accessed by power cable runs.

Number of Separate Circuits It is important to know how many separate electrical circuits are represented by the power outlets. This is a question for the facilities personnel/maintenance engineer. The power outlets and separate circuits should be noted on a location diagram.

Types of Fuses One liability of heavy electrical needs for video production equipment is the frequent blown fuse. In some facilities restoring power is not a matter of resetting a circuit, but replacing a fuse. A good example of the need for fuses is the older private home location environment. Fuses come in many sizes and wattages. It is important to know both size and wattage for the proposed location.

Number of Outlet Prongs There are at least two common types of electrical outlets: the two-prong and the three-prong. Many older environments have only the two-prong outlets. Almost all video production equipment utilize the three-prong plug. Hence, adapters will have to be used on all two-prong outlets. The number of two-prong outlets will have to be known during location scouting so that adapters can be provided.

Location of Circuit Breakers Given the common occurrence of overloading electrical circuits with video production equipment needs, the location of fuse boxes and circuit breakers should be known. Often crew members have to reset breakers and replace blown fuses.

Portable Generator Need It may happen that there is no power source available in a proposed location environment. The only possible source of electricity may be that generated by the production crew itself with a portable power generator. Power generators can be easily rented if needed. Caution must be exercised with the use of a power generator. They are a source of unwanted noise in the environment and can be difficult to control.

Audio Problems Defined This area of the form focuses on details that affect the production of audio recording in the proposed location environment.

Interior Environmental Sounds This entry should contain all perceived sound that is audible in the interior of the proposed location environment. This means careful listening for hums and buzzes from air conditioning, refrigerators, freezers, sound speakers, copying machines, and fluorescent lights. All sounds should be noted. Note should also be made on the ability to control or turn off the sounds.

Ceiling Composition The composition of a ceiling can

determine the quality of sound recordings made in the proposed location environment. For example, a hard composition ceiling reflects sound; sound proofing materials on a ceiling absorb sound. Both can make a difference in the quality of sound recorded in an environment.

Wall Composition The composition of the walls of a proposed location environment also makes a difference in the quality of sound recorded in that environment. For example, cork, carpet or cloth, and sound proofing absorb sound; tile, mirror, and plaster will reflect sound.

Exterior Environmental Sounds Location scouts must listen carefully to both interior and exterior sounds in an environment. Exterior sounds affect both an exterior and an interior shoot. For example, some common exterior sounds that can affect an interior shoot are airplanes, emergency vehicles, a school playground, busy highway, and noisy manufacturing plant. Make note of every perceivable sound.

Floor Covering Composition The composition of a floor also has an effect on sound recording in an environment. For example, a polished hardwood or tile floor reflects as well as creates sound (e.g., footsteps). Deep pile carpeting absorbs sound.

Playback Acoustics/PA System The acoustics of the location environment should be evaluated for audio playback quality. The existence of a public address system may serve as a playback system, but it should still be checked for sound reproduction quality.

Cast and Crew Needs This area of the form reminds location scouts that care and consideration of cast and crew needs will have to be accounted for during a location shoot.

Restroom Facilities Restroom facilities for men and women must be provided. Part of the location site survey is to note, perhaps on the diagram of the location, where the restroom facilities are closest to the shooting area.

Green Room Availability A green room is a theater term for a waiting area for actors. Some such waiting area may also be required for the cast for a video production. This should be a room close to the shooting area, but separate from the shooting area where cast can relax and await their blocking and videotaping calls.

Parking Arrangements A remote video production crew and cast can create a parking space demand on a neighborhood or public parking area. During scouting the question of special parking should be addressed. This may occasion some parking privileges or special directions or restrictions.

Freight Elevator In some location environments the number of crew, cast, and equipment involved in video production may require the use of a freight elevator in a facility. The location of the freight elevator should be part of a location environment diagram giving directions from the freight elevator to the shooting area.

Eating Facilities When the length of a shooting day requires a meal on location, some eating facility, special room, or vending machines should be noted. Some facilities may prohibit any eating on premises. Notation then will have to be made of restaurants in the vicinity of the proposed location.

Make-up Facilities If the video production requires that cast or talent appear in make-up, some facility will have to be provided for the application of the make-up. Ideally, make-up application requires mirrors, adequate lighting, and sinks. Restroom facilities make decent make-up preparation accommodations. If nothing else is available, a double set of restrooms can be designated for make-up and costuming.

Loading/Unloading Restrictions The amount of equipment needed for a remote video production may require special unloading and loading requirements at a location site, e.g., an outside loading dock area. Such a loading dock may also be close to a freight elevator. Location personnel should always be made aware of the great amount of equipment video production requires. They should be the judge of any special circumstances that might be required for so much equipment.

Hardware Store Because remote video production demands so much hardware equipment, there is often the need to purchase supplies or replace broken, lost, or forgotten supplies. Facilities representatives may be the persons to know where the closest hardware store is in the vicinity of the proposed location environment.

Civil Emergency Services This area of the form lists essential civil services in the service of both the production cast and crew and the location site.

Police Station The address and phone number of the police station that services the proposed location site is important contact information. With the number of individuals a remote video production crew involves, the amount of equipment and the use of an environment warrant the sensitivity to police presence and availability.

Fire Station The same holds true for the fire protection station within the environmental area of the proposed location shoot site. The heavy use of electrical power for a remote video production shoot should alert both producer and production crew to the potential dangers of so much power use. This holds especially true for an older facility, such as a private home used as a location site. The address and phone number of the fire station should be entered here.

Location Security and Equipment Safety This area of the form records important information on general personal and property security and safety.

Facility Security This entry records the general security of crew, cast, and equipment during the production shoot. Some proposed locations in highly public areas, such as a shopping mall, present a security risk; confined production sites, such as a private home, would be more secure. Note should be made of apparent security in general for all production elements.

Personnel Values Security Record should be made of the arrangements made with facilities personnel for the safety and security of personal belongings while crew and cast are involved in production. This includes wallets and purses especially. Facilities personnel often can provide a locked and secure room for the deposit of personal valuables during production.

Equipment Safe Storage   Arrangements should be made for the security of unused equipment and accessories that should be safely stored until needed or stored after use until the location strike. The facilities personnel can often provide a locked and secure room for equipment storage.

Overnight Storage/Security   Often remote location shoots take place over the period of more than one day. This entails the safe and secure storage of equipment overnight. Complete breakdown of all location equipment and loading, transport, and unloading a second day can result in the loss of valuable time and energy. Facilities personnel can often provide adequate overnight storage that is safe and secure.

Other Relevant Information   This area of the form records important information that falls outside the other areas of location details.

Public Area Power Source   Often in open public areas, such as a city park, the local power company may already provide a power box with electrical outlets for private use. This service has to be requested from the power company and a deposit made to secure power costs at the end of the production shoot. Location scouts should search a public area for some sign of power source facility. It may serve the site survey to make a call to the local power company and request a listing of outdoor power sources.

Clearance/Insurance   Personal security for the crew and talent and property damage insurance coverage should be secured before video production. Academic programs have personal insurance coverage for students and property damage and loss coverage for school equipment, which is active when the shoot is a valid academic project with a supervising faculty present. Other remote video production projects can easily receive coverage by contacting a reliable insurance agent. Some potential location facilities personnel require verification of insurance coverage before approval of their location for a shoot. Anticipating insurance notification before facilities personnel require it is a sign of professional competence.

Photographs Taken   When more than one location environment is being scouted for a shoot and a decision may be made away from a potential site, a producer will have to judge from the location scout's report. An important part of a location site survey is photographs of the proposed location. Instant developing film is most convenient. When adequate photographs of a location site are part of a survey, these photographs help a producer and camera operator plan a shoot and assist a crew after a location strike in replacing a location environment to the arrangement and condition it was in before the production crew arrived. The photographs taken should be listed. The photographer's camera position and direction of the lens of the photographed site should be noted on the location diagram as an aid in designing the video camera shots and lens framing for the production.

Location Environment Drawing/Map   Another important product of location scouting is a drawing or map of the proposed location site. This entails a rough pacing off of all environments, both interior and exterior, that are being considered as a video setting. Windows should be placed, compass direction indicated, power outlets and circuits noted, and existing furniture and other properties sketched. Everything should be included that may enter into the use of the location from the needs of the production and the adaptability of the location environment.

Traffic Control   At some exterior location environments, the extent of a video production crew, talent, and equipment necessitate some control of vehicular traffic. For example, parking restriction may be required along the area of a shooting set, moving traffic may have to be redirected during a shoot, or a street may have to be closed off entirely from traffic. Most police departments are cooperative to such requests but they need adequate advance time notification. In some instances the approval of a city or town council may be required. This too needs adequate lead time to process the request and get it to the council in good time for the shoot or a change of plans if the request should be denied.

Exterior Compass Direction   If the remote location site is an exterior shoot, an accurate assessment of the compass directions of the area should be made with respect to the proposed shooting site. The sun is the principal light source to an exterior shoot, and that source is in constant movement. Knowing the direction the sun takes from east to west on a proposed location environment is a most important variable to designing an outdoor video shoot. A compass is a necessity to scouting a location site. Many location personnel are not accurate about their recollection of east and west directions and are not reliable sources of information, given the importance that the sun's direction has on a remote video shoot.

Other Comments/Observations   This area should record any other details not covered in the form to this point. It is important to record all impressions of a proposed location site. Sometimes the smallest detail missed or the smallest detail included can become either an obstacle or an asset to the production later. When in doubt about including a detail, include it.

- **Production Schedule Form**

Production process: Music video preproduction

Responsibility: Producer

Purpose: To organize and schedule the videotape production of individual script and location units of the music video.

Objective: The production schedule form organizes the elements of each remote location into a production day and date for videotaping. The form serves to notify the production crew and talent of specific location address, date, time, and script pages of scheduling the videotape production of the music video. Because the music video genre is a short genre in length, rarely is more than a single production day needed. The schedule also sets an alternate date, projected equipment set-up and location strike time, and approximate times for completing each stage of the shoot.

Glossary

Shooting Day This area of the form sets the specific date (weekday, month, and day) for the shooting day. The production schedule form also firms up an alternate rain date.

Location Site The remote environment/place approved for the shoot after site survey was completed should be noted here. This names the building and geographic area where the videotaping is to take place.

Location Map No. This notation relates the location site and address to a municipal map of the geographic area (e.g., H-3).

Location Host The name of the location personnel responsible for the facility/area where the shoot is to occur should be recorded here. This is the everyday contact person with whom the producer will cooperate on details of the location and the shoot. A contact telephone number where the location host can be reached should be included.

Crew Call The time and place of the production crew starting crew call should be entered here.

Talent Call The time and place for the arrival call for talent is also listed. Because the talent do not need the lead time for equipment set-up as the production crew do, the talent call can be up to an hour later than the production crew call. Time should be allotted for make-up if make-up is required for talent.

Set-up This entry is a range of time including a deadline for the production crew to complete all equipment set-up and checks of the equipment.

Projected Strike Time This time sets an approximate termination hour for completing the shoot and striking the location.

Music Measure This column records the number(s) of the music measures being videotaped.

Storyboard Frames This column records the number(s) of the storyboard frames being videotaped.

Setting The specific setting within the location where the videotaping will occur is listed here.

Approx. Time A range of hours and minutes approximating the time needed to complete the music measures and/or storyboard frames proposed for production during the shooting day.

Artists(s)/Musician(s)/Actor(s) The talent who will be a part of the videotaping are listed here.

Action Properties On many location shoots, some action properties are required, e.g., an automobile, an animal, The action properties required for the respective script measures/frames are recorded here.

Comments The comments section allows the producer the opportunity to make any additional notes to be called to the attention of the crew or talent.

• Blocking Plot

Production process: Music video preproduction

Responsibility: Director

Purpose: To create the director's location storyboard, the location document from which the actors, dialogue, properties, camera operator(s), and camera framing will be directed.

Objective: This essential preproduction stage prepares the director for all details for directing the cast and talent while on location. From the location survey and photographs the director can design all production elements for location videotaping. The blocking plot serves to record the blocking of talent and sets and to record the storyboard sketch of every video frame proposed for production.

Notes on use: Many copies of the blocking plot form may be needed. Two blocking frames and storyboard frames are contained on each page. There is a lead page for the series and a secondary page for the remainder. Each page of the blocking plot form is designed to be inserted into the director's copy of the production storyboard facing the respective page of the storyboard.

The director should sketch the storyboard frame from the production storyboard. Then from the location site survey form and site survey photographs the bird's eye floor plan can be drawn. The director should then position the talent in the floor plan and indicate the blocking for the talent. Then the camera(s) should be sketched in place to achieve the shot(s) as proposed in the storyboard frame. Each separate bird's eye floor plan is drawn adjacent to a storyboard frame. Neither the floor plan nor storyboard frame need be redrawn each time if no major changes occur to the storyboard or the floor plan and nothing is to be added.

Glossary

Music Measure The number(s) of music measures as enumerated on the storyboard should be recorded here corresponding to the storyboard frames being blocked.

Storyboard Frame The number of the storyboard frame being blocked for the visualization for the music video is recorded here. Allow for dropping any number in enumeration of the frames.

Shot No. After the design of the blocking plot, the director creates a shot list from the storyboard frames. The shot list number for each storyboard frame is recorded here. This shot number should be entered at the corresponding in-cue on the storyboard opposite the blocking plot form page.

3:4 Video Frame This is the storyboard video aspect ratio frame. The sketch of the proposed shot from the production storyboard should be drawn in this frame.

Camera No. In designing the blocking plot the director should keep in mind the multiple isolated cameras in production. Each isolated camera should be numbered, and the number of the camera used to achieve the proposed shot should be recorded here.

Framing The choice of framing (XCU, CU, MS, LS, XLS) should be checked here. This facilitates calling out directions to the camera operator on location.

Change to If camera framing is to change during the shot, that camera framing change can be checked here.

Camera Motion The camera motion that is required as

part of the shot or the change of framing during the shot indicated in the storyboard frame can be checked here.

Lighting The director can check the kind of lighting required for the shot in this area of the form.

Sound The audio requirements for videotaping this shot can be checked here. Synchronous means that both audio and video will be recorded; silent means that the shot will not require any sound; wild means that the video need not be recorded, sound alone need be recorded. Because there is no need usually for audio recording on location for the music video, silent should be checked.

Bird's Eye Floor Plan The director should reproduce in reduced images the location environment for the set. This should include the properties on the location set. The director should then place the talent (using circles with the initial letter of the character for each talent) in the set and block them (using arrows and repeating the talent's circle). The director should then draw the camera in place to achieve the shot sketched in the storyboard frame for the shot.

Description of Take/Unit This area of the form allows for some notation of special directions for the particular take. This may involve the talent, some blocking movement, or the use of some prop.

In-cue This entry can be the first words of lyrics of the shot or some indication from the beat of the music for the beginning of the proposed shot.

Out-cue This entry can be the final words of lyrics of the shot or some indication from the beat of the music for the ending of the proposed shot.

• **Lighting Plot Form**

Production process: Music video preproduction

Responsibility: Lighting director

Purpose: To prepare and organize the lighting design of the music video remote location production shoot.

Objective: The lighting plot form is designed to facilitate the lighting design for the lighting director for every different location set. The plot serves to preplan the placement of lighting instruments, kind of lighting, lighting control, and lighting design. When lighting is preplanned, lighting equipment needs are easily realized and provided.

Notes on use: The lighting plot form is created to encourage preplanning for lighting design and production. Hence, the more lighting needs and aesthetics that can be anticipated, the better the lighting production tasks.

At the minimum, every different location set lighting design should be created in advance of the location production. Lighting design can begin after the production storyboard is complete. The basics to planning lighting design are the bird's eye floor plan, the talent's blocking, the time of day, and the mood of the script.

A different plot is not required for every shot on the shot list. Base lighting design need not change as camera placement changes, but changes of location require all

new lighting set-up and design. It is these changes that the lighting director needs to be aware of.

Glossary

Music Measure The numbers of the measures of music that are being videotaped on the current location are recorded here.

Storyboard Frame The numbers of the storyboard frame(s) being videotaped with this shot are recorded here.

Shot No. The number of the shot being videotaped from the shot list is a good determination for the lighting director of need or significant changes in lighting design during a shoot. The shot number from the production storyboard should be recorded here.

Location This notation is a reminder of the location environment in which the videotaping is to occur.

Lighting This area of the plot notes the basic facts for lighting design: inside or outside, day or night.

Light Change It is important to lighting design and lighting control to know if the script or the director plans any change of lighting during the shot being videotaped. This notation alerts the lighting director to that need.

Mood One of the functions of lighting design is to create mood. An indication of the mood to be created in the shot is noted here.

3:4 Video Frame Insofar as the lighting design of a shot is affected and in return affects what the shot shows, occasionally the composition of the framing dictates the lighting needs. The lighting director may sketch from the production storyboard elements of the storyboard frame as an aid to lighting design for specific shots of the production.

Framing The extent of the framing of subjects also determines lighting design. The composition of framing is indicated by checking the appropriate symbols for frame composition as checked on the production storyboard for the shot.

Change When a change in framing is indicated, it could trigger a change in lighting, or that the change in framing be calculated in the basic lighting design. The new framing composition is indicated by checking the appropriate symbols for new framing.

Bird's Eye Floor Plan The best preproduction information for the lighting director is the floor plan for the location with actor(s) blocking and movement indicated. This should be sketched in this box from the production storyboard. Where the camera is to be placed is also important to the lighting director and lighting design.

Description of Take/Unit Any director's notes on the elements of the take that will affect lighting design should be noted here.

Lighting Instruments/Lighting Accessories/Filters/Property Lights/Windows These lists in the plot form are designed to assist the lighting director in considering all elements of lighting design and materials in the preparation of the lighting plot. A lighting director can make notation in the proper space in planning for the particular design of each set.

In-cue A lighting director may find it convenient to make note of the in-cue from the lyrics when (on what action or lyrics) the lighting design is to begin.

Out-cue The same notation on an out-cue of action or lyrics for the end of a shot or a change of lighting may be advantageous to the lighting director.

• Equipment Checklist Form

Production process: Music video preproduction

Responsibility: Camera operator(s), videotape recorder operator(s), lighting director, audio director

Purpose: To suggest and account for all possible equipment and accessories necessary for a successful remote music video shoot.

Objective: The equipment checklist form is an all-inclusive checklist for equipment and accessories hardware that may be used or needed on a video production location site. The checklist notes first the equipment available to the production crew, usually the equipment owned by the production facility. Second, the list notes the equipment that may have to be purchased for the shoot. Third, the checklist allows for notation of any equipment that may have to be rented for the shoot. There are blank lines in equipment groups to personalize the checklist for an individual production or facility.

Glossary

Locations The location(s) for which the equipment will be needed should be noted here.

Avl This abbreviation stands for available equipment, which may be owned by the production facility itself. A check in this column indicates that the equipment or accessory is available to the production crew and free to be used on the scheduled production day.

Pch This abbreviation stands for purchase and indicates that the needed equipment or accessory will have to be purchased for the production project. Items checked as needed to be purchased will probably require some other requisition step and approval. The checklist also does not imply when or by whom the purchasing will be done. This is the responsibility of the production crew member.

Rnt This abbreviation stands for rent and indicates that the needed equipment or accessory is not available, perhaps too expensive to purchase for the shoot, and will have to be rented from a supplier. Similar to items checked in the purchase column, additional steps may be required in the process of obtaining the rented equipment. Some requisition may have to be made, approval received, and rental details made.

Camera/Recorder/Tripod/Test Equipment/Audio/Power Supplies/Lighting/Cables These areas of the form listed are an attempt to anticipate all possible equipment and accessories needs for a remote video production. Many items may be superfluous. They are listed as an attempt to suggest all possible production needs, and equally to suggest the use of some hardware that might be needed during a remote location shoot. One way to use this checklist is to permit it to suggest hardware elements to make the experience of a remote video shoot smooth and productive.

Miscellaneous This area of the form is the result of years of remote video production experience and represents many production disasters during which these elements could have made a difference. Some items are redundant; some may suggest a use not before anticipated. Most items are helpful to the good order and task facilitation on location.

• Shot List Form

Production process: Music video preproduction

Responsibility: Director

Purpose: To translate the proposed storyboard frames from the production storyboard and blocking plots into location videotape recording shots or camera shots.

Objective: The shot list form organizes each proposed storyboard frame into videotaping shots. Each shot should generate the necessary video to create the proposed edits as designed on the production storyboard. Each numbered shot is then entered on the storyboard at the spot where the proposed shot is to be edited. This preproduction task facilitates the "What's next" syndrome during location productions. The shot list should exactly define every camera set-up, lens framing, and video shot needed to achieve that video. The shot list form translates each proposed shot from the production storyboard to a simpler list for the advantage of the camera operator(s), videotape recorder operator(s), audio director, and lighting director.

Glossary

Location Every planned location site camera set-up and change of location site camera set-up should be noted in this column.

Shot No. From the production storyboard and blocking plot, every proposed shot needed to create the storyboard frame of the music video should be numbered consecutively. The respective number should be recorded here. The shot numbers are location-specific so that the shots can be numbered by one starting at each new location.

Master Shot If a proposed shot is a master shot or establishing shot (e.g., XLS) for a scene, it should be noted here. For example, a master shot might be an XLS of a couple walking toward the camera during dialogue.

Cut-in Shot If a proposed shot is a cut-in (from a master shot), it should be noted in this column. For example, a cut-in would be a CU shot of one of the couple in the master shot.

Cut-away Shot Unlike the cut-in (to a master shot), the cut-away shot is relevant but extraneous to (usually away from) the master scene shot. An example of a cut-away would be generic footage of a city street.

Shot Framing Shot framing directions for every proposed shot should make use of the symbols for the basic camera shot framing: XLS, LS, MS, CU, XCU. This would communicate to the camera operator the lens framing for the proposed shot. The framing choice for the shot should be checked on the production storyboard by the director. That framing direction should be recorded here.

Shot Motion Shot motion directions should indicate the kind of movement desired in the proposed shot. Movement in a shot can be either primary movement (on the part of the talent in front of the camera), the blocking of the talent; or secondary movement (on the part of the camera itself), the pan, tilt, arc, truck, dolly, pedestal, or zoom. This direction too should have been checked by the director on the production storyboard. That motion direction should be repeated here.

Content Notes Any particular details of any shots not covered in the previous directions can be noted here. Content notes may be found in the description of the take directions from the blocking plots. What is considered important to production crew members should be repeated here.

• **Video Continuity Notes Form**

Production process: Music video production

Responsibility: Continuity secretary

Purpose: To record during remote videotaping the details of all elements of the production as an aid to reestablishing details for sequential shots. The need is to facilitate a continuity of production details so that editing across takes is continuous.

Objective: The video continuity form is a record of all possible video production details (e.g., location, talent, properties, dialogue) that must carry over from shot to shot, i.e., across edits, in postproduction. The nature of single camera production is the fact that while videotaped shots are separate in production, the final video editing of various shots must look continuous. The continuity form records specific details at all facets of production and records them to reestablish the detail in subsequent videotaping.

Notes on use: The form is designed to be used for each separate shot being taken in single camera remote field production. This means that for any single shot with many takes, one continuity notes page should be used. In preparing for a lengthy remote shoot involving many shots to be achieved and many camera and lighting set-ups, many copies of this form will have to be made.

The person keeping continuity notes should be observant. The role demands attention to the slightest detail of the production that may have to be reestablished in another camera take. The role needs a crew person with 100% of the time spent on note taking.

Admittedly, the immediacy of replaying video on a playback monitor on location is a fast check on any detail in a previous videotaped take. Although playback is fast, it is time-consuming and it is not a habit that a director should have. Careful continuity notes are still a requirement in remote single camera music video production.

Not all the accounting enumeration (slate no., sequence no., shot no., storyboard frame no., music measure no.) need to be recorded for every shot. The preference is that of the director or the continuity secretary.

Glossary

Slate No. A production slate may have a number attached to it. That number is recorded here.

Continuity Secretary The continuity secretary's name should be recorded here. The extent of detail necessary in the production of remote single camera music video is so great that a full time continuity secretary is a necessity. Continuity note taking is not a hit or miss task in remote production.

Set-up/Location A description or sketch of the location or the set-up of the environment is required here. Note should be taken of things that were moved (e.g., action properties) that need to be replaced.

Interior/Exterior These choices allow the notation of whether the shoot is indoors or outdoors.

Day/Night These choices allow the notation of time of day.

Sync Cam 1/2 This alternative is the indication that the shoot is video and audio synchronous recording and indicates which audio channel is being used for recording the audio signal, channel 1 or channel 2.

Silent This choice indicates that the camera is taking video without recording any audio signal.

Wildtrack Wildtrack means that audio signals are being recorded without video. For example, to record a portion of location ambience for later audio mixing would not require video signals also.

WT with Cam This alternative, "wildtrack with camera," indicates that a wildtrack is being recorded with a video signal also.

Sequence No. Some remote production video units are parts of a numbered sequence. This entry is used to record the sequence number being videotaped.

Shot No. When a shot list is being followed on location, the sequential number of the shot being videotaped is recorded here.

Storyboard Frame No. The number of the storyboard frame being videotaped is recorded here.

Music Measure No. The number(s) of the music measures being videotaped are recorded here.

Costume/Make-up/Properties Notes This area should be used to verbally record all details noticed during production that may have to be reestablished for a subsequent shot. Note should be taken of any costume use (e.g., a tie off-centered, a pocket flap tucked in), make-up detail (e.g., smudged lipstick, position of a wound), or property use (e.g., half-smoked cigarette in the right hand between the index and middle finger or fresh ice cream cone in the left hand).

Tape No. This should be a record of the numerically coded videotape being recorded for this shot. This record should coordinate this shot with a particular videocassette.

Circle Takes (1–10) This area of the form facilitates record of each subsequent take of a shot or scene. The best use of these boxes is to circle each number representing the take in progress until the take is satisfactorily videotaped.

End Board The normal practice of indicating on the videotape leader what take of a shot is being recorded is to use the slate. If a particular take is flubbed for a minor problem (e.g., an actor missing a line), a producer might simply indicate that instead of stopping taping and beginning from scratch, the crew keep going by starting over without stopping. Because the slate then was not used to record at the beginning of the retake, an end board is used; the slate is recorded on tape at the end of the take instead of at the beginning. This note alerts the postproduction crew not to look for a slate at the beginning of that take but at the end.

Timer/Counter This area of the form should be used to record either a consecutive stopwatch time or the consecutive videotape recorder digital counter number. Both of these times should be a record of the length into the videotape where this take is recorded. Therefore, the stopwatch or the counter should be at zero when the tape is rewound to its beginning at the start of the tape. It is a good practice for the videotape recorder operator to have the habit of calling the counter numbers out aloud to the continuity notes taker at the beginning of every take.

Reason for Use/Not Good The benefit of the continuity notes is to save the tedium of reviewing all takes after a shoot to make a determination of the quality of each take. If conscientious notes are taken here, a judgmental notation on the quality of each take is recorded, and one postproduction chore is complete. Usually, a producer makes a judgment on location anyway in determining whether to retake a shot or to move on to a new shot. The continuity secretary should note whether the take is good or not, and the reason for that judgment.

Action Continuity details on any action during the take should be noted here. For example, the direction talent takes when turning, or the hand used to open the door should be noted.

Dialogue An area of continuity of interest can be the dialogue of the script. Here notation should be made of any quirk of dialogue used in a take that may have to be repeated in a take intended for a matched edit.

• **Talent Release Form**

Production process: Music video production

Responsibility: Producer

Purpose: To give the producer legal rights over the video recording of individual talent.

Objective: The talent release form is a legal document, which when filled out and signed by talent, gives to the producer and the producing organization the legal right to use the video recording of an individual for publication. This form is especially necessary in the case of talent when profit may be gained from the eventual sale of the video product. If talent contracts were completed and signed, talent releases were probably included. When talent volunteer their services or perform for only a nominal fee or other gratuity, a signed talent release is recommended. Generally, any talent being featured in video and audio taping should sign a talent release before the final video production is aired.

Glossary

Talent Name This entry should contain the name of the individual talent recorded on video for the music video production.
Recording Location The location site of the video recording should be entered here.
Producer The name of the supervising producer should be entered here.
Producing Organization The incorporated name of the video producing organization should be entered here.

Note: The expression, "For value received," may imply that some remuneration, even a token remuneration, is required for the form to be legally binding. When there is any doubt about the legal nature of the document, consult a lawyer.

MUSIC VIDEO CONCEPT FORM

Producer:

Director:

Album Title:
Cut Title:
Cut Length: :
Recording Artist:
Date: /   /

PRODUCTION BUDGET

MUSIC VIDEO PRODUCTION

Producer:
Director:

Song Title:
Artist:
Length: :

No. Preproduction Days: ☐ Hours: ☐
No. Studio Shoot Days: ☐ Hours: ☐
No. Location Days: ☐ Hours: ☐
No. Post Production Days: ☐ Hours: ☐

Shooting Date: /   /
Completion Date: /   /
Location Site(s):

SUMMARY OF PRODUCTION COSTS	ESTIMATED	ACTUAL
1. Preproduction crew		
2. Production crew		
3. Materials and expenses		
4. Location expenses		
5. Properties, costumes, animals		
6. Studio, hall, rental and expenses		
7. Set construction		
8. Set construction materials		
9. Equipment rental		
10. Videotape stock		
11. Miscellaneous		
12. Director fees		
13. Talent		
14. Talent expenses		
15. Sub-total		
16. Post Production editing		
17. Sound		
18. Personnel		
19. Art work		
20. Sub-total		
21. Contingency		
Grand Total		

COMMENTS:

PREPRODUCTION COSTS

CREW	ESTIMATED				ACTUAL			
	Days	Rate	O/T Hrs	Total	Days	Rate	O/T Hrs	Total
1. Producer								
2. Assoc Producer								
3.								
4. Asst Director								
5.								
6. Production Manager								
7.								
8. Camera Operator(s)								
9. VTR Operator(s)								
10.								
11. Lighting Director								
12. Electrician								
13.								
14. Grip								
15.								
16. Audio Director								
17.								
18. Make-Up								
19. Hair Stylist								
20. Costumes								
21.								
22.								
23. Location Scout(s)								
24. Production Assistant								
25.								
26.								
27. Storyboard Artist								
29.								
30.								
31.								
32.								
33.								
34.								
35.								
Sub-Total								

PRODUCTION COSTS

CREW	ESTIMATED				ACTUAL			
	Days	Rate	O/T Hrs	Total	Days	Rate	O/T Hrs	Total
36. Producer								
37. Assoc Producer								
38.								
39. Asst Director								
40.								
41. Production Manager								
42.								
43. Camera Operator(s)								
44. VTR Operator(s)								

CREW (Con't)	ESTIMATED				ACTUAL			
	Days	Rate	O/T Hrs	Total	Days	Rate	O/T Hrs	Total
45.								
46. Lighting Director								
47. Electrician								
48.								
49. Grip								
50.								
51. Audio Director								
52.								
53. Make-Up								
54. Hair Stylist								
55. Costumes								
56.								
57.								
58. Location Scout(s)								
59. Production Assistant								
60.								
61.								
62. Storyboard Artist								
63.								
64.								
65.								
66.								
67.								
68.								
69.								
Sub-Total								

PRODUCTION MATERIALS AND EXPENSES	ESTIMATED	ACTUAL
70. Auto Rentals: No. of Cars		
71. Air Fares: No. of People ( ) x Amt per Day ( )		
72. Per Diems: No. of People ( ) x Amt per Day ( )		
73.		
74.		
75. Trucking		
76. Deliveries and Taxis		
77.		
78. Casting: Prep Days Casting Days Call back		
79. Casting Facilities		
80. Working Meals		
81.		
Sub-Total		

LOCATION EXPENSES	ESTIMATED	ACTUAL
82. Location Fees		
83. Permits		
84. Insurance		
85. Vehicle Rental		
86. Parking, Tolls, and Gas		
87. Shipping/Trucking		

LOCATION EXPENSES (Con't)		ESTIMATED	ACTUAL
88. Scouting			
	Travel		
	Car Rental		
	Housing		
	Per Diem		
89. Celebrity Service			
90. Taxis/Other Transportation			
91. Location Police/Firemen			
92. Gratuities			
93. Miscellaneous			
94.			
	Sub Total		

PROPS, COSTUMES AND ANIMALS	ESTIMATED	ACTUAL
95. Prop Rental		
96. Prop Purchase		
97. Wardrobe Rental		
98. Wardrobe Purchase		
99. Picture Vehicles		
100. Animals and Handlers		
101. Wigs and Mustaches		
102.		
103. Miscellaneous		
104.		
Sub Total		

STUDIO AND HALL RENTAL AND EXPENSES	ESTIMATED				ACTUAL			
	Days	Rate	O/T Hrs	Total	Days	Rate	O/T Hrs	Total
105. Rental: Preproduction								
106. Rental: Production								
107. Rental: Post Product								
108.								
109. Generator/Operator								
110. Electrical Power								
111. Studio Charges								
112. Meals: Crew/Talent								
113. Security								
114. Miscellaneous								
115.								
Sub Total								

SET CONSTRUCTION	ESTIMATED				ACTUAL			
	Days	Rate	O/T Hrs	Total	Days	Rate	O/T Hrs	Total
116. Set Designer								
117. Carpenter(s)								
118. Grip(s)								
119. Outside Props								
120. Inside Props								
121. Scenics								
122. Electrician(s)								
123. Strike Personnel								
124.								
125. Miscellaneous								
126.								
Sub Total								

SET CONSTRUCTION MATERIALS	ESTIMATED	ACTUAL
127. Set Dressing Rentals		
128. Set Dressing Purchases		
129. Lumber		
130. Paint		
131. Hardware		
132. Special Effects		
133.		
134. Trucking		
135.		
136. Miscellaneous		
137.		
Sub Total		

EQUIPMENT RENTAL	ESTIMATED	ACTUAL
138. Camera Rental		
139. Videotape Recorder Rental		
140. Audio Rental		
141. Lighting Rental		
142.		
143. Generator Rental		
144. Crane/Cherry Picker Rental		
145. Walkie Talkies/Bull Horn(s)		
146. Dolly Rental		
147. Mobile Unit Rental		
148. Camera Plane/Chopper Rental		
149. Camera Car(s) Rental		
150. Camera Boat(s) Rental		
151. Production Supplies		
152.		
153. Miscellaneous		
154.		
Sub Total		

VIDEOTAPE STOCK	ESTIMATED	ACTUAL
155. Videotape:		
1" (:) x ($)		
3/4" (S 20:00) x ($)		
3/4" (30:00) x ($)		
3/4" (60:00) x ($)		
156.		
157. Miscellaneous		
Sub Total		

MISCELLANEOUS COSTS	ESTIMATED	ACTUAL
158. Petty Cash		
159. Air Shipping/Special Carriers		
160. Telephones/Cables		
161. Billing Costs		
162. Special Insurance		
162. Miscellaneous		
Sub Total		

DIRECTOR FEES	ESTIMATED	ACTUAL
163. Preproduction Fees		
164. Travel		
165. Per Diem		
166. Production Shoot Days Fees		
167. Post Production Fees		
168.		
169. Miscellaneous		
Sub Total		

TALENT	ESTIMATED				ACTUAL			
	Days	Rate	O/T Hrs	Total	Days	Rate	O/T Hrs	Total
170. Artists								
171.								
172. Musicians								
173.								
174.								
175. Extra								
176. Extra								
177.								
178.								
179.								
180. Dancer(s)								
181.								
182.								
183.								
184.								
185. Rehearsal Fees								
186.								
187. Audition Fees								
188.								

TALENT (Con't)	ESTIMATED				ACTUAL			
	Days	Rate	O/T Hrs	Total	Days	Rate	O/T Hrs	Total
189. Talent Transportation								
190. Miscellaneous								
191.								
Sub Total								

TALENT EXPENSES	ESTIMATED	ACTUAL
192. Per Diems: No. of Days ( ) x Amt per Day ( )		
193. Air Fare: No. of People ( ) x Amt per Fare ( )		
194. Taxis/Other Transportation		
195. Talent Handling		
196.		
197. Miscellaneous		
198.		
Sub Total		

POST PRODUCTION COSTS

EDITING	ESTIMATED				ACTUAL			
	Days	Rate	O/T Hrs	Total	Days	Rate	O/T Hrs	Total
199. SMPTE Time Coding								
200. On-Line Editing								
201.								
202. DVE Special Effects								
203. Tape-to-tape Duping								
204. Audio Mixing								
205. Audio Sweetening								
206. Sound Effects								
207. Character Generator								
208. Master(s)								
209. Dub(s)								
210. Tape Stock and Reels								
211. Paint Box								
212.								
213. Miscellaneous								
214.								
Sub Total								

SOUND	ESTIMATED				ACTUAL			
	Days	Rate	O/T Hrs	Total	Days	Rate	O/T Hrs	Total
215. Master Track								
216.								
217. Music Search								
218. Clearance Fees								
219. Synchonization Fees								
220.								
221. Miscellaneous								
Sub Total								

EDITING PERSONNEL	ESTIMATED				ACTUAL			
	Days	Rate	O/T Hrs	Total	Days	Rate	O/T Hrs	Total
222. Editor								
223. Asst Editor								
224.								
225. Miscellaneous								
Sub Total								

ART WORK	ESTIMATED				ACTUAL			
	Days	Rate	O/T Hrs	Total	Days	Rate	O/T Hrs	Total
226. Art Work								
227. Animator(s)								
228.								
229. Animation Materials								
230. Animation Photography								
231. Miscellaneous								
232.								
Sub Total								

COMMENTS

MUSIC VIDEO STORYBOARD

MUSIC VIDEO PRODUCTION

Producer:
Director:

Song Title:
Page   of

Lyrics

STORYBOARD BREAKDOWN
MUSIC VIDEO PRODUCTION

Producer:

Director:

Date: /   /

Song Title:
Artist:
Length: :
Music Measures:
Storyboard Frames:
Page   of

MUSIC MEA-SURE	STORY-BOARD FRMS	INT/EXT	TIME	SETTING	LOCATION	ARTIST(S), MUSICIAN(S), ACTOR(S)	SHOOT-ING ORDER

MUSIC VIDEO PRODUCTION STORYBOARD BREAKDOWN						Page of	
MUSIC MEA-SURE	STORY-BOARD FRMS	INT/ EXT	TIME	SETTING	LOCATION	ARTIST(S), MUSICIAN(S), ACTOR(S)	SHOOT-ING ORDER

LOCATION SITE SURVEY

MUSIC VIDEO PRODUCTION

Producer:	Song Title:
Director:	Artist:
Approval:	Music Measures:
Location Scout(s):	Storyboard Frames:
	Date: / /

Location: Site Identification:
Local Contact Person: Comments:
  Name:
  Title:
  Address:
  City: State:
  Phone No.: (   )   -
Facilities Personnel: Comments:
  Name:
  Position Title:
  Address:
  City: State:
  Phone No.: (   )   -

LIGHTING PROBLEMS DEFINED

Light contrast ratios	Existing light control
Lighting intensity	Lighting use
Ceiling height	Floor description
Windows/Compass direction	Special consideration

POWER PROBLEMS DEFINED

Number of power outlets	Number of outlet prongs
Number of separate circuits	Location of circuit breakers
Types of fuses	Portable generator need

AUDIO PROBLEMS DEFINED

Interior environmental sounds	Exterior environmental sounds
Ceiling composition	Floor covering composition
Wall composition	Playback acoustics/PA system

CAST AND CREW NEEDS

Restroom facilities	Eating facilities
Green room availability	Make-up facilities
Parking arrangements	Loading/unloading restrictions
Freight elevator	Hardware store

CIVIL EMERGENCY SERVICES

Police station   Fire station

LOCATION SECURITY AND EQUIPMENT SAFETY

Facility security   Equipment safe storage

Personnel values security   Overnight storage/security

OTHER RELEVANT INFORMATION

Public area power source   Traffic control

Clearance/Insurance needed   Exterior compass direction

Photographs taken   Location environment drawing/map

Other information:

OTHER COMMENTS/OBSERVATIONS

PRODUCTION SCHEDULE

MUSIC VIDEO PRODUCTION

Producer:

Director:

Song Title:
Artist: Length: :
Date: / /
Page   of

SHOOTING DAY   RAIN DATE
                                                        __/__/__
_____ , _____ , _____
    (Weekday)   (Month)   (Day)

Location Site:_____ Location Map No. _____

Address: _____
         City_____ State _____

Location Host: _____
Phone No.: (___)____-_____

Crew call:__:__ AM/PM

    Address:_____

Talent call:__:__ AM/PM

    Address:_____

Set-up:__:___ to ___:___   Projected Strike Time: ___:___

MUSIC MEA- SURE	STORY- BOARD FRMS	SETTING	APPROX. TIME	ARTIST(S), MUSICIAN(S), ACTOR(S)	ACTION PROPERTIES
			: to :		
			: to :		
			: to :		
			: to :		
			: to :		
			: to :		
			: to :		

Comments:

BLOCKING PLOT

MUSIC VIDEO PRODUCTION

Song Title: _____ Director: _____ Date: / /

Music Measure [ ] Storyboard Frame [ ] Shot No. [ ]

Lighting
☐ Interior
☐ Exterior
☐ Day
☐ Night

Sound
☐ Synchronous
☐ Silent
☐ Wild

Shot
☐ Master
☐ Cut-in
☐ Cut-away

Bird's Eye Floor Plan
Properties/Blocking/Camera(s)

3:4 Video Frame   Camera No. [ ]

Framing: ☐ XCU ☐ CU ☐ MS ☐ LS ☐ XLS   Change to: ☐ XCU ☐ CU ☐ MS ☐ LS ☐ XLS

Camera Motion: Pan ☐ Tilt ☐ Zoom ☐ Dolly ☐ Truck ☐ Arc ☐ Pedestal ☐ Defocus ☐

Description of Take/Unit   Actors/Movement/Properties

In-Cue   Action/Lyrics   Out-Cue   Action/Lyrics

Music Measure [ ] Storyboard Frame [ ] Shot No. [ ]

Lighting
☐ Interior
☐ Exterior
☐ Day
☐ Night

Sound
☐ Synchronous
☐ Silent
☐ Wild

Shot
☐ Master
☐ Cut-in
☐ Cut-away

Bird's Eye Floor Plan
Properties/Blocking/Camera(s)

3:4 Video Frame   Camera No. [ ]

Framing: ☐ XCU ☐ CU ☐ MS ☐ LS ☐ XLS   Change to: ☐ XCU ☐ CU ☐ MS ☐ LS ☐ XLS

Camera Motion: Pan ☐ Tilt ☐ Zoom ☐ Dolly ☐ Truck ☐ Arc ☐ Pedestal ☐ Defocus ☐

Description of Take/Unit   Actors/Movement/Properties

In-Cue   Action/Lyrics   Out-Cue   Action/Lyrics

MUSIC VIDEO PRODUCTION BLOCKING PLOT   Page   of

Music Measure [ ]   Storyboard Frame [ ]   Shot No. [ ]

3:4 Video Frame   Camera No. [ ]

Lighting
☐ Interior
☐ Exterior
☐ Day
☐ Night

Sound
☐ Synchronous
☐ Silent
☐ Wild

Shot
☐ Master
☐ Cut-in
☐ Cut-away

Bird's Eye Floor Plan
Properties/Blocking/Camera(s)

Framing: ☐ XCU ☐ CU ☐ MS ☐ LS ☐ XLS   Change to: ☐ XCU ☐ CU ☐ MS ☐ LS ☐ XLS
Camera Motion: Pan ☐ Tilt ☐ Zoom ☐ Dolly ☐ Truck ☐ Arc ☐ Pedestal ☐ Defocus ☐

Description of Take/Unit   Actors/Movement/Properties

In-Cue   Action/Lyrics   Out-Cue   Action/Lyrics

Music Measure [ ]   Storyboard Frame [ ]   Shot No. [ ]

3:4 Video Frame   Camera No. [ ]

Lighting
☐ Interior
☐ Exterior
☐ Day
☐ Night

Sound
☐ Synchronous
☐ Silent
☐ Wild

Shot
☐ Master
☐ Cut-in
☐ Cut-away

Bird's Eye Floor Plan
Properties/Blocking/Camera(s)

Framing: ☐ XCU ☐ CU ☐ MS ☐ LS ☐ XLS   Change to: ☐ XCU ☐ CU ☐ MS ☐ LS ☐ XLS
Camera Motion: Pan ☐ Tilt ☐ Zoom ☐ Dolly ☐ Truck ☐ Arc ☐ Pedestal ☐ Defocus ☐

Description of Take/Unit   Actors/Movement/Properties

In-Cue   Action/Lyrics   Out-Cue   Action/Lyrics

LIGHTING PLOT

MUSIC VIDEO PRODUCTION

Song Title: _____ Lighting Director: _____ Date: __/__/__

Music Measure [____] Storyboard Frame [____] Slot No. [____]

Lighting
- ☐ Interior
- ☐ Exterior
- ☐ Day
- ☐ Night

Light Change
- ☐ Yes
- ☐ No

Mood
_____
_____

3:4 Video Frame

Bird's Eye Floor Plan
Props/Blocking/Camera(s) Placement
Lighting Instruments

Framing: ☐ XCU ☐ CU ☐ MS ☐ LS ☐ XLS   Change to: ☐ XCU ☐ CU ☐ MS ☐ LS ☐ XLS

Description of Take/Unit	Actors/Movement/Properties

Lighting Instruments
Key Lights:

Fill Lights:

Soft Lights:

Lighting Accessories
Barn Doors:

Flags:

Gobo:

Filters
Spun Glass:

Gels:

Screens:

Scrims:

Neutral Density:

Property Lights
Lamps:

Ceiling:

Other:

Windows   N
Compass Directions: W   E
                         S
Blacked:

Gels:

In-Cue	Action/Lyrics	Out-Cue	Action/Lyrics

Comments:

315

EQUIPMENT CHECKLIST

MUSIC VIDEO PRODUCTION

Director:
Camera Operator(s):

Videotape Recorder Operator(s):

Audio Director:
Lighting Director:

Song Title:
Artist: Length: :
Shooting Day: / /
Location:
Date: / /

Avl Pch Rnt

CAMERA
- Video Camera
- Lenses
- Filters
- AC/DC Monitor
- Lg Screen Monitor
- _____

RECORDER
- Videotape Recorder
- _____
- _____

TRIPOD
- Tripod w/Head
- Camera Head Adapter
- Dolly
- _____

TEST EQUIPMENT
- Waveform Monitor
- Vectorscope
- Grey Scale
- Registration Chart
- White Card
- Headphones
- _____

AUDIO
- Shot gun Microphone
- Lavaliere Microphone
- Hand-held Microphone
- Fishpole
- Wind screens

Avl Pch Rnt

AUDIO (continued)
- Mixer
- Adapter plugs
- Earphone
- Headphones
- Playback Deck
- Speakers ☐
- _____

POWER SUPPLIES
- Batteries for Camera
- Batteries for Recorder
- Batteries for Monitor
- AC Power Converter
- Microphone Batteries

LIGHTING
- Light Kit
- Soft Light Kit
- Barn Doors
- Spun Glass Filters
- Blue Gels
- Orange Gels
- Screens
- Scrims
- ND Filters
- Aluminum Foil
- Wooden Clothes Pins
- Light Meter
- Reflector
- Spare Bulbs
- Flags
- _____
- _____

Avl Pch Rnt

CABLES

☐ ☐ ☐ Multi-pin Cable Camera
to Recorder
☐ ☐ ☐ Video Cable Camera
to Recorder
☐ ☐ ☐ Video Cable Camera
to Waveform Monitor/
Scope
☐ ☐ ☐ Video Cable Scope to
Monitor
☐ ☐ ☐ Audio Mixer Cable to
Recorder
☐ ☐ ☐ Audio Extension Cables
☐ ☐ ☐ Speaker Extension Cables

MISCELLANEOUS

☐ ☐ ☐ Video tape
☐ ☐ ☐ Teleprompter
☐ ☐ ☐ Teleprompter Script
☐ ☐ ☐ Cue Card Paper
☐ ☐ ☐ Duct Tape
☐ ☐ ☐ Masking Tape
☐ ☐ ☐ Spare Fuses
☐ ☐ ☐ Tool Kit
☐ ☐ ☐ Stopwatch
☐ ☐ ☐ Slate
☐ ☐ ☐ Chalk
☐ ☐ ☐ Eraser
☐ ☐ ☐ Bullhorn
☐ ☐ ☐ Walkie-Talkie
☐ ☐ ☐ Dulling Spray
☐ ☐ ☐ Talent Release Forms
☐ ☐ ☐ Step Ladder
☐ ☐ ☐ Lens Cleaner and Tissue

Avl Pch Rnt

☐ ☐ ☐ Sewing Kit
☐ ☐ ☐ Paper, Pens, Felt Markers
☐ ☐ ☐ Rope
☐ ☐ ☐ Barrier Cones
☐ ☐ ☐ Poster Board
☐ ☐ ☐ Flashlight
☐ ☐ ☐ Scissors
☐ ☐ ☐ 100' Power Cords
☐ ☐ ☐ Staple Gun and Staples
☐ ☐ ☐ Power Outlet Boxes
☐ ☐ ☐ _____
☐ ☐ ☐ _____
☐ ☐ ☐ _____
☐ ☐ ☐ _____
☐ ☐ ☐ _____
☐ ☐ ☐ _____
☐ ☐ ☐ _____
☐ ☐ ☐ _____
☐ ☐ ☐ _____
☐ ☐ ☐ _____
☐ ☐ ☐ _____
☐ ☐ ☐ _____
☐ ☐ ☐ _____

SHOT LIST

MUSIC VIDEO PRODUCTION

Producer:		Song Title:		
Director:		Artist:	Length: :
		Date: / /	
		Page of	

| LOCATION | SHOT | | | | | | CONTENT NOTES |
	NO.	MASTER	CUT-IN	CUT-AWAY	FRAMING	MOTION	

LOCATION	SHOT						CONTENT NOTES
	NO.	MASTER	CUT-IN	CUT-AWAY	FRAMING	MOTION	

MUSIC VIDEO PRODUCTION SHOT LIST   Page   of

VIDEO CONTINUITY NOTES

MUSIC VIDEO PRODUCTION

SONG TITLE:			ARTIST:		SLATE NO.
DIRECTOR:		CONTINUITY SEC'Y			DATE / /

SET-UP/LOCATION				
	INTERIOR	DAY	SYNC Cam 1/2 SILENT	SEQUENCE NO.
	EXTERIOR	NIGHT	WILDTRACK WT with Cam	SHOT NO.
	STORYBOARD FRAME NO.		MUSIC MEASURE NO.	

COSTUME/MAKE-UP/PROPERTIES NOTES

TAPE NO.										
CIRCLE TAKES	1	2	3	4	5	6	7	8	9	10
END BOARD										
TIMER										
COUNTER										
REASON FOR USE/ NOT GOOD										

ACTION   LYRICS

TALENT RELEASE FORM
MUSIC VIDEO PRODUCTION

Talent Name: _____
(Please Print)

Project Title: _____

For value received and without further consideration, I hereby consent to the use of all photographs, videotapes or film, taken of me and/or recordings made of my voice and/or written extraction, in whole or in part, of such recordings or musical performance

at _____ on _____ 19___
(Recording Location)   *(Month)*   *(Day)*   *(Year)*

by_____ for_____
(Producer)   *(Producing Organization)*

and/or others with its consent, for the purposes of illustration, advertising, or publication in any manner.

Talent Name_____
(Signature)

Address_____ City_____

State _____ Zip Code _____

Date:____/____/____

If the subject is a minor under the laws of the state where modeling, acting, or performing is done:

Guardian _____ Guardian _____
(Signature)   *(Please Print)*

Address _____ City _____

State _____ Zip Code _____

Date:____/____/____

Glossary

Action props Moving objects used by actors in drama production, e.g., an automobile, a horse and buggy.

Ambience Any background sound in a recording environment, e.g., city traffic sounds, an airplane flyover.

Aspect ratio frame The television screen proportional rectangle drawing, 3 units high, 4 units wide; drawings used in the design of storyboards. (See the storyboard form.)

Audio perspective The perception that longer video shots should have farther away sound and closer video shots should have a closer sound; an attempt to re-create the same sound distance perception of real life.

Audio plot A preproduction task requirement of an audio director that includes the judgment of type of microphone to record the required sound of a production, the microphone holder for picking up required sound, and physical placement of a microphone for a videotape shoot. (See the audio plot form.)

B-roll A second videotape source needed in postproduction to perform some video effects involving two video sources during editing such as a dissolve or a special wipe effect. The A-roll would be the first videotape source for such an effect.

Bite A portion of a video or audio recording actuality.

Blocking plot The preproduction task of a director consisting of a bird's eye view of a set or recording environment with major properties indicated. A director indicates with circles where talent are to be placed and move about. Circles for talent are combined with arrows to indicate movement of talent. From a blocking plot, a lighting director can create a lighting plot, and a camera operator can decide camera set-up and placement. (See the blocking plot form.)

Boom microphone A microphone, usually directional, designed to be mounted and held above the person speaking. A boom microphone must be aimed at the mouth of a speaker and raised and lowered depending on the camera framing of each camera shot.

Breakdown A preproduction analysis of either a script or a storyboard. It is intended to separate scene elements from the script or storyboard and arrange them in proposed videotaping order. A breakdown is a necessary component to the development of a production schedule. (See the script breakdown form.)

Bridge A video or audio segment that serves to connect, often in summary form, one video or audio subject to another.

Character generator A video effects generator that electronically produces text on a video screen. The text that is recorded in the memory of the character generator is usually used for purposes of matting over a color background or other video images.

Claims Product or service assertions made to the viewing or listening public audience usually in commercial advertising. Commercials often claim that the product or service advertised produces certain effects. Claims made by commercials should be verified.

Clipsheet A summary form of information about an edited master videotape. Clipsheets list such information as the title of an edited master video piece, the length of edited video, the character generator copy to be matted over the video during telecast, and the in-cues and out-cues of the video. (See the clipsheet form.)

Composition of a shot The subject and arrangement of a shot as framed in the viewfinder of a camera. The composition of a shot indicates the person or objects to be framed and the degree of the framing, e.g., CU, XLS.

Concept A preproduction stage in the process of music video production. A concept stage is similar to a proposal or treatment in film and video documentary and drama production. The concept consists of a creative description of the proposed imaging for the music track in music video preproduction. (See the concept form.)

Continuity The flow of edited images and the content details of edited images from shot to shot. Continuity observation entails the close scrutiny of talent, properties, and environment during video recording to assure accurate flow of edited images in postproduction. (See the continuity notes form.)

Control track A flow of electronic impulses recorded on the edge of videotape that serves as synchronization units for accurate videotape editing. They serve the same purpose as the sprocket holes do on film.

Copy Any scripted text to be recorded on the audio track of a videotape or recorded in the memory of a character generator for matting on a video image or background.

Copyright The legal right of an artist or author to the exclusive control of the artist's or author's original work. Copyrighted material is protected by law and the public use of such materials must always be cleared by a producer from the owner of the copyright.

Credits On-screen texts that list the names and roles played or performed by all members of the crew and cast of the videotape production.

Crew call The stated time for the rendezvous of production team members usually at a videotaping site.

Cut-away Video of related but extraneous video content inserted into primary video material. For example, video images of a hospital operating room (related but extraneous) would serve as a cut-away insert to video of an interview (primary video material) of a doctor/surgeon.

Cut-in Video of necessary and motivated video images to be edited into an established or master scene. For example, close-up shots (necessary and motivated) of two people in conversation serve as cut-ins to a long shot (master scene) of the two people walking and talking.

Decibel A unit of sound that measures the loudness or softness of the sound.

Edited master The final editing of a video piece from source tapes.

Editing cue sheet A listing or format of an edited master videotape developed from the editing work sheet. Entries on the editing cue sheet juxtapose take units from the video described on the editing work sheet into the order of the final edited master. The editing cue sheet is a written format of the final edited master tape. (See the editing cue sheet.)

Editing work sheet A set of notes that describe and time the in-cues and out-cues of all video takes on a source videotape. It can be thought of as a transcription of the source tape. Additional information on the editing work sheet should make some judgmental notation on the acceptability of video and/or audio of each take. The editing work sheet is a sequential listing of every video segment on a source tape. (See the editing work sheet form.)

End board The slate when a videotaped take is slated at the end of a take instead of at the front. The end board is used when a take is redone without stopping the camera and recorder. End board use often occurs when an actor simply flubs a line.

F-stop The calibrated units on the aperture of the lens of a camera. The f-stop units determine the amount of light entering the lens and falling on the pick-up tubes.

Final audio The last sound of copy material or music in a video piece. It is a designated end point to measure the length of time of an edited master video piece.

First audio The first sound of copy material or music in a video piece; a designated beginning point to measure the length of time of an edited video piece.

Fishpole An extendible holder for a directional microphone; usually handheld and extended into a set during dialogue for videotaping.

Format The listed order or outline of the content of a video product or program; also used to indicate the genre of a television program, e.g., talk show, documentary, musical.

Framing The composition and degree of image arrangement as seen through the viewfinder of a camera. The framing is usually described in terms of how close or far away the subject is perceived to be from the camera, e.g., a close-up or a long shot.

Freelancer A person who works in the film or video field on a production basis as opposed to full time employment. Writers, producers, and directors are examples.

Freeze The appearance of holding the video image on the screen still and static.

Gels Filters used in the control of light for videotaping. Gels (short for gelatin) are used on lighting instruments to filter light or change lighting temperature and on windows to change the temperature of light entering a videotaping environment.

Hand properties Objects needed (handled) by talent/actors in the production of teleplays and commercials e.g., a knife or a purse.

Hard news A news event that is most recent and fast breaking.

In-cue The beginning point of copy, music notes, or video screen at which timing or video or audio inserting is to occur.

Interviewee The person being interviewed.

Interviewer The person who interviews.

Isolated cameras The process of videotaping a scene with more than one camera, each camera recording its own video content. The opposite of the isolated camera operation is the multiple camera process in which more than one camera feeds video signals through a switcher to one recorder.

Jump cut An editing cut at which the image appears to jump. The cause of a jump cut is the necessity to edit content from some video during which significant camera change or talent change has occurred. For example, if a cameraperson has zoomed during an interview or if talent moved during an interview, editing some of that video will make the interviewee appear to jump at the edit.

Lead The beginning video and/or audio of a videotape piece; may be created as a voice-over, a stand-up, or with music.

Leader The beginning portion of audiotape or videotape that is used to record information about the subsequent video or audio. Most leaders, often called the academy leader, contain the record of the slate and an audio check, e.g., :30 of tone, with a portion of video black before the principal video content of the recording. Some leaders also contain a portion of color bars.

Legal clearance The process by which recording and reproduction rights are obtained to use copyrighted materials. Legal clearance must be obtained for copyrighted materials (e.g., music, photographs, film) and for synchronization (putting pictures to copyrighted music).

Levels Calibrated input units of light, sound, and video that have to be set to record at acceptable degrees of unity and definition for broadcast reproduction purposes.

Lighting design The preproduction stage during which the mood, intensity, and degree of light for a videotape production is created. The lighting design is the responsibility of the lighting director of a production. The lighting design can be done after location scouting is complete.

Lip syncing The process of coordinating prerecorded audio to the video recording of an individual mouthing the same audio; also called synchronization. This is required most frequently in the production of music videos.

Location The environment outside a recording studio in which some videotaping is to be done; often, the remote location or simply the remote.

Location log The record of all videotaping done on location. The log contains notation about each videotaped take during a remote shoot. The location log serves as the editing cue sheet before postproduction editing. (See the location log form.)

Location scouting The process of finding and describing potential remote environments for purposes of videotaping at a later date. (See the location scouting form.)

Logging The process of keeping the location log; also used to record continuity details during a videotaped shoot.

Master script The copy of the script for a production that contains the preproduction information for a videotape shoot; usually the director's copy which contains the final version of the copy, the storyboard, and the blocking of actors and action props.

Mike grip An individual who is responsible for holding the microphone or a microphone holder during the recording of audio on a videotaping location.

Mixing The process of combining two or more audio tracks into one. Mixing usually adds music or ambience sound to a track of voice recording. Mixing audio tracks in videotape editing refers to combining two recorded audio tracks into one audio channel.

Out-cue The end point of copy, music notes, or video screen at which timing or video or audio inserting is to end.

Pacing The perception of timing of a video piece. Pacing is not necessarily the actual speed of a production or production elements, but it is the coordinated flow and uniformity of sequencing of all production elements, e.g., music beat, copy rhythm, video cutting.

Package The production of short video pieces; often synonymous with soft news video production.

Pad Padding used whenever some flexible video, audio, black signal, or time may be needed.

Pick-up pattern The sound-sensitive area around the head of a microphone. It is the area within which sounds are picked up by the microphone.

Preproduction script A copy of the script for a video project that is considered subject to change. A preproduction script should contain sufficient audio and video material to judge the substance of the final proposed project.

Proposal The set of preproduction elements used to present the idea and request for a video production. Most proposals require at least a treatment and a budget. A proposal might also contain a preproduction script and a storyboard.

Record button A circular red insert plug found on the bottom of most videotape cassettes. Removing the record button serves as a safety check against recording over and erasing previously recorded video material. The absence of the record button will allow playback but not recording functions.

Roll tape An expression used to signal operation of the videotape recorder at the beginning of a videotape take. A location director uses the expression as a sign to begin the videotaping of a scene.

Rough edit The result of a first postproduction editing session in which accurate timing and tight edits are not required. A rough edit serves as a preliminary step to the final editing of tightly edited video genres such as commercials. A rough edit serves as the occasion to make final edit decisions on pacing and image transitions.

Script unit Section of a production script that designates a videotaping portion; similar to a scene of a larger act; any gratuitous unit that a director may define for production purposes. Many professional scripts number all script units consecutively in the right and left margins.

Secondary motion The movements in television that occur with the movement of the camera in production. Secondary movements include the pan, tilt, dolly, truck, arc, zoom, pedestal, and boom.

Serendipity syndrome The good and pleasant effects in television production that were unplanned and unexpected.

Shoot A slang term used to describe a remote location videotape production.

Shooting order The order in which a production schedule indicates the script units will be shot during production. Most often the shooting order is determined by the availability of location and actors.

Shot list A form created during preproduction in which a director indicates the types and order of shots to be videotaped during location production. A shot list differentiates between master or establishing shots and cut-ins, and indicates framing instructions and the duration of the each shot by out-cue. Shot lists are location-specific with the shot list for every location beginning with the count of one.

Slate An audio and video recording device that allows the labeling of the leader of each videotape take. A slate usually records the title of the production, the producer and/or director, the date, the take number, and the videotape code. The character generator can serve as a slate as does a blackboard or white showcard. The word slate also indicates the action of recording the slate on the videotape leader.

Society of Motion Picture and Television Engineers (SMPTE) time code   An electronic signal recorded on a secondary audio track of videotape stock to assist an editor in accurately creating a videotape edit. SMPTE time code records the hours, minutes, seconds, and frame numbers of elapsed time for each video frame.

Soft news   A news event that is not necessarily recent or timely. It is referred to as evergreen or timeless.

Source tape   Any videotape stock used to record video that will later be edited into a larger videotape project. Source tapes are edited onto a master tape.

Standby   A vocal command that indicates the director is ready to begin videotape recording at a location unit. Production and crew respond to a standby command with silence and readiness to begin.

Stand-up   The technique of a location news reporter when the reporter appears on camera standing in the foreground of the location; may be used as a lead, a bridge, or a tag for a video piece.

Storyboard   A series of aspect ratio frame forms used to sketch the proposed composition and framing of each shot to be videotaped for a video production. Storyboard frames are numbered consecutively, and the audio copy associated with each proposed shot is recorded under the frame. Storyboards are considered essential to some video genres (i.e., commercials) and are encouraged as a quality preproduction stage for all genres.

Stills   Static photographs or 35mm slides of some product or subject. Stills can be effected in video with a freeze frame. Stills are often used in commercial advertising production for the image of the product being advertised. Stills are often taken in the environment in which a commercial is being videotaped.

Strike   The final stage of a location shoot when all videotape production equipment is disassembled and packed for removal and the shooting environment restored to the arrangement and condition found at the arrival of the production crew.

Sweetening   The process in which audio and video signals are cleaned up and clarified electronically in postproduction. Sweetening audio refers to filtering out background noises such as hums and buzzes.

Synchronization rights   Legal clearances in which a producer receives the right to use copyrighted music in a videotape production.

Synopsis   An abbreviated description or statement of some longer or larger whole. A treatment usually contains a synopsis of the proposed video production.

Tag   The technique of a news reporter of summarizing and delivering closing remarks on a videotaped news piece. A tag can be a voice-over, a stand-up, or music.

Take   A single videotape unit from beginning recording to the end of recording; usually begins with a recording of the slate and ends with a director's call to cut. It is not uncommon to record many takes of any individual unit. Many takes may be required for one shot.

Talent   The term used to designate any person who appears in front of the cameras, both actors and extras. Even animals are referred to as talent.

Target audience   The designation of that subset of the mass public for whom a particular video piece is designed. Knowing a target audience permits a producer and director to make calculated choices of production values to attract and hold the interest of the targeted group.

Timing   The process of recording the length of a video piece from first audio to final audio. First audio and final audio might be music and not a vocal cue. Some video pieces may have a visual cue at the beginning or end of the piece.

Titling   The design and production of all those on-screen visual elements that create the title of a video production.

Trade papers   Magazines and newspapers that specialize in all the media and what media professionals are doing. The most common trade paper is *Variety*. These trade papers list music groups who are in production with a new album.

Treatment   A preproduction stage in which a producer describes a proposed video production for the purpose of soliciting approval to go into production with the project. The treatment may include a synopsis of a story, the goal and objective of a video piece, and the audience's need for the production. (See the treatment form.)

Vectorscope   An oscilloscope used to set and align the color of images as they are recorded by the videotape recorder.

Voice-over   A production technique in which an announcer's voice alone is heard without being seen in the video portion; a commonplace technique in news reporting. Leads, bridges, and tags may all be produced as voice-overs.

Volume (VU) meter   A measure of the degree of loudness of recorded or amplified sound.

White balance   The process that adjusts the colors to be seen by the camera to be recorded according to lighting intensity and contrast.

Wrap   The stage of location videotape production when the director indicates a good take has been videotaped and signals a move to another shot from the shot list. A wrap is distinguished from a strike.

Selected Bibliography

• General Production Texts

Armer, A. *Directing Television and Film.* Belmont, CA: Wadsworth, 1986.

Blum B. *Television Writing From Concept to Contract.* New York: Hastings House, 1980.

Blumenthal, H. J. *Television Producing & Directing.* New York: Harper & Row, 1988.

Carlson, V. & S. *Professional Lighting Handbook.* Stoneham, MA: Focal Press, 1985.

Fuller, B., Kanaba, S., & Kanaba, J. *Single Camera Video Production: Techniques, Equipment, and Resources for Producing Quality Video Programs.* Englewood Cliffs, NJ: Prentice-Hall, 1982.

Garvey, D., and Rivers, W. *Broadcast Writing.* New York: Longman, 1982.

Hubatka, M.C., Hull, F., & Sanders, R.W. *Audio Sweetening for Film and TV.* Blue Ridge Summit, PA: Tabs Books, 1985.

Huber, D. M. *Audio Production Techniques for Video.* Indianapolis: Howard Sams & Co., 1987.

Kehoe, V. *Technique of the Professional Make-up Artist.* Stoneham, MA: Focal Press, 1985.

Kennedy, T. *Directing the Video Production.* White Plains, NY: Knowledge Industry Publications, 1988.

Mathias, H., & Patterson, R. *Electronic Cinematography: Achieving Photographic Control over the Video Image.* Belmont, CA: Wadsworth Publishing, 1985.

McQuillin, L. *The Video Production Guide.* Sante Fe, NM: Video Info, 1983.

Miller, P. *Script Supervising and Film Continuity.* Stoneham, MA: Focal Press, 1986.

Millerson, G. *Video Production Handbook.* London: Focal Press, 1987.

Souter, G. A. *Lighting Techniques for Video Production: The Art of Casting Shadows.* White Plains, NY: Knowledge Industry Publications, 1987.

Utz, P. *Today's Video: Equipment, Set Up and Production.* Englewood Cliffs, NJ: Prentice Hall, 1987.

Weise, M. *Film and Video Budgets.* Stoneham, MA: Focal Press, 1980.

Wiegand, I. *Professional Video Production.* White Plains, NY: Knowledge Industry Publications, 1985.

Zettl, H. *Sight, Sound, Motion: Applied Media Aesthetics.* Belmont, CA: Wadsworth, 1973.

Zettl, H. *Television Production Handbook.* Belmont, CA: Wadsworth, 1984.

• Television News Production

Fang, I. *Television News, Radio News,* 3rd Ed. Minneapolis: Rada Press, 1980.

Shook, F. *The Process of Electronic News Gathering.* Englewood, CO: Morton Publishing, 1982.

Stephens, M. *Broadcast News,* 2nd Ed. New York: Holt, Rinehart and Winston, 1986.

Yoakam, R., & Cremer C. *ENG: Television News and the New Technology.* New York: Random House, 1985.

Yorke, I. *The Techniques of Television News,* 2nd Ed. Stoneham, MA: Focal Press, 1978.

• Documentary Production

Baddeley, W.H. *The Technique of Documentary Film Production,* 2nd Ed. New York: Hastings House, 1969.

Bluem, A.W. *Documentary in American Television: Form, Function, Method.* New York: Hastings House, 1977.

Rabiger, M. *Directing the Documentary.* Stoneham, MA: Focal Press 1987.

• Commercial Production

Gradus, B. *Directing: The Television Commercial.* New York: Hastings House, 1981.

Wainwright, C. *Television Commercials: How to Create Successful Advertising.* New York: Hastings House, 1970.

White, H. *How to Produce Effective TV Commercials,* 2nd Ed. Lincolnwood, IL: NTC Business Books, 1986.

• Music Video Production

See similar production techniques. (Nothing published)

• Drama Production

Chamness, D. *The Hollywood Guide to Film Budgeting and Script Breakdown.* Toluca Lake, CA: D. Chamness & Assoc., 1977.

Dmytryk, E. *On Screen Directing.* Stoneham, MA: Focal Press, 1984.

St. John Marner, T. *Directing Motion Pictures.* New York: A.S. Barnes, 1972.

Trapnell, C. *Teleplay.* New York: Hawthorn Books, 1974.

Index